P9-CMA-671

The Cultural Studies Reader

The Cultural Studies Reader offers the ideal introduction for students of this exciting discipline. It presents a selection of influential and innovative essays by writers such as Barthes, Adorno, Lyotard, Stuart Hall, and Gayatri Spivak, with a succinct preface to each. The book encompasses a wide range of topics – from sport to postmodernism, from museums to supermarkets, from gay writing to rock and roll – and covers every important cultural studies method and theory.

The Reader can be used as much more than an introductory anthology: it surveys the history and development of cultural studies from its origins in sociological analysis of post-war Britain to its present as a truly transnational discipline. Looking at the future, Simon During argues that cultural studies methodologies offer great potential for confronting such contemporary issues as postcolonialism, globalization, and multiculturalism.

This outstanding collection, which includes an extensive guide to further reading, will be of immense interest not only to those coming new to the field but also to those already involved in the teaching and practice of cultural studies.

Simon During teaches English and Cultural Studies at the University of Melbourne. He has written widely on cultural and literary history and theory, and is the author of *Foucault and Literature* (Routledge, 1992).

The Cultural Studies Reader

Edited by
SIMON DURING

London and New York

First published 1993
by Routledge
11 New Fetter Lane, London EC4P 4EE

Simultaneously published in the USA and Canada
by Routledge
29 West 35th Street, New York, NY 10001

Reprinted 1993, 1994

© 1993 This collection © Simon During; individual essays © individual
authors

Typeset in Palatino and Helvetica by Florencetype Ltd, Avon

Printed and bound in England by Clays Ltd, St Ives plc

All rights reserved. No part of this book may be reprinted or
reproduced or utilized in any form or by any electronic,
mechanical, or other means, now known or hereafter
invented, including photocopying and recording, or in any
information storage or retrieval system, without permission in
writing from the publishers.

British Library Cataloguing in Publication Data
A catalogue record for this book is available from the British Library

Library of Congress Cataloging in Publication Data
Also available

ISBN 0-415-07708-7   0-415-07709-5 (pbk)

Contents

Acknowledgements

I would like to thank Lisa O'Connell and Chris Healy for helping me clarify and organize the introduction to this collection; Rebecca Barden at Routledge for her encouragement and patience; and my helpful colleagues at Melbourne and Berkeley, too many to name, whom I consulted throughout the project.

Most of the essays in this collection have been edited both for reasons of space and to make them more accessible for readers new to cultural studies. Permission given by the following copyright holders and authors is gratefully acknowledged.

Theodor Adorno and Max Horkheimer, 'The culture industry: enlightenment as mass deception', extracted from *Dialectic of Enlightenment*, trans. John Cumming (New York: The Seabury Press 1972). © 1969 S. Fischer Verlag GmbH; English translation © 1972 Herder and Herder Ltd.

Ien Ang, '*Dallas* and the ideology of mass culture', extracted from *Watching Dallas: Soap Opera and the Melodramatic Imagination* (London: Methuen 1985). © 1985 Methuen & Co. Ltd.

Roland Barthes, 'Dominici, or the triumph of literature', from *Mythologies* (London: Jonathan Cape 1972). © 1957 Editions du Seuil, Paris; translation © 1972 Jonathan Cape.

Pierre Bourdieu, 'How can one be a sports fan?', extracted from *Social Science Information* 17/6 (1978). © 1978 Pierre Bourdieu and Sage Publications.

Rey Chow, 'Listening otherwise, music miniaturized: a different type of question about revolution', from *Discourse* 13/1 (Winter 1990–91). © 1990 Rey Chow.

James Clifford, 'On collecting art and culture', extracted from *The Predicament of Culture* (Cambridge, Mass.: Harvard University Press 1988). © 1988 President and Fellows of Harvard College.

Michel de Certeau, 'Walking in the city', extracted from *The Practice of Everyday Life* (Berkeley, Calif.: University of California Press 1984). © 1984 Regents of University of California Press.

Teresa de Lauretis, 'Upping the anti [*sic*] in feminist theory', extracted from *Conflicts in Feminism*, ed. Marianne Hirsch and Evelyn Fox Keller (New York: Routledge 1990). © 1990 Routledge and Kegan Paul.

Richard Dyer, 'Entertainment and utopia', from *Movie* 24 (Spring 1977). © 1977 Richard Dyer and *Movie*.

David Forgacs, 'National-popular: genealogy of a concept', from *Formations: Of Nations and Peoples* (London: Routledge and Kegan Paul 1984). © 1984 Formations Editorial Collective.

Michel Foucault, 'Space, power and knowledge', an interview with Paul Rabinow translated by Christian Hubert, extracted from *The Foucault Reader*, ed. Paul Rabinow (New York: Pantheon 1984). © 1984 Paul Rabinow.

Stuart Hall, 'Encoding, decoding', extracted from *Culture, Media, Language* (London: Unwin Hyman 1990). © 1990 Stuart Hall.

Dick Hebdige, 'From culture to hegemony', extracted from *Subculture: the Meaning of Style* (London: Methuen 1979). © 1979 Dick Hebdige.

Jean-François Lyotard, 'Defining the postmodern', from *Postmodernism ICA Documents*, ed. Lisa Appiganesi (London: Free Association Books 1989). © 1989 Jean-François Lyotard.

Armand Mattelart, Xavier Delcourt and Michèle Mattelart, 'International image markets', extracted from *International Image Markets*, trans. David Buxton (London: Comedia Publishing Co. 1984). © 1984 Armand Mattelart, Xavier Delcourt, Michèle Mattelart.

Meaghan Morris, 'Things to do with shopping centres', extracted from *Grafts: Feminist Cultural Criticism*, ed. Susan Sheridan (London: Verso 1988). © 1988 Meaghan Morris.

Janice A. Radway, 'The institutional matrix of romance', extracted from *Reading the Romance: Women, Patriarchy and Popular Literature* (Chapel

Hill: University of North Carolina 1984). © University of North Carolina Press.

Renato Rosaldo, 'After objectivism', extracted from *Culture and Truth: The Remaking of Social Analysis* (Boston: Beacon Press 1989). © 1989 Renato Rosaldo.

Andrew Ross, 'The popularity of pornography', extracted from *No Respect: Intellectuals and Popular Culture* (London: Routledge 1989). © 1989 Routledge, Chapman and Hall Inc.

Eve Kosofsky Sedgwick, 'Axiomatic', extracted from *Epistemology of the Closet* (Berkeley, Calif.: University of California Press 1990). © Regents of University of California Press.

Edward Soja, 'History: geography: modernity', extracted from *Postmodern Geographies: the Reassertion of Space in Critical Social Theory* (London: Verso 1989). © Edward Soja 1989.

Gayatri Spivak, 'Questions of multiculturalism', extracted from *The Postcolonial Critic: Interviews, Strategies, Dialogues*, ed. Sarah Harasym (London: Routledge 1990). © 1990 Gayatri Spivak and Sneja Gunew.

Peter Stallybrass and Allon White, 'Bourgeois hysteria and the carnivalesque', extracted from *The Politics and Poetics of Transgression* (London: Methuen 1986). © 1986 Peter Stallybrass and Allon White.

Will Straw, 'Characterizing rock music culture: the case of heavy metal', in *On Record: Rock, Pop and the Written Word*, eds Simon Frith and Andrew Goodwin (London: Routledge 1990). © 1990 Will Straw.

Michele Wallace, 'Negative images: towards a black feminist cultural criticism', extracted from *Invisibility Blues: From Pop to Theory* (London: Verso 1990). © 1990 Michele Wallace.

Cornel West, 'The new cultural politics of difference', extracted from *October* 53 (Summer 1990). © 1990 Massachusetts Institute of Technology and *October* Magazine.

Raymond Williams, 'Advertising: the magic system', extracted from *Problems in Materialism and Culture* (London: Verso 1980). © Raymond Williams 1980.

1 Simon During

Introduction

This book collects representative essays in cultural studies as an introduction to this increasingly popular field of study. Yet, as will become clearer after the essays have been read, cultural studies is not an academic discipline quite like others. It possesses neither a well-defined methodology nor clearly demarcated fields for investigation. Cultural studies is, of course, the study of culture, or, more particularly, the study of *contemporary* culture. But this does not take us very far. Even assuming that we know precisely what 'contemporary culture' is, it can be analysed in many ways – sociologically, for instance, by 'objectively' describing its institutions and functions as if they belong to a large, regulated system; or economically, by describing the effects of investment and marketing on cultural production. More traditionally, it can be studied 'critically' by celebrating either large forms (like literature) or specific texts or images (like *Waiting for Godot* or an episode of *Cheers*). The question remains: does cultural studies bring its own orientation to these established forms of analysis?

There is no easy answer, but to introduce the forms of analysis developed by the discipline we can point to two features that characterized it when it first appeared in Great Britain in the 1950s. It concentrated on 'subjectivity', which means that it studied culture in relation to individual lives, breaking with social scientific positivism or 'objectivism' (as Renato Rosaldo calls it in his essay included here). The book that is often said to inaugurate the subject, Richard Hoggart's *The Uses of Literacy* (1957), is a very personal work: it describes changes in working-class life in post-war Britain through Hoggart's own experiences. Hoggart wanted to show how those changes affected an individual's 'whole way of life'. For him culture was an important category because it helps us recognize that one life-practice (like reading) cannot be torn out of a large network constituted by many other life-practices – working, sexual orientation, family life, say.

The second distinguishing characteristic of early cultural studies was that it was an engaged form of analysis. Early cultural studies did not flinch from the fact that societies are structured unequally, that individuals are not all born with the same access to education, money, health-care, etc., and it worked in the interests of those who have fewest resources. In this it differed not only from the (apparently) objective social sciences but from the older forms of cultural criticism, especially literary criticism, which considered political questions as being of peripheral relevance to the appreciation of culture. For cultural studies, 'culture' was not an abbreviation of a 'high culture' assumed to have constant value across time and space. Another founding text of cultural studies, Raymond Williams's *Culture and Society: 1780–1950* (1958), criticized the consequences of uncoupling 'culture' from 'society', and 'high culture' from 'culture as a whole way of life', although Williams also conceded that it was through this uncoupling that modern culture acquires its particular energy, charm, and capacity to inform.

These two defining features of early cultural studies were closely connected because it is at the level of the individual life that the cultural effects of social inequality are most apparent. Most individuals aspire and struggle the greater part of their lives and it is easier to forget this if one is just interpreting texts rather than thinking about reading as a life-practice. Cultural studies insists one cannot just ignore – or accept – division and struggle. We can ask, how did an engaged discipline of this kind emerge within higher education? This is the question that lets us approach cultural studies most effectively, so let us turn to the historical conditions which made the discipline possible.

A BRIEF HISTORY OF CULTURAL STUDIES

Cultural studies appears as a field of study in Great Britain in the 1950s out of Leavisism, a form of literary studies named after F. R. Leavis, its most prominent member. Leavisism was an attempt to redisseminate what is now commonly called, after Pierre Bourdieu, 'cultural capital' – though this is not how it saw itself. Leavis wanted to use the educational system to distribute literary knowledge and appreciation more widely. To achieve this, the Leavisites argued for a very restricted canon, discarding modern experimental works like those of James Joyce or Virginia Woolf, for instance. Instead they primarily celebrated works directed towards developing the moral sensibility of readers, such as Jane Austen, Alexander Pope, or George Eliot – the 'great tradition'. Leavisites fiercely insisted that culture was not simply a leisure activity; reading 'the great tradition' was, rather, a means of forming mature individuals with a concrete and balanced sense of 'life'. And the main threat to this sense of life came from the pleasure offered by so-called 'mass culture'. In this, Leavisism was very much in tune with what cultural studies has come to call the 'social democratic power bloc', which dominated post-war Britain. After the war, Britain was administered by a sequence of governments that intervened in the private sector both socially (in areas like health and housing) and culturally (in education and the arts). When the education system expanded radically through the 1950s and 1960s, it turned to Leavisism to form citizens' sensibilities.

Cultural studies develops out of Leavisism through Hoggart and Williams, whose writings were taken up in secondary schools and tertiary colleges soon after they were written. Hoggart and Williams both came from working-class families; both had worked as teachers in post-compulsory education, though, importantly, in workers' education. Thus they experienced Leavisism ambivalently. On the one hand, they accepted that its canonical texts were richer than contemporary so-called 'mass culture' and that culture ought to be measured in terms of its capacity to deepen and widen experiences; on the other, they recognized that Leavisism at worst erased, and at the very least did not fully come into contact with, the communal forms of life into which they had been born. So Hoggart's *The Uses of Literacy*, in particular, is a schizophrenic book. Its first half contains a heartfelt evocation of traditional industrial working-class communities, relatively untouched by commercial culture and educational institutions, while its second half mounts a practical-critical attack on modern mass culture. When Hoggart went on to found the Birmingham Centre for Contemporary Cultural Studies (henceforth CCCS), a postgraduate and research institute designed to further his work, it began by having to deal with this tension.

Hoggart was able to believe that the celebration of old high culture could fit alongside an evocation of the culture of his youth because both stood apart from contemporary commercial popular culture and so were under threat. The threat to and final disappearance of traditional British working-class life need to be considered at some length because they were crucial for the early development of cultural studies. (See Laing 1986 for a good account of this history.) Before the war, since the early 1920s, the British economy had been dominated by unemployment – there were never less than a million people unemployed over the period. This was the background of Hoggart's 'traditional' working class. By the end of the 1940s, however, Britain had a full-employment economy, and by the end of the 1950s further shifts in the British economy were well under way. Jobs were moving into the state sector (in 1955 government expenditure had been 36.6 per cent of GDP as against 52.2 per cent in 1967 (Robbins 1983: 369)); small plants were being replaced by larger ones using 'Fordist' production techniques – that is, simplifying workers' tasks on assembly lines – which meant that labour became increasingly deskilled (between 1951 and 1973 the percentage of the work-force working in plants which employed over 1500 people increased by 50 per cent (Wright 1979: 40)). Simultaneously, the differential between lower-paid white-collar and the blue-collar workers was decreasing, and large-scale immigration from the colonies during the 1950s meant that many indigenous workers were no longer called upon to take the least desirable jobs. Workers, then, were becoming increasingly 'affluent' (to use a media term of the time), at least in so far as they were increasingly able to buy consumer goods like cars (numbers of which increased fivefold between 1950 and 1975), clothing, washing machines, refrigerators, record-players, telephone services (they increased fourfold between 1945 and 1970), and, most important of all, television sets (commercial television does not become widely available in Britain until 1957, the year Hoggart's book was published). Finally, the large state rehousing programme, compulsory national service in the army (which ended in 1958) and, to a lesser extent, educational reform, making higher education available to a fraction of the working class, also helped break up the culture that Hoggart described.

As the old working-class communal life fragmented, the cultural studies which followed Hoggart's *The Uses of Literacy* developed in two main ways. The old notion of culture as a whole way of life became increasingly difficult to sustain: attention moved from locally produced and often long-standing cultural forms (pub life, group singing, pigeon-fancying, attitudes to 'our mum', dances, holidays at camps and close-by seaside resorts, etc.) to culture as organized from afar – both by the state through its educational system, and by what Theodor Adorno and Max Horkheimer (in the essay included here) called the 'culture industry', that is, highly developed music, film and broadcasting businesses. This shift of focus could lead to a revision of older paradigms, as when Stuart Hall and Paddy Whannel in *The Popular Arts* (1964) gave the kind of status and attention reserved by the Leavisites for canonical literature to new forms (such as jazz and film) while devaluing others (especially television and rock music). Much more importantly, however, the logic by which culture was set apart from politics, already examined by Raymond Williams, was overturned. The historian E. P. Thompson, in his seminal book *The Making of the English Working Class* (1968) and elsewhere, had pointed out that the identity of the working class *as* working class had always had a strongly political and conflictual component – that identity was not just a matter of particular cultural interests and values. But the fragmentation of the old proletarian culture meant that a politics based on a strong working-class identity was less and less significant: people decreasingly identified themselves as workers (see Roberts *et al.* 1977).

It was in this context that cultural studies theorists began seriously to explore culture's own political function and to offer a critique of the social democratic power bloc which was drawing power into the state. From the early 1970s, culture was analysed through the concept 'hegemony' – a word associated with Antonio Gramsci, an Italian Marxist of the 1920s and 1930s. 'Hegemony' is a term to describe relations of domination which are not visible as such. It involves not coercion but consent on the part of the dominated (or 'subaltern'). Gramsci himself elaborated the concept to explain why Mussolini's fascism was so popular even though fascism curtailed the liberty of most Italians. For him, hegemonic forces constantly alter their content as social and cultural conditions change: they are improvised and negotiable, so that counter-hegemonic strategies must also be constantly revised. In the same spirit, if somewhat less subtly, culture could also be seen as what Michel Foucault was beginning to think of as a form of 'governmentality', that is, a means to produce conforming or 'docile' citizens, most of all through the education system.

As culture was thought about less as an expression of local communal lives linked to class identity and more as an apparatus within a large system of domination, cultural studies offered critiques of culture's hegemonic effects. At first, such critiques leant heavily on forms of semiotic analysis (represented in this collection in a sophisticated form by Stuart Hall's and James Clifford's essays). This meant in effect that culture was broken down into discrete messages, 'signifying practices' or 'discourses' which were distributed by particular institutions and media. To take a rather simplified example: a semiotic analysis of cigarette-smoking among workers would analyse smoking not as a life-practice, that is, in terms of its importance as a rite of passage, its use in structuring the flow of time and so on, but in terms of its being a signifier produced by images, like the 'Marlboro man', which connote masculinity, freedom and transcendence of workaday life. Semiotics' capacity to extend its analysis beyond particular texts or signs is limited: it remained an analysis of 'codings' and 'recodings', not of uses, practices or feelings (though Stuart Hall's essay collected here, which emphasized the concept 'decoding', has been influential because it articulates relations between uses and meanings).

It would be wrong to insist too strongly on what were called the 'culturalist' (emphasizing forms of life) and 'structuralist' (or semiotic) strands within the cultural studies of the period. But, in the 1970s, a hard form of structuralism did emerge, one that called upon the work of Louis Althusser, backed up by psychoanalytic notions developed by Jacques Lacan. For this theory, individuals were constructs of ideology, where ideology means not beliefs we disapprove of (as in 'racist ideology') but the set of discourses and images which constitute the most widespread knowledge and values – 'common sense'. Ideology, so the argument went, is required so that the state and capitalism can reproduce themselves without the threat of revolution. Here, as for Hoggart and Williams, the state's claim to neutrality is false, but this time for more classically Marxist reasons – because it protects the exploitative 'relations of production' (i.e. class differences) necessary to capitalism. For Althusser, dominant ideology turned what was in fact political, partial, and open to change into something seemingly 'natural', universal, and eternal. However, dominant ideology is not limited to politics or economics, so, though it may present a particular view of economic relations (as in the common idea that trade-unionism is a brake on economic competitiveness), its primary role is to construct an imaginary picture of civil life, especially the nuclear family, as natural and, most of all, each individual as 'unique' and 'free'. Ideology fragments real connections and interdependencies, producing a picture of social relations which overemphasizes individual freedom and autonomy.

For Althusser, individuals can be sucked into ideology so easily because it helps them make sense of the world, to enter the 'symbolic order' and ascribe power to themselves. They identify with ideology because they see themselves pictured as independent and strong in it – as an adolescent boy (or, indeed, adult) might picture himself, in a fantasy, as the Marlboro man. Dominant social values are internalized through this kind of identification. At this point, psychoanalysis was called upon to gird the theory. Once again, to state the argument very simply: individuals see themselves mirrored in dominant ideology and identify with it as a way of 'taking the father's place' in a process which is fuelled by the 'fear of castration', that is, anxieties that true autonomy or unique individuality can never be reached. So ideology does not just help reproduce inequitable social relations, it also provides a false resolution to private, familial tensions, a resolution that is, for Lacan if not for Althusser, finally enabled by the fact that no symbolic structure can offer final meaning or security. Its lure is always imaginary: the promise of a full 'I-ness' which can exist only where 'I am not'.

Politico-psychoanalytical structuralism of this kind never made as much headway in cultural studies as it did in film studies, say. It did not concede enough space to the capacity of the individual or community to act on the world on its own terms, to generate its own meanings and effects. It was too theoretical in the sense that it offered truths which took little or no account of local differences; indeed, its claims to be scientifically true lacked support from scientific method. And it did not pay enough heed to the actual techniques and practices by which individuals form themselves and their lives. But another strand of semiotic thought was able to enter the culturalist tradition with more vigour. This emphasized the concept of polysemy. 'Polysemy' is a technical word for the way in which a particular signifier always has more than one meaning, because 'meaning' is an effect of differences within a larger system.

[handwritten margin note: This is where psycho-analysis comes in]

This time the argument went: it is because meanings are not produced referentially (by pointing to specific objects in the world) but by one sign's difference from another that signs are polysemous. One sign can always both be substituted for by another (in what is called the 'paradigmatic' relation), and enter a sequence of other signs (the 'syntagmatic' relation). More loosely, a sign can 'connote' any number of others: the Marlboro man, for instance, connoting 'toughness' in one context and 'cancer' in another.

The notion of polysemy, however, remains limited in that it still works at the level of individual signs as discrete signifying units. Yet it did lead to more dynamic and complex theoretical concepts which help us describe how cultural products may be combined with new elements to produce different effects in different situations. In this way, cultural production is conceived of as a process of 'hybridization' and 'negotiation'. For instance, the Marlboro man might be made into a shiny, hard-edged polythene sculpture à la Jeff Koons to achieve a postmodern effect in an expensive Manhattan apartment; an ad using the image might be cut out of the magazine and used to furnish a poor dwelling in Lagos as an image of Western affluence and liberty; or it might be parodied on a CD/album cover. Concepts like hybridization, as they developed out of the notion of 'polysemy', return us to a renewed culturalism because they enable us to see how particular individuals and communities can actively create new meanings from signs and cultural products which come from afar. Yet a concept like 'hybridization' still does not account for the way that the meanings of particular signifiers or texts in a particular situation are, in part, ordered by material interests and power relations. The tobacco industry, the medical profession, and a certain stream within the women's movement might *struggle* over the meaning of 'Marlboro man' for political and commercial reasons: one in order to sell more product; the other to promote health, as well as their own status and earning power; the last to reject an insensitive mode of masculinity. Cultural studies has been, as we might expect, most interested in how groups with least power practically develop their own readings of, and uses for, cultural products – in fun, in resistance, or to articulate their own identity.

This brief historical account of cultural studies' key concepts has not focused on particular works at particular dates. The richness of the research promoted by the CCCS during the 1970s makes that research impossible adequately to represent here. But three particularly influential texts, Paul Willis's *Learning to Labour* (1977), David Morley's *The 'Nationwide' Audience* (1980), and the collectively written *Resistance through Rituals: Youth Subcultures in Post-War Britain* (1976), edited by Stuart Hall and Tim Jefferson, each of which was written from a different space in the spectrum thrown open by the history I have just sketched, can rewardingly be described.

First, Paul Willis's *Learning to Labour*. Willis used participant observer techniques to describe a group of disaffected boys in a working-class school (the 'lads'). He showed how they create a 'counter-school culture' in which they reject the official logic which legitimizes their education, that is, 'you obey the teachers because they teach you knowledge which will help you get a better job'. They reject this exchange for several reasons: partly because 'better jobs' (i.e. low-paid white-collar or apprentice jobs as against unskilled labouring jobs) involve moving out of the traditions of mateship, hard drinking, excitement, and strong male bonding passed down in their families; partly because those jobs were not necessarily 'better' financially, at least in the short and medium term, and didn't require the kind of knowledge on offer at school anyway; and partly because the lads had a strong sense that the economic system ultimately required the exploitation of some people's labour power so that the 'shit jobs' they would take were in fact necessary rather than worthless. Willis's work remains close to Hoggart's in that it involves a certain celebration of traditional working-class culture and it shows how that culture contains a quite accurate political understanding of the conditions of life, even though the lads have little conventional class-consciousness and absolutely no interest in formal political institutions. What is striking about the study, though, is how important both sexism and racism remain to this segment of British working-class culture. Unfortunately, Willis does not address this head-on.

Whereas Willis's *Learning to Labour* is a culturalist book in the traditional sense, David Morley's *The 'Nationwide' Audience* is one of the first ethnographic studies not of a community (defined in terms of locale and class) but of an audience (defined as a group of viewers/readers), in this case the audience of *Nationwide*, a BBC news-magazine programme widely watched through the late 1960s and the 1970s, and which broadcast mainly local, rather than national or international, stories, somewhat like a US breakfast show. Morley's study was ethnographic in that he did not simply analyse the programme, he organized open-ended group discussions between viewers, with each group from a homogeneous class/gender/work background (trade-unionists, managers, students, etc.). Indeed his book begins by contesting that image of a large audience as a 'mass' which had often been assumed by earlier sociological theorists of the media. His ethnographic approach was all the more a break within cultural studies work on media because, along with Charlotte Brunsdon, he had offered a conventional semiotic 'ideology-critique' of the programme in an earlier study, *Everyday Television: 'Nationwide'* (1978). There, Brunsdon and he had argued that the programme presented an image of the world in which gender, class, and ethnic differences were massively downgraded, and which assumed that 'we' (the programme's implied audience) possess a shared 'common sense' based on a practical view of the world, as against 'intellectual', political or culturally adventurous views. The programme's style or 'mode of address' was anchored in authoritarian but chatty presenters who embodied its values.

For Morley the textualist approach began to seem limited because it could not fully deal with polysemy. He had to go out into the field to discover what people actually thought about *Nationwide*. But this does not mean that, for him, the programme can be interpreted anyhow, precisely because its ideological orientation – that 'everyday life' view of the world – is the code which the programme itself presents as 'preferred'. To use Stuart Hall's phrase, the programme is 'structured in dominance' because it skews and restricts its audience's possibilities for interpreting the material it claims to present without bias. Though viewers need not accept the preferred code, they must respond to it in some way. Morley divides the possibilities of decoding *Nationwide* into three categories: (i) an acceptance of the preferred reading; (ii) flat opposition to it (mainly, as it turned out, by being extremely bored by it); and (iii) negotiation with it. His fieldwork findings were somewhat unexpected, though: there was no clear correlation between the socio-cultural position of the groups and their response to the programme, although those, like a group of Caribbean young women, furthest away from the common-sense 'we' embodied in the white (and mainly male) presenters, were least able to respond to it. Also some groups (especially students and trainee-managers) understood that the programme was biased (or 'structured in dominance') but still accepted its dominant code. Knowing how it worked, not being 'cultural dupes', did not mean refusal of its values. And, last, those groups with least social and cultural capital – like the Caribbean women – found the programme too distant from their own lives, preferring less newsy programmes with more 'human' stories – like those transmitted by the more market-orientated ITV companies. Though Morley makes little of it, for these groups it was the market rather than the state (through the state-funded BBC) that provided them with what they wanted. In a paradox that helps us understand certain problems at work at the heart of the social democratic power bloc, those who are most vulnerable to market forces respond most positively to its cultural products.

The third, and earliest, book, *Resistance through Rituals: Youth Subcultures in Post-War Britain*, is a collection of essays, each by different authors, each of which comes to grips with the fragmentation of traditional working-class culture in a different way. In general, the authors accepted that the working class was being split, one section being drawn into skilled jobs that would enable them to live like certain elements of the middle classes, another into deskilled, low-status, and often service jobs. However, they argued that jobs of this latter kind were especially taken by disadvantaged youth, who, inheriting neither a strong sense of communal identity nor values transmitted across generations in families, develop subcultures. These sub-cultures negotiate with and hybridize certain hegemonic cultural forms as modes of expression and opposition. Dick Hebdige (in an earlier essay than the one included here), for instance, shows how the Mods fetishized style itself as an element of life, borrowing elements from fashions, old and new, turning cultural consumption (the crucial element in the life-practices of the 'affluent' worker) to their own ends. These subcultures are much more creative than Willis's lads or Morley's audience, and, at least in some cases, they use commodities, the primary products of the system that disadvantages them, as forms of resistance and grounds on which to construct a communal identity. Yet, while *Learning to Labour* allowed the 'lads'' voices a great deal of space in the text, and Morley too transcribed actual voices, *Resistance through Rituals* is primarily concerned to develop a *theory* of hegemony under the conditions it encounters. This more theoretical approach, characteristic of an earlier phase of cultural studies, has its limits. It means that the writers find resistance to 'hegemony' in subcultural styles rather too easily. The book does not emphasize the way in which newly developed 'youth markets' influenced and promoted subcultural systems – especially in the music and fashion businesses. It also underestimates the impact of the education sys-tem, which streamed children after 11 and kept them at school until they were 15 (16 after 1972), generating intense inter-generational bondings unknown before the war. Neither are the Mods, Teds, hippies, and so on seen as trying to have fun or to construct a mode of life for themselves; they are primarily viewed as being engaged in symbolic struggle with the larger social system. But, as we are about to see, categories like 'struggle' and resistance against the 'dominant' become increasingly difficult for cultural studies to sustain.

Despite their use of semiotic and Gramscian concepts, *Learning to Labour*, *The 'Nationwide' Audience*, and *Resistance through Rituals* remain within the tradition established by Hoggart's *The Uses of Literacy*. In the late 1970s things changed. Cultural studies came increasingly under the influence of forms of thought associated with French theorists, in particular Pierre Bourdieu, Michel de Certeau, and Michel Foucault. I will present their work in a general model – though it is important to remember that this model is an abstraction and presents no specific individual's work. Indeed, Bourdieu and Foucault, especially, had little time for each other's approach.

For French theory, individuals live in a setting constituted by various institutions, or what we can call, following Bourdieu, 'fields' – families, work, peer groups, educational apparatuses, political parties, and so on. Each field takes a particular material form, most having a characteristic space and time attached to them (the private home for family life and most media reception, weekdays for work, etc.). The relation of space to social fields is the theme of the essays by Foucault and Edward Soja collected here. Each field is future-directed and contains its own 'imaginary', its own promise and image of satisfaction and success, its own possibilities for pleasure. Family life, for instance, depends upon images of the perfect family (mum, dad, and a new-born baby, say) and members may feel pleasure when they reproduce that image, even if only for a moment. This 'imaginary' *is* imaginary because of the limits and scarcities which organize fields – family life is constrained by finances, ageing, and inter-generational conflict, for example. Because of these limits, too, fields are suffused by power relations and tend to be structured hierarchically. After all, not everyone can have equal experience, knowledge, money, or authority. Very hierarchical fields (like schools and offices) are most disciplined and rationalized: in them all activities are directed to a fixed purpose – education in a school, profit in a business. Further, each field has characteristic signifying practices more or less tightly attached to it: the same person may well talk, walk, and dress differently at school (or work) from the way they do in the family, and differently again when socializing with their peers. These signifying practices are structured through scarcity as well. Dick Hebdige has pointed out that punks worked on their body rather than consumption as a means of expression because it was one of the few materials that they could afford.

Each field also contains a variety of styles of belonging: one can be this kind of student or that kind, for instance, a casual filmgoer or a film buff. These fields, then, contain choices of 'self-formation' or what Foucault called 'self-government', though, in highly disciplined and rationalized fields like schools or businesses, these choices are more directed from above than in others. Likewise, individuals can work out strategies by which to advance in a field or to reconcile themselves to their current position: Bourdieu famously showed how members of the working class, unable to afford certain goods or tastes, made a virtue of necessity by saying they didn't like them anyway. On the other hand, possibilities exist for 'transgressive' undermining or 'festive' over-turning of routines and hierarchies through passive resistance, ironical mimicry, symbolic inversion, orgiastic letting go, even day-dreaming – as the essays by Richard Dyer, Peter Stallybrass and Allon White, and Michel de Certeau here show. Especially in societies where hierarchies in many fields are rigid, these forms of transgression may themselves become institution-alized – as in Brazil today with its carnival samba schools, or early capitalist Europe with its pantomimes. Finally, each field, to some degree, both defines itself against and is suffused by others: for instance, relations in the workplace may be modelled on the family ('paternalism'), though the family is simultaneously a 'haven' from work. However, highly rationalized fields (like schools and factories) interact least directly with other fields – they form their own 'world'. None the less, it is where fields are most rationalized and disciplined that positions held in one internal hierarchy may be converted into a position held in another. Reaching the 'top' of the education system helps you start 'higher' in the world of work.

What about subjectivity in this schema? The important point is that actual individuals are not 'subjects' wholly positioned by the system these fields constitute or the strategies the fields provide. There are several reasons for this: in theory at least, individuals can always make choices which take into account, and thus avoid, the forces they know to be positioning them. Also, because human beings exist as 'embodied social subjects' (as Teresa de Lauretis puts it in her essay in this volume), an individual's relation to the fields continually incorporates and shifts under the impact of contingent givens (skin colour, physical appearance, and so on) and material events (illness, technological breakdowns, and so on) which are not simply determinants of social or cultural forces. Third, language itself intervenes between the individual and the socio-cultural fields that construct his or her positions. Our sense of uniqueness is grounded on our sense that we can *say* what we like – at least to ourselves – and we have that sense because language is both a resource that costs nothing (a basic but often ignored point) and complex enough to enable an infinite number of individual speech acts. As deconstructive theorists have pointed out, this is true because of, rather than despite, the fact that private discourse always comes from somewhere else and its meanings cannot be wholly mastered by those who use it. Last, given that individuals live (i) in symbolic structures which let them (within limits) speak for themselves; (ii) in bodies that are their own but not wholly under control; and (iii) in a temporality which flows towards the unknowable and uncontainable, they may find in themselves 'deep' selves which cannot be reduced either to the self that freely chooses styles, strategies, and techniques of self-formation or to the subject positioned by external fields and discourses. Modern Western culture, in particular, has given a great deal of value to this form of subjectivity, and cultural studies' insistence that subjectivity primarily consists of practices and strategies has been targeted against it.

The French model breaks from earlier forms of cultural studies. To begin with, it downgrades the way that economic scarcities operate systematically across *many* fields. Because it conceives of social fields as 'partially autonomous', the French model cannot affirm a central agency that might direct a number of fields to provide a more equitable distribution of resources. In this, it is remote from traditional social democratic politics. Instead, there is a drift to affirm both culture's Utopian force and those forms of resistance (such as de Certeau's 'walking in the city' in this collection) only possible in the cracks and gaps of the larger, apparently impregnable, system. Somewhat paradoxically, that system is impregnable just because it is less centred around a 'dominant' set of institutions or ideology. Why did cultural studies accept relatively depoliticized analyses of this kind? The reasons are to be found in the decline of the social democratic power bloc from the mid-1970s onwards which enabled the so-called 'new right's' emergence – in the US under Ronald Reagan (1981) and in the UK under Margaret Thatcher (1979). Furthermore, it was in the context of the new right's emergence that (as we shall see), after absorbing French theory, the discipline orientated itself towards what Cornel West in his essay here calls the 'culture of difference' and became a genuinely global movement. In part, cultural studies changed because the student body changed. Students who identified themselves as feminists, members of a particular ethnic or sexual-preference group rather than of a class or a nation, say, were interested in studying culture and theory on their terms, and were ready for more fragmented models of culture and society – models which, strangely enough, echoed Mrs Thatcher's famous and radical apothegm: 'There is no such thing as "society".'

The new right (or 'Thatcherism' as I shall often call it, following Stuart Hall) countered the social democrats by arguing, first, that the state should intervene in citizens' lives to the minimum possible extent so that market forces can structure as many social relations and exchanges as possible, and, next, that the affirmation of internal differences (especially between classes, ethnic groups, and genders) could threaten national unity. The nation was defined in terms of traditional and popular national-cultural images of 'Englishness' in Thatcher's case and 'Americanness' in Reagan's. This was a politics that appealed at least as much to the 'affluent worker' as to traditional conservative (in the US, Republican) voters. As long ago as 1957, Richard Hoggart had noted how, with increased spending power, the working class were increasingly evaluating the world in economic, rather than class, terms. Thatcherism was also the product of the social democratic interventionist state's failure to manage the economy without playing inflation off against unemployment, a failure which itself followed increasing economic globalization (especially of the financial sector) and the appearance of economic powers outside the West. (The most prominent events in the process of economic globalization were the 1971 end of the old Bretton Woods agreement by which all major currencies had been pegged against the US dollar; the 1973–4 OPEC cartel; the radical increase of Japanese competitiveness in key consumer-durable markets; the movement of Western manufacturing 'off shore' through the 1970s and 1980s, and the immense increase of capacity for information about commodity and money markets to be disseminated quickly and globally.) In these terms, Thatcherism is the political reflex of an affluent but threatened first-world society in a post-colonial world order. As Stuart Hall pointed out (Hall 1988), it was able to counter a widespread sense of fragility by taking advantage of a mass of 'popular knowledge' which put the family, respectability, hard work, 'practicality', and order first – a 'popular knowledge' which, as Morley demonstrated, had been, for years, transmitted in shows like *Nationwide* and its US equivalents. At this level at least, Thatcherism does not draw on the values of traditional high culture; instead it appeals to the social imaginary produced by the market-orientated media.

Thatcherism contains an internal contradiction – between its economic rationalism and its consensual cultural nationalism. The more the market is freed from state intervention and trade and finance cross national boundaries, the more the nation will be exposed to foreign influences and the greater the gap between rich and poor. Thatcherite appeals to popular values can be seen as an attempt to overcome this tension. In particular, the new right gives the family extraordinary value and aura just because a society organized by market forces is one in which economic life expectations are particularly insecure (as well as one in which, for some, rewards are large and life exciting). In the same way, a homogeneous image of national culture is celebrated and enforced to counter the dangers posed by the increasingly global nature of economic exchanges and widening national, economic divisions. The new right image of a monoculture and hard-working family life, organized through traditional gender roles, requires a devaluation not just of other nations and their cultural identities but of 'enemies within': those who are 'other' racially, sexually, intellectually. It was in this situation that the Birmingham school focused more intensely, on the one hand, on feminist work (as by Charlotte Brunsdon, Angela McRobbie, and Dorothy Hobson) as well as on the analysis of racism and a counter-celebration of black cultures (most painstakingly in Paul Gilroy's *There Ain't No Black in the Union Jack*, 1987); and, on the other hand, on a more straightforward critique of Thatcherism itself, as in the essays collected in Stuart Hall's *The Hard Road to Renewal* (1988) as well as the earlier collectively written *Policing the Crisis* (1979). This last book latches on to the mechanisms by which law-and-order issues and racism were gaining ground in the last days of the social democratic power bloc, convincingly demonstrating that law-and-order panics in Britain in the 1970s were produced by tacit alliances between the media and the police – being, in that sense, organized.

As cultural studies responded to the conditions surrounding the new right's emergence, the discipline became internationalized. The main reason for this is simple: analyses of racism, sexism, and the culture industry possessed a wider appeal than analysis of the British working-class culture, particularly in the US or Australia ('New World' states who fancied themselves relatively 'classless' societies). But, when cultural studies moved away from a marxian analysis based on class, it began to approach, if in a different spirit and register, certain Thatcherite themes. After all, both movements were strongly anti-statist; both affirmed, within limits, a decentred view of social organization.

What were the analogies between Thatcherism and cultural studies, politically so opposed to one another? Perhaps most importantly, where new right discourse argued that no state institution could transcend particular interests and legitimately control individual choices best represented in the market, cultural studies criticized the notion that any theory could stand outside the field it claimed to tell the truth about as if it were a 'meta-discourse'. For French theory, 'theory' itself was a discursive practice produced in a particular field with particular power effects: it offers, for instance, the ability rhetorically to master other people's values and 'common sense'. That there could be no transcendental 'meta-discourse' was a crucial thesis in what is sometimes also called theoretical 'postmodernism' – the end of any appeal to those 'grand narratives' by which institutions and discourses bearing the modernizing values of universal liberty, equality and progress were affirmed in the name of a trans-historical, meta-discursive subject. (See the essay by Lyotard below for a description of post-modernism.)

The new mode of cultural studies no longer concentrated on reading culture as primarily directed against the state. Mainly under the impact of new feminist work at first, it began to affirm 'other' ways of life on their own terms. Emphasis shifted from communities positioned against large power blocs and bound together as classes or subcultures to ethnic and women's groups committed to maintaining and elaborating autonomous values, identities, and ethics. This moment in cultural studies pictured society as much more decentred than either the CCCS had in its earliest work or than the French theorists had, as they focused on discipline, rationalization, and institutional fields. However, an immediate problem confronted this new model as it broke society down into fractions united by sexuality, gender, or ethnicity: how to conceive of relations between these dispersed communities? Two solutions were offered, both rather utopian and future-directed: first, new 'rainbow' alliances and cross-identifications could be worked out for particular and provisional social or 'micro-political' ends; second, relations between these groups would be 'dialogic' – a concept borrowed from Mikhail Bakhtin and in which the otherness of each interacting participant remains intact. Whatever the effectiveness of these solutions, celebrations of the 'other' sounded a powerful oppositional note where governments attempted to encourage or enforce monoculturalism and traditional gender models on the nation. None the less, the affirmation of 'otherness' and 'difference' in what is sometimes called a 'politics of survival' belong to a looser, more pluralistic and post-modern, conceptual model than those which insist that capitalism and the free market produce interests that are *structurally* unequal and in conflict with each other. Unlike social democratic thought, the new cultural studies no longer aimed at a radical transfiguration of the whole system of social fields.

radical transformation no longer the aim

Cultural studies' affirmation of otherness and negation of meta-discourse must also be understood in terms of the accelerated globalizing of cultural production and distribution from the 1970s on. This is the theme of the essay by Armand Mattelart and his colleagues in this volume, and they show how multidirectional the process of 'globalization' has been. In some areas, it has involved a breakdown of distinctions between 'first'- and 'third'-world nations: new technologies (such as satellite broadcasting) produced international audiences, as for Bob Geldoff's 'Live Aid' 1985 concert, which belonged to what might be called the 'global popular', while, to similar ends, and on the back of the global popular, non-governmental agencies like Greenpeace established new transnational organizations. The globalization of the media had one especially important consequence: through the 1970s and 1980s it accelerated the concentration of the cultural industry, largely because the global market requires increased investment in marketing and distribution. Now, for instance, the international recording industry is an oligopoly consisting of six majors: three European, one American, and two Japanese. But in other ways globalization has produced new local 'vertical' differences – as where, for instance, first-world encouragement to modernize and develop led simultaneously to massive third-world indebtedness with an increase in local poverty and to urbanization and rural deculturalization. In other ways still, however, globalization has generated diversity and autonomy – as when sophisticated cultural and media industries began to develop outside the West in places as different as Brazil and Hong Kong (increasing the amount of local news world-wide, for instance) or when, as James Clifford points out in his essay in this collection, non-Western communities were able creatively to commodify or museumify their cultures or, finally, when vibrant independent rock groups and fans have emerged in Europe, Australasia, Asia (especially Japan), and the US, touring globally without much hype and bouncing off each other, while often maintaining local differences.

globalization

One effect of the large and very various process of globalization has been especially important to cultural studies: Eurocentric concepts of 'primitive', 'underdeveloped', or superstitious peoples (that is, so-called 'fourth-world' people) became difficult to sustain on a variety of registers. In his influential essay 'On ethnographic authority' (in Clifford 1988b), Clifford again showed that anthropologists' 'native informants' could now speak for themselves to 'us' without the mediation of the anthropologists and their 'science'. To somewhat similar ends, Edward Said drew attention to 'orientalism' – the history of those images of the 'orient' produced to help the West dominate the East, and in which what non-Westerners said about themselves was systematically discounted. As cultural studies became the voice of the other, the 'marginal' in the academy, it absorbed a radical wing of anthropology, just as it had earlier absorbed a wing of sociology in Britain. The literary world threw up another case in which the processes of globalization were shown to trouble any simplistic or conventional analysis: protests against Salman Rushdie's *The Satanic Verses* (started by migrant communities in Britain) undercut assumptions about the naturalness (or dominance) of Western notions of how particular cultural formations relate to one another, in particular the Western sense of literature's transcendence of religion and politics. In sum, globalization meant that the role that subcultures and the working class played in earlier cultural studies began to be replaced and transformed by communities outside the West or internal migrant (or 'diasporic') communities – in a move which involved new theoretical and political problems and intensities.

Conceiving of cultural studies as the academic site for marginal/minority discourses had another, very different but no less visible and globalizing consequence, one which took it further from its original attack on mass culture. The discipline began to celebrate commercial culture, in a move I will call 'cultural populism'. Cultural populism became possible within the cultural studies anti-hegemonic tradition because, despite the new right's reliance on values disseminated through the cultural market, the right also buttressed its monoculturalism by traditionalist appeals to the canon. (This play between popular knowledge and celebration of the canon marks another tension within contemporary conservative thought.) In its turn, cultural populism helped cultural studies to become global just because, as we have seen, commercial culture has an increasingly transnational reach. What form has cultural populism taken in cultural studies? It too turned away from the highly theoretical attacks on hegemony so important in the 1970s, this time by arguing that at least some popular-cultural products themselves have positive quasi-political effects independently of education and critical discourse.

To take one instance: in his 1987 essay, 'British cultural studies and television', John Fiske, after reading *Magnum P.I.* through the classic distinction between 'preferred', 'negotiated', and 'oppositional' readings developed by Hall and Morley, goes on to claim that Madonna (c. 1986) offered fans her own form of feminist ideology-critique. Madonna 'calls into question' 'binary oppositions as a way of conceptualizing women' (Fiske 1987a: 275). Elsewhere Fiske emphasized that popular culture provided 'pleasure in the processes of making meanings' (Fiske 1987b: 239) in a move that relied on Roland Barthes's later view that markedly polysemous texts generate particularly intense and liberating pleasures. Such work is refreshing because it rejects the hierarchies that support monocultures, as well as because, unlike the 'hegemony' theorists, it does not condescend to actual popular-cultural practices. But it leaves many questions open. The theorist is still telling the 'popular' audience how their pleasure works in terms which owe much more to the history of theory than they do to what people actually say or think. ✓ Camille Pesta

This form of cultural populism also passes over the question of co-option. Madonna's later work shows us that 'needs of capital' (i.e. the requirement that investments make profits) has not been exactly irrelevant to her career. By calling herself a 'material girl', by daring to screen for us some familial truths in *Truth or Dare/In Bed with Madonna*, and by drawing from the iconography of sexuality (including 'perverse' sex like S and M) for her playful, ironic posing and so making that iconography available to new and larger markets, she helps keep the industry in business. In this light a comparison between Madonna and even a star as musically and stylistically as mainstream as Sinead O'Connor, who has sinned more openly against American patriotism, might be revealing. It would help show how a 'cultural populism' which can celebrate Madonna (whom the industry also loves) as transgressive is subtly, if unconsciously, connected to the promotion of market forces. This is not to say that Madonna is not an important agent in breaking down the barriers which organized the relation between the popular and the sexual as well as the popular and feminity, nor is it to say that entering cultural markets means co-option in any rigid or formal way. Indeed the expansion and differentiation of cultural markets have been tremendously fruitful in all kinds of ways – they are perhaps the major force that will keep cultural studies alive. But cultural populism requires a very nuanced account of the relations between cultural markets and cultural products, and between culture and politics, in order convincingly to celebrate (some) popular culture as 'progressive' – perhaps along the lines taken by Janice Radway in her essay in this collection.

Finally, another kind of cultural studies, which has recently emerged under the title 'cultural policy studies', responds to the decline of the social democratic power bloc in yet other ways. Indeed, cultural policy studies itself takes two distinguishable forms, one economically orientated and pragmatic, the other more theoretical. The first, economic cultural policy analysis, starts from the recognition that much cultural production and distribution requires allocation of scarce resources – the limits to the number of stations that can operate in the radio spectrum for instance. It also takes account of the fact that cultural labour and consumption are increasingly important to national economies, especially those of highly 'advanced' post-industrial countries. For reasons like this, governments are called upon to set parameters for cultural production and distribution – to provide public broadcasting for instance, or to protect local workers against imported labour or products. (See Collins, Garnham, and Locksley (1988) for an excellent example of a policy document in this spirit aimed at the debate over UK public television.) At the micro-level, local communities too may need policy advice, in order, for instance, to establish a museum that best provides for both local and tourist needs. Cultural policy studies helps us think about the frameworks and methods of articulating policy in such situations.

The other branch of cultural policy theory derives from Michel Foucault's later work, though Foucault himself, despite advising a number of French governments, was ambivalent about this development of his thought. He encouraged intellectuals to be more critical than is possible when offering policy advice. (Ian Hunter's *Culture and Government* is the book which theorizes this form of neo-Foucauldianism in most detail; see Foucault's essay 'Practicing criticism' (in Foucault 1988) for a rejection, in advance, of the position.) In its most radical guise, the neo-Foucauldian thesis argues that culture is neither an end in itself nor the product of autonomous agents – whether individuals or communities – but a mechanism for transmitting forms of 'governmentality', for ordering how we act, think, live. Indeed, so the argument goes, cultural work and effects only exist in relation to other governmental structures. Thus Tony Bennett has recently argued that 'policy and governmental conditions and processes should be thought of as constitutive of different forms and fields of culture' (Bennett 1992, 25). The implication is that the least mystified task of the cultural studies analyst is to enter into alliances with, and attempt to influence, the processes of governmentality.

A number of strong arguments can be urged against neo-Foucauldian cultural policy theory. In particular, such theory possesses a rudimentary account of subjectivity. For it, the individual tends to be just a product of 'governmental' protocols or of 'techniques of self-formation'. This matters because questions of pleasure, corporeality, fantasy, identification, affect, desire, critique, transgression, and so on disappear – which is crippling to rich analysis of cultural work and reception. The theory also relies on a reductive sense of politics. 'Policy' becomes a word which, almost magically, neutralizes the more stubborn, conflictual, and critical relations between the various individuals and groups which constitute the social fields in which culture is produced, disseminated, and received.

Leaving these important theoretical difficulties aside for a minute, we can say that both forms of cultural policy studies mark an acceptance of the state hitherto unknown in cultural studies. It traditionally resisted the state's hegemony. There is, indeed, a sense in which cultural policy studies resists new right thinking by returning to statism.

Cultural policy studies also breaks with the history of cultural studies in that the discipline has not traditionally produced neutral expertise. Here the difficulties just noted return. It is all the harder to see how cultural studies might provide (apparently) neutral expertise when one considers the kinds of case that cultural policy characteristically address. How much 'local content' should a particular television industry have? What kind of museum should be constructed in this locality? From the bureaucratic point of view, questions like these require information to be gathered, costs and benefits to be projected, various economic models to be debated. In this, individuals trained in policy-orientated cultural studies (and in other disciplines) might, of course, have a productive role to play. But apart from that, such questions are best argued over not by experts but by (representatives of) interested parties – that is, democratically and politically. As a transnational academic discipline cultural studies itself does not represent such an interest. And, in fact, policy advice does not uncover truths which can be immediately used and applied. On the contrary, outside the academy, it tends to become a pawn in wider political engagements between such interests.

CULTURAL STUDIES NOW: SOME DIRECTIONS AND PROBLEMS

So cultural studies is a discipline continuously shifting its interests and methods, both because it is in constant and engaged interaction with its larger historical context and because it cannot be complacent about its authority. After all, it has taken the force of arguments against 'meta-discourses' and does not want the voice of the academic theorist to drown out other less often heard voices. As we have begun to see, the discipline's turn to ethnography in particular was motivated by the desire to move beyond theoretical discourses which, however insightful, have been restricted to higher education institutions. Ethnography of the kind developed by Willis and Morley was important to cultural studies because it provided a method by which the discipline could escape such restrictions, and it remains crucial to an understanding of the current and future directions of the discipline. It is crucial just because the turn to ethnography highlights the difficulty of *either* claiming *or* disclaiming academic and, more especially, ethnographic authority. For, if we accept that the academic humanities are a field in which power and cultural capital are generated and transmitted and so do not simply articulate 'true' meta-discourses, we must also accept that non-academic or 'popular' cultural institutions require critique from a distance because they have their limits and power effects as well. To put it another way, cultural studies today is situated between its pressing need to question its own institutional and discursive legitimation and its fear that cultural practices outside the institution are becoming too organized and too dispersed to appeal to in the spirit it has hitherto appealed to subcultures, the women's movement, and other 'others' in its (always somewhat compromised) repudiation of statism and the new right.

In this situation, we need to consider the question of ethnographic or academic authority a little more carefully. Of course, ethnography has a long history in the positive social sciences. Social scientists and market re-searchers have traditionally employed three modes of ethnographic investi-gation: (i) large-scale 'surveys' (or 'quantitative research') using formal questionnaires on a sample large enough to provide 'correlation coefficients' or measures of the degree to which one variable (like a taste for reading Charles Dickens) relates to another (like one's parents' jobs); (ii) 'qualitative research' or in-depth or 'focus' interviews, which claim no statistical validity (though they are often used alongside large-scale surveys) and do not rely on formal questionnaires but on (usually group) discussion; (iii) 'participant ob-servation' in which researchers live alongside their subjects – this having been most common in anthropology. Cultural studies ethnography, particularly of media audiences, has mainly used qualitative research in order to avoid the pitfalls of sociological objectivity and to give room to voices other than the theorist's own. The problem of representativeness has been discounted (for example, the people who wrote to Ien Ang about *Dallas* and whom she analysed in her essay collected here are not statistically representative of anything). For cultural studies, knowledge based on statistical techniques belongs to the processes which 'normalize' society and stand in opposition to cultural studies' respect for the marginal subject.

In early cultural studies ethnographic work like Morley's *The 'Nationwide' Audience*, the researcher played the role of a neutral narrator – using research subjects as the basis upon which to elaborate theory. Later participant ob-servers, like Paul Willis, tried to articulate their subjects' perceptions into a more abstract and rigorous lexicon: for Willis good theory was continuous with the 'practical consciousness' of those he studied. The bonding between ethnographer and subject became even more crucial when women began working with women – of which Dorothy Hobson's work on the soap opera

[handwritten marginal note: But what of the fact that those who espouse the post modern most compliantly, who worry least about the problem of representativeness, are able to do so because they are among the economic elite?]

Crossroads is a well-known early instance (Hobson 1982). To think about the importance of the ethnographer's gender – consider how difficult it would have been for a woman to have had Willis's relation to the 'lads'! A sense of shared values, identities, and purposes between the researcher and the researched often elicits richer responses and transactions in the field. To take an instance where the researcher is not immediately participating with her subjects in the field: when Ien Ang invited letters from *Dallas* viewers, she positioned herself as a fan (as she was) so as to encourage engaged replies. But – and here we strike a crucial problem – the ethnographer is not simply a fan; there is an irreducible rift between the position of being a researcher and that of being a fan, though of course a single individual can be both. There are two ways of dealing with this: one is to accept it and the ambivalence or contradiction it generates as productive – as Meaghan Morris does in her essay collected here; the other is for the researcher simultaneously to ethnographize herself in relation to her subjects and to allow her subjects as much exposure as possible to her own, more academic, discourses. At which point ethnography can involve two-way transmission of information and maybe even passion.

With the category 'being a fan', the question of populism reappears. But now we need to draw a distinction between cultural populism and that form of academic populism which (like Paul Willis) argues that, in cultural studies, academic knowledge ought to formalize what is already popularly known. A difficulty for both these populisms is that, when we think of either a 'culture of differences' engaged in a 'politics of survival' or a society as structured by various, interacting fields through which various discursive/cultural practices are transmitted, then the *binary* opposition 'popular' versus 'élite' begins to fall away. The assault on this form of binary thinking has been all the stronger because recent historical research has shown that the separation between popular and élite culture has historically been more fluid than cultural histor- ians have believed. (See Levine 1988 and Collins 1989.) Nevertheless the 'popular' as a category is unlikely to fall out of sight in cultural studies. To begin with, as we have seen, the distribution networks of concentrated cultural markets are increasingly gaining access to communities from different locali- ties, ethnicities, and cultural background to produce ever larger popular audiences: after all, Disneyland, Teenage Ninja Turtles, Michael Jackson, Arnold Schwarzenegger, and even Bart Simpson, like Coke, McDonald's, and Sony Walkmans, belong to the global popular. At a more local level, notions of popular wants and desires are powerfully appealed to both by national politicians (nowhere more so than in Thatcherism) and by managers of large-scale cultural industries as they attempt to organize consumers' tastes, desires, and pleasures. As Meaghan Morris in her essay in the collection notes, politicians construct an imaginary through figures such as 'the silent majority', or the 'man' (less often 'woman') 'in the street'. These figures are sometimes literally fake: in the 1930s and 1940s, Hollywood habitually produced 'documentaries' using actors as supposedly 'real' interviewees. Fake or not, these figures become *embodied* in our national social imaginary. For the politicians, it is as if a certain kind of individual possesses the opinions, tastes, and values which polls, charts, ratings, and elections reveal to be popular. In the culture industries, the figure of the 'popular' mediates between producers and audiences. Using its own sophisticated ethnographic techniques, the industry attempts to produce what the public (or, at any rate, the more affluent sections of it) wants. But at the same time it generates public desire by marketing its products (both hardware and software) as if they were already popular. That 'nothing sells like a hit' is more than a tautology, it is the most successful formula for cultural marketing. People will buy what other people love and desire. Through these political and commercial tactics and logics, the popular is constantly pushed towards the normal, even the universal.

Yet, as a concept like the global popular makes apparent, no single kind of person embodies the popular. Cultural studies can provide space for, and knowledge of, the multiple audiences and communities who, in various combinations, vote, buy records, watch television and films, etc., without ever fitting the 'popular', 'ordinary', or 'normal'. This is another reason for examining the techniques by which social values, attitudes, and desires are measured, as well as demystifying the political uses of representations like the 'silent majority' and 'ordinary American'. In this way, cultural studies can begin to intervene on the cultural market's failure to admit full cultural multiplicity – particularly if it accepts that, in principle, cultural markets can provide a variety of products, pleasures, and uses, including transgressive and avant-garde ones. Although cultural multiplicity is appealed to by many theoretical articles in this anthology, especially Michele Wallace's, Cornel West's, and Gayatri Spivak and Sneja Gunew's, it is useful to cite a well-known recent example of how audience measurement affects cultural production and images of the 'popular' within a particular nation state. When, in the US, *Billboard* stopped producing its charts by measuring radio play and sales in an unrepresentative sample of shops and began using information based directly on bar-coded sales, it immediately became apparent that 'genre' music – country, rap, heavy metal – was selling much better than anyone had suspected. These music forms began to enter a redefined main stream. The sense of what was 'popular' shifted. This is not to say that these new techniques perfectly represent public preferences: *Billboard*'s measurement of purchase doesn't measure real consumption, let alone tastes. For example, not all social groups have the same capacity to turn their taste into purchases, not all sold product

[handwritten margin note: N.B. See Xtian rock]

is listened to as often as others, and some music genres are more often taped than others. Images of 'popular listening' based on *Billboard*'s information would still be awry – though this information will also allow the music business oligopolies to restructure their production and hence (within limits) popular tastes and desires.

The deeper question that quantitative market research and ratings fail to answer is how cultural products are valued and used – this is especially important because this failure, too, has important effects on our construction of the popular. Take television, for instance. Ratings are still mainly produced by measuring how many televisions are turned on to each channel at any particular moment, though techniques to measure actual audience attention are also employed, including videoing viewers! But (leaving the question of VCR recorders aside) we know that television is watched in many ways: for information, for comforting background noise and flicker, as a neutral flow which helps to reduce (or increase) family tensions, for relaxation after working hours, for fans to watch a favourite programme intensely, to produce a sense of cultural superiority through a careful, but ironical and distanced, mode of viewing, as a medium for programmes which are received as great art, and so on. At any one time any programme is available for many of these viewing practices. However, at certain times of the week certain such practices dominate. 'Prime time' is the period in which most people watch for relaxation, for instance. What the ratings measure, then, is not *one* kind of viewing: like is not being compared with like. Rather, a good rating is a sign that a particular television use value dominates at a particular moment within the larger rhythms of the working/schooling week. It is not a simple index of popular will or taste. Again, by turning a good rating into an expression of the 'popular', less widespread practices and preferences are marginalized as 'unpopular'.

Partly because the notion of the 'popular' carries with it these problems, cultural studies is increasingly drawing attention to another, closely connected, category, one which does not compound divisiveness for the simple reason that (at least apparently) no one, anywhere, can avoid it. This category is 'everyday life'. Ironically, however, cultural studies (as in the essay by Michel de Certeau collected here) derives the notion from an avant-garde tradition which turned to everyday life not as a basis for reassuring consensus but as an arena capable of radical transformation just because it was being increasingly disciplined, commodified, and rationalized in so-called 'modernity'. In particular, Henri Lefebvre believed that intellectuals could drive the 'organized passivity' and banality out of everyday life, drawing attention to its tragedies, sublimity, and magic (Lefebvre 1971 and 1991). This was to be achieved by showing, first, that everyday life is *constructed* as the sphere in which, as the writer Maurice Blanchot put it, 'nothing happens' (Blanchot 1987: 15), and, then, by writing about it carefully and affectionately, to defamiliarize it and reaffirm its true value. Lefebvre's desire to play everyday life against modernity was elaborated by Michel de Certeau, who found a dreamlike logic or 'grammar' in overlooked and habitual acts (like walking) which countered disciplining routines. Given de Certeau's and Morris's marvellous essays, there can be little doubt that everyday life does provide an area where imaginative intellectual analysis and description may produce liberating effects. Partly by bringing academic analysis closer to the aims and techniques of older, non-academic essay-writing, the textualizers of everyday life help us accept academic authority at the same time as they loosen and disseminate it. None the less, theory which grounds itself on a sense of the everyday does not avoid the problems associated with populism. Most relevantly, within a discipline that has globalized itself through affirming otherness, it is important to remember the obvious point that everyday life is not everywhere the same, despite those modernizing effects of uniformity that Lefebvre was obsessed by. Think about walking in the city: doesn't it make a difference if one walks in Paris, down-town Detroit, Melbourne, Mexico City, or Hong Kong just for starters? And, in each of these places, does a woman have the same experience as a man, a gay as a straight, a young person as an old one? The everyday, too, is produced and experienced at the intersection of many fields by embodied individuals. At times and in places it may also be a limit that cultural practices, especially those that attempt to move across cultures, aim to escape. And, as Meaghan Morris's essay reminds us, the everyday does not possess a single history. It exists within multiple histories, many of which escape the way the past is remembered and stored officially, in universities for instance. Here, perhaps more than elsewhere, cultural studies merges into those modes of history-writing which reconnect us to the world in ways that cannot be taken for granted, and in which our given identities, our 'origins', begin to seem less secure. So it is not as though appeal to everyday life can avoid the intractable questions as to relations between social differences, life-practices, and cultural expression which cultural studies began by addressing. But the fact that textualizing and historicizing everyday life, with all its seduction, lead to these kinds of difficulties is another sign that the discipline has real vitality. There remains much work to do.

Part I *Theory and method*

2 Theodor Adorno and Max Horkheimer

The culture industry: enlightenment as mass deception

EDITOR'S INTRODUCTION

Adorno and Horkheimer's essay, published in the mid-1940s, remains the classic denunciation of the 'culture industry'. It offers a vision of a society that has lost its capacity to nourish true freedom and individuality – as well as the ability to represent the real conditions of existence. Adorno and Horkheimer believe this loss results from the fact that cultural production has moved from an artisanal stage, which depended on individual effort and required little or no investment, to an industrial stage. For them, the modern culture industry produces safe, standardized products geared to the larger demands of the capitalist economy. It does so by representing 'average' life for purposes of pure entertainment or distraction as seductively and realistically as possible. Thus, for them, Hollywood movies, radio, mass-produced journalism, and advertising are only different at the most superficial level. Furthermore, the culture industry has become so successful that 'art' and 'life' are no longer wholly separable – which is the theme later theorists of postmodernity took from the essay. (See Jameson 1990; and the Lyotard essay in this volume.) Of course, 'high' art still exists as 'mass culture''s opposite, but for Adorno, in a famous phrase, these are two halves of a whole that do not add up.

Debate about the essay continues, but it is important to remember the situation in which it was written. The Second World War had not quite ended, and Adorno and Horkheimer were refugees from Nazi Germany living in the US. Hitler's totalitarianism (with its state control of cultural production) and the American market system are fused in their thought – all the more easily because, for them as members of the German (or rather the secularized German Jewish) bourgeoisie, high culture, particularly drama and music, is a powerful vehicle of civil values. It is also worth emphasizing that when this essay was written the cultural industry was less variegated than it was to become, during the 1960s in particular. Hollywood, for instance, was still 'vertically integrated' so that the five major studios owned the production, distribution, and exhibition arms of the film business between them; television was still in its infancy; the LP and the single were unknown; the cultural market had not been broken into various demographic sectors – of which, in the 1950s, the youth segment was to become the most energetic. This helps explain how Adorno and Horkheimer neglect what was to become central to cultural studies: the ways in which the cultural industry, while in the service of organized capital, also provides the opportunities for all kinds of individual and collective creativity and decoding.

Further reading: Adorno 1991; Berman 1989; Connerton 1980; Jameson 1990; Jay 1984a.

S.D.

The sociological theory that the loss of the support of objectively established religion, the dissolution of the last remnants of precapitalism, together with technological and social differentiation or specialization, have led to cultural chaos is disproved every day; for culture now impresses the same stamp on everything. Films, radio and magazines make up a system which is uniform as a whole and in every part. Even the aesthetic activities of political opposites are one in their enthusiastic obedience to the rhythm of the iron system. The decorative industrial management buildings and exhibition centres in authoritarian countries are much the same as anywhere else. The huge gleaming towers that shoot up everywhere are outward signs of the ingenious planning of international concerns, toward which the unleashed entrepreneurial system (whose monuments are a mass of gloomy houses and business premises in grimy, spiritless cities) was already hastening. Even now the older houses just outside the concrete city centres look like slums, and the new bungalows on the outskirts are at one with the flimsy structures of world fairs in their praise of technical progress and their built-in demand to be discarded after a short while like empty food cans. Yet the city housing projects designed to perpetuate the individual as a supposedly independent unit in a small hygienic dwelling make him all the more subservient to his adversary – the absolute power of capitalism. Because the inhabitants, as producers and as consumers, are drawn into the centre in search of work and pleasure, all the living units crystallize into well-organized complexes. The striking unity of microcosm and macrocosm presents men with a model of their culture: the false identity of the general and the particular. Under monopoly all mass culture is identical, and the lines of its artificial framework begin to show through. The people at the top are no longer so interested in concealing monopoly: as its violence becomes more open, so its power grows. Movies and radio need no longer pretend to be art. The truth that they are just business is made into an ideology in order to justify the rubbish they deliberately produce. They call themselves industries; and when their directors' incomes are published, any doubt about the social utility of the finished products is removed.

Interested parties explain the culture industry in technological terms. It is alleged that because millions participate in it, certain reproduction processes are necessary that inevitably require identical needs in innumerable places to be satisfied with identical goods. The technical contrast between the few production centres and the large number of widely dispersed consumption points is said to demand organization and planning by management. Furthermore, it is claimed that standards were based in the first place on consumers' needs, and for that reason were accepted with so little resistance. The result is the circle of manipulation and retroactive need in which the unity of the system grows ever stronger. No mention is made of the fact that the basis on which technology acquires power over society is the power of those whose economic hold over society is greatest. A technological rationale is the rationale of domination itself. It is the coercive nature of society alienated from itself. Automobiles, bombs, and movies keep the whole thing together until their levelling element shows its strength in the very wrong which it furthered. It has made the technology of the culture industry no more than the achievement of standardization and mass production, sacrificing whatever involved a distinction between the logic of the work and that of the social system. This is the result not of a law of movement in technology as such but of its function in today's economy. The need which might resist central control has already been suppressed by the control of the individual consciousness. The step from the telephone to the radio has clearly distinguished the roles. The former still allowed the subscriber to play the role of subject, and was liberal. The latter is democratic: it turns all participants into listeners and authoritatively subjects them to broadcast programmes which are all exactly the same. No machinery of rejoinder has been devised, and private broadcasters are denied any freedom. They are confined to the apocryphal field of the 'amateur', and also have to accept organization from above. But any trace of spontaneity from the public in official broadcasting is controlled and absorbed by talent scouts, studio competitions and official programmes of every kind selected by professionals. Talented performers belong to the industry long before it displays them;

otherwise they would not be so eager to fit in. The attitude of the public, which ostensibly and actually favours the system of the culture industry, is a part of the system and not an excuse for it. If one branch of art follows the same formula as one with a very different medium and content; if the dramatic intrigue of broadcast soap operas becomes no more than useful material for showing how to master technical problems at both ends of the scale of musical experience – real jazz or a cheap imitation; or if a movement from a Beethoven symphony is crudely 'adapted' for a film sound-track in the same way as a Tolstoy novel is garbled in a film script: then the claim that this is done to satisfy the spontaneous wishes of the public is no more than hot air. We are closer to the facts if we explain these phenomena as inherent in the technical and personnel apparatus which, down to its last cog, itself forms part of the economic mechanism of selection. In addition there is the agreement – or at least the determination – of all executive authorities not to produce or sanction anything that in any way differs from their own rules, their own ideas about consumers, or above all themselves.

In our age the objective social tendency is incarnate in the hidden subjective purposes of company directors, the foremost among whom are in the most powerful sectors of industry – steel, petroleum, electricity, and chemicals. Culture monopolies are weak and dependent in comparison. They cannot afford to neglect their appeasement of the real holders of power if their sphere of activity in mass society (a sphere producing a specific type of commodity which anyhow is still too closely bound up with easygoing liberalism and Jewish intellectuals) is not to undergo a series of purges. The dependence of the most powerful broadcasting company on the electrical industry, or of the motion picture industry on the banks, is characteristic of the whole sphere, whose individual branches are themselves economically interwoven. All are in such close contact that the extreme concentration of mental forces allows demarcation lines between different firms and technical branches to be ignored. The ruthless unity in the culture industry is evidence of what will happen in politics. Marked differentiations such as those of A and B films, or of stories in magazines in different price ranges, depend not so much on subject matter as on classifying, organizing, and labelling consumers. Something is provided for all so that none may escape; the distinctions are emphasized and extended. The public is catered for with a hierarchical range of mass-produced products of varying quality, thus advancing the rule of complete quantification. Everybody must behave (as if spontaneously) in accordance with his previously determined and indexed level, and choose the category of mass product turned out for his type. Consumers appear as statistics on research organization charts, and are divided by income groups into red, green, and blue areas; the technique is that used for any type of propaganda.

How formalized the procedure is can be seen when the mechanically differentiated products prove to be all alike in the end. That the difference between the Chrysler range and General Motors products is basically illusory strikes every child with a keen interest in varieties. What connoisseurs discuss as good or bad points serve only to perpetuate the semblance of competition and range of choice. The same applies to the Warner Brothers and Metro Goldwyn Mayer productions. But even the differences between the more expensive and cheaper models put out by the same firm steadily diminish: for automobiles, there are such differences as the number of cylinders, cubic capacity, details of patented gadgets; and for films there are the number of stars, the extravagant use of technology, labour, and equipment, and the introduction of the latest psychological formulas. The universal criterion of merit is the amount of 'conspicuous production', of blatant cash investment. The varying budgets in the culture industry do not bear the slightest relation to factual values, to the meaning of the products themselves. Even the technical media are relentlessly forced into uniformity. Television aims at a synthesis of radio and film, and is held up only because the interested parties have not yet reached agreement, but its consequences will be quite enormous and promise to intensify the impoverishment of aesthetic matter so drastically, that by tomorrow the thinly veiled identity of all industrial culture products can come triumphantly out into the open, derisively fulfilling the Wagnerian dream of the *Gesamtkunstwerk* – the fusion of all the arts in one work. The alliance of word, image, and music is all the more perfect than in *Tristan* because the sensuous elements which all approvingly reflect the surface of social reality are in principle embodied in the same technical process, the unity of which becomes its distinctive content. This process integrates all the elements of the production, from the novel (shaped with an eye to the film) to the last sound effect. It is the triumph of invested capital, whose title as absolute master is etched deep into the hearts of the dispossessed in the employment line; it is the meaningful content of every film, whatever plot the production team may have selected.

The whole world is made to pass through the filter of the culture industry. The old experience of the movie-goer, who sees the world outside as an extension of the film he has just left (because the latter is intent upon reproducing the world of everyday perceptions), is now the producer's guideline. The more intensely and flawlessly his techniques duplicate empirical objects, the easier it is today for the illusion to prevail that the outside world is the straightforward continuation of that presented on the screen. This purpose has been furthered by mechanical reproduction since the lightning takeover by the sound film.

Real life is becoming indistinguishable from the movies. The sound film, far surpassing the theatre of illusion, leaves no room for imagination or reflection on the part of the audience, who is unable to respond within the structure of the film, yet deviate from its precise detail without losing the thread of the story; hence the film forces its victims to equate it directly with reality. The stunting of the mass-media consumer's powers of imagination and spontaneity does not have to be traced back to any psychological mechanisms; he must ascribe the loss of those attributes to the objective nature of the products themselves, especially to the most characteristic of them, the sound film. They are so designed that quickness, powers of observation, and experience are undeniably needed to apprehend them at all; yet sustained thought is out of the question if the spectator is not to miss the relentless rush of facts. Even though the effort required for his response is semi-automatic, no scope is left for the imagination. Those who are so absorbed by the world of the movie – by its images, gestures, and words – that they are unable to supply what really makes it a world, do not have to dwell on particular points of its mechanics during a screening. All the other films and products of the entertainment industry which they have seen have taught them what to expect; they react automatically. The might of industrial society is lodged in men's minds. The entertainments manufacturers know that their products will be consumed with alertness even when the customer is distraught, for each of them is a model of the huge economic machinery which has always sustained the masses, whether at work or at leisure – which is akin to work. From every sound film and every broadcast programme the social effect can be inferred which is exclusive to none but is shared by all alike. The culture industry as a whole has moulded men as a type unfailingly reproduced in every product. All the agents of this process, from the producer to the women's clubs, take good care that the simple reproduction of this mental state is not nuanced or extended in any way.

The art historians and guardians of culture who complain of the extinction in the West of a basic style-determining power are wrong. The stereotyped appropriation of everything, even the inchoate, for the purposes of mechanical reproduction surpasses the rigour and general currency of any 'real style', in the sense in which cultural *cognoscenti* celebrate the organic precapitalist past. No Palestrina could be more of a purist in eliminating every unprepared and unresolved discord than the jazz arranger in suppressing any development which does not conform to the jargon. When jazzing up Mozart he changes him not only when he is too serious or too difficult but when he harmonizes the melody in a different way, perhaps more simply, than is customary now. No medieval builder can have scrutinized the subjects for church windows and sculptures more suspiciously than the studio hierarchy scrutinizes a work by Balzac or Hugo before finally approving it. No medieval theologian could have determined the degree of the torment to be suffered by the damned in accordance with the *ordo* of divine love more meticulously than the producers of shoddy epics calculate the torture to be undergone by the hero or the exact point to which the leading lady's hemline shall be raised. The explicit and implicit, exoteric and esoteric catalogue of the forbidden and tolerated is so extensive that it not only defines the area of freedom but is all-powerful inside it. Everything down to the last detail is shaped accordingly. Like its counterpart, avant-garde art, the entertainment industry determines its own language, down to its very syntax and vocabulary, by the use of anathema. The constant pressure to produce new effects (which must conform to the old pattern) serves merely as another rule to increase the power of the conventions when any single effect threatens to slip through the net. Every detail is so firmly stamped with sameness that nothing can appear which is not marked at birth, or does not meet with approval at first sight. And the star performers, whether they produce or reproduce, use this jargon as freely and fluently and with as much gusto as if it were the very language which it silenced long ago. Such is the ideal of what is natural in this field of activity, and its influence becomes all the more powerful, the more technique is perfected and diminishes the tension between the finished product and everyday life. The paradox of this routine, which is essentially travesty, can be detected and is often predominant in everything that the culture industry turns out. A jazz musician who is playing a piece of serious music, one of Beethoven's simplest minuets, syncopates it involuntarily and will smile superciliously when asked to follow the normal divisions of the beat. This is the 'nature' which, complicated by the ever-present and extravagant demands of the specific medium, constitutes the new style and is a 'system of non-culture, to which one might even concede a certain "unity of style" if it really made any sense to speak of stylized barbarity'.

The universal imposition of this stylized mode can even go beyond what is quasi-officially sanctioned or forbidden; today a hit song is more readily forgiven for not observing the 32 beats or the compass of the ninth than for containing even the most clandestine melodic or harmonic detail which does not conform to the idiom. Whenever Orson Welles offends against the tricks of the trade, he is forgiven because his departures from the norm are regarded as calculated mutations which serve all the more strongly to confirm the validity of the system. The constraint of the technically conditioned idiom which stars and directors have to produce as 'nature' so that the people can appropriate it, extends to such fine nuances that they almost attain the subtlety of the devices of an avant-garde work as against those of truth. The rare capacity minutely to fulfil the obligations of the natural idiom in all branches of the culture industry becomes the criterion of efficiency. What and how they say it must be measurable by everyday language, as in logical positivism. The producers are experts. The idiom demands an astounding productive power, which it absorbs and squanders. In a diabolical way it has overreached the culturally conservative distinction between genuine and artificial style. A style might be called artificial which is imposed from without on the refractory impulses of a form. But in the culture industry every element of the subject matter has its origin in the same apparatus as that jargon whose stamp it bears. The quarrels in which the artistic experts become involved with sponsor and censor about a lie going beyond the bounds of credibility are evidence not so much of an inner aesthetic tension as of a divergence of interests. The reputation of the specialist, in which a last remnant of objective independence sometimes finds refuge, conflicts with the business politics of the Church, or the concern which is manufacturing the cultural commodity. But the thing itself has been essentially objectified and made viable before the established authorities began to argue about it. Even before Zanuck acquired her, Saint Bernadette was regarded by her latter-day hagiographer as brilliant propaganda for all interested parties. That is what became of the emotions of the character. Hence the style of the culture industry, which no longer has to test itself against any refractory material, is also the negation of style. The reconciliation of the general and particular, of the rule and the specific demands of the subject matter, the achievement of which alone gives essential, meaningful content to style, is futile because there has ceased to be the slightest tension between opposite poles: these concordant extremes are dismally identical; the general can replace the particular, and vice versa.

Nevertheless, this caricature of style does not amount to something beyond the genuine style of the past. In the culture industry the notion of genuine style is seen to be the aesthetic equivalent of domination. Style considered as mere aesthetic regularity is a romantic dream of the past. The unity of style not only of the Christian Middle Ages but of the Renaissance expresses in each case the different structure of social power, and not the obscure experience of the oppressed in which the general was enclosed. The great artists were never those who embodied a wholly flawless and perfect style, but those who used style as a way of hardening themselves against the chaotic expression of suffering, as a negative truth. The style of their works gave what was expressed that force without which life flows away unheard. Those very art forms which are known as classical, such as Mozart's music, contain objective trends which represent something different to the style which they incarnate. As late as Schönberg and Picasso, the great artists have retained a mistrust of style, and at crucial points have subordinated it to the logic of the matter. What Dadaists and Expressionists called the untruth of style as such triumphs today in the sung jargon of a crooner, in the carefully contrived elegance of a film star, and even in the admirable expertise of a photograph of a peasant's squalid hut. Style represents a promise in every work of art. That which is expressed is subsumed through style into the dominant forms of generality, into the language of music, painting, or words, in the hope that it will be reconciled thus with the idea of true generality. This promise held out by the work of art that it will create truth by lending new shape to the conventional social forms is as necessary as it is hypocritical. It uncondi-tionally posits the real forms of life as it is by suggesting that fulfilment lies in their aesthetic derivatives. To this extent the claim of art is always ideology too. However, only in this confrontation with tradition of which style is the record can art express suffering. That factor in a work of art which enables it to transcend reality certainly cannot be detached from style; but it does not consist of the harmony actually realized, of any doubtful unity of form and content, within and without, of indi-vidual and society; it is to be found in those features in which discrep-ancy appears: in the necessary failure of the passionate striving for identity. Instead of exposing itself to this failure in which the style of the great work of art has always achieved self-negation, the inferior work has always relied on its similarity with others – on a surrogate identity.

In the culture industry this imitation finally becomes absolute. Having ceased to be anything but style, it reveals the latter's secret: obedience to the social hierarchy. Today aesthetic barbarity completes what has threatened the creations of the spirit since they were gathered together as culture and neutralized. To speak of culture was always contrary to culture. Culture as a common denominator already contains in embryo that schematization and process of cataloguing and classification which bring culture within the sphere of administration. And it is precisely the industrialized, the consequent, subsumption which entirely accords with this notion of culture. By subordinating in the same way and to the same end all areas of intellectual creation, by occupying men's senses from the time they leave the factory in the evening to the time they clock in again the next morning with matter that bears the impress of the labour process they themselves have to sustain throughout the day, this subsumption mockingly satisfies the concept of a unified culture which the philosophers of personality contrasted with mass culture.

The culture industry perpetually cheats its consumers of what it perpetually promises. The promissory note which, with its plots and staging, it draws on pleasure is endlessly prolonged; the promise, which is actually all the spectacle consists of, is illusory: all it actually confirms is that the real point will never be reached, that the diner must be satisfied with the menu. In front of the appetite stimulated by all those brilliant names and images there is finally set no more than a commendation of the depressing everyday world it sought to escape. Of course works of art were not sexual exhibitions either. However, by representing deprivation as negative, they retracted, as it were, the prostitution of the impulse and rescued by mediation what was denied. The secret of aesthetic sublimation is its representation of fulfilment as a broken promise. The culture industry does not sublimate; it represses. By repeatedly exposing the objects of desire, breasts in a clinging sweater or the naked torso of the athletic hero, it only stimulates the unsublimated forepleasure which habitual deprivation has long since reduced to a masochistic semblance. There is no erotic situation which, while insinuating and exciting, does not fail to indicate unmistakably that things can never go that far. The Hays Office merely confirms the ritual of Tantalus that the culture industry has established anyway. Works of art are ascetic and unashamed; the culture industry is pornographic and prudish. Love is downgraded to romance. And, after the descent, much is permitted; even licence as a marketable speciality has its quota bearing the trade description 'daring'. The mass production of the sexual automatically achieves its repression. Because of his ubiquity, the film star with whom one is meant to fall in love is from the outset a copy of himself. Every tenor voice comes to sound like a Caruso record, and the 'natural' faces of Texas girls are like the successful models by whom Hollywood has typecast them. The mechanical reproduction of beauty, which reactionary cultural fanaticism wholeheartedly serves in its methodical idolization of individuality, leaves no room for that unconscious idolatry which was once essential to beauty. The triumph over beauty is celebrated by humour – the *Schadenfreude* that every successful deprivation calls forth. There is laughter because there is nothing to laugh at. Laughter, whether conciliatory or terrible, always occurs when some fear passes. It indicates liberation either from physical danger or from the grip of logic. Conciliatory laughter is heard as the echo of an escape from power; the wrong kind overcomes fear by capitulating to the forces which are to be feared. It is the echo of power as something inescapable. Fun is a medicinal bath. The pleasure industry never fails to prescribe it. It makes laughter the instrument of the fraud practised on happiness. Moments of happiness are without laughter; only operettas and films portray sex to the accompaniment of resounding laughter. But Baudelaire is as devoid of humour as Hölderlin. In the false society laughter is a disease which has attacked happiness and is drawing it into its worthless totality. To laugh at something is always to deride it, and the life which, according to Bergson, in laughter breaks through the barrier, is actually an invading barbaric life, self-assertion prepared to parade its liberation from any scruple when the social occasion arises. Such a laughing audience is a parody of humanity. Its members are monads, all dedicated to the pleasure of being ready for anything at the expense of everyone else. Their harmony is a caricature of solidarity. What is fiendish about this false laughter is that it is a compelling parody of the best, which is conciliatory. Delight is austere: *res severa verum gaudium*. The monastic theory that not asceticism but the sexual act denotes the renunciation of attainable bliss receives negative confirmation in the gravity of the lover who with foreboding commits his life to the fleeting moment. In the culture industry, jovial denial takes the place of the pain found in ecstasy and in asceticism. The supreme law is that they shall not satisfy their desires at any price; they must laugh and be content with laughter. In every product of the culture industry, the permanent denial imposed by civilization is once again unmistakably demonstrated and inflicted on its victims. To offer and to deprive them of something is one and the same. This is what happens in erotic films. Precisely because it must never take place, everything centres upon copulation. In films it is more strictly forbidden for an illegitimate relationship to be admitted without the parties being punished than for a millionaire's future son-in-law to be active in the labour movement. In contrast to the liberal era, industrialized as well as popular culture may wax indignant at capitalism, but it cannot renounce the threat of castration. This is fundamental. It outlasts the organized acceptance of the uniformed seen in the films which are produced to that end, and in reality. What is decisive today is no longer puritanism, although it still asserts itself in the form of women's organizations, but the necessity inherent in the system not to leave the customer alone, not for a moment to allow him any suspicion that resistance is possible. The principle dictates that he should be shown all his needs as capable of fulfilment, but that those needs should be so predetermined that he feels himself to be the eternal consumer, the object of the culture industry. Not only does it make him believe that the deception it practises is satisfaction, but it goes further and implies that, whatever the state of affairs, he must put up with what is offered. The escape from everyday drudgery which the whole culture industry promises may be compared to the daughter's abduction in the cartoon: the father is holding the ladder in the dark. The paradise offered by the culture industry is the same old drudgery. Both escape and elopement are predesigned to lead back to the starting point. Pleasure promotes the resignation which it ought to help to forget.

Amusement, if released from every restraint, would not only be the antithesis of art but its extreme role. The Mark Twain absurdity with which the American culture industry flirts at times might be a corrective of art. The more seriously the latter regards the incompatibility with life, the more it resembles the seriousness of life, its antithesis; the more effort it devotes to developing wholly from its own formal law, the more effort it demands from the intelligence to neutralize its burden. In some revue films, and especially in the grotesque and the funnies, the possibility of this negation does glimmer for a few moments. But of course it cannot happen. Pure amusement in its consequence, relaxed self-surrender to all kinds of associations and happy nonsense, is cut short by the amusement on the market: instead, it is interrupted by a surrogate overall meaning which the culture industry insists on giving to its products, and yet misuses as a mere pretext for bringing in the stars. Biographies and other simple stories patch the fragments of nonsense into an idiotic plot. We do not have the cap and bells of the jester but the bunch of keys of capitalist reason, which even screens the pleasure of achieving success. Every kiss in the revue film has to contribute to the career of the boxer, or some hit song expert or other whose rise to fame is being glorified. The deception is not that the culture industry supplies amusement but that it ruins the fun by allowing business considerations to involve it in the ideological clichés of a culture in the process of self-liquidation. Ethics and taste cut short unrestrained amusement as 'naïve' – naïveté is thought to be as bad as intellectualism – and even restrict technical possibilities. The culture industry is corrupt; not because it is a sinful Babylon but because it is a cathedral dedicated to elevated pleasure. On all levels, from Hemingway to Emil Ludwig, from Mrs Miniver to the Lone Ranger, from Toscanini to Guy Lombardo, there is untruth in the intellectual content taken ready-made from art and science. The culture industry does retain a trace of something better in those features which bring it close to the circus, in the self-justifying and nonsensical skill of riders, acrobats and clowns, in the 'defence and justification of physical as against intellectual art'. But the refuges of a mindless artistry which represents what is human as opposed to the social mechanism are being relentlessly hunted down by a schematic reason which compels everything to prove its significance and effect. The consequence is that the nonsensical at the bottom disappears as utterly as the sense in works of art at the top.

In the culture industry the individual is an illusion not merely because of the standardization of the means of production. He is tolerated only so long as his complete identification with the generality is unquestioned. Pseudo individuality is rife: from the standardized jazz improvization to the exceptional film star whose hair curls over her eye to demonstrate her originality. What is individual is no more than the generality's power to stamp the accidental detail so firmly that it is accepted as such. The defiant reserve or elegant appearance of the individual on show is mass-produced like Yale locks, whose only difference can be measured in fractions of millimetres. The peculiarity of the self is a monopoly commodity determined by society; it is falsely represented as natural. It is no more than the moustache, the French accent, the deep voice of the woman of the world, the Lubitsch touch: finger prints on identity cards which are otherwise exactly the same, and into which the lives and faces of every single person are transformed by the power of the generality. Pseudo individuality is the prerequisite for comprehending tragedy and

removing its poison: only because individuals have ceased to be themselves and are now merely centres where the general tendencies meet, is
it possible to receive them again, whole and entire, into the generality.
In this way mass culture discloses the fictitious character of the 'individual' in the bourgeois era, and is merely unjust in boasting on account
of this dreary harmony of general and particular. The principle of
individuality was always full of contradiction. Individuation has never
really been achieved. Self-preservation in the shape of class has kept
everyone at the stage of a mere species being. Every bourgeois characteristic, in spite of its deviation and indeed because of it, expressed the
same thing: the harshness of the competitive society. The individual
who supported society bore its disfiguring mark; seemingly free, he was
actually the product of its economic and social apparatus. Power based
itself on the prevailing conditions of power when it sought the approval
of persons affected by it. As it progressed, bourgeois society did also
develop the individual. Against the will of its leaders, technology has
changed human beings from children into persons. However, every
advance in individuation of this kind took place at the expense of the
individuality in whose name it occurred, so that nothing was left but the
resolve to pursue one's own particular purpose. The bourgeois whose
existence is split into a business and a private life, whose private life is
split into keeping up his public image and intimacy, whose intimacy is
split into the surly partnership of marriage and the bitter comfort of
being quite alone, at odds with himself and everybody else, is already
virtually a Nazi, replete both with enthusiasm and abuse; or a modern
city-dweller who can now only imagine friendship as a 'social contact':
that is, as being in social contact with others with whom he has no
inward contact. The only reason why the culture industry can deal so
successfully with individuality is that the latter has always reproduced
the fragility of society. On the faces of private individuals and movie
heroes put together according to the patterns on magazine covers
vanishes a pretence in which no one now believes; the popularity of the
hero models comes partly from a secret satisfaction that the effort to
achieve individuation has at last been replaced by the effort to imitate,
which is admittedly more breathless. It is idle to hope that this self-
contradictory, disintegrating 'person' will not last for generations, that
the system must collapse because of such a psychological split, or that
the deceitful substitution of the stereotype for the individual will of itself
become unbearable for mankind. Since Shakespeare's *Hamlet*, the unity
of the personality has been seen through as a pretence. Synthetically

produced physiognomies show that the people of today have already forgotten that there was ever a notion of what human life was. For centuries society has been preparing for Victor Mature and Mickey Rooney. By destroying they come to fulfil.

3 Roland Barthes

Dominici, or the triumph of literature

EDITOR'S INTRODUCTION

This essay, which originally appeared as a column in a newspaper, was first published in book form, in *Mythologies*, in 1957.

    Mythologies has been such an important book because it begins to examine, concretely, how ideology works. It is the founding text of practical ideology-critique. And 'Dominici, or the triumph of literature' is especially interesting because it points forward to a later-period Barthes, for whom the concept of 'mythology' would be replaced by that of discourse (see Barthes 1977). Here Barthes shows that 'literature' is not separate from everyday life and its power flows. On the contrary, he analyses a case in which an inarticulate rural labourer is condemned in terms of a discourse which is profoundly literary: the judges describe Dominici's motives in terms borrowed from literary clichés; they gain their sense of superiority because they speak 'better' French than he – where 'better' means more like written prose. And, in reporting the trial, the journalists turn it into more literature – where 'literature' does not just mean the literary canon but the conventional system of writing and representation in which the canon remains uncontested.

    Although the essay does not use the term, this remains a classic account of how hegemony is produced through interactions between various institutions and discourses – in this case, literature, the law, and journalism – over the body of those who can hardly talk back. In a later overview of his journalistic columns, published at the end of *Mythologies*, Barthes theorized the mode of analysis he had used. He argues that the way discourse (or 'mythology') is circulated through society makes a particular representation of the world seem natural and universal, so that an outsider to it cannot be imagined except as 'unnatural', 'perverse', 'exotic', 'abnormal', 'stupid', and so on. This analysis is finally of a piece with Adorno and Horkheimer's line of thought, though, in his description of the Citroën also published in *Mythologies*, the young Barthes expressed his belief that mass-produced commodities can be beautiful. One cannot imagine Theodor Adorno, in particular, conceding that.

Further reading: Barthes 1972 and 1977; Belsey 1980; Bennett and Woollacott 1988; Ray 1984.

S.D.

The whole Dominici trial[1] was enacted according to a certain idea of psychology, which happens to be, as luck would have it, that of the Literature of the bourgeois Establishment. Since material evidence was uncertain or contradictory, one had to resort to evidence of a mental kind; and where could one find it, except in the very mentality of the accusers? The motives and sequence of actions were therefore reconstituted off-hand but without a shadow of a doubt; in the manner of those archaeologists who go and gather old stones all over the excavation site and with their cement, modern as it is, erect a delicate wayside altar of Sesostris, or else, who reconstitute a religion which has been dead for two thousand years by drawing on the ancient fund of universal wisdom, which is in fact nothing but their own brand of wisdom, elaborated in the schools of the Third Republic.

The same applies to the 'psychology' of old Dominici. Is it really his? No one knows. But one can be sure that it is indeed that of the Presiding Judge of the Assizes or the Public Prosecutor. Do these two mentalities, that of the old peasant from the Alps and that of the judiciary, function in the same way? Nothing is less likely. And yet it is in the name of a 'universal' psychology that old Dominici has been condemned: descending from the charming empyrean of bourgeois novels and essentialist psychology, Literature has just condemned a man to the guillotine. Listen to the Public Prosecutor:

> Sir Jack Drummond, I told you, was afraid. But he knows that in the end the best way to defend oneself is to attack. So he throws himself on this fierce-looking man and takes the old man by the throat. Not a word is spoken. But to Gaston Dominici, the simple fact that someone should want to hold him down by both shoulders is unthinkable. It was physically impossible for him to bear this strength which was suddenly pitted against him.

This is credible like the temple of Sesostris, like the Literature of M. Genevoix. Only, to base archaeology or the novel on a 'Why not?' does not harm anybody. But Justice? Periodically, some trial, and not necessarily fictitious like the one in Camus's *The Outsider*, comes to remind you that the Law is always prepared to lend you a spare brain in order to condemn you without remorse, and that, like Corneille, it depicts you as you should be, and not as you are.

This official visit of Justice to the world of the accused is made possible thanks to an intermediate myth which is always used abundantly by all official institutions, whether they are the Assizes or the periodicals of literary sects: the transparence and universality of language. The Presiding Judge of the Assizes, who reads *Le Figaro*, has obviously no scruples in exchanging words with the old 'uneducated' goatherd. Do they not have in common the same language, and the clearest there is, French? O wonderful self-assurance of classical education, in which shepherds, without embarrassment, converse with judges! But here again, behind the prestigious (and grotesque) morality of Latin translations and essays in French, what is at stake is the head of a man.

And yet the disparity of both languages, their impenetrability to each other, have been stressed by a few journalists, and Giono has given numerous examples of this in his accounts of the trial. Their remarks show that there is no need to imagine mysterious barriers, Kafka-like misunderstandings. No: syntax, vocabulary, most of the elementary, analytical materials of language grope blindly without ever touching, but no one has any qualms about it (*'Êtes-vous allé au pont? – Allée? il n'y a pas d'allée, je le sais, j'y suis été*).[2] Naturally, everyone pretends to believe that it is the official language which is common sense, that of Dominici being only one of its ethnological varieties, picturesque in its poverty. And yet, this language of the president is just as peculiar, laden as it is with unreal clichés; it is a language for school essays, not for a concrete psychology (but perhaps it is unavoidable for most men, alas, to have the psychology of the language which they have been taught). These are in actual fact two particular uses of language which confront each other. But one of them has honours, law and force on its side.

And this 'universal' language comes just at the right time to lend a new strength to the psychology of the masters: it allows it always to take other men as objects, to describe and condemn at one stroke. It is an adjectival psychology, it knows only how to endow its victims with epithets, it is ignorant of everything about the actions themselves, save the guilty category into which they are forcibly made to fit. These categories are none other than those of classical comedy or treatises of graphology: boastful, irascible, selfish, cunning, lecherous, harsh, man exists in their eyes only through the 'character traits' which label him for society as the object of a more or less easy absorption, the subject of a more or less respectful submission. Utilitarian, taking no account of any state of consciousness, this psychology has nevertheless the pretension of giving as a basis for actions a pre-existing inner person, it postulates 'the soul': it judges man as a 'conscience' without being embarrassed by having previously described him as an object.

Now that particular psychology, in the name of which you can very well today have your head cut off, comes straight from our traditional literature, that which one calls in bourgeois style literature of the Human Document. It is in the name of the human document that the old Dominici has been condemned. Justice and literature have made an alliance, they have exchanged their old techniques, thus revealing their basic identity, and compromising each other barefacedly. Behind the judges, in curule chairs, the writers (Giono, Salacrou). And on the prosecution side, do we see a lawyer? No, an 'extraordinary story-teller', gifted with 'undeniable wit' and a 'dazzling verve' (to quote the shocking testimonial granted to the Public Prosecutor by *Le Monde*). Even the police are here seen practising fine writing:

> Police Superintendent: 'Never have I met such a dissembling liar, such a wary gambler, such a witty narrator, such a wily trickster, such a lusty septuagenarian, such a self-assured despot, such a devious schemer, such a cunning hypocrite . . . Gaston Dominici is an astonishing quick-change artist playing with human souls, and animal thoughts . . . This false patriarch of the Grand'Terre has not just a few facets, he has a hundred!'

Antithesis, metaphors, flights of oratory, it is the whole of classical rhetoric which accuses the old shepherd here. Justice took the mask of Realist literature, of the country tale, while Literature itself came to the court-room to gather new 'human' documents, and naïvely to seek from the face of the accused and the suspects the reflection of a psychology which, however, it had been the first to impose on them by the arm of the law.

Only, confronting the literature of repletion (which is always passed off as the literature of the 'real' and the 'human'), there is a literature of poignancy; the Dominici trial has also been this type of literature. There have not been here only writers hungering for reality and brilliant narrators whose 'dazzling' verve carries off a man's head; whatever the degree of guilt of the accused, there was also the spectacle of a terror which threatens us all, that of being judged by a power which wants to hear only the language it lends us. We are all potential Dominicis, not as murderers but as accused, deprived of language, or worse, rigged out in that of our accusers, humiliated and condemned by it. To rob a man of his language in the very name of language: this is the first step in all legal murders.

NOTES

1. Gaston Dominici, the 80-year-old owner of the Grand'Terre farm in Provence, was convicted in 1952 of murdering Sir Jack Drummond, his wife and daughter, whom he found camping near his land.
2. 'Did you go to the bridge? – A path? There is no path, I know, I've been there!' *Allé* = 'gone', *allée* = a path, but Dominici uses *été*, 'been'.

4 James Clifford

On collecting art and culture

EDITOR'S INTRODUCTION

James Clifford's brilliant essay describes an 'art–culture' system in which art, as something to be possessed and collected by individuals, becomes the pivot around which culture, as a seemingly communal and transcendental tradition, turns. He analyses the system using both structural and historical techniques and comes to the conclusion that it has been crucial to the formation of 'Western subjectivity'. For him, however, the system is surprisingly open and fluid. Though it transforms sacred and utilitarian objects from distant cultures into art to be owned and contemplated, it also exoticizes home cultures. Further, the system allows all kinds of groups to use art for their own ends: for instance, new kinds of museums are being created by post-colonized peoples all over the world.

This is a much more optimistic and vibrant representation of cultural practices than Adorno's or Barthes's. But it is worth asking: what has happened to categories like exploitation or even power here? – or, in the particular case of collecting so-called 'tribal artefacts', what about the sacred? After all, the Maori exhibition Clifford mentions took place only against protests against the exportation of sacred *taonga* (treasures) to foreign museums. As an essay at the forefront of contemporary cultural studies it demands more study and debate.

Further reading: Appadurai 1986; Clifford 1988a, 1988b; During 1989; Haraway 1984; Karp and Lavine 1991.

S.D.

There is a Third World in every First World, and vice-versa.
– Trinh T. Minh-ha, 'Difference', *Discourse* 8

This chapter is composed of four loosely connected parts, each concerned with the fate of tribal artefacts and cultural practices once they are relocated in Western museums, exchange systems, disciplinary archives, and discursive traditions. The first part proposes a critical, historical approach to collecting, focusing on subjective, taxonomic, and political processes. It sketches the 'art–culture system' through which in the last century exotic objects have been contextualized and given value in the West. This ideological and institutional system is further explored in the second part, where cultural description is presented as a form of collecting. The 'authenticity' accorded to both human groups and their artistic work is shown to proceed from specific assumptions about temporality, wholeness, and continuity. The third part focuses on a revealing moment in the modern appropriation of non-Western works of 'art' and 'culture', a moment portrayed in several memoirs by Claude Lévi-Strauss of his wartime years in New York. A critical reading makes explicit the redemptive metahistorical narrative these memoirs presuppose. The general art–culture system supported by such a narrative is contested throughout the chapter and particularly in the fourth part, where alternative 'tribal' histories and contexts are suggested.

Collecting Ourselves

Entering
You will find yourself in a climate of nut castanets,
A musical whip
From the Torres Straits, from Mirzapur a sistrum
Called Jumka, 'used by Aboriginal
Tribes to attract small game
On dark nights,' coolie cigarettes
And mask of Saagga, the Devil Doctor,
The eyelids worked by strings.

James Fenton's poem 'The Pitt Rivers Museum, Oxford', from which this stanza is taken, rediscovers a place of fascination in the ethnographic collection. For this visitor even the museum's descriptive labels seem to increase the wonder ('. . . attract small game/on dark nights') and the fear. Fenton is an adult-child exploring territories of danger and desire, for to be a child in this collection ('Please sir, where's the withered/Hand?') is to ignore the serious admonitions about human evolution and cultural diversity posted in the entrance hall. It is to be interested instead by the claw of a condor, the jaw of a dolphin, the hair of a witch, or 'a jay's feather worn as a charm/In Buckinghamshire'. Fenton's ethnographic museum is a world of intimate encounters with inexplicably fascinating objects: personal fetishes. Here collecting is inescapably tied to obsession, to recollection. Visitors 'find the landscape of their childhood marked out/Here in the chaotic piles of souvenirs . . . boxroom of the forgotten or hardly possible'.

> Go
> As a historian of ideas or a sex-offender,
> For the primitive art,
> As a dusty semiologist, equipped to unravel
> The seven components of that witch's curse
> Or the syntax of the mutilated teeth. Go
> In groups to giggle at curious finds.
> But do not step into the kingdom of your promises
> To yourself, like a child entering the forbidden
> Woods of his lonely playtime.

Do not step in this tabooed zone 'laid with the snares of privacy and fiction/And the dangerous third wish'. Do not encounter these objects except as *curiosities* to giggle at, *art* to be admired, or *evidence* to be understood scientifically. The tabooed way, followed by Fenton, is a path of too-intimate fantasy, recalling the dreams of the solitary child 'who wrestled with eagles for their feathers' or the fearful vision of a young girl, her turbulent lover seen as a hound with 'strange pretercanine eyes'. This path through the Pitt Rivers Museum ends with what seems to be a scrap of autobiography, the vision of a personal 'forbidden woods' – exotic, desired, savage, and governed by the (paternal) law:

> He had known what tortures the savages had prepared
> For him there, as he calmly pushed open the gate
> And entered the wood near the placard: 'TAKE NOTICE MEN
> MEN-TRAPS AND SPRING-GUNS ARE SET ON THESE
> PREMISES.'
> For his father had protected his good estate.

Fenton's journey into otherness leads to a forbidden area of the self. His intimate way of engaging the exotic collection finds an area of desire, marked off and policed. The law is preoccupied with *property*.

C. B. Macpherson's classic analysis of Western 'possessive individualism' (1962) traces the seventeenth-century emergence of an ideal self as owner: the individual surrounded by accumulated property and goods. The same ideal can hold true for collectivities making and remaking their cultural 'selves'. For example Richard Handler (1985) analyses the making of a Québécois cultural 'patrimoine', drawing on Macpherson to unravel the assumptions and paradoxes involved in 'having a culture', selecting and cherishing an authentic collective 'property'. His analysis suggests that this identity, whether cultural or personal, presupposes acts of collection, gathering up possessions in arbitrary systems of value and meaning. Such systems, always powerful and rule governed, change historically. One cannot escape them. At best, Fenton suggests, one can transgress ('poach' in their tabooed zones) or make their self-evident orders seem strange. In Handler's subtly perverse analysis a system of retrospection – revealed by a Historic Monuments Commission's selection of ten sorts of 'cultural property' – appears as a taxonomy worthy of Borges's 'Chinese encyclopedia': '(1) commemorative monuments; (2) churches and chapels; (3) forts of the French Regime; (4) windmills; (5) roadside crosses; (6) commemorative inscriptions and plaques; (7) devotional monuments; (8) old houses and manors; (9) old furniture; (10) "les choses disparues"'. In Handler's discussion the collection and preservation of an authentic domain of identity cannot be natural or innocent. It is tied up with nationalist politics, with restrictive law, and with contested encodings of past and future.

Some sort of 'gathering' around the self and the group – the assemblage of a material 'world', the marking-off of a subjective domain that is not 'other' – is probably universal. All such collections embody hierarchies of value, exclusions, rule-governed territories of the self. But the notion that this gathering involves the accumulation of possessions, the idea that identity is a kind of wealth (of objects, knowledge, memories, experience), is surely not universal. The individualistic accumulation of Melanesian 'big men' is not possessive in Macpherson's sense, for in Melanesia one accumulates not to hold objects as private goods but to give them away, to redistribute. In the West, however, collecting has long been a strategy for the deployment of a possessive self, culture, and authenticity.

Children's collections are revealing in this light: a boy's accumulation of miniature cars, a girl's dolls, a summer-vacation 'nature museum' (with labelled stones and shells, a hummingbird in a bottle), a treasured bowl filled with the bright shavings of crayons. In these small rituals we observe the channellings of obsession, an exercise in how to make the world one's own, to gather things around oneself tastefully, appropriately. The inclusions in all collections reflect wider cultural rules – of rational taxonomy, of gender, of aesthetics. An excessive, sometimes even rapacious need to *have* is transformed into rule-governed, meaningful desire. Thus the self that must possess but cannot have it all learns to select, order, classify in hierarchies – to make 'good' collections.

Whether a child collects model dinosaurs or dolls, sooner or later she or he will be encouraged to keep the possessions on a shelf or in a special box or to set up a doll house. Personal treasures will be made public. If the passion is for Egyptian figurines, the collector will be expected to label them, to know their dynasty (it is not enough that they simply exude power or mystery), to tell 'interesting' things about them, to distinguish copies from originals. The good collector (as opposed to the obsessive, the miser) is tasteful and reflective. Accumulation unfolds in a pedagogical, edifying manner. The collection itself – its taxonomic, aesthetic structure – is valued, and any private fixation on single objects is negatively marked as fetishism. Indeed a 'proper' relation with objects (rule-governed possession) presupposes a 'savage' or deviant relation (idolatry or erotic fixation). In Susan Stewart's gloss, 'The boundary between collection and fetishism is mediated by classification and display in tension with accumulation and secrecy' (1984: 163).

Stewart's wide-ranging study *On Longing* traces a 'structure of desire' whose task is the repetitious and impossible one of closing the gap that separates language from the experience it encodes. She explores certain recurrent strategies pursued by Westerners since the sixteenth century. In her analysis the miniature, whether a portrait or doll's house, enacts a bourgeois longing for 'inner' experience. She also explores the strategy of gigantism (from Rabelais and Gulliver to earthworks and the billboard), the souvenir, and the collection. She shows how collections, most notably museums, create the illusion of adequate representation of a world by first cutting objects out of specific contexts (whether cultural, historical, or intersubjective) and making them 'stand for' abstract wholes – a 'Bambara mask', for example, becoming an ethnographic metonym for Bambara culture. Next a scheme of classification is elaborated for storing or displaying the object so that the reality of the collection itself, its coherent order, overrides specific histories of the object's production and appropriation (pp. 162–5). Paralleling Marx's account of the fantastic objectification of commodities, Stewart argues that in the modern Western museum 'an illusion of a relation between things takes the place of a social relation' (p. 165). The collector discovers, acquires, salvages objects. The objective world is given, not produced, and thus historical relations of power in the work of acquisition are occulted. The *making* of meaning in museum classification and display is mystified as adequate *representation*. The time and order of the collection erase the concrete social labour of its making.

Stewart's work brings collecting and display sharply into view as crucial processes of Western identity formation. Gathered artefacts – whether they find their way into curio cabinets, private living rooms, museums of ethnography, folklore, or fine art – function within a developing capitalist 'system of objects' (Baudrillard 1968). By virtue of this system a world of *value* is created and a meaningful deployment and circulation of artefacts maintained. For Baudrillard collected objects create a structured environment that substitutes its own temporality for the 'real time' of historical and productive processes: 'The environment of private objects and their possession – of which collections are an extreme manifestation – is a dimension of our life that is both essential and imaginary. As essential as dreams' (1968: 135).

A history of anthropology and modern art needs to see in collecting both a form of Western subjectivity and a changing set of powerful institutional practices. The history of collections (not limited to museums) is central to an understanding of how those social groups that invented anthropology and modern art have *appropriated* exotic things, facts, and meanings. (*Appropriate*: 'to make one's own', from the Latin *proprius* 'proper', 'property'.) It is important to analyse how powerful discriminations made at particular moments constitute the general system of objects within which valued artefacts circulate and make sense. Far-reaching questions are thereby raised.

What criteria validate an authentic cultural or artistic product? What are the differential values placed on old and new creations? What moral and political criteria justify 'good', responsible, systematic collecting practices? Why, for example, do Leo Frobenius's wholesale acquisitions of African objects around the turn of the century now seem excessive? How is a 'complete' collection defined? What is the proper balance between scientific analysis and public display? (In Santa Fe a superb collection of Native American art is housed at the School of American Research in a building constructed, literally, as a vault, with access carefully restricted. The Musée de l'Homme exhibits less than a tenth of its collections; the rest is stored in steel cabinets or heaped in corners of the vast basement.) Why has it seemed obvious until recently that non-Western objects should be preserved in European museums, even when this means that no fine specimens are visible in their country of origin? How are 'antiquities', 'curiosities', 'art', 'souvenirs', 'monuments', and 'ethnographic artefacts' distinguished – at different historical moments and in specific market conditions? Why have many anthropological museums in recent years begun to display certain of their objects as 'masterpieces'? Why has tourist art only recently come to the serious attention of anthropologists? What has been the changing interplay between natural-history collecting and the selection of anthropological artefacts for display and analysis? The list could be extended.

The critical history of collecting is concerned with what from the material world specific groups and individuals choose to preserve, value, and exchange. Although this complex history, from at least the Age of Discovery, remains to be written, Baudrillard provides an initial framework for the deployment of objects in the recent capitalist West. In his account it is axiomatic that all categories of meaningful objects – including those marked off as scientific evidence and as great art – function within a ramified system of symbols and values.

To take just one example: the *New York Times* of December 8, 1984, reported the widespread illegal looting of Anasazi archaeological sites in the American Southwest. Painted pots and urns thus excavated in good condition could bring as much as $30,000 on the market. Another article in the same issue contained a photograph of Bronze Age pots and jugs salvaged by archaeologists from a Phoenician shipwreck off the coast of Turkey. One account featured clandestine collecting for profit, the other scientific collecting for knowledge. The moral evaluations of the two acts of salvage were sharply opposed, but the pots recovered were all meaningful, beautiful, and old. Commercial, aesthetic, and scientific worth in both cases presupposed a given system of value. This system finds intrinsic interest and beauty in objects from a past time, and it assumes that collecting everyday objects from ancient (preferably vanished) civilizations will be more *rewarding* than collecting, for example, decorated thermoses from modern China or customized T-shirts from Oceania. Old objects are endowed with a sense of 'depth' by their historically minded collectors. Temporality is reified and salvaged as origin, beauty, and knowledge.

This archaizing system has not always dominated Western collecting. The curiosities of the New World gathered and appreciated in the sixteenth century were not necessarily valued as antiquities, the products of primitive or 'past' civilizations. They frequently occupied a category of the marvellous, of a present 'Golden Age'. More recently the retrospective bias of Western appropriations of the world's cultures has come under scrutiny (Fabian 1983; Clifford 1986). Cultural or artistic 'authenticity' has as much to do with an inventive present as with a past, its objectification, preservation, or revival.

Since the turn of the century objects collected from non-Western sources have been classified in two major categories: as (scientific) cultural artefacts or as (aesthetic) works of art. Other collectables – mass-produced commodities, 'tourist art', curios, and so on – have been less systematically valued; at best they find a place in exhibits of 'technology' or 'folklore'. These and other locations within what may be called the 'modern art–culture system' can be visualized with the help of a (somewhat procrustian) diagram.

A. J. Greimas's 'semiotic square' (Greimas and Rastier 1968) shows us 'that any initial binary opposition can, by the operation of negations and the appropriate syntheses, generate a much larger field of terms which, however, all necessarily remain locked in the closure of the initial system' (Jameson 1981: 62). Adapting Greimas for the purposes of cultural criticism, Fredric Jameson uses the semiotic square to reveal 'the limits of a specific ideological consciousness, [marking] the conceptual points beyond which that consciousness cannot go, and between which it is condemned to oscillate' (1981: 47). Following his example, I offer the following map (see diagram) of a historically specific, contestable field of meanings and institutions.

Beginning with an initial opposition, by a process of negation four terms are generated. This establishes horizontal and vertical axes and between them four semantic zones: (1) the zone of authentic masterpieces, (2) the zone of authentic artefacts, (3) the zone of inauthentic masterpieces, (4) the zone of inauthentic artefacts. Most objects – old and new, rare and common, familiar and exotic – can be located in one of these zones or ambiguously, in traffic, between two zones.

The system classifies objects and assigns them relative value. It establishes the 'contexts' in which they properly belong and between which they circulate. Regular movements toward positive value proceed from bottom to top and from right to left. These movements select artefacts of enduring worth or rarity, their value normally guaranteed by a 'vanishing' cultural status or by the selection and pricing mechanisms of the art market. The value of Shaker crafts reflects the fact that Shaker society no longer exists: the stock is limited. In the art world work is

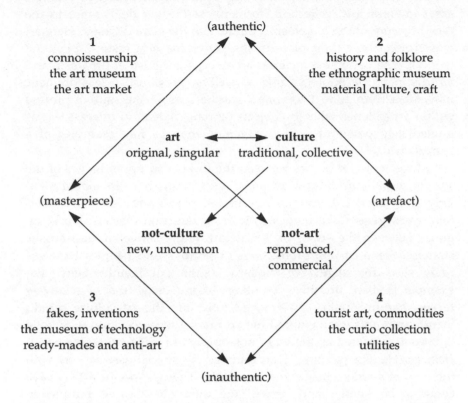

recognized as 'important' by connoisseurs and collectors according to criteria that are more than simply aesthetic (see Becker 1982). Indeed, prevailing definitions of what is 'beautiful' or 'interesting' sometimes change quite rapidly.

An area of frequent traffic in the system is that linking zones 1 and 2. Objects move in two directions along this path. Things of cultural or historical value may be promoted to the status of fine art. Examples of movement in this direction, from ethnographic 'culture' to fine 'art', are plentiful. Tribal objects located in art galleries (the Rockefeller Wing at the Metropolitan Museum in New York) or displayed anywhere according to 'formalist' rather than 'contextualist' protocols move in this way. Crafts (Shaker work collected at the Whitney Museum in 1986), 'folk art', certain antiques, 'naïve' art all are subject to periodic promotions. Movement in the inverse direction occurs whenever art masterworks are culturally and historically 'contextualized', something that has been occurring more and more explicitly.

Perhaps the most dramatic case has been the relocation of France's great impressionist collection, formerly at the Jeu de Paume, to the new Museum of the Nineteenth Century at the Gare d'Orsay. Here art masterpieces take their place in the panorama of a historical-cultural 'period'. The panorama includes an emerging industrial urbanism and its triumphant technology, 'bad' as well as 'good' art. A less dramatic movement from zone 1 to zone 2 can be seen in the routine process within art galleries whereby objects become 'dated', of interest less as immediately powerful works of genius than as fine examples of a period style.

Movement also occurs between the lower and upper halves of the system, usually in an upward direction. Commodities in zone 4 regularly enter zone 2, becoming rare period pieces and thus collectables (old green glass Coke bottles). Much current non-Western work migrates between the status of 'tourist art' and creative cultural–artistic strategy. Some current productions of Third World peoples have entirely shed the stigma of modern commercial inauthenticity. For example Haitian 'primitive' painting – commercial and of relatively recent, impure origin – has moved fully into the art–culture circuit. Significantly this work entered the art market by association with zone 2, becoming valued as the work not simply of individual artists but of *Haitians*. Haitian painting is surrounded by special associations with the land of voodoo, magic and negritude. Though specific artists have come to be known and prized, the aura of 'cultural' production attaches to them much more than, say, to Picasso, who is not in any essential way valued as a 'Spanish artist'. The same is true, as we shall see, of many recent works of tribal art, whether from the Sepik or the American Northwest Coast. Such works have largely freed themselves from the tourist or commodity category to which, because of their modernity, purists had often relegated them; but they cannot move directly into zone 1, the art market, without trailing clouds of authentic (traditional) culture. There can be no direct movement from zone 4 to zone 1.

Occasional travel occurs between zones 4 and 3, for example when a commodity or technological artefact is perceived to be a case of special inventive creation. The object is selected out of commercial or mass culture, perhaps to be featured in a museum of technology. Sometimes such objects fully enter the realm of art: 'technological' innovations or commodities may be contextualized as modern 'design', thus passing through zone 3 into zone 1 (for example the furniture, household machines, cars, and so on displayed at the Museum of Modern Art in New York).

There is also regular traffic between zones 1 and 3. Exposed art forgeries are demoted (while nonetheless preserving something of their original aura). Conversely various forms of 'anti-art' and art parading its unoriginality or 'inauthenticity' are collected and valued (Warhol's soup can, Sherrie Levine's photo of a photo by Walker Evans, Duchamp's urinal, bottle rack, or shovel). Objects in zone 3 are all potentially collectable within the general domain of art: they are uncommon, sharply distinct from or blatantly cut out of culture. Once appropriated by the art world, like Duchamp's ready-mades, they circulate within zone 1.

The art–culture system I have diagrammed excludes and marginalizes various residual and emergent contexts. To mention only one: the categories of art and culture, technology and commodity are strongly secular. 'Religious' objects can be valued as great art (an altarpiece by Giotto), as folk art (the decorations on a Latin American popular saint's shrine), or as cultural artefact (an Indian rattle). Such objects have no individual 'power' or mystery – qualities once possessed by 'fetishes' before they were reclassified in the modern system as primitive art or cultural artefact. What 'value', however, is stripped from an altarpiece when it is moved out of a functioning church (or when its church begins to function as a museum)? Its specific power or sacredness is relocated to a general aesthetic realm.

While the object systems of art and anthropology are institutionalized and powerful, they are not immutable. The categories of the beautiful, the cultural, and the authentic have changed and are changing. Thus it is important to resist the tendency of collections to be self-sufficient, to suppress their own historical, economic, and political processes of production. Ideally the history of its own collection and display should be a visible aspect of any exhibition. It had been rumoured that the Boas Room of Northwest Coast artefacts in the American Museum of Natural History was to be refurbished, its style of display modernized. Apparently (or so one hopes) the plan has been abandoned, for this atmospheric, dated hall exhibits not merely a superb collection but a moment in the history of collecting. The widely publicized Museum of Modern Art show of 1984, '"Primitivism" in Twentieth-Century Art', made apparent (as it celebrated) the precise circumstance in which certain ethnographic objects suddenly became works of universal art.

More historical self-consciousness in the display and viewing of non-Western objects can at least jostle and set in motion the ways in which anthropologists, artists, and their publics collect themselves and the world.

At a more intimate level, rather than grasping objects only as cultural signs and artistic icons, we can return to them, as James Fenton does, their lost status as fetishes – not specimens of a deviant or exotic 'fetishism' but *our own* fetishes. This tactic, necessarily personal, would accord to things in collections the power to fixate rather than simply the capacity to edify or inform. African and Oceanian artefacts could once again be *objets sauvages*, sources of fascination with the power to disconcert. Seen in their resistance to classification they could remind us of our *lack* of self-possession, of the artifices we employ to gather a world around us.

CULTURE COLLECTING

Found in *American Anthropologist*, n.s. 34 (1932): 740:

> Note from New Guinea
> Aliatoa, Wiwiak District, New Guinea
>
> *April 21, 1932*
> We are just completing a culture of a mountain group here in the lower Torres Chelles. They have no name and we haven't decided what to call them yet. They are a very revealing people in spots, providing a final basic concept from which all the mother's brothers' curses and father's sisters' curses, etc. derive, and having articulated the attitude toward incest which Reo [Fortune] outlined as fundamental in his Encyclopedia article. They have taken the therapeutic measures which we recommended for Dobu and Manus – having a devil in addition to the neighbor sorcerer, and having got their dead out of the village and localized. But in other ways they are annoying: they have bits and snatches of all the rag tag and bob tail of magical and ghostly belief from the Pacific, and they are somewhat like the Plains in their receptivity to strange ideas. A picture of a local native reading the index to the *Golden Bough* just to see if they had missed anything, would be appropriate. They are very difficult to work, living all over the place with half a dozen garden houses, and never staying put for a week at a time. Of

course this offered a new challenge in method which was interesting. The difficulties incident upon being two days over impossible mountains have been consuming and we are going to do a coastal people next.

Sincerely yours,
Margaret Mead

'Cultures' are ethnographic collections. Since Tylor's founding definition of 1871 the term has designated a rather vague 'complex whole' including everything that is learned group behaviour, from body techniques to symbolic orders. There have been recurring attempts to define culture more precisely (see Kroeber and Kluckhohn 1952) or, for example, to distinguish it from 'social structure'. But the inclusive use persists. For there are times when we still need to be able to speak holistically of Japanese or Trobriand or Moroccan culture in the confidence that we are designating something real and differentially coherent. It is increasingly clear, however, that the concrete activity of representing a culture, subculture, or indeed any coherent domain of collective activity is always strategic and selective. The world's societies are too systematically interconnected to permit any easy isolation of separate or independently functioning systems. The increased pace of historical change, the common recurrence of stress in the systems under study, forces a new self-consciousness about the way cultural wholes and boundaries are constructed and translated. The pioneering *élan* of Margaret Mead 'completing a culture' in highland New Guinea, collecting a dispersed population, discovering its key customs, naming the result – in this case 'the Mountain Arapesh' – is no longer possible.

To see ethnography as a form of culture collecting (not, of course, the *only* way to see it) highlights the ways that diverse experiences and facts are selected, gathered, detached from their original temporal occasions, and given enduring value in a new arrangement. Collecting – at least in the West, where time is generally thought to be linear and irreversible – implies a rescue of phenomena from inevitable historical decay or loss. The collection contains what 'deserves' to be kept, remembered, and treasured. Artefacts and customs are saved out of time. Anthropological culture collectors have typically gathered what seems 'traditional' – what by definition is opposed to modernity. From a complex historical reality (which includes current ethnographic encounters) they select what gives form, structure, and continuity to a world. What is hybrid or 'historical' in an emergent sense has been less commonly collected and presented as a system of authenticity. For example in New Guinea Margaret Mead and Reo Fortune chose not to study groups that were, as Mead wrote in a letter, 'badly missionized'; and it had been self-evident to Malinowski in the Trobriands that what most deserved scientific attention was the circumscribed 'culture' threatened by a host of modern 'outside' influences. The experience of Melanesians becoming Christians for their own reasons – learning to play, and play with, the outsiders' games – did not seem worth salvaging.

Every appropriation of culture, whether by insiders or outsiders, implies a specific temporal position and form of historical narration. Gathering, owning, classifying, and valuing are certainly not restricted to the West; but elsewhere these activities need not be associated with accumulation (rather than redistribution) or with preservation (rather than natural or historical decay). The Western practice of culture collecting has its own local genealogy, enmeshed in distinct European notions of temporality and order. It is worth dwelling for a moment on this genealogy, for it organizes the assumptions being arduously unlearned by new theories of practice, process, and historicity (Bourdieu 1977, Giddens 1979, Ortner 1984, Sahlins 1985).

A crucial aspect of the recent history of the culture concept has been its alliance (and division of labour) with 'art'. Culture, even without a capital c, strains toward aesthetic form and autonomy. I have already suggested that modern culture ideas and art ideas function together in an 'art–culture system'. The inclusive twentieth-century culture category – one that does not privilege 'high' or 'low' culture – is plausible only within this system, for while in principle admitting all learned human behavior, this culture with a small c orders phenomena in ways that privilege the coherent, balanced, and 'authentic' aspects of shared life. Since the mid-nineteenth century, ideas of culture have gathered up those elements that seem to give continuity and depth to collective existence, seeing it whole rather than disputed, torn, intertextual, or syncretic. Mead's almost postmodern image of 'a local native reading the index to *The Golden Bough* just to see if they had missed anything' is not a vision of authenticity.

Mead found Arapesh receptivity to outside influences 'annoying'. *Their* culture collecting complicated hers. Historical developments would later force her to provide a revised picture of these difficult Melanesians. In a new preface to the 1971 reprint of her three-volume ethnography *The Mountain Arapesh* Mead devotes several pages to letters from Bernard Narakobi, an Arapesh then studying law in Sydney,

Australia. The anthropologist readily admits her astonishment at hearing from him: 'How was it that one of the Arapesh – a people who had had such a light hold on any form of collective style – should have come further than any individual among the Manus, who had moved as a group into the modern world in the years between our first study of them, in 1928, and the beginning of our restudy, in 1953?' (Mead 1971: ix). She goes on to explain that Narakobi, along with other Arapesh men studying in Australia, had 'moved from one period in human culture to another' as 'individuals'. The Arapesh were 'less tightly bound within a coherent culture' than Manus (pp. ix–x). Narakobi writes, however, as a member of his 'tribe', speaking with pride of the values and accomplishments of his 'clansfolk'. (He uses the name Arapesh sparingly.) He articulates the possibility of a new multiterritorial 'cultural' identity: 'I feel now that I can feel proud of my tribe and at the same time feel I belong not only to Papua–New Guinea, a nation to be, but to the world community at large' (p. xiii). Is not this modern way of being 'Arapesh' already prefigured in Mead's earlier image of a resourceful native paging through *The Golden Bough*? Why must such behaviour be marginalized or classed as 'individual' by the anthropological culture collector?

Expectations of wholeness, continuity, and essence have long been built into the linked Western ideas of culture and art. A few words of recent background must suffice, since to map the history of these concepts would lead us on a chase for origins back at least to the Greeks. Raymond Williams provides a starting point in the early nineteenth century – a moment of unprecedented historical and social disruption. In *Culture and Society* (1958), *Keywords* (1983), and elsewhere Williams has traced a parallel development in usage for the words *art* and *culture*. The changes reflect complex responses to industrialism, to the spectre of 'mass society', to accelerated social conflict and change.[1]

According to Williams in the eighteenth century the word *art* meant predominantly 'skill'. Cabinetmakers, criminals, and painters were each in their way artful. *Culture* designated a tendency to natural growth, its uses predominantly agricultural and personal: both plants and human individuals could be 'cultured'. Other meanings also present in the eighteenth century did not predominate until the nineteenth. By the 1820s *art* increasingly designated a special domain of creativity, spontaneity, and purity, a realm of refined sensibility and expressive 'genius'. The 'artist' was set apart from, often against, society – whether 'mass' or 'bourgeois'. The term *culture* followed a parallel course, coming to mean what was most elevated, sensitive, essential, and precious – most uncommon – in society. Like art, culture became a general category; Williams calls it a 'final court of appeal' against threats of vulgarity and levelling. It existed in essential opposition to perceived 'anarchy'.

Art and culture emerged after 1800 as mutually reinforcing domains of human *value*, strategies for gathering, marking off, protecting the best and most interesting creations of 'Man'. In the twentieth century the categories underwent a series of further developments. The plural, anthropological definition of culture (lower-case *c* with the possibility of a final *s*) emerged as a liberal alternative to racist classifications of human diversity. It was a sensitive means for understanding different and dispersed 'whole ways of life' in a high colonial context of unprecedented global interconnection. *Culture* in its full evolutionary richness and authenticity, formerly reserved for the best creations of modern Europe, could now be extended to all the world's populations. In the anthropological vision of Boas's generation 'cultures' were of equal value. In their new plurality, however, the nineteenth-century definitions were not entirely transformed. If they became less elitist (distinctions between 'high' and 'low' culture were erased) and less Eurocentric (every human society was fully 'cultural'), nevertheless a certain body of assumptions were carried over from the older definitions. George Stocking (1968: 69–90) shows the complex interrelations of nineteenth-century humanist and emerging anthropological definitions of culture. He suggests that anthropology owes as much to Matthew Arnold as to its official founding father, E. B. Tylor. Indeed much of the vision embodied in *Culture and Anarchy* has been transferred directly into relativist anthropology. A powerful structure of feeling continues to see culture, wherever it is found, as a coherent *body* that lives and dies. Culture is enduring, traditional, structural (rather than contingent, syncretic, historical). Culture is a process of ordering, not of disruption. It changes and develops like a living organism. It does not normally 'survive' abrupt alterations.

In the early twentieth century, as *culture* was being extended to all the world's functioning societies, an increasing number of exotic, primitive, or archaic objects came to be seen as 'art'. They were equal in aesthetic and moral value with the greatest Western masterpieces. By midcentury the new attitude toward 'primitive art' had been accepted by large numbers of educated Europeans and Americans. Indeed from the standpoint of the late twentieth century it becomes clear that the parallel concepts of art and culture did successfully, albeit temporarily, comprehend and incorporate a plethora of non-Western artefacts and customs.

This was accomplished through two strategies. First, objects reclassified as 'primitive art' were admitted to the imaginary museum of human creativity and, though more slowly, to the actual fine arts museums of the West. Second, the discourse and institutions of modern anthropology constructed comparative and synthetic images of Man drawing evenhandedly from among the world's authentic ways of life, however strange in appearance or obscure in origin. Art and culture, categories for the best creations of Western humanism, were in principle extended to all the world's peoples.

It is perhaps worth stressing that nothing said here about the historicity of these cultural or artistic categories should be construed as claiming that they are false or denying that many of their values are worthy of support. Like any successful discursive arrangement the art–culture authenticity system articulates considerable domains of truth and scientific progress as well as areas of blindness and controversy. By emphasizing the transience of the system I do so out of a conviction (it is more a feeling of the historical ground moving underfoot) that the classifications and generous appropriations of Western art and culture categories are now much less stable than before. This instability appears to be linked to the growing interconnection of the world's populations and to the contestation since the 1950s of colonialism and Eurocentrism. Art collecting and culture collecting now take place within a changing field of counterdiscourses, syncretisms, and reappropriations originating both outside and inside 'the West'. I cannot discuss the geopolitical causes of these developments. I can only hint at their transforming consequences and stress that the modern genealogy of culture and art that I have been sketching increasingly appears to be a local story. 'Culture' and 'art' can no longer be simply *extended* to non-Western peoples and things. They can at worst be *imposed*, at best *translated* – both historically and politically contingent operations.

Before I survey some of the current challenges to Western modes of collection and authentication, it may be worth portraying the still-dominant form of art and culture collecting in a more limited, concrete setting. The system's underlying historical assumptions will then become inescapable. For if collecting in the West salvages things out of non-repeatable time, what is the assumed direction of this time? How does it confer rarity and authenticity on the varied productions of human skill? Collecting presupposes a story; a story occurs in a 'chronotope'.

A CHRONOTOPE FOR COLLECTING

> Dans son effort pour comprendre le monde, l'homme dispose donc
> toujours d'un surplus de signification.
>
> – Claude Lévi-Strauss

The term *chronotope*, as used by Bakhtin, denotes a configuration of
spatial and temporal indicators in a fictional setting where (and when)
certain activities and stories *take place*. One cannot realistically situate
historical detail – putting something 'in its time' – without appealing to
explicit or implicit chronotopes. Claude Lévi-Strauss's pointed, nostalgic
recollections of New York during the Second World War can serve as a
chronotope for modern art and culture collecting. The setting is elaborated in an essay whose French title, 'New York post- et préfiguratif'
(1983), suggests its underlying spatio-temporal predicament more
strongly than the published English translation, 'New York in 1941'
(1985). The essay falls within a microgenre of Lévi-Strauss's writing, one
he developed with virtuosity in *Tristes tropiques*. Specific places – Rio,
Fire Island, new Brazilian cities, Indian sacred sites – appear as moments
of intelligible human order and transformation surrounded by the destructive, entropic currents of global history.

In what follows I have supplemented the essay on New York with
passages from other texts written by Lévi-Strauss either during the war
years or in recollection of them. In reading them as a unified chronotope, one ought to bear in mind that these are not historical records but
complex literary commemorations. The time–space in question has been
retrospectively composed by Lévi-Strauss and recomposed, for other
purposes, by myself.

A refugee in New York during the Second World War, the anthropologist is bewildered and delighted by a landscape of unexpected juxtapo-
sitions. His recollections of those seminal years, during which he
invented structural anthropology, are bathed in a magical light. New
York is full of delightful incongruities. Who could resist

> the performances that we watched for hours at the Chinese opera
> under the first arch of the Brooklyn Bridge, where a company that
> had come long ago from China had a large following. Every day,
> from mid-afternoon until past midnight, it would perpetuate the
> traditions of classical Chinese opera. I felt myself going back in time
> no less when I went to work every morning in the American room of

the New York Public Library. There, under its neo-classical arcades and between walls paneled with old oak, I sat near an Indian in a feather headdress and a beaded buckskin jacket – who was taking notes with a Parker pen. (1985: 266)

As Lévi-Strauss tells it, the New York of 1941 is an anthropologist's dream, a vast selection of human culture and history. A brief walk or subway ride will take him from a Greenwich Village reminiscent of Balzac's Paris to the towering skyscrapers of Wall Street. Turning a corner in this jumble of immigrants and ethnic groups, the stroller suddenly enters a different world with its own language, customs, cuisine. Everything is available for consumption. In New York one can obtain almost any treasure. The anthropologist and his artistic friends André Breton, Max Ernst, André Masson, Georges Duthuit, Yves Tanguy, and Matta find masterpieces of pre-Columbian, Indian, Oceanic, or Japanese art stuffed in dealers' closets or apartments. Everything somehow finds it way here. For Lévi-Strauss New York in the 1940s is a wonderland of sudden openings to other times and places, of cultural matter out of place:

New York (and this is the source of its charm and its peculiar fascination) was then a city where anything seemed possible. Like the urban fabric, the social and cultural fabric was riddled with holes. All you had to do was pick one and slip through it if, like Alice, you wanted to get to the other side of the looking glass and find worlds so enchanting that they seemed unreal. (p. 261)

The anthropological *flâneur* is delighted, amazed, but also troubled by the chaos of simultaneous possibilities. This New York has something in common with the early-century dada-surrealist flea market – but with a difference. Its *objets trouvés* are not just occasions for reverie. This they surely are, but they are also signs of vanishing worlds. Some are treasures, works of great art.

Lévi-Strauss and the refugee surrealists were passionate collectors. The Third Avenue art dealer they frequented and advised, Julius Carlebach, always had several Northwest Coast, Melanesian, or Eskimo pieces on hand. According to Edmund Carpenter, the surrealists felt an immediate affinity with these objects' predilection for 'visual puns'; their selections were nearly always of a very high quality. In addition to the art dealers another source for this band of primitive-art connoisseurs was the Museum of the American Indian. As Carpenter tells it:

The Surrealists began to visit the Bronx warehouse of that Museum, selecting for themselves, concentrating on a collection of magnificent Eskimo masks. These huge visual puns, made by the Kuskokwim Eskimo a century or more ago, constituted the greatest collection of its kind in the world. But the Museum Director, George Heye, called them 'jokes' and sold half for $38 and $54 each. The Surrealists bought the best. Then they moved happily through Heye's Northwest Coast collection, stripping it of one masterwork after another. (Carpenter 1975: 10)

In 1946 Max Ernst, Barnett Newman, and several others mounted an exhibit of Northwest Coast Indian painting at the Betty Parsons Gallery. They brought together pieces from their private collections and artefacts from the American Museum of Natural History. By moving the museum pieces across town, 'the Surrealists declassified them as scientific specimens and reclassified them as art' (Carpenter 1975: 11).

The category of primitive art was emerging, with its market, its connoisseurship, and its close ties to modernist aesthetics. What had begun with the vogue for *l'art nègre* in the twenties would become institutionalized by the fifties and sixties; but in wartime New York the battle to gain widespread recognition for tribal objects was not yet won. Lévi-Strauss recalls that as cultural attaché to the French Embassy in 1946 he tried in vain to arrange a trade: for a massive collection of American Indian art a few Matisses and Picassos. But 'the French authorities turned a deaf ear to my entreaties, and the Indian collections wound up in American museums' (1985: 262). The collecting of Lévi-Strauss and the surrealists during the forties was part of a struggle to gain aesthetic status for these increasingly rare masterworks.

Modern practices of art and culture collecting, scientific and avant-garde, have situated themselves at the end of a global history. They have occupied a place – apocalyptic, progressive, revolutionary, or tragic – from which to gather the valued inheritances of Man. Concretizing this temporal setup, Lévi-Strauss's 'post- and prefigurative' New York anticipates humanity's entropic future and gathers up its diverse pasts in decontextualized, collectable forms. The ethnic neighbourhoods, the provincial reminders, the Chinese Opera Company, the feathered Indian in the library, the works of art from other continents and eras that turn up in dealers' closets: all are survivals, remnants of threatened or vanished traditions. The world's cultures appear in the chronotope as shreds of humanity, degraded commodities, or elevated great art but always functioning as vanishing 'loopholes' or 'escapes' from a one-dimensional fate.

In New York a jumble of humanity has washed up in one vertiginous place and time, to be grasped simultaneously in all its precious diversity and emerging uniformity. In this chronotope the pure products of humanity's pasts are rescued by modern aesthetics only as sublimated art. They are salvaged by modern anthropology as consultable archives for thinking about the range of human invention. In Lévi-Strauss's setting the products of the present-becoming-future are shallow, impure, escapist, and 'retro' rather than truly different – 'antiques' rather than genuine antiquities. Cultural invention is subsumed by a commodified 'mass culture'.

The chronotope of New York supports a global allegory of fragmentation and ruin. The modern anthropologist, lamenting the passing of human diversity, collects and values its survivals, its enduring works of art. Lévi-Strauss's most prized acquisition from a marvellous New York where everything seemed available was a nearly complete set of volumes 1 through 48 of the *Annual Reports* of the Bureau of American Ethnology. These were, he tells us in another evocation of the war years, 'sacrosanct volumes, representing most of our knowledge about the American Indians . . . It was as though the American Indian cultures had suddenly come alive and become almost tangible through the physical contact that these books, written and published before these cultures' definite extinction, established between their times and me' (Lévi-Strauss 1960: 50). These precious records of human diversity had been recorded by an ethnology still in what he calls its 'pure' rather than 'diluted' state. They would form the authentic ethnographic material from which structuralism's metacultural orders were constructed.

Anthropological collections and taxonomies, however, are constantly menaced by temporal contingencies. Lévi-Strauss knows this. It is a disorder he always holds at bay. For example in *Tristes tropiques* he is acutely aware that focusing on a tribal past necessarily blinds him to an emergent present. Wandering through the modern landscape of New York, far from encountering less and less to know, the anthropologist is confronted with more and more – a heady mix-and-match of possible human combinations. He struggles to maintain a unified perspective; he looks for order in deep 'geological' structures. But in Lévi-Strauss's work generally, the englobing 'entropological' narrative barely contains a current history of loss, transformation, invention, and emergence.

Toward the end of his brilliant inaugural lecture at the Collège de France, 'The Scope of Anthropology', Lévi-Strauss evokes what he calls 'anthropological doubt', the inevitable result of ethnographic risk-taking, the 'buffetings and denials directed at one's most cherished ideas and habits by other ideas and habits best able to rebut them' (1960: 26). He poignantly recalls a Kwakiutl visitor, hosted in New York by Franz Boas, transfixed by the freaks and automats of Times Square, and he wonders whether anthropology may not be condemned to equally bizarre perceptions of the distant societies and histories it seeks to grasp. New York was perhaps Lévi-Strauss's only true 'fieldwork': for once he stayed long enough and mastered the local language. Aspects of the place, such as Boas's Kwakiutl, have continued to charm and haunt his anthropological culture collecting.

But one New York native sits with special discomfort in the chrono-tope of 1941. This is the feathered Indian with the Parker pen working in the Public Library. For Lévi-Strauss the Indian is primarily associated with the past, the 'extinct' societies recorded in the precious Bureau of American Ethnology *Annual Reports*. The anthropologist feels himself 'going back in time' (1985: 266). In modern New York an Indian can appear only as a survival or a kind of incongruous parody.

Another historical vision might have positioned the two scholars in the library differently. The decade just preceding Lévi-Strauss's arrival in New York had seen a dramatic turnaround in federal policy. Under John Collier's leadership at the Bureau of Indian Affairs a 'New Indian Policy' actively encouraged tribal reorganization all over the country. While Lévi-Strauss studied and collected their pasts, many 'extinct' Native American groups were in the process of reconstituting them-selves culturally and politically. Seen in this context, did the Indian with the Parker pen represent a 'going back in time' or a glimpse of another future? That is a different story.

OTHER APPROPRIATIONS

To tell these other stories, local histories of cultural survival and emerg-ence, we need to resist deep-seated habits of mind and systems of authenticity. We need to be suspicious of an almost-automatic tendency to relegate non-Western peoples and objects to the pasts of an increasingly homogeneous humanity. A few examples of current invention and contestation may suggest different chronotopes for art and culture collecting.

Anne Vitart-Fardoulis, a curator at the Musée de l'Homme, has published a sensitive account of the aesthetic, historical, and cultural discourses routinely used to explicate individual museum objects. She discusses a famous intricately painted animal skin (its present name: M.H. 34.33.5), probably originating among the Fox Indians of North America. The skin turned up in Western collecting systems some time ago in a 'cabinet of curiosities'; it was used to educate aristocratic children and was much admired for its aesthetic qualities. Vitart-Fardoulis tells us that now the skin can be decoded ethnographically in terms of its combined 'masculine' and 'feminine' graphic styles and understood in the context of a probable role in specific ceremonies. But the meaningful contexts are not exhausted. The story takes a new turn:

> The grandson of one of the Indians who came to Paris with Buffalo Bill was searching for the [painted skin] tunic his grandfather had been forced to sell to pay his way back to the United States when the circus collapsed. I showed him all the tunics in our collection, and he paused before one of them. Controlling his emotion, he spoke. He told the meaning of this lock of hair, of that design, why this color had been used, the meaning of that feather . . . This garment, formerly beautiful and interesting but passive and indifferent, little by little became meaningful, active testimony to a living moment through the mediation of someone who did not observe and analyze but who lived the object and for whom the object lived. It scarcely matters whether the tunic is really his grandfather's. (Vitart-Fardoulis 1986: 12)

Whatever is happening in this encounter, two things are clearly *not* happening. The grandson is not replacing the object in its original or 'authentic' cultural context. That is long past. His encounter with the painted skin is part of a modern recollection. And the painted tunic is not being appreciated as art, as an aesthetic object. The encounter is too specific, too enmeshed in family history and ethnic memory. Some aspects of 'cultural' and 'aesthetic' appropriation are certainly at work, but they occur within a *current tribal history*, a different temporality from that governing the dominant systems I diagrammed earlier. In the context of a present-becoming-future the old painted tunic becomes newly, traditionally meaningful.

The currency of 'tribal' artefacts is becoming more visible to non-Indians. Many new tribal recognition claims are pending at the Department of the Interior. And whether or not they are formally successful matters less than what they make manifest: the historical and political reality of Indian survival and resurgence, a force that impinges on Western art and culture collections. The 'proper' place of many objects in museums is now subject to contest. The Zuni who prevented the loan of their war god to the Museum of Modern Art were challenging the dominant art–culture system, for in traditional Zuni belief war god figures are sacred and dangerous. They are not ethnographic artefacts, and they are certainly not 'art'. Zuni claims on these objects specifically reject their 'promotion' (in all senses of the term) to the status of aesthetic or scientific treasures.

I would not claim that the only true home for the objects in question is in 'the tribe' – a location that, in many cases, is far from obvious. My point is just that the dominant, interlocking contexts of art and anthropology are no longer self-evident and uncontested. There are other contexts, histories, and futures in which non-Western objects and cultural records may 'belong'. The rare Maori artefacts that in 1984–5 toured museums in the United States normally reside in New Zealand museums. But they are controlled by the traditional Maori authorities, whose permission was required for them to leave the country. Here and elsewhere the circulation of museum collections is significantly influenced by resurgent indigenous communities.

What is at stake is something more than conventional museum programmes of community education and 'outreach'. Current developments question the very status of museums as historical-cultural theatres of memory. Whose memory? For what purposes? The Provincial Museum of British Columbia has for some time encouraged Kwakiutl carvers to work from models in its collection. It has lent out old pieces and donated new ones for use in modern potlatches. Surveying these developments, Michael Ames, who directs the University of British Columbia Museum, observes that 'Indians, traditionally treated by museums only as objects and clients, add now the role of patrons'. He continues: 'The next step has also occurred. Indian communities establish their own museums, seek their own National Museum grants, install their own curators, hire their own anthropologists on contract, and call for repatriation of their own collections' (Ames 1986: 57). The Quadra Island Kwakiutl Museum located in Quathraski Cove, British Columbia, displays tribal work returned from the national collections in

Ottawa. The objects are exhibited in glass cases, but arranged according to their original family ownership. In Alert Bay, British Columbia, the U'mista Cultural Centre displays repatriated artefacts in a traditional Kwakiutl 'big house' arranged in the sequence of their appearance at the potlatch ceremony. The new institutions function both as public exhibits and as cultural centres linked to ongoing tribal traditions (Clifford 1991 provides a fuller account). Two Haida museums have also been established in the Queen Charlotte Islands, and the movement is growing elsewhere in Canada and the United States.

Resourceful Native American groups may yet appropriate the Western museum – as they have made their own another European institution, the 'tribe'. Old objects may again participate in a tribal present-becoming-future. Moreover, it is worth briefly noting that the same thing is possible for written artefacts collected by salvage ethnography. Some of these old texts (myths, linguistic samples, lore of all kinds) are now being recycled as local history and tribal 'literature'. The objects of both art and culture collecting are susceptible to other appropriations.

NOTE

1. Although Williams's analysis is limited to England, the general pattern applies elsewhere in Europe, where the timing of modernization differed or where other terms were used. In France, for example, the words *civilisation* or, for Durkheim, *société* stand in for *culture*. What is at issue are general qualitative assessments of collective life.

5 Teresa de Lauretis

Upping the anti [sic] in feminist theory

EDITOR'S INTRODUCTION

De Lauretis's essay contributes to the feminist debate over 'essentialism'. The debate arises because, for structuralist and post-structuralist thought, identity is always articulated within a system of differences and is therefore never fixed. To take a concrete example: a signifier like 'women' which is important to forming identities (in statements like 'I am a woman') does not, for instance, refer transparently to a particular kind of body – as if that kind of body were the essence of 'being-woman'. After all, individuals who do not have a woman's body can still possess a woman's identity, and structuralists argue that this is possible just because 'woman' means something, not in relation to any essential quality of womanhood, but in distinction to other categories like, most obviously, 'maleness'.

The debate between essentialists and (post)structuralists had been productively elaborated during the 1970s, but, in this essay, de Lauretis proposes a new move. She turns towards what she calls feminism's 'essential differences'. This phrase brings both sides of the debate together, not in the spirit of synthesis, but to point to the structure of differences in which feminism carries out its work. Feminism's 'essential difference' is to be found in its 'historical specificity' and in the sites, bodies, discourses in and through which women live differently both from men and from each other. De Lauretis further suggests that analysis of feminism's historical specificity has to begin its work not with a category as unnuanced as 'woman' but with the more subtle one of the 'female-embodied social subject'.

By suggesting we might return to the history and cultural formations in which 'women' are constructed, de Lauretis is not so much depriving cultural studies of feminist theory as using cultural studies to make theory less routine.

Further reading: Butler 1990; de Lauretis 1987; Gallop 1982; Haraway 1988; Hirsch and Fox Keller 1990; Jardine 1985; Mohanty 1984.

S.D.

ESSENTIALISM AND ANTI-ESSENTIALISM

Nowadays, the term *essentialism* covers a range of metacritical meanings and strategic uses that go the very short distance from convenient label to buzzword. Many who, like myself, have been involved with feminist critical theory for some time and who did use the term, initially, as a serious critical concept, have grown impatient with this word – essentialism – time and again repeated with its reductive ring, its self-righteous tone of superiority, its contempt for 'them' – those guilty of it. Yet, few would deny that feminist theory is all about an essential difference, an irreducible difference, though not a difference between woman and man, nor a difference inherent in 'woman's nature' (in woman as nature), but a difference in the feminist conception of woman, women, and the world.

Let us say, then, that there is an essential difference between a feminist and a non-feminist understanding of the subject and its relation to institutions; between feminist and non-feminist knowledges, discourses, and practices of cultural forms, social relations, and subjective processes; between a feminist and a non-feminist historical consciousness. That difference is essential in that it is constitutive of feminist thinking and thus of feminism: it is what makes the thinking feminist, and what constitutes certain ways of thinking, certain practices of writing, reading, imaging, relating, acting, etc., into the historically diverse and culturally heterogeneous social movement which, qualifiers and distinctions notwithstanding, we continue with good reasons to call feminism. Another way to say this is that the essential difference of feminism lies in its historical specificity – the particular conditions of its emergence and development, which have shaped its object and field of analysis, its assumptions and forms of address; the constraints that have attended its conceptual and methodological struggles; the erotic component of its political self-awareness; the absolute novelty of its radical challenge to social life itself.

But even as the specific, essential difference of feminism may not be disputed, the question of the nature of its specificity or what is of the essence in feminist thought and self-representation has been an object of contention, an issue over which divisions, debates, and polarizations have occurred consistently, and without resolution, since the beginning of that self-conscious critical reflection that constitutes the theory of feminism. The currency of the term 'essentialism' may be based on nothing more than its capacity to circumvent this very question – the nature of the specific difference of feminism – and thus to polarize feminist thought on what amounts to a red herring. I suggest that the current enterprise of 'anti-essentialist' theorists engaged in typologizing, defining and branding various 'feminisms' along an ascending scale of theoretico-political sophistication where 'essentialism' weighs heavy at the lower end, may be seen in this perspective.

Which is not to say that there should be no critique of feminist positions or no contest for the practical as well as the theoretical meanings of feminism, or even no appeal for hegemony by participants in a social movement which, after all, potentially involves all women. My polemical point here is that either too much or too little is made of the 'essentialism' imputed to most feminist positions (notably those labelled cultural, separatist or radical, but others as well, whether labelled or not), so that the term serves less the purposes of effective criticism in the ongoing elaboration of feminist theory than those of convenience, conceptual simplification or academic legitimation. Taking a more discerning look at the *essence* that is in question in both *essentialism* and *essential difference*, therefore, seems like a very good idea.

Among the several acceptations of 'essence' (from which 'essentialism' is apparently derived) in the OED, the most pertinent to the context of use that is in question here are the following:

1. Absolute being, substance in the metaphysical sense; the reality underlying phenomena.

2. That which constitutes the being of a thing; that 'by which it is what it is'. In two different applications (distinguished by Locke as *nominal essence* and *real essence* respectively):

a. of a conceptual entity: The totality of the properties, constituent elements, etc., without which it would cease to be the same thing; the indispensable and necessary attributes of a thing as opposed to those which it may have or not . . .

b. of a real entity: Objective character, intrinsic nature as a 'thing-in-itself'; 'that internal constitution, on which all the sensible properties depend'.

Examples of a., dated from 1600 to 1870, include Locke's statement in the *Essay on Human Understanding*: 'The Essence of a Triangle, lies in a very little compass . . . three Lines meeting at three Angles, make up that Essence'; and all the examples given for b., from 1667 to 1856, are to the effect that the essence of a real entity, the 'thing-in-itself',is either unknown or unknowable.

Which of these 'essences' are imputed to feminist 'essentialists' by their critics? If most feminists, however one may classify trends and positions – cultural, radical, liberal, socialist, poststructuralist, and so forth – agree that women are made, not born, that gender is not an innate feature (as sex may be) but a sociocultural construction (and precisely for that reason it is oppressive to women), that patriarchy is historical (especially so when it is believed to have superseded a previous matriarchal realm), then the 'essence' of woman that is described in the writings of many so-called essentialists is not the *real essence*, in Locke's terms, but more likely a *nominal* one. It is a totality of qualities, properties, and attributes that such feminists define, envisage, or enact for themselves (and some in fact attempt to live out in 'separatist' communities), and possibly also wish for other women. This is more a project, then, than a description of existent reality; it is an admittedly feminist project of 're-vision', where the specifications *feminist* and *re-vision* already signal its historical location, even as the (re)vision projects itself outward geographically and temporally (universally) to recover the past and to claim the future. This may be utopian, idealist, perhaps misguided or wishful thinking, it may be a project one does not want to be a part of, but it is not essentialist as is the belief in a God-given or otherwise immutable nature of woman.

In other words, barring the case in which woman's 'essence' is taken as absolute being or substance in the traditional metaphysical sense (and this may actually be the case for a few, truly fundamentalist thinkers to whom the term essentialist would properly apply), for the great majority of feminists the 'essence' of woman is more like the essence of the triangle than the essence of the thing-in-itself: it is the specific properties (e.g., a female-sexed body), qualities (a disposition to nurturance, a certain relation to the body, etc.), or necessary attributes (e.g., the experience of femaleness, of living in the world as female) that women have developed or have been bound to historically, in their differently patriarchal sociocultural contexts, which make them women, and not men. One may prefer one triangle, one definition of women and/or feminism, to another and, within her particular conditions and possibilities of existence, struggle to define the triangle she wants or wants to be – feminists do want differently. And in these very struggles, I suggest, consist the historical development and the specific difference of feminist theory, the essence of the triangle.

It would be difficult to explain, otherwise, why thinkers or writers with political and personal histories, projects, needs, and desires as different as those of white women and women of colour, of lesbians and heterosexuals, of differently abled women, and of successive gener-ations of women, would all claim feminism as a major – if not the only – ground of difference; why they would address both their critiques or accusations and their demands for recognition to other women, femi-nists in particular; why the emotional and political stakes in feminist theorizing should be so high, dialogue so charged, and confrontation so impassioned; why, indeed, the proliferation of typologies and the wide currency of 'essentialism' on one hand, countered by the equally wide currency of the term 'male theory' on the other. It is one of the projects of this paper to up the *anti* in feminist theoretical debates, to shift the focus of the controversy from 'feminist essentialism', as a category by which to classify feminists or feminisms, to the historical specificity, the essential difference of feminist theory itself. To this end I first turn to two essays which prompted my reflection on the uses of 'essentialism' in current Anglo-American feminist critical writing, Chris Weedon's *Feminist Practice and Poststructuralist Theory*, published in London in 1987, and Linda Alcoff's 'Cultural Feminism versus Post-Structuralism: The Identity Crisis in Feminist Theory', published in the Spring 1988 issue of *Signs*. Then I will go on to argue that the essential difference of feminist theory must be looked for in the form as well as the contents of its political, personal, critical, and textual practices, in the diverse oppo-sitional stances feminism has taken vis-à-vis social and cultural forma-tions, and in the resulting divisions, self-conscious reflection, and conceptual elaboration that constitute the effective history of feminism. And thus a division such as the one over the issue of 'essentialism' only *seems* to be a purely 'internal', intra-feminist one, a conflict within feminism. In fact, it is not.

The notion of an 'essential womanhood, common to all women, sup-pressed or repressed by patriarchy' recurs in Weedon's book as the mark of 'radical-feminist theory', whose cited representatives are Mary Daly, Susan Griffin, and Adrienne Rich. 'Radical-feminist theory' is initially listed together with 'socialist-feminist and psychoanalytic-feminist theories' as 'various attempts to systematize individual insights about the oppression of women into relatively coherent theories of patriarchy', in spite of the author's statement, on the same page, that radical-feminist writers are hostile to theory because they see it as a form of male dominance which co-opts women and suppresses the feminine (p. 6). As one reads on, however, socialist feminism drops out altogether while psychoanalytic feminism is integrated into a new and more 'politically' sophisticated discourse called 'feminist poststructuralism'. Thus, three-fourths of the way through the book, one finds this summary statement:

> For poststructuralist feminism, neither the liberal-feminist attempt to redefine the truth of women's nature within the terms of exist-ing social relations and to establish women's full equality with men, nor the radical-feminist emphasis on fixed difference, reali-zed in a separatist context, is politically adequate. Poststructuralist feminism requires attention to historical specificity in the pro-duction, for women, of subject positions and modes of femininity and their place in the overall network of social power relations. In this the meaning of biological sexual difference is never finally fixed. . . . An understanding of how discourses of biological sexual difference are mobilized, in a particular society, at a particular moment, is the first stage in intervening in order to initiate change. (p. 135)

There is more than simple irony in the claim that this late-comer, poststructuralist feminism, dark horse and winner of the feminist theory contest, is the 'first stage' of feminist intervention. How can Weedon, at one and the same time, so strongly insist on attention to historical specificity and social – not merely individual – change, and yet disregard the actual historical changes in Western culture brought about in part, at least, by the women's movement and at least in some measure by feminist critical writing over the past twenty years?

One could surmise that Weedon does not like the changes that have taken place (even as they allow the very writing and publication of her book), or does not consider them sufficient, though that would hardly be reason enough to disregard them so blatantly. A more subtle answer may lie in the apologetic and militant project of her book, a defence of poststructuralism vis-à-vis both the academic establishment and the general educated reader, but with an eye to the women's studies corner of the publishing market; whence, one must infer, the lead position in the title of the other term of the couple, feminist practice. For, as the Preface states, 'the aim of this book is to make poststructuralist theory accessible to readers to whom it is unfamiliar, to argue its political usefulness to feminism and to consider its implications for feminist critical practice' (p. vii). Somehow, however, in the course of the book, the Preface's modest claim 'to point to a possible direction for future feminist cultural criticism' (p. vii) is escalated into a peroration for the new and much improved feminist theory called feminist poststructuralism or, indifferently, poststructural feminism.

In the concluding chapter on 'Feminist Critical Practice' (strangely in the singular, as if among so many feminisms and feminist theories, only one practice could properly be called both feminist and critical), the academic contenders are narrowed down to two. The first is the poststructural criticism produced by British feminists (two are mentioned, E. Ann Kaplan and Rosalind Coward) looking 'at the mechanisms through which meaning is constructed' mainly in popular culture and visual representation; the second is 'the other influential branch of feminist criticism [that] looks to fiction as an expression of an already constituted gendered experience' (p. 152). Reappearing here, the word 'experience', identified earlier on as the basis for radical-feminist politics ('many feminists assume that women's experience, unmediated by further theory, is the source of true knowledge', p. 8), links this second branch of feminist (literary) criticism to radical-feminist ideology. Its standardbearers are Americans, Showalter's gynocritics and the 'woman-centred criticism' of Gilbert and Gubar, whose reliance on the concept of authorship as a key to meaning and truth also links them with 'liberalhumanist criticism' (pp. 154–5).

A particular subset of this – by now radical-liberal – feminist criticism 'dedicated to constructing traditions' (p. 156) is the one concerned with 'black and lesbian female experience'; here the problems and ideological traps appear most clearly, in Weedon's eyes, and are 'most extreme in the case of lesbian writing and the construction of a lesbian aesthetic' (p. 158). The reference works for her analysis, rather surprisingly in view of the abundance of Black and lesbian feminist writings in the 1980s, are a couple of rather dated essays by Barbara Smith and Bonnie Zimmerman reprinted in a collection edited by Elaine Showalter and, in fact, misnamed *The New Feminist Criticism*. But even more surprisingly – or not at all so, depending on one's degree of optimism – it is again poststructuralist criticism that, with the help of Derridean deconstruction, can set all of these writers straight, as it were, as to the real, socially constructed and discursively produced nature of gender, race, class, and sexuality – as well as authorship and experience! Too bad for us that no exemplary poststructuralist feminist works or critics are discussed in this context (Cixous, Kristeva, and Irigaray figure prominently, but as psychoanalytic feminists earlier in the book).

Now, I should like to make it clear that I have no quarrel with poststructuralism as such, or with the fundamental importance for all critical thinking, feminist theory included, of many of the concepts admirably summarized by Weedon in passages such as the following:

> For a theoretical perspective to be politically useful to feminism, it should be able to recognize the importance of the *subjective* in constituting the meaning of women's lived reality. It should not deny subjective experience, since the ways in which people make sense of their lives is a necessary starting point for understanding how power relations structure society. Theory must be able to address women's experience by showing where it comes from and how it relates to material social practices and the power relations which structure them. . . . In this process subjectivity becomes available, offering the individual both a perspective and a choice, and opening up the possibility of political change. (pp. 8–9)

But while I am in complete agreement that experience is a difficult, ambiguous, and often oversimplified term, and that feminist theory needs to elaborate further 'the relationship between experience, social power and resistance' (p. 8), I would insist that the notion of experience in relation both to social-material practices and to the formation and processes of subjectivity is a feminist concept, not a poststructuralist one (this is an instance of that essential difference of feminism which I want to reclaim from Weedon's all-encompassing 'poststructuralism'), and would be still unthinkable were it not for specifically feminist practices, political, critical, and textual: consciousness raising, the rereading and revision of the canon, the critique of scientific discourses, and the imaging of new social spaces and forms of community. In short, the very practices of those feminist critics Weedon allocates to the 'essentialist' camp. I would also add that 'a theory of the relationship between experience, social power and resistance' is precisely one possible definition of feminist, not of poststructuralist, theory, as Weedon would have it, since the latter does not countenance the notion of experience within its conceptual horizon or philosophical presuppositions; and that, moreover, these issues have been posed and argued by several non-denominational feminist theories in the United States for quite some time: for example, in the works of Biddy Martin, Nancy K. Miller, Tania Modleski, Mary Russo, Kaja Silverman, as well as myself, and even more forcefully in the works of feminist theorists and writers of colour such as Gloria Anzaldúa, Audre Lorde, Chandra Mohanty, Cherríe Moraga, and Barbara Smith.

So my quarrel with Weedon's book is about its reductive opposition

– all the more remarkable coming from a proponent of deconstruction – of a *lumpen* feminist essentialism (radical-liberal-separatist and American) to a phantom feminist poststructuralism (critical-socialist-psychoanalytic and Franco-British), and with the by-products of such a *parti-pris*: the canonization of a few (in)famous feminists as signposts of the convenient categories set up by the typology, the agonistic narrative structure of its account of 'feminist theories', and finally its failure to contribute to the elaboration of feminist critical thought, however useful the book may be to its other intended readers, who can thus rest easy in the fantasy that poststructuralism is the theory and feminism is just a practice.

The title of Alcoff's essay, 'Cultural Feminism versus Post-Structuralism: The Identity Crisis in Feminist Theory', bespeaks some of the same problems: a manner of thinking by mutually oppositional categories, an agonistic frame of argumentation, and a focus on division, a 'crisis in feminist theory' that may be read not only as a crisis *over* identity, a metacritical doubt and a dispute among feminists as to the notion of identity, but also as a crisis *of* identity, of self-definition, implying a theoretical impasse for feminism as a whole. The essay, however, is more discerning, goes much further than its title suggests, and even contradicts it in the end, as the notion of identity, far from fixing the point of an impasse, becomes an active shifter in the feminist discourse of woman.

Taking as its starting point 'the concept of woman', or rather, its redefinition in feminist theory ('the dilemma facing feminist theorists today is that our very self-definition is grounded in a concept that we must deconstruct and de-essentialize in all of its aspects'), Alcoff finds two major categories of responses to the dilemma, or what I would call the paradox of woman (p. 406). Cultural feminists, she claims, 'have not challenged the defining of woman but only that definition given by men' (p. 407), and have replaced it with what they believe a more accurate description and appraisal, 'the concept of the essential female' (p. 408). On the other hand, the poststructuralist response has been to reject the possibility of defining woman altogether and to replace 'the politics of gender or sexual difference . . . with a plurality of difference where gender loses its position of significance' (p. 407). A third category is suggested, but only indirectly, in Alcoff's unwillingness to include among cultural feminists certain writers of colour such as Moraga and Lorde in spite of their emphasis on cultural identity, for in her view 'their work has consistently rejected essentialist conceptions of gender' (p. 412). Why an emphasis on racial, ethnic, and/or sexual identity need not be seen as essentialist is discussed more fully later in the essay with regard to identity politics and in conjunction with a third trend in feminist theory which Alcoff sees as a new course for feminism, 'a theory of the gendered subject that does not slide into essentialism' (p. 422).

Whereas the narrative structure underlying Weedon's account of feminist theories is that of a contest where one actor successively engages and defeats or conquers several rivals, Alcoff's develops as a dialectic. Both the culturalist and the poststructuralist positions display internal contradictions: for example, not all cultural feminists 'give explicitly essentialist formulations of what it means to be a woman' (p. 411), and their emphasis on the affirmation of women's strength and positive cultural roles and attributes has done much to counter images of woman as victim or of woman as male when in a business suit; but insofar as it reinforces the essentialist explanations of those attributes that are part and parcel of the traditional notion of womanhood, cultural feminism may, and for some women does, foster another form of sexist oppression. Conversely, if the poststructuralist critique of the unified, authentic subject of humanism is more than compatible with the feminist project to 'deconstruct and de-essentialize' woman (as Alcoff puts it, in clearly poststructuralist terms), its absolute rejection of gender and its negation of biological determinism in favour of a cultural-discursive determinism result, as concerns women, in a form of nominalism. If 'woman' is a fiction, a locus of pure difference and resistance to logocentric power, and if there are no women as such, then the very issue of women's oppression would appear to be obsolete and feminism itself would have no reason to exist (which, it may be noted, is a corollary of poststructuralism and the stated position of those who call themselves 'post-feminists'). 'What can we demand in the name of women,' Alcoff asks, 'if "women" do not exist and demands in their name simply reinforce the myth that they do?' (p. 420).

The way out – let me say, the sublation – of the contradictions in which are caught these two mainstream feminist views lies in 'a theory of the subject that avoids both essentialism and nominalism' (p. 421), and Alcoff points to it in the work of a few theorists, 'a few brave souls', whom she rejoins in developing her notion of 'woman as positionality': 'woman is a position from which a feminist politics can emerge rather than a set of attributes that are "objectively identifiable"' (pp. 434–5). In becoming feminist, for instance, women take up a position, a point of perspective, from which to interpret or (re)construct values and meanings. That position is also a politically assumed identity, and one relative to their sociohistorical location, whereas essentialist definitions would have woman's identity or attributes independent of her external situation; however, the positions available to women in any sociohistorical location are neither arbitrary nor undecidable. Thus, Alcoff concludes,

> If we combine the concept of identity politics with a conception of the subject as positionality, we can conceive of the subject as nonessentialized and emergent from a historical experience and yet retain our political ability to take gender as an important point of departure. Thus we can say at one and the same time that gender is not natural, biological, universal, ahistorical, or essential and yet still claim that gender is relevant because we are taking gender as a position from which to act politically. (p. 433)

I am, of course, in agreement with her emphases on issues and arguments that have been central in my work, such as the necessity to theorize experience in relation to practices, the understanding of gendered subjectivity as 'an emergent property of a historicized experience' (p. 431), and the notion that identity is an active construction and a discursively mediated political interpretation of one's history. What I must ask, and less as a criticism of Alcoff's essay than for the purposes of my argument here, is: why is it still necessary to set up two opposing categories, cultural feminism and poststructuralism, or essentialism and anti-essentialism, thesis and antithesis, when one has already achieved the vantage point of a theoretical position that overtakes them or sublates them?

Doesn't the insistence on the 'essentialism' of cultural feminists reproduce and keep in the foreground an image of 'dominant' feminism that is at least reductive, at best tautological or superseded, and at worst not in our interests? Doesn't it feed the pernicious opposition of low versus high theory, a low-grade type of critical thinking (feminism) that is contrasted with the high-test theoretical grade of a poststructuralism from which some feminists would have been smart enough to learn? As one feminist theorist who's been concurrently involved with feminism, women's studies, psychoanalytic theory, structuralism, and film theory from the beginning of my critical activity, I know that learning to be a feminist has grounded, or embodied, all of my learning and so engendered thinking and knowing itself. That engendered thinking and that embodied, situated knowledge (in Donna Haraway's phrase) are the stuff of feminist theory, whether by 'feminist theory' is meant one of a growing number of feminist critical discourses – on culture, science, subjectivity, writing, visual representation, social institutions, etc. – or, more particularly, the critical elaboration of feminist thought itself and the ongoing (re)definition of its specific difference. In either case, feminist theory is not of a lower grade than that which some call 'male theory', but different in kind; and it is its essential difference, the essence of that triangle, that concerns me here as a theorist of feminism.

Why then, I ask again, continue to constrain it in the terms of essentialism and anti-essentialism even as they no longer serve (but did they ever?) to formulate our questions? For example, in her discussion of cultural feminism, Alcoff accepts another critic's characterization despite some doubt that the latter 'makes it appear too homogeneous and . . . the charge of essentialism is on shaky ground' (p. 411). Then she adds:

> In the absence of a clearly stated position on the ultimate source of gender difference, Echols *infers* from their emphasis on building a feminist free-space and woman-centered culture that cultural feminists hold some version of essentialism. I share Echols's *suspicion*. Certainly, *it is difficult to render the views of Richard Daly into a coherent whole without supplying a missing premise* that there is an innate female essence. (p. 412; emphasis added)

But why do it at all? What is the purpose, or the gain, of supplying a missing premise (innate female essence) in order to construct a coherent image of feminism which thus becomes available to charges (essentialism) based on the very premise that had to be supplied? What motivates such a project, the suspicion, and the inferences?

THEORIZING BEYOND RECONCILIATION

For a theorist of feminism, the answer to these questions should be looked for in the particular history of feminism, the debates, internal divisions, and polarizations that have resulted from its engagement with the various institutions, discourses, and practices that constitute the social, and from its self-conscious reflection on that engagement; that is to say, the divisions that have marked feminism as a result of the divisions (of gender, sex, race, class, ethnicity, sexuality, etc.) in the social itself, and the discursive boundaries and subjective limits that feminism has defined and redefined for itself contingently, historically, in the process of its engagement with social and cultural formations. The answer should be looked for, in other words, in the form as well as the contents that are specific to feminist political practices and conceptual elaboration, in the paradoxes and contradictions that constitute the effective history, the essential difference, of feminist thought.

In one account that can be given of that history, feminist theory has developed a series of oppositional stances not only vis-à-vis the wider, 'external' context (the social constraints, legislation, ideological apparati, dominant discourses and representations against which feminism has pitched its critique and its political strategies in particular historical locations), but also, concurrently and interrelatedly, in its own 'internal', self-critical processes. For instance, in the seventies, the debates on academic feminism vs. activism in the United States defined an opposition between theory and practice which led, on the one hand, to a polarization of positions either *for* theory or *against* theory in nearly all cultural practices and, on the other, to a consistent, if never fully successful, effort to overcome the opposition itself. Subsequently, the internal division of the movement over the issue of separatism or 'mainstreaming', both in the academy and in other institutional contexts, recast the practice/theory opposition in terms of lesbian vs. heterosexual identification, and of women's studies vs. feminist cultural theory, among others. Here, too, the opposition led to both polarization (e.g., feminist criticism vs. feminist theory in literary studies) and efforts to overcome it by an expanded, extremely flexible, and ultimately unsatisfactory redefinition of the notion of 'feminist theory' itself.

Another major division and the resulting crucial shift in feminist thought were prompted, at the turn of the decade into the eighties, by the wider dissemination of the writings of women of colour and their critique of racism in the women's movement. The division over the issue of race vs. gender, and of the relative importance of each in defining the modes of women's oppression, resistance, and agency, also produced an opposition between a 'white' or 'Western feminism' and a 'U.S. Third World feminism' articulated in several racial and ethnic hyphenations, or called by an altogether different name (e.g., black 'womanism'). Because the oppositional stance of women of colour was markedly, if not exclusively, addressed to white women in the context of feminism – that is to say, their critique addressed more directly white feminists than it did (white) patriarchal power structures, men of colour, or even white women in general – once again that division on the issue of race vs. gender led to polarization as well as to concerted efforts to overcome it, at least internally to feminist theoretical and cultural practices. And once again those efforts met with mostly unsatisfactory or inadequate results, so that no actual resolution, no dialectic sublation has been achieved in this opposition either, as in the others. For even as the polarization may be muted or displaced by other issues that come to the fore, each of those oppositions remains present and active in feminist consciousness and, I want to argue, must so remain in a feminist theory of the female-sexed or female-embodied social subject that is based on its specific and emergent history.

Since the mid-eighties, the so-called feminist sex wars (Ruby Rich) have pitched 'pro-sex' feminists vs. the anti-pornography movement in a conflict over representation that recast the sex/gender distinction into the form of a paradoxical opposition: sex and gender are either collapsed together, and rendered both analytically and politically indistinguishable (MacKinnon, Hartsock) or they are severed from each other and seen as endlessly recombinable in such figures of boundary crossing as transsexualism, transvestism, bisexualism, drag and impersonation (Butler), cyborgs (Haraway), etc. This last issue is especially central to the lesbian debate on sadomasochism (*Coming to Power*, *Against Sadomasochism*), which recasts the earlier divisions of lesbians between the women's liberation movement, with its more or less overt homophobia (Bearchell, Clark), and the gay liberation movement, with its more or less overt sexism (Frye), into the current opposition of radical S/M lesbianism to mainstream-cultural lesbian feminism (Rubin, Califia), an opposition whose mechanical binarism is tersely expressed by the recent magazine title *On Our Backs* punning on the long-established feminist periodical *Off Our Backs*. And here may be also mentioned the opposition pro and against psychoanalysis (e.g., Rose and Wilson) which, ironically, has been almost completely disregarded in these sexuality debates, even as it determined the conceptual elaboration of sexual difference in the seventies and has since been fundamental to the feminist critique of representation in the media and the arts.

This account of the history of feminism in relation to both 'external' and 'internal' events, discourses, and practices suggests that two concurrent drives, impulses or mechanisms, are at work in the production of its self-representation: *an erotic, narcissistic drive* that enhances images of feminism as difference, rebellion, daring, excess, subversion, disloyalty, agency, empowerment, pleasure and danger, and rejects all images of powerlessness, victimization, subjection, acquiescence, passivity, conformism, femininity; and *an ethical drive* that works toward community, accountability, entrustment, sisterhood, bonding, belonging to a common world of women or sharing what Adrienne Rich has poignantly called 'the dream of a common language'. Together, often in mutual contradiction, the erotic and ethical drives have fuelled not only the various polarizations and the construction of oppositions but also the invention or conceptual imaging of a 'continuum' of experience, a global feminism, a 'house of difference', or a separate space where 'safe words' can be trusted and 'consent' be given uncoerced. And, as I suggest in my discussion of a recent text of Italian feminism by the Milan Women's Bookstore collective, an erotic and an ethical drive may be seen to underlie and sustain at once the possibility of, and the difficulties involved in, the project of articulating a female symbolic. Are these two drives together, most often in mutual contradiction, what particularly distinguishes lesbian feminism, where the erotic is as necessary a condition as the ethical, if not more?

That the two drives often clash or bring about political stalemates and conceptual impasses is not surprising, for they have contradictory objects and aims, and are forced into open conflict in a culture where women are not supposed to be, know, or see themselves as subjects. And for this very reason perhaps, the two drives characterize the movement of feminism, and more emphatically lesbian feminism, its historically intrinsic, essential condition of contradiction, and the processes constitutive of feminist thought in its specificity. As I have written elsewhere, 'the tension of a twofold pull in contrary directions – the critical negativity of its theory, and the affirmative positivity of its politics – is both the historical condition of existence of feminism and its theoretical condition of possibility'. That tension, as the condition of possibility and effective elaboration of feminist theory, is most productive in the kind of critical thinking that refuses to be pulled to either side of an opposition and seeks instead to deconstruct it, or better, to disengage it from the fixity of polarization in an 'internal' feminist debate and to reconnect it to the 'external' discursive and social context from which it finally cannot be severed except at the cost of repeatedly reducing a historical process, a movement, to an ideological stalemate. This may be the approach of those writers whom Alcoff would call 'brave souls . . . attempting to map out a new course' (p. 407). But that course, I would argue, does not proceed in the manner of a dialectic, by resolving or reconciling the given terms of an opposition – say, essentialism/anti-essentialism or pro-sex/anti-pornography – whether the resolution is achieved discursively (for example, alleging a larger, tactical or political perspective on the issue) or by pointing to their actual sublation in existing material conditions (for example, adducing socio-logical data or statistical arguments). It proceeds, in my view, by what I call upping the 'anti': by analysing the undecidability, conceptual as well as pragmatic, of the alternative *as given*, such critical works release its terms from the fixity of meaning into which polarization has locked them, and reintroduce them into a larger contextual and conceptual frame of reference; the tension of positivity and negativity that marks feminist discourse in its engagement with the social can then displace the impasse of mere 'internal' opposition to a more complex level of analysis.

Seen in this larger, historical frame of reference, feminist theory is not merely a theory of gender oppression in culture, as both MacKinnon and Rubin maintain, from the respective poles of the sex/gender and pro-sex/anti-pornography debates, and as is too often reiterated in women's studies textbooks; nor is it the essentialist theory of women's nature which Weedon opposes to an anti-essentialist, poststructuralist theory of culture. It is instead a developing theory of the female-sexed or female-embodied social subject, whose constitution and whose modes of social and subjective existence include most obviously sex and gender, but also race, class, and any other significant sociocultural divisions and representations; a developing theory of the female-embodied social subject that is based on its specific, emergent, and conflictual history.

NOTE

Another version of this essay was published in *Differences: A Journal of Feminist Cultural Studies* 1, no. 2 (Fall 1989) with the title 'The Essence of the Triangle or, Taking the Risk of Essentialism Seriously: Feminist Theory in Italy, the U.S., and Britain'. The essay was initially written for the issue of *Differences* devoted to 'The Essential Difference: Another Look at Essentialism', but then rethought in the context of the project of a book addressing the problem of 'conflicts in feminism'. The two versions have in common the arguments set out in Part I, but then, in Parts II and III, present two quite distinct accounts of what I call the effective history of feminist theory and its specific, essential difference as a developing theory of the female-sexed or female-embodied social subject: there, an account, one possible history of feminist theory in Italy, here one account of feminist theory in North America.

6 Stuart Hall

Encoding, decoding

EDITOR'S INTRODUCTION

Stuart Hall's influential essay offers a densely theoretical account of how messages are produced and disseminated, referring particularly to television. He suggests a four-stage theory of communication: production, circulation, use (which here he calls distribution or consumption), and reproduction. For him each stage is 'relatively autonomous' from the others. This means that the coding of a message *does* control its reception but not transparently – each stage has its own determining limits and possibilities. The concept of relative autonomy allows him to argue that polysemy is not the same as pluralism: messages are not open to any interpretation or use whatsoever – just because each stage in the circuit limits possibilities in the next.

In actual social existence, Hall goes on to argue, messages have a 'complex structure of dominance' because at each stage they are 'imprinted' by institutional power relations. Furthermore, a message can only be received at a particular stage if it is recognizable or appropriate – though there is space for a message to be used or understood at least somewhat against the grain. This means that power relations at the point of production, for example, will loosely fit those at the point of consumption. In this way, the communication circuit is also a circuit which reproduces a pattern of domination.

This analysis allows Hall to insert a semiotic paradigm into a social framework, clearing the way both for further textualist and ethnographic work. His essay has been particularly important as a basis on which fieldwork like David Morley's has proceeded.

Further reading: Hall 1977, 1980; Morley 1980, 1989.

S.D.

Traditionally, mass-communications research has conceptualized the process of communication in terms of a circulation circuit or loop. This model has been criticized for its linearity – sender/message/receiver – for its concentration on the level of message exchange and for the absence of a structured conception of the different moments as a complex structure of relations. But it is also possible (and useful) to think of this process in terms of a structure produced and sustained through the articulation of linked but distinctive moments – production, circulation, distribution/consumption, reproduction. This would be to think of the process as a 'complex structure in dominance', sustained through the articulation of connected practices, each of which, however, retains its distinctiveness and has its own specific modality, its own forms and conditions of existence.

The 'object' of these practices is meanings and messages in the form of sign-vehicles of a specific kind organized, like any form of communication or language, through the operation of codes within the syntagmatic chain of a discourse. The apparatuses, relations and practices of production thus issue, at a certain moment (the moment of 'production/ circulation') in the form of symbolic vehicles constituted within the rules of 'language'. It is in this discursive form that the circulation of the 'product' takes place. The process thus requires, at the production end, its material instruments – its 'means' – as well as its own sets of social (production) relations – the organization and combination of practices within media apparatuses. But it is in the *discursive* form that the circulation of the product takes place, as well as its distribution to different audiences. Once accomplished, the discourse must then be translated – transformed, again – into social practices if the circuit is to be both completed and effective. If no 'meaning' is taken, there can be no 'consumption'. If the meaning is not articulated in practice, it has no effect. The value of this approach is that while each of the moments, in articulation, is necessary to the circuit as a whole, no one moment can fully guarantee the next moment with which it is articulated. Since each has its specific modality and conditions of existence, each can constitute its own break or interruption of the 'passage of forms' on whose continuity the flow of effective production (that is, 'reproduction') depends.

Thus while in no way wanting to limit research to 'following only those leads which emerge from content analysis', we must recognize that the discursive form of the message has a privileged position in the communicative exchange (from the viewpoint of circulation), and that the moments of 'encoding' and 'decoding', though only 'relatively autonomous' in relation to the communicative process as a whole, are *determinate* moments. A 'raw' historical event cannot, *in that form*, be transmitted by, say, a television newscast. Events can only be signified within the aural-visual forms of the televisual discourse. In the moment when a historical event passes under the sign of discourse, it is subject to all the complex formal 'rules' by which language signifies. To put it paradoxically, the event must become a 'story' before it can become a *communicative event*. In that moment the formal sub-rules of discourse are 'in dominance', without, of course, subordinating out of existence the historical event so signified, the social relations in which the rules are set to work or the social and political consequences of the event having been signified in this way. The 'message form' is the necessary 'form of appearance' of the event in its passage from source to receiver. Thus the transposition into and out of the 'message form' (or the mode of symbolic exchange) is not a random 'moment', which we can take up or ignore at our convenience. The 'message form' is a determinate moment; though, at another level, it comprises the surface movements of the communications system only and requires, at another stage, to be integrated into the social relations of the communication process as a whole, of which it forms only a part.

From this general perspective, we may crudely characterize the television communicative process as follows. The institutional structures of broadcasting, with their practices and networks of production, their organized relations and technical infrastructures, are required to produce a programme. Production, here, constructs the message. In one sense, then, the circuit begins here. Of course, the production process is not without its 'discursive' aspect: it, too, is framed throughout by meanings and ideas: knowledge-in-use concerning the routines of production, historically defined technical skills, professional ideologies, institutional knowledge, definitions and assumptions, assumptions about the audience and so on frame the constitution of the programme through this production structure. Further, though the production structures of television originate the television discourse, they do not constitute a closed system. They draw topics, treatments, agendas, events, personnel, images of the audience, 'definitions of the situation' from other sources and other discursive formations within the wider socio-cultural and political structure of which they are a differentiated part. Philip Elliott has expressed this point succinctly, within a more traditional framework, in his discussion of the way in which the audience is both the 'source' and the 'receiver' of the television message. Thus – to borrow Marx's terms – circulation and reception are, indeed, 'moments' of the production process in television and are reincorporated, via a number of skewed and structured 'feedbacks', into the production process itself. The consumption or reception of the television message is thus also itself a 'moment' of the production process in its larger sense, though the latter is 'predominant' because it is the 'point of departure for the realization' of the message. Production and reception of the television message are not, therefore, identical, but they are related: they are differentiated moments within the totality formed by the social relations of the communicative process as a whole.

At a certain point, however, the broadcasting structures must yield encoded messages in the form of a meaningful discourse. The institution-societal relations of production must pass under the discursive rules of language for its product to be 'realized'. This initiates a further differentiated moment, in which the formal rules of discourse and language are in dominance. Before this message can have an 'effect' (however defined), satisfy a 'need' or be put to a 'use', it must first be appropriated as a meaningful discourse and be meaningfully decoded. It is this set of decoded meanings which 'have an effect', influence, entertain, instruct or persuade, with very complex perceptual, cognitive, emotional, ideological or behavioural consequences. In a 'determinate' moment the structure employs a code and yields a 'message': at another determinate moment the 'message', via its decodings, issues into the structure of social practices. We are now fully aware that this re-entry into the practices of audience reception and 'use' cannot be understood in simple behavioural terms. The typical processes identified in positivistic research on isolated elements – effects, uses, 'gratifications' – are themselves framed by structures of understanding, as well as being produced by social and economic relations, which shape their 'realization' at the reception end of the chain and which permit the meanings signified in the discourse to be transposed into practice or consciousness (to acquire social use value or political effectivity).

Clearly, what we have labelled in the diagram (below) 'meaning structures 1' and 'meaning structures 2' may not be the same. They do not constitute an 'immediate identity'. The codes of encoding and decoding may not be perfectly symmetrical. The degrees of symmetry – that is, the degrees of 'understanding' and 'misunderstanding' in the communicative exchange – depend on the degrees of symmetry/asymmetry (relations of equivalence) established between the positions of the 'personifications', encoder-producer and decoder-receiver. But this in turn depends on the degrees of identity/non-identity between the codes which perfectly or imperfectly transmit, interrupt or systematically

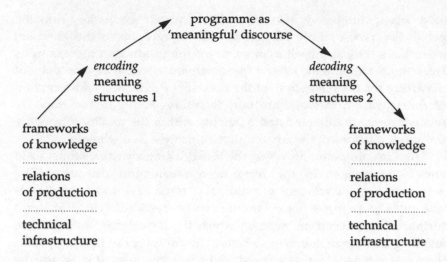

distort what has been transmitted. The lack of fit between the codes has a great deal to do with the structural differences of relation and position between broadcasters and audiences, but it also has something to do with the asymmetry between the codes of 'source' and 'receiver' at the moment of transformation into and out of the discursive form. What are called 'distortions' or 'misunderstandings' arise precisely from the *lack of equivalence* between the two sides in the communicative exchange. Once again, this defines the 'relative autonomy', but 'determinateness', of the entry and exit of the message in its discursive moments.

The application of this rudimentary paradigm has already begun to transform our understanding of the older term, television 'content'. We are just beginning to see how it might also transform our understanding of audience reception, 'reading' and response as well. Beginnings and endings have been announced in communications research before, so we must be cautious. But there seems some ground for thinking that a new and exciting phase in so-called audience research, of a quite new kind, may be opening up. At either end of the communicative chain the use of the semiotic paradigm promises to dispel the lingering behaviourism which has dogged mass-media research for so long, especially in its approach to content. Though we know the television programme is not a behavioural input, like a tap on the knee cap, it seems to have been almost impossible for traditional researchers to conceptualize the communicative process without lapsing into one or other variant of low-flying behaviourism. We know, as Gerbner has remarked, that representations of violence on the TV screen 'are not violence but messages about violence': but we have continued to research the question of violence, for example, as if we were unable to comprehend this epistemological distinction.

The televisual sign is a complex one. It is itself constituted by the combination of two types of discourse, visual and aural. Moreover, it is an iconic sign, in Peirce's terminology, because 'it possesses some of the properties of the thing represented'. This is a point which has led to a great deal of confusion and has provided the site of intense controversy in the study of visual language. Since the visual discourse translates a three-dimensional world into two-dimensional planes, it cannot, of course, *be* the referent or concept it signifies. The dog in the film can bark but it cannot bite! Reality exists outside language, but it is constantly mediated by and through language: and what we can know and say has to be produced in and through discourse. Discursive 'knowledge' is the product not of the transparent representation of the 'real' in language but of the articulation of language on real relations and conditions. Thus there is no intelligible discourse without the operation of a code. Iconic signs are therefore coded signs too – even if the codes here work differently from those of other signs. There is no degree zero in language. Naturalism and 'realism' – the apparent fidelity of the representation to the thing or concept represented – is the result, the effect, of a certain specific articulation of language on the 'real'. It is the result of a discursive practice.

Certain codes may, of course, be so widely distributed in a specific language community or culture, and be learned at so early an age, that they appear not to be constructed – the effect of an articulation between sign and referent – but to be 'naturally' given. Simple visual signs appear to have achieved a 'near-universality' in this sense: though evidence remains that even apparently 'natural' visual codes are culture-specific. However, this does not mean that no codes have intervened; rather, that the codes have been profoundly *naturalized*. The operation of naturalized codes reveals not the transparency and 'naturalness' of language but the depth, the habituation and the near-universality of the codes in use. They produce apparently 'natural' recognitions. This has the (ideological) effect of concealing the practices of coding which are present. But we must not be fooled by appearances. Actually, what naturalized codes demonstrate is the degree of habituation produced when there is a fundamental alignment and reciprocity – an achieved equivalence – between the encoding and decoding sides of an exchange of meanings. The functioning of the codes on the decoding side will frequently assume the status of naturalized perceptions. This leads us to think that the visual sign for 'cow' actually *is* (rather than *represents*) the animal, cow. But if we think of the visual representation of a cow in a manual on animal husbandry – and, even more, of the linguistic sign 'cow' – we can see that both, in different degrees, are *arbitrary* with respect to the concept of the animal they represent. The articulation of an arbitrary sign – whether visual or verbal – with the concept of a referent is the product not of nature but of convention, and the conventionalism of discourses requires the intervention, the support, of codes. Thus Eco has argued that iconic signs 'look like objects in the real world because they reproduce the conditions (that is, the codes) of perception in the viewer'. These 'conditions of perception' are, however, the result of a highly coded, even if virtually unconscious, set of operations – decodings. This is as true of the photographic or televisual image as it is of any other sign. Iconic signs are, however, particularly vulnerable to being 'read' as natural because visual codes of perception are very widely distributed and because this type of sign is less arbitrary than a linguistic sign: the linguistic sign, 'cow', possesses *none* of the properties of the thing represented, whereas the visual sign appears to possess *some* of those properties.

This may help us to clarify a confusion in current linguistic theory and to define precisely how some key terms are being used in this article. Linguistic theory frequently employs the distinction 'denotation' and 'connotation'. The term 'denotation' is widely equated with the literal meaning of a sign: because this literal meaning is almost universally recognized, especially when visual discourse is being employed, 'denotation' has often been confused with a literal transcription of 'reality' in language – and thus with a 'natural sign', one produced without the intervention of a code. 'Connotation', on the other hand, is employed simply to refer to less fixed and therefore more conventionalized and changeable, associative meanings, which clearly vary from instance to instance and therefore must depend on the intervention of codes.

We do *not* use the distinction – denotation/connotation – in this way. From our point of view, the distinction is an *analytic* one only. It is useful, in analysis, to be able to apply a rough rule of thumb which distinguishes those aspects of a sign which appear to be taken, in any language community at any point in time, as its 'literal' meaning (denotation) from the more associative meanings for the sign which it is possible to generate (connotation). But analytic distinctions must not be confused with distinctions in the real world. There will be very few instances in which signs organized in a discourse signify *only* their 'literal' (that is, near-universally consensualized) meaning. In actual discourse most signs will combine both the denotative and the connotative *aspects* (as redefined above). It may, then, be asked why we retain the distinction at all. It is largely a matter of analytic value. It is because signs appear to acquire their full ideological value – appear to be open to articulation with wider ideological discourses and meanings – at the level of their 'associative' meanings (that is, at the connotative level) – for here 'meanings' are *not* apparently fixed in natural perception (that is, they are not fully naturalized), and their fluidity of meaning and association can be more fully exploited and transformed. So it is at the connotative *level* of the sign that situational ideologies alter and transform signification. At this level we can see more clearly the active intervention of ideologies in and on discourse: here, the sign is open to new accentuations and, in Vološinov's terms, enters fully into the struggle over meanings – the class struggle in language. This does not mean that the denotative or 'literal' meaning is outside ideology. Indeed, we could say that its ideological value is strongly *fixed* – because it has become so fully universal and 'natural'. The terms 'denotation' and 'connotation', then, are merely useful analytic tools for distinguishing, in particular contexts, between not the presence/absence of ideology in language but the different levels at which ideologies and discourses intersect.

The level of connotation of the visual sign, of its contextual reference and positioning in different discursive fields of meaning and association, is the point where *already coded* signs intersect with the deep semantic codes of a culture and take on additional, more active ideological dimensions. We might take an example from advertising discourse. Here, too, there is no 'purely denotative', and certainly no 'natural', representation. Every visual sign in advertising connotes a quality, situation, value or inference, which is present as an implication or implied meaning, depending on the connotational positioning. In Barthes's example, the sweater always signifies a 'warm garment' (denotation) and thus the activity/value of 'keeping warm'. But it is also possible, at its more connotative levels, to signify 'the coming of winter' or 'a cold day'. And, in the specialized sub-codes of fashion, sweater may also connote a fashionable style of *haute couture* or, alternatively, an informal style of dress. But set against the right visual background and positioned by the romantic sub-code, it may connote 'long autumn walk in the woods'. Codes of this order clearly contract relations for the sign with the wider universe of ideologies in a society. These codes are the means by which power and ideology are made to signify in particular discourses. They refer signs to the 'maps of meaning' into which any culture is classified; and those 'maps of social reality' have the whole range of social meanings, practices, and usages, power and interest 'written in' to them. The connotative levels of signifiers, Barthes remarked, 'have a close communication with culture, knowledge, history, and it is through them, so to speak, that the environmental world invades the linguistic and semantic system. They are, if you like, the fragments of ideology'.

The so-called denotative *level* of the televisual sign is fixed by certain, very complex (but limited or 'closed') codes. But its connotative *level*, though also bounded, is more open, subject to more active *transformations*, which exploit its polysemic values. Any such already constituted sign is potentially transformable into more than one connotative configuration. Polysemy must not, however, be confused with pluralism. Connotative codes are *not* equal among themselves. Any society/ culture tends, with varying degrees of closure, to impose its classifications of the social and cultural and political world. These constitute a *dominant cultural order*, though it is neither univocal nor uncontested. This question of the 'structure of discourses in dominance' is a crucial point. The different areas of social life appear to be mapped out into discursive domains, hierarchically organized into *dominant or preferred meanings*. New, problematic or troubling events, which breach our expectancies and run counter to our 'common-sense constructs', to our 'taken-for-granted' knowledge of social structures, must be assigned to their discursive domains before they can be said to 'make sense'. The most common way of 'mapping' them is to assign the new to some domain or other of the existing 'maps of problematic social reality'. We say *dominant*, not 'determined', because it is always possible to order, classify, assign and decode an event within more than one 'mapping'. But we say 'dominant' because there exists a pattern of 'preferred readings'; and these both have the institutional/political/ideological order imprinted in them and have themselves become institutionalized. The domains of 'preferred meanings' have the whole social order embedded in them as a set of meanings, practices and beliefs: the everyday knowledge of social structures, of 'how things work for all practical purposes in this culture', the rank order of power and interest and the structure of legitimations, limits and sanctions. Thus to clarify a 'misunderstanding' at the connotative level, we must refer, *through* the codes, to the orders of social life, of economic and political power and of ideology. Further, since these mappings are 'structured in dominance' but not closed, the communicative process consists not in the unproblematic assignment of every visual item to its given position within a set of prearranged codes, but of *performative rules* – rules of competence and use, of logics-in-use – which seek actively to *enforce* or *pre-fer* one semantic domain over another and rule items into and out of their appropriate meaning-sets. Formal semiology has too often neglected this practice of *interpretative work*, though this constitutes, in fact, the real relations of broadcast practices in television.

In speaking of *dominant meanings*, then, we are not talking about a one-sided process which governs how all events will be signified. It consists of the 'work' required to enforce, win plausibility for and command as legitimate a *decoding* of the event within the limit of dominant definitions in which it has been connotatively signified. Terni has remarked:

> By the word *reading* we mean not only the capacity to identify and decode a certain number of signs, but also the subjective capacity to put them into a creative relation between themselves and with other signs: a capacity which is, by itself, the condition for a complete awareness of one's total environment.

Our quarrel here is with the notion of 'subjective capacity', as if the referent of a televisional discourse were an objective fact but the interpretative level were an individualized and private matter. Quite the opposite seems to be the case. The televisual practice takes 'objective' (that is, systemic) responsibility precisely for the relations which disparate signs contract with one another in any discursive instance, and thus continually rearranges, delimits and prescribes into what 'awareness of one's total environment' these items are arranged.

This brings us to the question of misunderstandings. Television producers who find their message 'failing to get across' are frequently concerned to straighten out the kinks in the communication chain, thus facilitating the 'effectiveness' of their communication. Much research which claims the objectivity of 'policy-oriented analysis' reproduces this administrative goal by attempting to discover how much of a message the audience recalls and to improve the extent of understanding. No doubt misunderstandings of a literal kind do exist. The viewer does not know the terms employed, cannot follow the complex logic of argument or exposition, is unfamiliar with the language, finds the concepts too alien or difficult or is foxed by the expository narrative. But more often broadcasters are concerned that the audience has failed to take the meaning as they – the broadcasters – intended. What they really mean to say is that viewers are not operating within the 'dominant' or 'preferred' code. Their ideal is 'perfectly transparent communication'. Instead, what they have to confront is 'systematically distorted communication'.

In recent years discrepancies of this kind have usually been explained by reference to 'selective perception'. This is the door via which a residual pluralism evades the compulsions of a highly structured, asymmetrical and non-equivalent process. Of course, there will always be private, individual, variant readings. But 'selective perception' is almost never as selective, random or privatized as the concept suggests. The patterns exhibit, across individual variants, significant clusterings. Any new approach to audience studies will therefore have to begin with a critique of 'selective perception' theory.

It was argued earlier that since there is no necessary correspondence between encoding and decoding, the former can attempt to 'pre-fer' but cannot prescribe or guarantee the latter, which has its own conditions of existence. Unless they are wildly aberrant, encoding will have the effect of constructing some of the limits and parameters within which decodings will operate. If there were no limits, audiences could simply read whatever they liked into any message. No doubt some total misunderstandings of this kind do exist. But the vast range must contain *some* degree of reciprocity between encoding and decoding moments, otherwise we could not speak of an effective communicative exchange at all. Nevertheless, this 'correspondence' is not given but constructed. It is not 'natural' but the product of an articulation between two distinct moments. And the former cannot determine or guarantee, in a simple sense, which decoding codes will be employed. Otherwise communication would be a perfectly equivalent circuit, and every message would be an instance of 'perfectly transparent communication'. We must think, then, of the variant articulations in which encoding/decoding can be combined. To elaborate on this, we offer a hypothetical analysis of some possible decoding positions, in order to reinforce the point of 'no necessary correspondence'.

We identify *three* hypothetical positions from which decodings of a televisual discourse may be constructed. These need to be empirically tested and refined. But the argument that decodings do not follow inevitably from encodings, that they are not identical, reinforces the argument of 'no necessary correspondence'. It also helps to deconstruct the common-sense meaning of 'misunderstanding' in terms of a theory of 'systematically distorted communication'.

The first hypothetical position is that of the *dominant-hegemonic position*. When the viewer takes the connoted meaning from, say, a television newscast or current affairs programme full and straight, and decodes the message in terms of the reference code in which it has been encoded, we might say that the viewer *is operating inside the dominant code*. This is the ideal-typical case of 'perfectly transparent communication' – or as close as we are likely to come to it 'for all practical purposes'. Within this we can distinguish the positions produced by the *professional code*. This is the position (produced by what we perhaps ought to identify as the operation of a 'metacode') which the professional broadcasters assume when encoding a message which has *already* been signified in a hegemonic manner. The professional code is 'relatively independent' of the dominant code, in that it applies criteria and transformational operations of its own, especially those of a technico-practical nature. The professional code, however, operates *within* the 'hegemony' of the dominant code. Indeed, it serves to reproduce the dominant definitions precisely by bracketing their hegemonic quality and operating instead with displaced professional codings which foreground such apparently neutral-technical questions as visual quality, news and presentational values, televisual quality, 'professionalism' and so on. The hegemonic interpretations of, say, the politics of Northern Ireland, or the Chilean *coup* or the Industrial Relations Bill are principally generated by political and military elites: the particular choice of presentational occasions and formats, the selection of personnel, the choice of images, the staging of debates are selected and combined through the operation of the professional code. How the broadcasting professionals are able *both* to operate with 'relatively autonomous' codes of their own *and* to act in such a way as to reproduce (not without contradiction) the hegemonic signification of events is a complex matter which cannot be further spelled out here. It must suffice to say that the professionals are linked with the defining elites not only by the institutional position of broadcasting itself as an 'ideological apparatus', but also by the structure of *access* (that is, the systematic 'over-accessing' of selective elite personnel and their 'definition of the situation' in television). It may even be said that the professional codes serve to reproduce hegemonic definitions specifically by *not overtly* biasing their operations in a dominant direction: ideological reproduction therefore takes place here inadvertently, unconsciously, 'behind men's backs'. Of course, conflicts, contradictions and even misunderstandings regularly arise between the dominant and the professional significations and their signifying agencies.

The second position we would identify is that of the *negotiated code* or position. Majority audiences probably understand quite adequately what has been dominantly defined and professionally signified. The dominant definitions, however, are hegemonic precisely because they represent definitions of situations and events which are 'in dominance' (*global*). Dominant definitions connect events, implicitly or explicitly, to grand totalizations, to the great syntagmatic views-of-the-world: they take 'large views' of issues: they relate events to the 'national interest' or to the level of geo-politics, even if they make these connections in truncated, inverted or mystified ways. The definition of a hegemonic viewpoint is (a) that it defines within its terms the mental horizon, the universe, of possible meanings, of a whole sector of relations in a society or culture; and (b) that it carries with it the stamp of legitimacy – it appears coterminous with what is 'natural', 'inevitable', 'taken for granted' about the social order. Decoding within the *negotiated version* contains a mixture of adaptive and oppositional elements: it acknowledges the legitimacy of the hegemonic definitions to make the grand significations (abstract), while, at a more restricted, situational (situated) level, it makes its own ground rules – it operates with exceptions to the rule. It accords the privileged position to the dominant definitions of events while reserving the right to make a more negotiated application to 'local conditions', to its own more *corporate* positions. This negotiated version of the dominant ideology is thus shot through with contradictions, though these are only on certain occasions brought to full visibility. Negotiated codes operate through what we might call particular or situated logics: and these logics are sustained by their differential and unequal relation to the discourses and logics of power. The simplest example of a negotiated code is that which governs the response of a worker to the notion of an Industrial Relations Bill limiting the right to strike or to arguments for a wages freeze. At the level of the 'national interest' economic debate the decoder may adopt the hegemonic definition, agreeing that 'we must all pay ourselves less in order to combat inflation'. This, however, may have little or no relation to his/her willingness to go on strike for better pay and conditions or to oppose the Industrial Relations Bill at the level of shop-floor or union organization. We suspect that the great majority of so-called 'misunderstandings' arise from the contradictions and disjunctures between hegemonic-dominant encodings and negotiated-corporate decodings. It is just these mismatches in the levels which most provoke defining elites and professionals to identify a 'failure in communications'.

Finally, it is possible for a viewer perfectly to understand both the literal and the connotative inflection given by a discourse but to decode the message in a *globally* contrary way. He/she detotalizes the message in the preferred code in order to retotalize the message within some alternative framework of reference. This is the case of the viewer who listens to a debate on the need to limit wages but 'reads' every mention of the 'national interest' as 'class interest'. He/she is operating with what we must call an *oppositional code*. One of the most significant political moments (they also coincide with crisis points within the broadcasting organizations themselves, for obvious reasons) is the point when events which are normally signified and decoded in a negotiated way begin to be given an oppositional reading. Here the 'politics of signification' – the struggle in discourse – is joined.

NOTE

This article is an edited extract from 'Encoding and Decoding in Television Discourse', CCCS Stencilled Paper no. 7.

7 Renato Rosaldo

After objectivism

EDITOR'S INTRODUCTION

This lucid essay, like James Clifford's, assumes a different global geography from that of earlier Birmingham and Euro-orientated cultural studies. It recognizes that the 'critical readership' of cultural studies can no longer be narrowly circumscribed; it is to be found as much in the Philippines, for instance, as in Los Angeles, in Suva as much as in Birmingham. Rosaldo argues that full recognition of the discipline's global nature requires the discipline both to employ a wider range of 'rhetorical forms in social description' and to edge closer to participant observation in its ethnography. No longer does the ethnographer have an unproblematic authority. This argument needs to be read alongside other contributions to the 'new ethnography' – like those listed in the 'Further reading' below.

Subtly, Rosaldo enacts his own thesis as he presents it, by drawing upon his own family life as an example. This kind of auto-ethnography is very far from self-indulgent just because it embodies an argument. It helps us refuse one of the most powerful seductions of the kind of knowledge generated by cultural studies: the confusion of theoretical and academic recodings with objectivity.

Further reading: Chabram 1990; Clifford and Marcus 1986; Dwyer 1979; Fabian 1983; Marcus and Fischer 1986; Rosaldo 1989.

S.D.

After falling head over heels in love, I paid a ceremonial visit, during the summer of 1983, to the 'family cottage' on the shores of Lake Huron in western Ontario. Much as one would expect (unless one was, as I was, too much in the thick of things), my prospective parents-in-law treated me, their prospective son-in-law, with reserve and suspicion. Such occasions are rarely easy, and this one was no exception. Not unlike other rites of passage, my mid-life courtship was a blend of conventional form and unique personal experience.

My peculiar position, literally surrounded by potential in-laws, nourished a project that unfolded over a two-week period in barely conscious daydreams. The daily family breakfast started turning in my mind into a ritual described in the distanced normalizing mode of a classic ethnography. On the morning of my departure, while we were eating breakfast, I revealed my feelings of tender malice by telling my potential in-laws the 'true' ethnography of their family breakfast: 'Every morning the reigning patriarch, as if just in from the hunt, shouts from the kitchen, "How many people would like a poached egg?" Women and children take turns saying yes or no.

'In the meantime, the women talk among themselves and designate one among them the toast maker. As the eggs near readiness, the reigning patriarch calls out to the designated toast maker, "The eggs are about ready. Is there enough toast?"

'"Yes," comes the deferential reply. "The last two pieces are about to pop up." The reigning patriarch then proudly enters bearing a plate of poached eggs before him.

'Throughout the course of the meal, the women and children, including the designated toast maker, perform the obligatory ritual praise song, saying, "These sure are great eggs, Dad."'

My rendition of a family breakfast in the ethnographic present transformed a relatively spontaneous event into a generic cultural form. It became a caricatured analysis of rituals of dominance and deference organized along lines of gender and generation.

This microethnography shifted jaggedly between words ordinarily used by the family (mainly in such direct quotes as 'These sure are great eggs, Dad') and those never used by them (such as 'reigning patriarch', 'designated toast maker', and 'obligatory ritual praise song'). The jargon displayed a degree of hostility toward my potential father-in-law (the reigning patriarch) and hesitant sympathy with my potential sisters-in-law (the designated toast maker and the singers of the praise song). Far from being a definitive objective statement, my microethnography turned out to be a timely intervention that altered mealtime practices without destroying them. The father approaching retirement and his daughters already established in their careers were in the process of remoulding their relations with one another. For all its deliberate carica-ture, my description contained an analysis that offered my potential in-laws a measure of insight into how their family breakfast routines, by then approaching empty ritual, embodied increasingly archaic familial relations of gender and hierarchy. Indeed, subsequent observations have confirmed that the ritual praise songs honouring the poached eggs and their maker have continued to be sung, but with tongue in cheek. To defamiliarize the family breakfast was to transform its taken-for-granted routines.

The reader will probably not be surprised to hear that my potential in-laws laughed and laughed as they listened to the microethnography about (and with which I had interrupted) their family breakfast. Without taking my narrative literally, they said they learned from it because its objectifications made certain patterns of behaviour stand out in stark relief – the better to change them. The reception of my tale, as became evident in retrospect, was conditioned by their family practice of taking pleasure in witty teasing banter laced with loving malice.

The experience of having gales of laughter greet my microethnography made me wonder why a manner of speaking that sounds like the literal 'truth' when describing distant cultures seems terribly funny as a description of 'us'. Why does a mode of composition flip between being parodic or serious depending in large measure on whether it is applied to 'ourselves' or to 'others'? Why does the highly serious classic ethnographic idiom almost inevitably become parodic when used as self-description?

Elsewhere I have argued that during the classic period (roughly 1921–1971), norms of distanced normalizing description gained a monopoly on objectivity. Their authority appeared so self-evident that they became the one and only legitimate form for telling the literal truth about other cultures. Proudly called the ethnographic present, these norms prescribed, among other things, the use of the present tense to depict social life as a set of shared routines and the assumption of a certain distance that purportedly conferred objectivity. All other modes of composition were marginalized or suppressed altogether.

In my view, no mode of composition is a neutral medium, and none should be granted exclusive rights to scientifically legitimate social description. Consider, for a moment longer, my mini-ethnography of the family breakfast. Although classic norms only rarely allowed for variants, mine was not the only possible version of the family meal. One could have told the tale of how this breakfast differed from all others. Such a telling could include specific conversations, the intrusive potential son-in-law, and the moods and rhythms with which the event unfolded. In addition, the narrator could have assumed the father's point of view and described how the 'family provider' distributed his gifts to the 'starving horde'. Or the tone of this account could have been droll, or sincere, or whimsical, or earnest, or angry, or detached, rather than mockingly parodic.

One plausible criterion for assessing the adequacy of social descriptions could be a thought experiment: How valid would we find ethnographic discourse about others if it were used to describe ourselves? The available literature, not to mention the family breakfast episode, indicates that a division between serious conception and laughing reception can separate the author's intentions from the reader's responses. Human subjects have often reacted with bemused puzzlement over the ways they have been depicted in anthropological writings.

The problem of validity in ethnographic discourse has reached crisis proportions in a number of areas over the past fifteen years. In Chicano responses to anthropological depictions of themselves, the most balanced yet most devastating assessment has been put forth by Américo Paredes. He begins rather gently by saying, 'I find the Mexicans and Chicanos pictured in the usual ethnographies somewhat unreal.' He goes on to suggest that the people studied find ethnographic accounts written about them more parodic than telling: 'It is not so much a sense of outrage, that would betray wounded egos, as a feeling of puzzlement, that *this* is given as a picture of the communities they have grown up in. Many of them are more likely to laugh at it all than feel indignant.' His critique of the somewhat unreal picture put forth in ethnographies about Chicanos continues with a stunning item-by-item enumeration of such errors as mistranslations, taking jokes seriously, missing double meanings, and accepting an apocryphal story as the literal truth about brutal initiation rites in youth gangs.

Paredes's diagnosis is that most ethnographic writing on Mexicans and Chicanos has failed to grasp significant variations in the tone of cultural events. In an ethnography he sees as representative, Paredes observes that the Chicanos portrayed 'are not only literal-minded, they never crack a joke'. He argues that ethnographers who attempt to interpret Chicano culture should recognize 'whether a gathering is a wake, a beer bust, or a street-corner confabulation'. Knowledge about the cultural framing of events would aid the ethnographer in distinguishing an earnest speech from a joking speech. Even when using technical concepts, the analysis should not lose sight of whether the event was serious (to be taken literally) or deadpan (to be read as farce).

Lest there be any confusion, I am saying neither that the native is always right nor that Paredes as native ethnographer could never be wrong. Instead, my claim is that we should take the criticisms of our subjects in much the same way that we take those of our colleagues. Not unlike other ethnographers, so-called natives can be insightful, sociologically correct, axe-grinding, self-interested, or mistaken. They do know their own cultures, and rather than being ruled out of court, their criticisms should be listened to and taken into account, to be accepted, rejected, or modified, as we reformulate our analyses. At issue is not the real truth versus the ethnographic lie. After all, the pragmatic concerns of everyday life can diverge from those of disciplined enquiry. A person 'falling in love' speaks with quite different desires and purposes than the psychiatrist who describes the 'same' phenomenon as 'object cathexis'. Technical and everyday vocabularies differ in large measure because their respective projects are oriented to different goals. In this case, Paredes has called attention to how the 'objects' of study can find an earnest ethnography about themselves as parodic as did the participants in the Canadian family breakfast. His incisive critique calls for ethnographers to reassess their rhetorical habits.

The difficulties of using ethnographic discourse for self-description should have long been apparent to anthropologists, most of whom have read Horace Miner's classic (if heavy-handed) paper, 'Body Ritual among the Nacirema'. (Nacirema spelled backwards, of course, is American.) In that paper, an ethnographic sketch of Nacirema 'mouth-rites', written in accord with classic norms, was parodic in its application to Americans:

> The daily body ritual performed by everyone includes a mouth-rite. Despite the fact that these people are so punctilious about care of the mouth, this rite involves a practice which strikes the uninitiated stranger as revolting. It was reported to me that the ritual consists of inserting a small bundle of hog hairs into the mouth, along with certain magical powders, and then moving the bundle in a highly formalized series of gestures.

His essay thus defamiliarizes both through the narrator's position as uninitiated stranger and through the distanced idiom that transforms everyday life practices into more elevated ritual and magical acts.

Clearly there is a gap between the technical idiom of ethnography and the language of everyday life. Miner's description employs terms used by a certain group of professionals rather than the words most of 'us' Americans usually use in talking about brushing 'our' teeth. The article becomes parodic precisely because of the discrepancy between what we all know about brushing our teeth and the ethnographer's elevated, distanced, normalizing discourse. Unlike my account of the family breakfast, jarring discordance here does not become fully explicit in the text (despite what text positivists may think). Instead, it resides in the disjunction between Miner's technical jargon and the North American reader's knowledge that the mouth-rites refer to brushing one's teeth in the morning.

In retrospect, one wonders why Miner's article was taken simply as a good-natured joke rather than as a scathing critique of ethnographic discourse. Who could continue to feel comfortable describing other people in terms that sound ludicrous when applied to ourselves? What if the detached observer's authoritative objectivity resides more in a manner of speaking than in apt characterizations of other forms of life?

Lest it appear that no ethnography has ever been written in the manner of Miner's Nacirema mouth-rites, one should probably cite an actual case. Otherwise, the reader could regard the classic norms as a figment of my imagination rather than as the discipline's until recently (and, in many quarters, still) dominant mode of representing other cultures.

Consider, for example, the description of 'weeping rites' in A. R. Radcliffe-Brown's classic ethnography about the Andaman Islanders, a hunter-gatherer group residing south-east of India:

> When two friends or relatives meet after having been separated, the social relation between them that has been interrupted is about to be renewed. This social relation implies or depends upon the existence of a specific bond of solidarity between them. The weeping rite (together with the subsequent exchange of presents) is the affirmation of this bond. The rite, which, it must be remembered, is obligatory, compels the two participants to act as though they felt certain emotions, and thereby does, to some extent, produce these emotions in them.

The reader should keep in mind that this passage describes tears of greeting between long-separated old friends. Nonetheless, the ethnographer manifests scepticism about whether or not the weepers actually feel anything. Evidently, he regards their tears as mere playacting. To the limited extent that emotions are present, the ethnographer explains them as the consequence of having performed the obligatory weeping rites.

Yet the status of Radcliffe-Brown's term 'obligatory' remains obscure. Does it mean that when he witnessed weeping greeters, they always turned out to be long-lost intimates? How could he have observed greetings without tears between long-lost intimates? Or did people simply tell the ethnographer that when long-lost intimates greet one another, they weep? Despite its analytical import, the reader is left to wonder what Radcliffe-Brown means by the term *obligatory*.

Nonetheless, most anthropological readers of Radcliffe-Brown probably take his account at face value. When, for example, I told a colleague about my dissatisfaction with Radcliffe-Brown's depiction of Andaman weeping rites, she correctly followed the code for ethnographic readers and replied, 'Yes, but for them, unlike for us, the rites are obligatory.' Such are the costs of following rarely examined habits of reading.

The problem resides less in the use of such descriptions than in an uncritical attachment to them as the sole vehicle for literal objective truth. Radcliffe-Brown so detached himself from his human subjects that his account lends itself to being read as unwittingly parodic, and even absurd. When tearful greetings between long-lost intimates are described as obligatory weeping rites, they become so defamiliarized as to appear simply bizarre.

The idiom of classic ethnography characteristically describes specific events as if they were programmed cultural routines and places the observer at a great distance from the observed. The systematic effects of classic modes of composition were rarely explored because they purportedly held a monopoly on objectivity. The point, however, is not to discard classic norms but to displace them so that they become only one among a number of viable forms of social description rather than the one and only mode of writing about other cultures. Radcliffe-Brown's detached, dehumanizing descriptive idiom potentially offers analytical insight not available through concepts more frequently used in everyday life. The Canadian breakfast episode, as I said, suggests that distanced normalizing descriptions can be used with a deliberately satirical intent to jolt people into thinking afresh about their everyday lives.

Although my description of the family breakfast formally resembles Radcliffe-Brown's, the objectifications differ markedly in their impact. When read in accord with classic norms, Radcliffe-Brown's account appears to be the only objective way of describing social reality. It is the literal truth. My more parodic account stands as one among a number of possible descriptions. Its accuracy matters, but it objectifies more with a view to speeding a process of change than with producing a timeless truth. How social descriptions are read depends not only on their formal linguistic properties but also on their content and their context. Who is speaking to whom, about what, for what purposes, and under what circumstances? The differences between distinct forms of objectification reside in the analyst's position within a field of social interaction rather than in the text regarded as a document with intrinsic meaning.

What follows deliberately objectifies classic canons of objectivity with a view to moving not beyond conventions (which, in any case, is impossible) but toward the use of a wider range of rhetorical forms in social description. As a corrective to the literal-mindedness with which classic social descriptions are habitually read, this chapter deliberately defamiliarizes the rhetoric of objectivism (which, arguably, unwittingly defamiliarizes the everyday world) in order to indicate how short the gap is between objective characterization and objectifying caricature. My goal in thus objectifying objectivism is to speed a process of change already underway in the modes of composition for ethnography as a form of social analysis.

DEATH IN NORTH AMERICAN CULTURE

In what follows I will discuss anthropological writings on death and mourning, with a view toward exploring the limits of classic norms for social description. In a manner peculiarly at odds with the intense emotions it arouses, the topic of death has proven a particularly fertile area in the production of distanced normalizing accounts. The analytical problems that emerge so clearly with reference to mourning and be-reavement also are present in a number of other areas, including passio-nate love, social improvisations, and spontaneous fun. Death, however, has the virtue of being relatively well represented in the anthropological literature.

The fact that death has proven so vexing for ethnographic analysis probably does not surprise most North American readers. The majority of intensive ethnographic studies have been conducted by relatively young people who have no personal experience of devastating personal losses. Furthermore, such researchers usually come from upper-middle-class Anglo-American professional backgrounds, where (unlike those with higher mortality rates, such as policemen and crop dusters) people often shield themselves by not talking about death and other people's bereave-ment. Such ethnographers probably have grown up with the notion that it is rude and intrusive to ask the chief mourners about their experience of grieving.

My characterization of bereavement in upper-middle-class Anglo-American culture represents a central tendency, more a statistical probability than a monolithic certainty. Since readers can usually judge the representativeness of anecdotes about their own culture, a brief example from my local newspaper, a familiar source rarely used in academic writing, probably will suffice as an illustration. This story, about how parents react to their children's deaths, claimed that most upper-middle-class people strive to live out the illusion of being in control of their lives. Death, however, threatens their fiction of being in control. Listen to Pamela Mang, whose daughter Jessica died of cancer: 'One of the most profound insights I got out of Jessica's illness was that most of us try to protect ourselves from disasters and difficulties, and that we miss a lot of life because of that. . . . Oh, God, you just want to get it out, to talk about it, because somehow getting it out into the air makes it something of a size that is manageable, that you can handle.' Yet most North Americans, especially those without personal experience of loss, find death a subject best avoided. In trying to shield themselves from their own mortality, North Americans often claim that the bereaved don't want to speak about their losses (despite what Pamela Mang says). Although other cultures focus lavish attention on death, most ethnographers would find it extremely difficult to interview chief mourners because, for 'us', grief is a private and personal matter. Hence the ethnography of death's striking adherence to classic norms that verbally transform particular losses into general descriptions of what all funeral rituals share.

Classic norms especially shaped Jack Goody's ethnography of death among the West African LoDagaa. The chapter called 'The Day of Death: Mourning the Dead', for example, begins with a composite account of patterns of mourning among the close kin of the deceased ('the immediate mourners'):

> While the xylophones are playing, the lineage 'wives' and 'sisters' of the dead man walk and run about the area in front of the house, crying lamentations and holding their hands behind the nape of the neck in the accepted attitude of grief. . . . From time to time, one of the immediate mourners breaks into a trot, even a run, and a bystander either intercepts or chases after the bereaved and quietens him by seizing his wrist.

The analyst positions himself as a spectator who looks on from the outside. Are the lamentations of the dead man's wives and sisters little more than conventional gestures, as the description suggests? What about the intensely bereaved person who is being restrained?

Goody goes on to discuss, not bereavement, but how people's relations of kinship to the deceased determine the means – tying by hide, tying by fibre, and tying with string around the ankle – by which bystanders restrain them when, in their grief, they attempt to injure or kill themselves. He presents the following table:

MAN'S FUNERAL

Father	Tied by hide
Mother	Tied by hide
Wife	Tied by hide
Brother	Tied by fibre
Sister	Tied by fibre
Son	String tied around the ankle
Daughter	String tied around the ankle

Put into words, the table simply says that when the bereaved attempt to injure or kill themselves, bystanders use ties of hide to restrain a dead man's parents and wife, ties of fibre to restrain his siblings, and ties of string around the ankle to restrain his children. (One can only wonder at the objectifying impulse to present such a readily verbalized statement in tabular form.) The ethnographer's position as uninvolved spectator becomes yet more evident when he says, 'Before analyzing these categories of bereaved in greater detail, note should be taken of some other ways in which mourners are visually differentiated.' The spectacle itself, seen from the outside, is largely visual. The violent upheaval of grief, its wailing and attempts at self-injury and suicide, appear under this description as normal routines.

Most ethnographic descriptions of death stand at a peculiar distance from the obviously intense emotions expressed, and they turn what for the bereaved are unique and devastating losses into routine happenings. In following classic norms, Goody consistently links intense expressions of bereavement to conventional expectations:

A man *will be expected* to display great grief at the death of a young son.

Another indication of the same imbalance in the parent–child relationship is to be seen in the occurrence of suicide attempts, which are a *standardized method* of demonstrating grief at the loss of a relative.

The passages cited above substitute the term *conventional* for Radcliffe-Brown's key term, *obligatory*. Why do ethnographers so often write as if a father losing a son or a bereaved person attempting suicide were doing little more than following convention? Unreflective talk about culturally expected expressions of grief easily slips into scepticism about the reality of the emotions expressed. It is all too easy to elide the force of conventional forms of life with the merely conventional, as if forceful emotions were mere motions.

Neither one's ability to anticipate appropriately other people's reactions nor the fact that people express their grief in culturally specific ways should be conflated with the notion that the devastatingly bereaved are merely conforming to conventional expectations. Even eyewitness reports cast in the normalizing ethnographic idiom trivialize the events they describe by reducing the force of intense emotions to spectacle. Such accounts visualize people's actions from the outside and fail to provide the participants' reflections on their own experiences. They normalize by presenting generalized recipes for ritual action rather than attempting to grasp the particular content of bereavement.

Classic norms of ethnographic discourse make it difficult to show how social forms can be both imposed by convention *and* used spontaneously and expressively. In relying exclusively on such an idiom, ethnographies can represent other lives *as if* they doubted even the most visible agonies of the bereaved, including, for instance, a father mourning a son or a husband grieving for his wife who died in childbirth.

THEORY AS THE REIFICATION OF CLASSIC NORMS

Most prominently, Claude Lévi-Strauss has taken the classic norms and dressed them in their most general theoretical garb:

> Men do not act, as members of a group, in accordance with what each feels as an individual; each man feels as a function of the way in which he is permitted or obliged to act. Customs are given as external norms before giving rise to internal sentiments, and these non-sentient norms determine the sentiments of individuals as well as the circumstances in which they may, or must, be displayed.

Lévi-Strauss dismisses not only the explanatory import but the very reality of emotions:

> Moreover, if institutions and customs drew their vitality from being continually refreshed and invigorated by individual sentiments, like those in which they originated, they ought to conceal an affective richness, continually replenished, which would be their positive content. We know that this is not the case, and that the constancy which they exhibit usually results from a conventional attitude.

In his view, institutions and customs appear so emotionally barren that he claims that human beings experience affect only in the violation, not in the performance, of conventional acts: 'Emotion is indeed aroused, but when the custom, in itself indifferent, is violated.' If people suffer through their bereavement, it hardly appears objective to represent their experiences as if they were merely conforming with conventions by going through the expected motions. Yet, evidence presented in accord with the classic norms of social description appears to support abstract theoretical statements that are neither humane nor accurate. In attempting to apprehend the complexities of other cultures, disciplined enquiry can ill afford to build its theories on such a questionable foundation.

When classic norms gain exclusive rights to objective truth, ethnography becomes as likely to reveal where objectivity lies as where it tells the truth. What, then, can supplement normalizing distanced discourse in ethnographic writing? Myriad modes of composition, of course, are possible – moral indignation, satire, critique, and others. Several have been used, even in this chapter. For present illustrative purposes, however, I shall consider how personal narratives offer an alternative mode of representing other forms of life.

Although personal narratives often appear in ethnographies written in the classic mode, they usually have been relegated quite literally to the margins: prefaces, introductions, afterwords, footnotes, and italicized or small-print case histories. In fact, the classic norms usually achieved their authority at the expense of personal narratives and case histories. Yet the latter forms often facilitate the analysis of social processes that have proven difficult even to perceive through distanced normalizing discourse.

Anthropologist Clifford Geertz, for example, has described the dilemmas that surfaced during an Indonesian funeral on the island of Java. After opening his account with a brief normalizing description ('the men begin to cut wooden grave markers and to dig a grave'), he shifts to the past tense and describes a particular boy's funeral where one thing after another went wrong. The cutting of wooden grave markers, just cited as recipe, becomes transformed: 'After a half hour or so, a few of the abangans began to chip half-heartedly away at pieces of wood to make grave markers and a few women began to construct small flower offerings for want of anything better to do; but it was clear that the ritual was arrested and that no one quite knew what to do next. Tension slowly rose.' Always at risk in living through the anguish of loss, routine funerary rites broke down as conflicts erupted between Moslem and Hindu-Buddhist participants. Delving into the particulars of this agonizing event rather than the generalities of a composite construction revealed the severe limits of collapsing mourning with ritual and ritual with routine.

In yet another instance, anthropologist Loring Danforth provides an account that moves from spectacle to rather more intimate biographical portraits of mourners. His account begins in a vivid, though external manner:

> Soon the graveyard was alive with activity, and a forest of candles burned at the foot of each grave. About ten women, all dressed in shades of black, brown, or blue, busied themselves lighting lamps and sweeping around the graves. Several women began hauling water in large buckets from the faucet in the church courtyard nearby.

Danforth depicts a visual spectacle the mood of which is one of bucolic calm and routine. Yet as the account proceeds, the analysis shifts so that the reader soon learns the particular histories of the mourners:

> The death of Irini's twenty-year-old daughter Eleni was generally acknowledged to have been the most tragic the village of Potamia had experienced in many years. Eleni died almost five years earlier, in August 1974. She had been a very attractive young woman, tall, with long black hair. . . . One month before she was to begin her first teaching job, Eleni was struck by a car and killed in a hit-and-run accident in the city of Thessaloniki.

The reader then hears verbatim laments, learns how Irini did not leave her house for a full year following her daughter's death, discovers how a friendship developed between Irini and another bereaved mother, and witnesses the daughter's exhumation as the participants, by then known in certain biographical particulars, find themselves overcome with emotion. The ethnographer provides a sense of the emotions experienced by the actors through their words, their gestures, and their biographies.

There is no single recipe for representing other cultures. Indeed, my observations on the Canadian family breakfast suggest that the classic norms, used in a deliberately parodic or distorting manner, can at times yield forceful accounts. Normalizing descriptions can both reveal *and* conceal aspects of social reality. Ethnographies written in accord with classic norms need to be reread, not banished from anthropology. Rather than discarding distanced normalizing accounts, the discipline should recover them, but with a difference. They must be cut down to size and relocated, not replaced. No longer enshrined as ethnographic realism, the sole vehicle for speaking the literal truth about other cultures, the classic norms should become one mode of representation among others. Thus, for example, their satirical potential could be explored in cross-cultural studies as well as in reflections on North American society. They could be used alongside other modes of composition in exploring the interplay between routine and improvisation in everyday life.

Certainly, standing current fashion on its head by substituting tales of specific cases for distanced normalizing discourse will not yield a solution to the vexed problem of representing other lives. Instead, an increased disciplinary tolerance for diverse legitimate rhetorical forms will allow for any particular text to be read against other possible versions. Allowing forms of writing that have been marginalized or banned altogether to gain legitimacy could enable the discipline to approximate people's lives from a number of angles of vision. Such a tactic could enable us better to advance the ethnographic project of apprehending the range of human possibilities in their fullest complexity.

8 Michele Wallace

Negative images: towards a black feminist cultural criticism

EDITOR'S INTRODUCTION

Like Renato Rosaldo's piece, this essay is addressed to those who do not live, think, or work under Eurocentric paradigms. But it reminds us that Eurocentrism (like other centrisms) does not disappear as easily as all that. For even to celebrate the 'other' is to reaffirm a structure of centre/margin: indeed, the otherness of the other may be strengthened by moves to critique it. This has widespread theoretical implications. After all, critical distinctions, like that of 'myth' against 'history' and minority against hegemonic discourse, continue to work in terms articulated by those who decide what constitutes history and what formations *are* hegemonic. So, at least at one level, these distinctions hinder the development of autonomous non-centrist lifestyles and values.

Using Oprah Winfrey's spectacular career as an example, Michele Wallace suggests that 'the black feminist vision' is most trapped by the way in which centres may be strengthened through the very concepts used to disarticulate them. And she suggests, compellingly, that one of the means of avoiding this problem is to work towards a clear-sighted view of the institutions in which theory and discourse are articulated, in particular focusing on their material interests.

Further reading: Anzaldúa and Moraga 1982; Carby 1986a, 1986b; Christian 1987; Mercer 1987; Wallace 1990; Willis 1991.

S.D.

It is useless to argue with the point of view that sees every successful and controversial black female publication as a monolithic conspiracy to undo the race. I am even ready to concede that the participation of black women (and black men) in American cultural production and reproduction, from TV to literary criticism, shows signs of some regrettable trends. While I am enjoying the increasing visibility of blacks on TV and in films as much as anybody else, I feel compelled to remember the downside: material conditions are not changing for the masses of blacks. Moreover, it may even be that the economic and political victimization of the urban and rural black poor in the US and worldwide is somehow exacerbated by the deeply flawed and inadequate representations of 'race' currently sponsored by both blacks and non-blacks in both 'high' and 'low' culture.

I think, however, that this dilemma is best confronted in an ongoing critical dialectic, not by censorship and foregone conclusions. The possibility that something I've written, or will write, might be part of the problem makes me interested in the problem in general. Because black feminism all but entirely lacks an analytical or self-critical sphere (such as the complex network of conference-journal-and-book production that generally supports the speculation of white, and often 'minority' or 'Third World' male scholars and intellectuals), I would like to take this opportunity to write about how my view of black feminism has evolved under the pressure of the criticism of *Black Macho* and in the light of black feminism's increasingly public presence within literature, film and television.

It is necessary to realize that the voices of black feminism in the US emerge today from a long tradition of the structural 'silence' of women of colour within the sphere of global knowledge production. Rarely addressed by mainstream or radical feminism – or indeed by anyone – this 'silence' has doomed to failure most efforts to change the black woman's status or condition within society. There is presently a further danger that in the proliferation of black female images on TV, in music videos and, to a lesser extent, in film, we are witnessing merely a postmodern variation of this phenomenon of black female 'silence'.

I think it is imperative that we begin to develop a radical black feminist perspective. It may build upon the work of Trinh Minh-ha, Gayatri Spivak, Hazel Carby, Bell Hooks and Hortense Spillers by examining the interplay of 'sex', 'race' and 'class' in Anglo-American and Afro-American culture as they may shape the 'production' of knowledge, the structure, content and 'circulation' of the 'text', as well as the 'audience' of consumption.

It is crucial that a diagnostic focus on how 'black' and 'white' culture progresses or regresses on issues of race, class, gender and sexuality should not preclude that much delayed 'close reading' or textual analysis of black feminist creativity, particularly in mass culture where it is most neglected. Such textual analysis might begin in several places, but I am particularly interested in the foregrounding and contrasting of psychoanalytic and ethnographic perspectives on the 'other'. As the two sides of a Western modernist regression/progression on 'race' and 'sexuality', they need to be reunited in discussions of postcolonial 'minority' discourse, which is where I would situate black feminist cultural production at present.

In particular, I would emphasize Claude Lévi-Strauss's notion of 'myth' in his work with 'primitive' people of colour, and Roland Barthes's notion of 'myth' in his reading of contemporary mass culture, precisely because they both emerge out of modernism's frustration with 'history' as a linear and ideological narrative. Also, both interpretations still seem influential in determining contemporary 'political' definitions (in postmodernism and cultural studies) of incorrect thinking.

In a recent essay called 'Mythology and History: An Afro-centric Perspective of the World', Amon Saba Saakana talks about the juxtaposition of 'myth' and 'history' in terms of Western science's rationalizing the murder of Native Americans and the enslavement and colonization of Africans and Asians. In Saakana's account, European imperialism in the seventeenth and eighteenth centuries was inevitably accompanied by the development of 'history', a form of narrative discourse considered by the Enlightenment as infinitely superior to 'myth', which then was made to stand in for all other approaches to the past. Although the roots of Greek culture in Egyptian and Ethiopian cultures were once recognized as African, these roots were then denied and effaced, even as 'civilization' became the polite word for 'the ability to define, through the power of conquest, the control of knowledge, and the framing of meanings' (Saakana 1988: 144).

A priority continues to be given to 'history' over 'myth' in even the most sophisticated cases of cultural critique, forming the basis for a much preferred 'historical consciousness' of the kind conventionally necessary to leftist and/or Marxist intellectual production in the West.

To be more specific, I am less interested in the way that Barthes's and Lévi-Strauss's uses of 'myth' are customarily read as colourblind in a secondary process of signification than I am in the distinctions made by these authors between two different kinds of 'readings' of culture on the part of distinct categories of the population of the world. The 'masses' in Barthes's *Mythologies*, and 'primitive' non-white peoples in Lévi-Strauss's *Tristes Tropiques* and *The Savage Mind* (the bulk of the postcolonial, non-white populations in Europe and the Americas of today could be seen as a combination of the two), are presumed to be less literate, less 'historical' in their thinking, and, therefore, less knowledgeable than that white, male, educated elite who are always in the know.

Beginning with the work of Zora Neale Hurston as anthropologist under Franz Boas at Columbia, the Afro-American literary tradition acquires its present character as the writing down, or the translation, of a predominantly oral or mythic tradition previously sealed off from mainstream white American culture, not only by economic and political disenfranchisement, but also by its enclosure in a system that Barthes and Lévi-Strauss will later bracket as 'myth', and which Trinh Minh-ha has lately called 'separate development'. This is just how people who lack the broader, more 'universal' knowledge of the scholar and the historian think about, or fail to think about, 'History'.

Even as Hurston, Lévi-Strauss and Afro-American literary critic Henry Louis Gates, Jr, insist that the formulations of 'myth' or the 'oral tradition' are just as good, just as complex and rigorous, this focus emphasizes the comparative inadequacy of black culture. For it is always in the terms of the dominant critical discourse that the alternative mythic practice is being described and named, not the other way around. Nor does the reversal of the terms of interpretation, so that 'myth' or the 'oral tradition' reads 'History' (as Toni Morrison attempts to do in *Beloved*, for instance), do anything but further mystify the grossly unequal relation between the two discourses.

Psychoanalytic readings, too, will need to be revised in terms of race in order to interpret the complex priority quite typically given to 'family' or its aberrations, in fictional texts by Afro-American women especially. That the development of the Afro-American family bears a necessarily problematic relationship to the Oedipal myth, and that that relationship might potentially reveal much about issues of orality vs. literacy vs. 'silence' in Afro-American culture, is borne out by the narrative choices of Afro-American writers beginning with Ralph Ellison's *Invisible Man*, where folk artist Trueblood's 'incest' is used to bring together psychoanalytical (familial-sexual) and anthropological (ethnographic-racial) notions of 'taboo'.

If the 'close reading' of Afro-American literature or culture is thus attempted by black feminists, it becomes impossible not to draw upon the relationship of the text to other texts that precede and surround it in a web of signification and 'history', as Barthes reads Balzac in *S/Z* but with 'race', class, gender included this time. Yet the 'close reading' should not be employed as the automatic first move, but rather as the subsequent stage of an institutional, theoretical and political critique that leaves key textual issues unresolved. If after one has demystified issues of production and how and where the audience receives or views the text, there is still a 'text' remaining, then the 'close reading' can and should be employed as a means of further investigation and analysis.

The point, finally, is not only to write such cultural criticism but also to promulgate 'cultural reading' as an act of resistance. Whereas most people concerned with political repression in the US seem to view such an analysis of culture as a low priority, particularly when that analysis asks questions about 'race' and 'sex' as well as 'class', I can't any longer imagine how one manages, as a black woman, to get through a single day of television, film, advertising, magazines and newspapers, without interpretation and analysis. For instance, I can't imagine experiencing the recent presidential election process in the US without employing some mode of interpretation that acknowledges the exclusion of 'black women' or 'women of colour' from 'the issues'. Black women never came up, even though they might have been considered the object, along with their children, of some of the most repressive policies in both the Democratic and the Republican Parties. So where and how were we then to read ourselves into events? As blacks who are not men, and women who are not white, it simply wasn't safe to accept any represen-tation of the candidates, in television news, in the televised debates, in the newspapers and magazines, or on the 'left' or the 'right', without thinking for oneself. To do so involves 'interpretation', that is, bringing some other information gathered from elsewhere to bear upon the 'official' information so freely and repetitively given.

By contrast, consider some recent instances in which mass culture addresses the black woman in an attempt to mainstream 'black femi-nism'. You will remember that most of us became familiar with the name Oprah Winfrey when she appeared in the role of Sofia in the movie *The Color Purple*, which was adapted from the black feminist novel by Alice Walker, but which became, under the guidance and supervision of Hollywood director Steven Spielberg, a sentimental tale having little to do with 'black feminism' – that is, little to do with changing the status and condition of black women as a group. As the most successful daytime television talk-show host the networks have ever seen, and as the first black female ever to own a prosperous TV and film production company, Oprah Winfrey is buying up TV and film rights to all the 'black feminist' literature she can lay her hands on. Not only does she own rights to *Beloved* by Toni Morrison, and *Their Eyes Were Watching God* by Zora Neale Hurston (with Quincy Jones), her production of Gloria Naylor's novel *The Women of Brewster Place*, starring herself in the lead role, was recently aired on network television.

For the Sunday and Monday that the mini-series played, network viewers could witness the contrast of a bubbly, carefree Oprah on her daytime talk show versus a downtrodden, unhappy Oprah playing 'Mattie Michaels' at night. Fat, old and poor, Mattie demonstrated the murky immutability of black female life 'as it really is', even as she was the exact opposite of the daytime Oprah who has all the answers to such problems as domestic violence, marital strife, mental illness and other forms of social 'immorality' and disorder. Don't worry, be 'rich', the talk-show Oprah seems to say via her 'Valley Girl' speech, her straightened hair in a different style on every other show, her elegant couture wardrobe, her much celebrated weight loss, her meteoric industry success.

By contrast, the television version of *Women of Brewster Place* is about a collection of black women who live on a dead-end urban street. It is their 'choice' of men that dooms them to remain there. For instance, Mattie Michaels, Oprah's character, begins the show by mortgaging her house in order to post bail for her 'no-good' son. Predictably, he runs off to avoid trial. Mattie loses the house and ends up in a slum apartment on Brewster Place. While Mattie's son was not exactly her 'choice' in the way that one might choose a lover, it was her 'choice', the drama leads us to believe, as a teenager to have sex with the 'no-good' boy who got her pregnant, and it was her 'choice' to 'spoil' the son that resulted by allowing him to sleep in bed with her because he was 'afraid of the dark'. Whether or not Mattie has also chosen the racism of whites and the poverty of blacks, without which this television drama would make no sense, is a question rendered irrelevant by this story's ideological presupposition, which is that any black woman may freely choose to follow the example of the daytime or the night-time Oprah.

When Mattie and her friends start to take down that wall blocking off Brewster Place with their bare hands in the rain one night towards the end of the second and final instalment of the mini-series, my attention was not focused on the relationship these women have to the 'real world', which is presumably beyond the wall. My attention was focused on their relationship to the discourse of network night-time television: the series simply confirmed television's currently deplorable record on black female characterization. Black women play two kinds of parts: tragic chippies and weeping mothers. If a black female actress can't or won't cry, she can forget about working in TV drama. What this means, quite simply, is that black women are turned into an unspeakable, unknowable 'other' by night-time network television.[1]

Before television can be about the politics of real life, it must confront television's own inner politics. Quite predictably, despite her superficially 'feminist' agenda reported in the pages of *TV Guide* in a story titled 'There's Oprah, Jackee, Robin Givens – and a Break Men May Not Deserve', Winfrey's *Women of Brewster Place* has left that picture unchanged. For this reason, the melodramatic, maudlin portrayal of lesbianism and the flat, stereotypical portrayal of black men, despite the effort to provide in casting and script 'a break men may not deserve', seem to me only symptomatic of this production's larger failure to address the underlying problems of television's discourse.

In 1986, in response to the controversy in the 'black community' over 'negative images' of black men in the movie *The Color Purple*, I was asked by an organization of Third World women graduate students at the University of California in Berkeley to speak on the issue of black feminist intellectual responsibility. The organizer of this conference, Carrie Mae Weems (now a well-known artist in New York City), asked me because she saw parallels in the promotion of my book *Black Macho and the Myth of the Superwoman* as a *Ms* magazine cover in 1979, and the translation of Alice Walker's novel *The Color Purple* into a successful movie. Both Alice Walker and I had somehow been used by the white power structure to hurt the image of blacks, or as she put it in a letter to me:

> You experienced a backlash after the publication of your *Black Macho and the Myth of the Superwoman*. Some folks felt that your analysis seemed to validate, for whites, the negative and stereotypic views of Black men held by whites; you were thus 'used' by the media, and the White Feminist Movement. Does a book like *The Color Purple* operate in a similar way?

In 1979, a large number of black critics in *The Black Scholar*, among them a few black feminists, had linked *Black Macho* with Ntozake Shange's *For Colored Girls Who Have Considered Suicide/When the Rainbow is Enuf*, which became a successful Broadway show, in order to make the same kind of argument. The commercially profitable Broadway show, Hollywood movie or 'bestselling' book issuing from mostly lily-white theatre, film and book industries, which rarely provide a hospitable environment for 'black talent', was and is as much the rub as the idea of black women criticizing black men in permanent and public ways. The problem reached critical mass in regard to *Black Macho*, also in 1979, when the book was reviewed in *The Sunday New York Times* by black feminist poet and essayist June Jordan, who characterized its production as part of a massive media conspiracy to deny the historical significance of the Civil Rights Movement (Jordan 1981: 164).

At Berkeley in 1986, in my first concerted effort to respond to such criticisms, I did not try to defend my version of 'history' against such attacks, especially since the views of people who actually participated in the Civil Rights Movement in the South were clearly more reliable and authoritative than my own. Instead, I made a blanket defence of black feminist creativity as inherently subversive of a racist and exclusionary status quo. The point was to go beyond an argument about 'facts' to a general observation about how rarely black women participate in the production of 'fact' and 'history'. When they make *any* move to do so, it is potentially subversive of a repressive status quo.

I used a black w/hole as a metaphor – a hole in space which appears empty but is actually intensely full – to portray a black feminist creativity that appeared to authorize a 'negative' view of the black community but was, in fact, engaged in reformulating black female subjectivity as the product of a complex structure of American (US) inequality. By black feminist creativity, I meant all public creative acts inaugurated by black women, primarily because I never questioned until recently the intrinsic 'feminism' or progressive politics of black female expression, or, more-over, the power of feminist thought to transform society in a way beneficial to all.

In the process, I advocated a more dialectical and less paranoid interpretation of cultural hegemony which, somewhat randomly, drew upon the insights of Hegel, Gramsci, Raymond Williams, Kenneth Burke and Fredric Jameson. In particular, hegemony as Raymond Williams defined and employed it, together with Jameson's notion of a 'political unconscious', helped to explain how cultural production represents a complex process that is not fundamentally altered by any single cultural event. The individual act of writing a book, regardless of whether Shange or Walker or I was the author, was less significant than the absence of published black female critical voices, the void we wrote into and could never hope to fill.

Since then, I've become more concerned about incorporating the method (not necessarily exhaustively) of Marxist cultural criticism, structuralism, psychoanalysis, deconstruction and postmodernism in the development of a critical practice designed to grapple with the complexities of racial/sexual politics as a constellation of increasingly global issues. I am firmly convinced that if black feminism, or the feminism of women of colour, is going to thrive on any level as a cultural analysis, it cannot continue to ignore the way that Freud, Marx, Saussure, Nietzsche, Lévi-Strauss, Lacan, Derrida and Foucault have forever altered the credibility of obvious truth, 'common sense' or any unitary conception of reality. Moreover, there are many feminists who are practising cultural studies, postmodernist, deconstructive and psychoanalytic criticism who can contribute to our formulations if we read them against the grain. Since the concerns and issues of women of colour are so often not included in prevailing definitions of 'reality', any analysis suggesting that 'reality', or 'knowledge', is not simply given but rather produced, seems to me particularly welcome.

Yet this theoretically engaged stance of black feminist cultural theory I advocate challenges some more cautious and sceptical tendencies within Afro-American literary theory. Such theorists emphasize that the canonical texts of the West have never included anything but the most derogatory perception of 'blackness'. As the preeminent Afro-American literary critic, Henry Louis Gates, puts it, the question is whether we as theorists can 'escape a "mockingbird" relation to "theory"'. Is our use of theory 'destined to be derivative, often to the point of parody', as he worries? Can we 'escape the racism of so many critical theorists, from Hume and Kant through the Southern Agrarians and the Frankfurt School?' (Gates 1987: 35).

Gates's critical work is preoccupied with the idea that a black person will appear ridiculous in the act of adopting the white man's critical discourses. In his introduction to the anthology 'Race', Writing and Difference, while he argues that racial categories are essentially mythological and pernicious, he makes it just as clear that the Afro-American writer and critic is in the uncomfortable position of claiming an intellectual heritage designed to make it impossible for him (never mind her) to write a single word. In Figures in Black, his first book-length study, Gates invokes the Afro-American folk figure of the Signifying Monkey in order to describe the modern black critic's necessarily subversive and problematic relationship to Western critical approaches. Just as blacks have 'imitated' white Western languages, literatures, religions, music, dance, dress and family life, but with a critical 'signifyin'' difference, so shall Afro-American literary criticism steal the meat from the sandwich but leave the white bread untouched.

Yet for some black critics of deconstructive and postmodern approaches, it's as though white people had come up with critical theory precisely in order to avoid the question that the persistence of racial inequality poses to the epoch. From an 'Afro-centric' perspective, current trends in critical theory look mighty like an exercise in self-absorption designed to reconsolidate the canon of Western Masters (not just Milton and Shakespeare but Hegel, Marx and Freud, too!), thus trivializing the analysis of any aspect of Afro-American or African diasporic cultural development.

But, more to the point, Gates's primary concern is the consolidation of an Afro-American literary tradition. I appreciate this work since it is a fairly futile exercise to try to critique the need for an Afro-American canon when it remains completely questionable, within the dominant discourse, whether such a thing could possibly exist. On the other hand, as Raymond Williams has pointed out, 'canon' and 'tradition' invariably involve highly selective and exclusionary processes which tend to reinforce the status quo. In Gates's case in particular, he often fails to portray Afro-American writing as a 'minority' literature engaged in a contemporary dialogue with a majority 'white' culture for the specific purpose of transcending and/or transforming it. This failure becomes particularly unfortunate in regard to contemporary Afro-American literature by women. Having encountered considerable commercial success and publicity, this literature calls into question, even more than women's books or black books in general, conventional academic notions of a canonical literary tradition, as well as art-world concepts of an elite 'avant-garde', as inconsistent with mass appeal.

Any 'close reading' of these texts disassociated from their cultural and political context is only adequate to the task of a superficial and temporary canonization. However 'close' that reading may be, it won't provide much information about how literature by black women alternately conspires with and rebels against our present cultural and political arrangements. In feminist terms, it is just as important to have a way of talking about *The Color Purple*'s impact on how racism or sexism is perceived in contemporary culture, as it is to talk about *The Color Purple* as a symbolic (literary) resolution of racism's concrete irresolvability.

Gates began to venture into the field of such a cultural problematic when he wrote recently,

And, if only for the record, let me state clearly here that only a
black person alienated from black language-use could fail to understand that we have been deconstructing white people's languages
and discourse since that dreadful day in 1619 when we were
marched off the boat in Virginia. Derrida did not invent deconstruction, *we* did! That is what the blues and signifying are all
about. Ours must be a signifying, vernacular criticism, related to
other critical theories, yet indelibly black, a critical theory of our
own. (Gates 1987: 38)

But a continuation of his own discussion here of the social and political
roots of what might be called a nascent Afro-American 'deconstruction'
and 'postmodernism' only becomes viable in the context of a broader
reading of culture as a complex network of patterns and processes which
coordinate the influence of 'high' and 'low' art, vernacular expression,
and mass culture in a newly variegated field of contemporary mainstream cultural hegemony. Yet the problem here may be that such an
analysis would require the freedom to say less than glowingly compli-
mentary things about black women writers on all occasions and as dean
of Afro-American Studies, he is not free to do so. Instead, Gates's
primary intention, which seems to be to establish an Afro-American
literary tradition on firm ground, may have a most unfortunate side
effect in regard to black women writers of repressing those black women
writers who wish to engage in political/critical discourse and favouring
those black women writers who want to ride the bonanza of mainstream
popularity for all it's worth.

Raymond Williams's discussion of a hegemonic impulse towards an
exclusionary elitism embedded in the concept of literary 'traditions'
remains relevant here. But the process bears particular watching in this
case because of the potential danger of metamorphosing contemporary
political texts into dead, historical monuments in order to enshrine
them. That is to say, to pre-select, praise and revere a subset of Afro-
American literature (to be designated the canon) is a process totally
antithetical to that of becoming critically engaged by the inevitable
political and cultural questions raised by an Afro-American Literature
(either inside or outside of the canon).

So what is a black feminist to say about the fact that Gates is not only
the editor of the first *Norton Anthology of Afro-American Literature*, but also
the editor of an extensive Oxford series of republications of black
women writers? He is singlehandedly reshaping, codifying and con-

solidating the entire field of Afro-American Studies, including black feminist studies.

While Gates is, no doubt, well-intentioned in his efforts to recognize and acknowledge the contributions of black women writers, *The New York Times Book Review* presentation of his recent essay 'Whose Canon Is It, Anyway?' seems to me to alter the stakes, as he demonstrates an ability to define black feminist enquiry for the dominant discourse in a manner as yet unavailable to black female critics. The results, so far, are inevitably patriarchal. Having established himself as the father of Afro-American Literary Studies, with the help of *The New York Times Book Review*, he now proposes to become the phallic mother of a newly depoliticized, mainstreamed and commodified black feminist literary criticism.

There's a clue to this agenda in the anecdote that introduces this essay's black feminist catharsis: at age four, Gates was supposed to perform in church the speech 'Jesus was a boy like me/And like him I want to be', but he couldn't remember it to save his life so his mother, from the back of the church, stood up and said it for him in 'her strong compelling cadences'. Everybody in the church laughed. While Gates presents this anecdote as an example of his symbiotic relationship with his mother, it seems on the contrary a story that justifies, as revenge for this humiliating incident, his appropriation of black female subjectivity or 'voice'. The hostile twist is embedded in the lines themselves, for there was never any question of his mother being a 'boy' anything like 'Jesus'.

Whereas she is powerless to appropriate his 'voice' in any mean-ingful sense, he is perfectly free to speak for her – and for the rest of us besides: 'learning to speak in the voice of the black mother', Gates ends his article ominously, 'is perhaps the ultimate challenge of producing a discourse of the Other' (Gates 1989: 45). Not only is it impossible for anybody to speak in anybody else's voice, such a project tends to further consolidate the lethal global presupposition (which is unconscious) in the dominant discourse that women of colour are incapable of describing, much less analysing, reality, themselves, or their place within the world.

In every case, public statements of black feminism have been contro-versial in their relationship to an idealized and utopian black feminism, which, nevertheless, remains almost entirely unarticulated and untheor-ized. It is almost as if black feminism were only called upon to deny all attempts to attach its name to an agenda. Yet I have not abandoned the notion that black feminist creativity is inherently (potentially) subversive of a patriarchal hegemony, as well as of a racist and exclusionary white cultural hegemony.

Let me focus briefly upon the external limitations placed upon a black feminist vision by a society that feeds upon and subsumes all resistance and critique, even as it is broadcasting its open-mindedness via the massive proliferation of the 'mechanical reproduction' of representation, interpretation and analysis in the form of TV, film and print journalism. Again and again, when the negative space of the woman of colour meets the Age of Mechanical Reproduction or, worse yet, Baudrillard's 'simulations', the resulting effect is a 'strong black woman' floating above our heads like one of the cartoon characters in Macy's Christmas Parade, a form larger than life, and yet a deformation powerless to speak. This is not so because any black woman anywhere ever meant to come before the American public without a message, but because the culture routinely and automatically denies her the opportunity of producing autonomous or productive meanings.

The genesis of *The Color Purple* as bestselling novel, then blockbuster movie, seems to me to provide an excellent example of a text initially proposing a complex rereading of Afro-American history and Afro-American literature becoming something else entirely in the process of its own success. Finally, the overwhelming urgency of form associated with mass appeal – a Spielberg movie as compelling as *E.T.*, and for all the same reasons – seemed to supersede all other considerations. None of this means that I do not endorse the black feminist voice in such a production, nor does it mean I didn't 'enjoy' *The Color Purple* on some level. It only means that I now better understand how the feminist project, which is actually part of the same scheme as that production of knowledge that trivialized the 'silence' of women of colour in the first place, needs profound and multiple acts of revision. It is not enough merely to address the dilemma posed by the black female condition in the US or the world as an object of misery and pathos. Black feminism must insist upon a critical oppositional representation of the black female subject.

While black feminism remains largely undeveloped in terms of its programme, it can no longer be regarded as the same mystery that it was in 1976 when *For Colored Girls* was first produced. Although I may be disappointed about its public progress, I can no longer deny that some manifestations of black feminism have entered the public arena. In retrospect, the movie *The Color Purple* seems to have initiated this second stage in the process of black feminism's public articulation.

In 1987, Toni Morrison published *Beloved* to a very warm critical reception by the mass media and book industry. While there were no commensurate changes in the status or condition of black women in general, there was nothing remotely 'marginal' about Morrison's success. Our enemies thus take some pleasure in pointing out that black women writers are now enjoying a certain vogue as publishable authors and as topics of literary critical speculation.

The key event may be the Oxford series of reissues of books by black women writers, the key figure Gates, and the key idea that every book black women have ever written should be in print. As for the status of black feminist interpretation, all of which now springs from the largesse of the 'mother' of them all, Gates himself, the fortunes of a small number of black female academic literary critics are rising.

While I am not suggesting that this movement to canonize black women writers is reactionary, it does seem as though the participants take for granted that the revision of a once all-white, all-male canon is as progressive as anybody needs to get. Perhaps they are right, for this task is far from safely accomplished. But it seems to me that one must also consider whether relations of power in higher education or relations of representation in the production of knowledge are significantly altered by any of this. When I see 'black feminism' being touted by the safest of all possible 'spokesmen' on the cover of the safest of all cultural venues – *The New York Times Book Review* – I say the time has arrived to start asking such questions.

NOTE

1. This situation is changing as a middle-class black woman, usually as 'wife of' a black male lead, as on *The Cosby Show*, *In The Heat of The Night* or the new show *Men*, becomes more visible. Yet there is little connection between these bourgeois simulations of the 'white woman' and the signifier 'black woman' as it is understood by the rest of television, particularly news shows and documentaries.

Part II *Space and time*

9 Edward Soja

History: geography: modernity

[handwritten: time has been privileged over space in theory.]

EDITOR'S INTRODUCTION

Edward Soja presents a lucid defence of the demand for 'geographical and spatial imagination' in theoretical work. He argues that modern academic study has, in the modern era, privileged time and history over space and geography. This has meant that modernity has been interpreted too quickly and simply as destroying and replacing traditions – whereas, Soja argues, it is more sensitively to be interpreted as a complex reorganization of temporal and spatial relations. For instance, a crucial feature of modernity is how change itself becomes increasingly globally synchronous, especially in the technological and economic spheres. Postmodern social transformations, in particular, involve a reordering of space: speed and accessibility triumph over distance, though the shrinking of the world can lead to strong barriers being placed between margins and centres from either side.

In this selection from a longer piece of work, Soja gives a brief account of Michel Foucault's demand for a 'history of space' and of Marshall Berman's description of modernity's embrace of speed and simultaneity. Berman and Foucault, however, do not quite lead in the same direction. As the interview with Foucault in this collection makes clear, he is interested in making changes reversible by emphasizing the gaps between the intentions behind, and the effects of, the reorganization of space by planners, architects, and so on; Berman, on the other hand, has a stronger sense of an increasingly impregnable global system moving in an irreversible direction.

Further reading: Berman 1982; Foucault 1986; Harvey 1989; Jameson 1990; Kern 1983.

S.D.

Did it start with Bergson or before? Space was treated as the dead, the fixed, the undialectical, the immobile. Time, on the contrary was richness, fecundity, life, dialectic. (Foucault, 1980: 70)

The great obsession of the nineteenth century was, as we know, history: with its themes of development and of suspension, of crisis and cycle, themes of the ever-accumulating past, with its great preponderance of dead men and the menacing glaciation of the world. . . . The present epoch will perhaps be above all the epoch of space. We are in the epoch of simultaneity: we are in the epoch of juxtaposition, the epoch of the near and far, of the side-by-side, of the dispersed. We are at a moment, I believe, when our experience of the world is less that of a long life developing through time than that of a network that connects points and intersects with its own skein. One could perhaps say that certain ideological conflicts animating present-day polemics oppose the pious descendants of time and the determined inhabitants of space. (Foucault 1986: 22)

The nineteenth-century obsession with history, as Foucault described it, did not die in the *fin de siècle*. Nor has it been fully replaced by a spatialization of thought and experience. An essentially historical epistemology continues to pervade the critical consciousness of modern social theory. It still comprehends the world primarily through the dynamics arising from the emplacement of social being and becoming in the interpretive contexts of time: in what Kant called *nacheinander* and Marx defined so transfiguratively as the contingently constrained 'making of history'. This enduring epistemological presence has preserved a privileged place for the 'historical imagination' in defining the very nature of critical insight and interpretation.

So unbudgeably hegemonic has been this historicism of theoretical consciousness that it has tended to occlude a comparable critical sensibility to the spatiality of social life, a practical theoretical consciousness that sees the lifeworld of being creatively located not only in the making of history but also in the construction of human geographies, the social production of space and the restless formation and reformation of geographical landscapes: social being actively emplaced in space *and* time in an explicitly historical *and* geographical contextualization. Although others joined Foucault to urge a rebalancing of this prioritization of time over space, no hegemonic shift has yet occurred to allow the critical eye – or the critical I – to see spatiality with the same acute depth of vision that comes with a focus on *durée*. The critical hermeneutic is still enveloped in a temporal master-narrative, in a historical but not yet comparably geographical imagination. Foucault's revealing glance back over the past hundred years thus continues to apply today. Space still tends to be treated as fixed, dead, undialectical; time as richness, life, dialectic, the revealing context for critical social theorization.

As we move closer to the end of the twentieth century, however, Foucault's premonitory observations on the emergence of an 'epoch of space' assume a more reasonable cast. The material and intellectual contexts of modern critical social theory have begun to shift dramatically. In the 1980s, the hoary traditions of a space-blinkered historicism are being challenged with unprecedented explicitness by convergent calls for a far-reaching spatialization of the critical imagination. A distinctively postmodern and critical human geography is taking shape, brashly reasserting the interpretive significance of space in the historically privileged confines of contemporary critical thought. Geography may not yet have displaced history at the heart of contemporary theory and criticism, but there is a new animating polemic on the theoretical and political agenda, one which rings with significantly different ways of seeing time and space together, the interplay of history and geography, the 'vertical' and 'horizontal' dimensions of being in the world freed from the imposition of inherent categorical privilege.

It remains all too easy for even the best of the 'pious descendants of time' to respond to these pesky postmodern intrusions with an antidisestablishmentarian wave of a still confident upper hand or with the presumptive yawns of a seen-it-all-before complacency. In response, the determined intruders often tend to overstate their case, creating the unproductive aura of an anti-history, inflexibly exaggerating the critical privilege of contemporary spatiality in isolation from an increasingly silenced embrace of time. But from these confrontational polemics is also arising something else, a more flexible and balanced critical theory that re-entwines the making of history with the social production of space, with the construction and configuration of human geographies. New possibilities are being generated from this creative commingling, possibilities for a simultaneously historical and geographical materialism; a triple dialectic of space, time, and social being; a transformative re-theorization of the relations between history, geography, and modernity.

LOCATING THE ORIGINS OF POSTMODERN GEOGRAPHIES

The first insistent voices of postmodern critical human geography appeared in the late 1960s, but they were barely heard against the then prevailing temporal din. For more than a decade, the spatializing project remained strangely muted by the untroubled reaffirmation of the primacy of history over geography that enveloped both Western Marxism and liberal social science in a virtually sanctified vision of the ever-accumulating past. One of the most comprehensive and convincing pictures of this continuously historical contextualization was drawn by C. Wright Mills in his paradigmatic portrayal of the sociological imagination (Mills 1959). Mills's work provides a useful point of departure for spatializing the historical narrative and reinterpreting the course of critical social theory.

The silenced spatiality of historicism

Mills maps out a sociological imagination that is deeply rooted in a historical rationality – what Martin Jay (1984b) would call a 'longitudinal totalization' – that applies equally well to critical social science and to the critical traditions of Marxism.

> [The sociological imagination] is a quality of mind that will help [individuals] to use information and to develop reason in order to achieve lucid summations of what is going on in the world and of what may be happening within themselves. (1959: 11)

> The first fruit of this imagination – and the first lessons of the social science that embodies it – is the idea that the individual can understand his own experience and gauge his own fate only by locating himself within his period, that he can know his own chances in life only by becoming aware of those of all individuals in his circumstances. . . . We have come to know that every individual lives, from one generation to the next, in some society; that he lives out a biography, and that he lives it out within some historical sequence. By the fact of his living he contributes, however minutely, to the shaping of this society and to the course of history, even as he is made by society and by its historical push and shove. (12)

He goes further:

> The sociological imagination enables us to grasp history and biogra-

phy and the relations of the two within society. This is its task and its promise. To recognize this task and this promise is the mark of the classic social analyst. . . . *No social study that does not come back to the problems of biography, of history, and of their intersections within society, has completed its intellectual journey.* (Ibid., emphasis added)

I draw upon Mills's depiction of what is essentially a historical imagination to illustrate the alluring logic of historicism, the rational reduction of meaning and action to the temporal constitution and experience of social being. This connection between the historical imagination and historicism needs further elaboration. First, there is the easier question of why 'sociological' has been changed to 'historical'. As Mills himself notes, 'every cobbler thinks leather is the only thing', and as a trained sociologist Mills names his leather after his own disciplinary specialization and socialization. The nominal choice personally specifies what is a much more widely shared 'quality of mind' that Mills claims should pervade, indeed embody, all social theory and analysis, an emancipatory rationality grounded in the intersections of history, biography, and society.

To be sure, these 'life-stories' have a geography too; they have milieux, immediate locales, provocative emplacements which affect thought and action. The historical imagination is never completely spaceless and critical social historians have written, and continue to write, some of the best geographies of the past. But it is always time and history that provide the primary 'variable containers' in these geographies. This would be just as clear whether the critical orientation is described as sociological or political or anthropological – or for that matter phenomenological, existential, hermeneutic, or historical materialist. The particular emphases may differ, but the encompassing perspective is shared. An already-made geography sets the stage, while the wilful making of history dictates the action and defines the story line.

It is important to stress that this historical imagination has been particularly central to critical social theory, to the search for practical understanding of the world as a means of emancipation versus maintenance of the status quo. Social theories which merely rationalize existing conditions and thereby serve to promote repetitive behaviour, the continuous reproduction of established social practices, do not fit the definition of critical theory. They may be no less accurate with respect to what they are describing, but their rationality (or irrationality, for that matter) is likely to be mechanical, normative, scientific, or instrumental rather than critical. It is precisely the critical and potentially emancipatory value of the historical imagination, of people 'making history' rather than taking it for granted, that has made it so compulsively appealing. The constant reaffirmation that the world can be changed by human action, by praxis, has always been the centrepiece of critical social theory whatever its particularized source and emphasis.

The development of critical social theory has revolved around the assertion of a mutable history against perspectives and practices that mystify the changeability of the world. The critical historical discourse thus sets itself against abstract and transhistorical universalizations (including notions of a general 'human nature' which explain everything and nothing at the same time); against naturalisms, empiricisms, and positivisms which proclaim physical determinations of history apart from social origins; against religious and ideological fatalisms which project spiritual determinations and teleologies (even when carried forward in the cloak of human consciousness); against any and all conceptualizations of the world which freeze the frangibility of time, the possibility of 'breaking' and remaking history.

Both the attractive critical insight of the historical imagination and its continuing need to be forcefully defended against distracting mystifications have contributed to its exaggerated assertion as historicism. Historicism has been conventionally defined in several different ways. Raymond Williams's *Keywords* (1983), for example, presents three contemporary choices, which he describes as: 1) 'neutral' – a method of study using facts from the past to trace the precedents of current events; 2) 'deliberate' – an emphasis on variable historical conditions and contexts as a privileged framework for interpreting all specific events; and 3) 'hostile' – an attack on all interpretation and prediction which is based on notions of historical necessity or general laws of historical development.

I wish to give an additional twist to these options by defining historicism as an overdeveloped historical contextualization of social life and social theory that actively submerges and peripheralizes the geographical or spatial imagination. This definition does not deny the extraordinary power and importance of historiography as a mode of emancipatory insight, but identifies historicism with the creation of a critical silence, an implicit subordination of space to time that obscures geographical interpretations of the changeability of the social world and intrudes upon every level of theoretical discourse, from the most abstract ontological concepts of being to the most detailed explanations of empirical events.

This definition may appear rather odd when set against the long tradition of debate over historicism that has flourished for centuries. The failure of this debate to recognize the peculiar theoretical peripheralization of space that has accompanied even the most neutral forms of historicism is, however, precisely what began to be discovered in the late 1960s, in the ragged beginnings of what I have called a postmodern critical human geography. Even then, the main currents of critical social thought had become so spatially-blinkered that the most forceful reassertions of space versus time, geography versus history, had little effect. The academic discipline of Modern Geography had, by that time, been rendered theoretically inert and contributed little to these first reassertions. And when some of the most influential social critics of the time took a bold spatial turn, not only was it usually seen by the unconverted as something else entirely, but the turners themselves often chose to muffle their critiques of historicism in order to be understood at all.

The ambivalent spatiality of Michel Foucault

The contributions of Foucault to the development of critical human geography must be drawn out archeologically, for he buried his precursory spatial turn in brilliant whirls of historical insight. He would no doubt have resisted being called a postmodern geographer, but he was one, *malgré lui*, from *Madness and Civilization* (1961) to his last works on *The History of Sexuality* (1978). His most explicit and revealing observations on the relative significance of space and time, however, appear not in his major published works but almost innocuously in his lectures and, after some coaxing interrogation, in two revealing interviews: 'Questions on Geography' (Foucault 1980) and 'Space, Knowledge, and Power' (see Foucault below; see also Wright and Rabinow 1982).

The epochal observations which head this chapter, for example, were first made in a 1967 lecture entitled '*Des Espaces Autres*'. They remained virtually unseen and unheard for nearly twenty years, until their publication in the French journal *Architecture-Mouvement-Continuité* in 1984 and, translated by Jay Miskowiec as 'Of Other Spaces', in *Diacritics* (1986). In these lecture notes, Foucault outlined his notion of 'heterotopias' as the characteristic spaces of the modern world, superseding the hierarchic 'ensemble of places' of the Middle Ages and the enveloping 'space of emplacement' opened up by Galileo into an early-modern, infinitely unfolding, 'space of extension' and measurement. Moving away from both the 'internal space' of Bachelard's brilliant poetics (1969) and the intentional regional descriptions of the phenome- nologists, Foucault focused our attention on another spatiality of social life, an 'external space', the actually lived (and socially produced) space of sites and the relations between them:

> The space in which we live, which draws us out of ourselves, in which the erosion of our lives, our time and our history occurs, the space that claws and gnaws at us, is also, in itself, a heterogeneous space. In other words, we do not live in a kind of void, inside of which we could place individuals and things. We do not live inside a void that could be colored with diverse shades of light, we live inside a set of relations that delineates sites which are irreducible to one another and absolutely not superimposable on one another. (1986: 23)

These heterogeneous spaces of sites and relations – Foucault's heteroto- pias – are constituted in every society but take quite varied forms and change over time, as 'history unfolds' in its adherent spatiality. He identifies many such sites: the cemetery and the church, the theatre and the garden, the museum and the library, the fairground and the 'vaca- tion village', the barracks and the prison, the Moslem hammam and the Scandinavian sauna, the brothel and the colony. Foucault contrasts these 'real places' with the 'fundamentally unreal spaces' of utopias, which present society in either 'a perfected form' or else 'turned upside down':

> The heterotopia is capable of juxtaposing in a single real place several spaces, several sites that are in themselves incompatible . . . they have a function in relation to all the space that remains. This function unfolds between two extreme poles. Either their role is to create a space of illusion that exposes every real space, all the sites inside of which human life is partitioned, as still more illusory. . . . Or else, on the contrary, their role is to create a space that is other, another real space, as perfect, as meticulous, as well arranged as ours is messy, ill constructed, and jumbled. The latter type would be the heterotopia, not of illusion, but of compensation, and I wonder if certain colonies have not functioned somewhat in this manner. (1986: 25, 27).

With these remarks, Foucault exposed many of the compelling

directions he would take in his lifework and indirectly raised a powerful argument against historicism – and against the prevailing treatments of space in the human sciences. Foucault's heterogeneous and relational space of heterotopias is neither a substanceless void to be filled by cognitive intuition nor a repository of physical forms to be phenomenologically described in all its resplendent variability. It is another space, what Lefebvre would describe as *l'espace vécu*, actually lived and socially created spatiality, concrete and abstract at the same time, the habitus of social practices. It is a space rarely seen for it has been obscured by a bifocal vision that traditionally views space as either a mental construct or a physical form.

To illustrate his innovative interpretation of space and time and to clarify some of the often confusing polemics which were arising around it, Foucault turned to the then current debates on structuralism, one of the twentieth century's most important avenues for the reassertion of space in critical social theory. Foucault vigorously insisted that he himself was not (just?) a structuralist, but he recognized in the development of structuralism a different and compelling vision of history and geography, a critical reorientation that was connecting space and time in new and revealing ways.

> Structuralism, or at least that which is grouped under this slightly too general name, is the effort to establish, between elements that could have been connected on a temporal axis, an ensemble of relations that makes them appear as juxtaposed, set off against one another, in short, as a sort of configuration. Actually structuralism does not entail a denial of time; it does involve a certain manner of dealing with what we call time and what we call history.(1986: 22)

This synchronic 'configuration' is the spatialization of history, the making of history entwined with the social production of space, the structuring of a historical geography.

Foucault refused to project his spatialization as an anti-history but his history was provocatively spatialized from the very start. This was not just a shift in metaphorical preference, as it frequently seemed to be for Althusser and others more comfortable with the structuralist label than Foucault. It was the opening up of history to an interpretive geography. To emphasize the centrality of space to the critical eye, especially regarding the contemporary moment, Foucault becomes most explicit:

> In any case I believe that the anxiety of our era has to do fundamen-
> tally with space, no doubt a great deal more than with time. Time
> probably appears to us only as one of the various distributive
> operations that are possible for the elements that are spread out in
> space. (Ibid.: 23)

He would never be quite so explicit again. Foucault's spatialization took
on a more demonstrative rather than declarative stance, confident perhaps that at least the French would understand the intent and significance of his strikingly spatialized historiography.

In an interview conducted shortly before his death (see Foucault
below), Foucault reminisced on his exploration 'Of Other Spaces' and
the enraged reactions it engendered from those he once identified as the
'pious descendants of time'. Asked whether space was central to the
analysis of power, he answered:

> Yes. Space is fundamental in any form of communal life; space is
> fundamental in any exercise of power. To make a parenthetical
> remark, I recall having been invited, in 1966, by a group of architects
> to do a study of space, of something that I called at that time
> 'heterotopias', those singular spaces to be found in some given
> social spaces whose functions are different or even the opposite of
> others. The architects worked on this, and at the end of the study
> someone spoke up – a Sartrean psychologist – who firebombed me,
> saying that *space* is reactionary and capitalist, but *history* and *becom-
> ing* are revolutionary. This absurd discourse was not at all unusual
> at the time. Today everyone would be convulsed with laughter at
> such a pronouncement, but not then.

Amidst today's laughter – still not as widespread and convulsive as
Foucault assumed it would be – one can look back and see that Foucault
persistently explored what he called the 'fatal intersection of time with
space' from the first to the last of his writings. And he did so, we are
only now beginning to realize, infused with the emerging perspective of
a post-historicist and postmodern critical human geography.

Few could see Foucault's geography, however, for he never ceased
to be a historian, never broke his allegiance to the master identity of
modern critical thought. To be labelled a geographer was an intellectual
curse, a demeaning association with an academic discipline so far
removed from the grand houses of modern social theory and philosophy
as to appear beyond the pale of critical relevance. Foucault had to be

coaxed into recognizing his formative attachment to the geographer's spatial perspective, to admit that geography was always at the heart of his concerns. This retrospective admission appeared in an interview with the editors of the French journal of radical geography, *Herodote*, and was published in English as 'Questions on Geography', in *Power/Knowledge* (Foucault 1980). In this interview, Foucault expanded upon the observations he made in 1967, but only after being pushed to do so by the interviewers.

At first, Foucault was surprised – and annoyed – at being asked by his interviewers why he had been so silent about the importance of geography and spatiality in his works despite the profuse use of geographical and spatial metaphors. The interviewers suggested to him:

> If geography is invisible or ungrasped in the area of your explorations and excavations, this may be due to the deliberately historical or archeological approach which privileges the factor of time. Thus one finds in your work a rigorous concern with periodization that contrasts with the vagueness of your spatial demarcations.

Foucault responded immediately by diversion and inversion, throwing back the responsibility for geography to his interviewers (while remembering the critics who reproached him for his 'metaphorical obsession' with space). After further questioning, however, he admitted (again?) that space has been devalued for generations by philosophers and social critics, reasserted the inherent spatiality of power/knowledge, and ended with a *volte face*:

> I have enjoyed this discussion with you because I've changed my mind since we started. I must admit that I thought you were demanding a place for geography like those teachers who protest when an education reform is proposed because the number of hours of natural sciences or music is being cut. . . . Now I can see that the problems you put to me about geography are crucial ones for me. Geography acted as the support, the condition of possibility for the passage between a series of factors I tried to relate. Where geography itself was concerned, I either left the question hanging or established a series of arbitrary connections. . . . Geography must indeed lie at the heart of my concerns. (Foucault 1980: 77)

Foucault's argument here takes a new turn, from simply looking at 'other spaces' to questioning the origins of 'this devaluation of space that has prevailed for generations'. It is at this point that he makes the comment cited earlier on the post-Bergsonian treatment of space as passive and lifeless, time as richness, fecundity, dialectic.

Here then are the inquisitive ingredients for a direct attack on historicism as the source of the devaluation of space, but Foucault had other things in mind. In a revealing aside, he takes an integrative rather than deconstructive path, holding on to his history but adding to it the crucial nexus that would flow through all his work: the linkage between space, knowledge, and power.

> For all those who confuse history with the old schemas of evolution, living continuity, organic development, the progress of conscious-ness or the project of existence, the use of spatial terms seems to have an air of an anti-history. If one started to talk in terms of space that meant one was hostile to time. It meant, as the fools say, that one 'denied history', that one was a 'technocrat'. They didn't under-stand that to trace the forms of implantation, delimitation and demarcation of objects, the modes of tabulation, the organisation of domains meant the throwing into relief of processes – historical ones, needless to say – of power. The spatialising description of discursive realities gives on to the analysis of related effects of power. (Ibid.)

In 'The Eye of Power', published as a preface to Jeremy Bentham, *La Panoptique* (1977) and reprinted in *Power/Knowledge* (Foucault 1980: 149), he restates his ecumenical project:

> A whole history remains to be written of *spaces* – which would at the same time be the history of *powers* (both of these terms in the plural) – from the great strategies of geopolitics to the little tactics of the habitat.

Foucault thus postpones a direct critique of historicism with an acute lateral glance, at once maintaining his spatializing project but preserving his historical stance. 'History will protect us from historicism,' he opti-mistically concludes.

THE DECONSTRUCTION AND RECONSTITUTION OF MODERNITY

In *All That is Solid Melts Into Air: The Experience of Modernity* (1982), Marshall Berman explores the multiple reconfigurations of social life that have characterized the historical geography of capitalism over the past four hundred years. At the heart of his interpretive outlook is a revealing periodization of changing concepts of modernity from the formative sixteenth-century clash between the 'Ancients' and the 'Moderns' to the contemporary debates that herald still another conceptual and social reconfiguration, another reconsideration of what it means to be modern. In this concatenation of modernities is a history of historicism that can now begin to be written from a postmodern geographical perspective.

Berman broadly defines modernity as 'a mode of vital experience', a collective sharing of a particularized sense of 'the self and others', of 'life's possibilities and perils'. In this definition, there is a special place given to the ways we think about and experience time and space, history and geography, sequence and simultaneity, event and locality, the immediate period and region in which we live. Modernity is thus comprised of both context and conjuncture. It can be understood as the specificity of being alive, in the world, at a particular time and place; a vital individual and collective sense of contemporaneity. As such, the experience of modernity captures a broad mesh of sensibilities that reflects the specific and changing meanings of the three most basic and formative dimensions of human existence: space, time, and being. Herein lies its particular usefulness as a means of resituating the debates on history and geography in critical social theory and for defining the context and conjuncture of postmodernity.

Just as space, time, and matter delineate and encompass the essential qualities of the physical world, spatiality, temporality, and social being can be seen as the abstract dimensions which together comprise all facets of human existence. More concretely specified, each of these abstract existential dimensions comes to life as a social construct which shapes empirical reality and is simultaneously shaped by it. Thus, the spatial order of human existence arises from the (social) production of space, the construction of human geographies that both reflect and configure being in the world. Similarly, the temporal order is concretized in the making of history, simultaneously constrained and constraining in an evolving dialectic that has been the ontological crux of Marxist thought for over a hundred years. To complete the necessary existential triad, the social order of being-in-the-world can be seen as revolving around the constitution of society, the production and reproduction of social relations, institutions, and practices. How this ontological nexus of space–time–being is conceptually specified and given particular meaning in the explanation of concrete events and occurrences is the generative source of all social theory, critical or otherwise.

It provides an illuminating motif through which to view the interplay between history, geography, and modernity.

Sequences of modernity, modernization and modernism

In the experience of modernity, the ontological nexus of social theory becomes specifically and concretely composed in a changing 'culture of time and space', to borrow the felicitous phrase used by Stephen Kern (1983) to describe the profound reconfiguration of modernity that took place in the previous *fin de siècle*.

> From around 1880 to the outbreak of World War I a series of sweeping changes in technology and culture created distinctive new modes of thinking about and experiencing time and space. Technological innovations including the telephone, wireless telegraph, x-ray, cinema, bicycle, automobile and airplane established the material foundation for this reorientation; independent cultural developments such as the stream of consciousness novel, psychoanalysis, Cubism, and the theory of relativity shaped consciousness directly. The result was a transformation of the dimensions of life and thought. (1983: 1–2)

During this expanded *fin de siècle*, from the aftermath of the defeat of the Paris Commune to the events which would lead up to the Russian Revolution (to choose somewhat different turning points), the world changed dramatically. Industrial capitalism survived its predicted demise through a radical social and spatial restructuring which both intensified (or deepened, as in the rise of corporate monopolies and mergers) and extensified (or widened, as in the global expansion of imperialism) its definitive production relations and divisions of labour. Accompanying the rise of this new political economy of capitalism was an altered culture of time and space, a restructured historical geography taking shape from the shattered remains of an older order and infused with ambitious new visions and designs for the future as the very nature and experience of modernity – what it meant to be modern – was significantly reconstituted. A similar reconstitution took place in the prevailing forms of social theorization, equally attuned to the changing nature of capitalist modernity. But before turning to this restructuring of social theory, there is more to be derived from Berman's conceptualization of modernity and the recognition of the parallelism between the past and present *fins de siècle*.

As so many have begun to see, both *fin de siècle* periods resonate with similarly transformative, but not necessarily revolutionary, socio-spatial processes. As occurred roughly a century ago, there is currently a complex and conflictful dialectic developing between urgent socio-economic modernization sparked by the system-wide crises affecting contemporary capitalist societies; and a responsive cultural and political modernism aimed at making sense of the material changes taking place in the world and gaining control over their future directions. Modernization and modernism interact under these conditions of intensified crisis and restructuring to create a shifting and conflictful social context in which everything seems to be 'pregnant with its contrary', in which all that was once assumed to be solid 'melts into air', a description Berman borrows from Marx and represents as an essential feature of the vital experience of modernity-in-transition.

Modernization can be directly linked to the many different 'objective' processes of structural change that have been associated with the ability of capitalism to develop and survive, to reproduce successfully its fundamental social relations of production and distinctive divisions of labour despite endogenous tendencies towards debilitating crisis. This defining association between modernization and the survival of capitalism is crucial, for all too often the analysts of modernity extract social change from its social origins in modes of production to 'stage' history in idealized evolutionary modellings. From these perspectives, change just seems to 'happen' in a lock-step march of modernity replacing tradition, a mechanical teleology of progress. Modernization is not entirely the product of some determinative inner logic of capitalism, but neither is it a rootless and ineluctable idealization of history.

Modernization, as I view it here, is a continuous process of societal restructuring that is periodically accelerated to produce a significant recomposition of space–time–being in their concrete forms, a change in the nature and experience of modernity that arises primarily from the historical and geographical dynamics of modes of production. For the past four hundred years, these dynamics have been predominantly capitalist, as has been the very nature and experience of modernity during that time. Modernization is, like all social processes, unevenly developed across time and space and thus inscribes quite different historical geographies across different regional social formations. But on occasion, in the ever-accumulating past, it has become systemically synchronic, affecting all predominantly capitalist societies simultaneously. This synchronization has punctuated the historical geography of capitalism since at least the early nineteenth century with an increasingly recognizable macro-rhythm, a wave-like periodicity of societal crisis and restructuring that we are only now beginning to understand in all its ramifications.

Perhaps the earliest of these prolonged periods of 'global' crisis and restructuring stretched through what Hobsbawm termed the 'age of revolution' and peaked in the turbulent years between 1830 and 1848–51. The following decades were a time of explosive capitalist expansion in industrial production, urban growth, and international trade, the florescence of a classical, competitive, entrepreneurial regime of capital accumulation and social regulation. During the last three decades of the nineteenth century, however, boom turned largely into bust for the then most advanced capitalist countries as the Long Depression, as it was called, accentuated the need for another urgent restructuring and modernization, a new 'fix' for a capitalism forever addicted to crisis.

The same rollercoaster sequence of crisis-induced restructuring, leading to an expansionary boom, and then to crisis and restructuring again, marked the first half of the twentieth century, with the Great Depression echoing the conflictful system-wide downturns of the past and initiating the transition from one distinctive regime of accumulation to another. And as it now seems increasingly clear, the last half of the twentieth century has followed a similar broad trajectory, with a prolonged expansionary period after the Second World War and a still ongoing, crisis-filled era of attempted modernization and restructuring taking us toward the next *fin de siècle*.

10 Michel de Certeau

Walking in the city

EDITOR'S INTRODUCTION

In this remarkable essay, carefully poised between poetry and semiotics, Michel de Certeau analyses an aspect of daily urban life. He presents a theory of the city, or rather an ideal for the city, against the theories and ideals of urban planners and managers. To do so, he does not look down at the city as if from a high-rise building, he walks in it.

Walking in the city turns out to have its own logic, or, as de Certeau puts it, its own 'rhetoric'. The walker individuates and makes ambiguous the 'legible' order given to cities by planners, a little like the way waking life is displaced and ambiguated by dreaming – to take one of de Certeau's several analogies.

This is a Utopian essay: it conceives of the 'everyday' as different from the official in the same way that poetry is different from a planning manual. And it grants twentieth-century urban experience, for whicn walking is a secondary form of locomotion (often a kind of drifting), the glamour that a writer such as Walter Benjamin found in the nineteenth-century leisured observer or *flâneur*. 'Walking in the city' has been very influential in recent cultural studies just because it works both as an imaginative essay and as a piece of technical semiotic analysis. That double mode is particularly effective in showing how everyday life has a special value when it takes place in the gaps of larger power structures.

Further reading: de Certeau 1984; Frow 1991; Harvey 1985; Lefebvre 1971; Morris 1990; Rigby 1991.

S.D.

Seeing Manhattan from the 110th floor of the World Trade Center. Beneath the haze stirred up by the winds, the urban island, a sea in the middle of the sea, lifts up the skyscrapers over Wall Street, sinks down at Greenwich, then rises again to the crests of Midtown, quietly passes over Central Park and finally undulates off into the distance beyond Harlem. A wave of verticals. Its agitation is momentarily arrested by vision. The gigantic mass is immobilized before the eyes. It is transformed into a texturology in which extremes coincide – extremes of ambition and degradation, brutal oppositions of races and styles, contrasts between yesterday's buildings, already transformed into trash cans, and today's urban irruptions that block out its space. Unlike Rome, New York has never learned the art of growing old by playing on all its pasts. Its present invents itself, from hour to hour, in the act of throwing away its previous accomplishments and challenging the future. A city composed of paroxysmal places in monumental reliefs. The spectator can read in it a universe that is constantly exploding. In it are inscribed the architectural figures of the *coincidatio oppositorum* formerly drawn in miniatures and mystical textures. On this stage of concrete, steel and glass, cut out between two oceans (the Atlantic and the American) by a frigid body of water, the tallest letters in the world compose a gigantic rhetoric of excess in both expenditure and production.

VOYEURS OR WALKERS

To what erotics of knowledge does the ecstasy of reading such a cosmos belong? Having taken a voluptuous pleasure in it, I wonder what is the source of this pleasure of 'seeing the whole', of looking down on, totalizing the most immoderate of human texts.

To be lifted to the summit of the World Trade Center is to be lifted out of the city's grasp. One's body is no longer clasped by the streets that turn and return it according to an anonymous law; nor is it possessed, whether as player or played, by the rumble of so many differences and by the nervousness of New York traffic. When one goes up there, he leaves behind the mass that carries off and mixes up in itself any identity of authors or spectators. An Icarus flying above these waters, he can ignore the devices of Daedalus in mobile and endless labyrinths far below. His elevation transfigures him into a voyeur. It puts him at a distance. It transforms the bewitching world by which one was 'possessed' into a text that lies before one's eyes. It allows one to read it, to be a solar Eye, looking down like a god. The exaltation of a scopic and gnostic drive: the fiction of knowledge is related to this lust to be a viewpoint and nothing more.

Must one finally fall back into the dark space where crowds move back and forth, crowds that, though visible from on high, are themselves unable to see down below? An Icarian fall. On the 110th floor, a poster, sphinx-like, addresses an enigmatic message to the pedestrian who is for an instant transformed into a visionary: *It's hard to be down when you're up.*

The desire to see the city preceded the means of satisfying it. Medieval or Renaissance painters represented the city as seen in a perspective that no eye had yet enjoyed. This fiction already made the medieval spectator into a celestial eye. It created gods. Have things changed since technical procedures have organized an 'all-seeing power'? The totalizing eye imagined by the painters of earlier times lives on in our achievements. The same scopic drive haunts users of architectural productions by materializing today the utopia that yesterday was only painted. The 1370 foot high tower that serves as a prow for Manhattan continues to construct the fiction that creates readers, makes the complexity of the city readable, and immobilizes its opaque mobility in a transparent text.

Is the immense texturology spread out before one's eyes anything more than a representation, an optical artefact? It is the analogue of the facsimile produced, through a projection that is a way of keeping aloof, by the space planner urbanist, city planner or cartographer. The panorama-city is a 'theoretical' (that is, visual) simulacrum, in short a picture, whose condition of possibility is an oblivion and a misunderstanding of practices.

The ordinary practitioners of the city live 'down below', below the thresholds at which visibility begins. They walk – an elementary form of this experience of the city; they are walkers, *Wandersmänner*, whose bodies follow the thicks and thins of an urban 'text' they write without being able to read it. These practitioners make use of spaces that cannot be seen; their knowledge of them is as blind as that of lovers in each other's arms. The paths that correspond in this intertwining, unrecognized poems in which each body is an element signed by many others, elude legibility. It is as though the practices organizing a bustling city were characterized by their blindness. The networks of these moving, intersecting writings compose a manifold story that has neither author nor spectator, shaped out of fragments of trajectories and alterations of spaces: in relation to representations, it remains daily and indefinitely other.

Escaping the imaginary totalizations produced by the eye, the everyday has a certain strangeness that does not surface, or whose surface is only its upper limit, outlining itself against the visible. Within this ensemble, I shall try to locate the practices that are foreign to the 'geometrical' or 'geographical' space of visual, panoptic, or theoretical constructions. These practices of space refer to a specific form of *operations* ('ways of operating'), to 'another spatiality' (an 'anthropological', poetic and mythic experience of space), and to an *opaque and blind* mobility characteristic of the bustling city. A *migrational*, or metaphorical, city thus slips into the clear text of the planned and readable city.

1. FROM THE CONCEPT OF THE CITY TO URBAN PRACTICES

The World Trade Center is only the most monumental figure of Western urban development. The atopia-utopia of optical knowledge has long had the ambition of surmounting and articulating the contradictions arising from urban agglomeration. It is a question of managing a growth of human agglomeration or accumulation. 'The city is a huge monastery,' said Erasmus. Perspective vision and prospective vision constitute the twofold projection of an opaque past and an uncertain future onto a surface that can be dealt with. They inaugurate (in the sixteenth century?) the transformation of the urban *fact* into the *concept* of a city. Long before the concept itself gives rise to a particular figure of history, it assumes that this fact can be dealt with as a unity determined by an urbanistic *ratio*. Linking the city to the concept never makes them identical, but it plays on their progressive symbiosis: to plan a city is both to *think the very plurality* of the real and to make that way of thinking the plural *effective*; it is to know how to articulate it and be able to do it.

An operational concept?

The 'city' founded by utopian and urbanistic discourse is defined by the possibility of a threefold operation:

    1. The production of its *own* space (*un espace propre*): rational organization must thus repress all the physical, mental and political pollutions that would compromise it;

    2. the substitution of a nowhen, or of a synchronic system, for the indeterminable and stubborn resistances offered by traditions; univocal scientific strategies, made possible by the flattening out of all the data in a plane projection, must replace the tactics of users who take advantage

of 'opportunities' and who, through these trap-events, these lapses in visibility, reproduce the opacities of history everywhere;

3. finally, the creation of a *universal* and anonymous *subject* which is the city itself: it gradually becomes possible to attribute to it, as to its political model, Hobbes's State, all the functions and predicates that were previously scattered and assigned to many different real subjects – groups, associations, or individuals. 'The city', like a proper name, thus provides a way of conceiving and constructing space on the basis of a finite number of stable, isolatable, and interconnected properties.

Administration is combined with a process of elimination in this place organized by 'speculative' and classificatory operations. On the one hand, there is a differentiation and redistribution of the parts and functions of the city, as a result of inversions, displacements, accumulations, etc.; on the other there is a rejection of everything that is not capable of being dealt with in this way and so constitutes the 'waste products' of a functionalist administration (abnormality, deviance, illness, death, etc.). To be sure, progress allows an increasing number of these waste products to be reintroduced into administrative circuits and transforms even deficiencies (in health, security, etc.) into ways of making the networks of order denser. But in reality, it repeatedly produces effects contrary to those at which it aims: the profit system generates a loss which, in the multiple forms of wretchedness and poverty outside the system and of waste inside it, constantly turns production into 'expenditure'. Moreover, the rationalization of the city leads to its mythification in strategic discourses, which are calculations based on the hypothesis or the necessity of its destruction in order to arrive at a final decision. Finally, the functionalist organization, by privileging progress (i.e., time), causes the condition of its own possibility – space itself – to be forgotten; space thus becomes the blind spot in a scientific and political technology. This is the way in which the Concept-city functions; a place of transformations and appropriations, the object of various kinds of interference but also a subject that is constantly enriched by new attributes, it is simultaneously the machinery and the hero of modernity.

Today, whatever the avatars of this concept may have been, we have to acknowledge that if in discourse the city serves as a totalizing and almost mythical landmark for socioeconomic and political strategies, urban life increasingly permits the re-emergence of the element that the urbanistic project excluded. The language of power is in itself 'urbanizing', but the city is left prey to contradictory movements that counterbalance and combine themselves outside the reach of panoptic power. The city becomes the dominant theme in political legends, but it is no longer a field of programmed and regulated operations. Beneath the discourses that ideologize the city, the ruses and combinations of powers that have no readable identity proliferate; without points where one can take hold of them, without rational transparency, they are impossible to administer.

The return of practices

The Concept-city is decaying. Does that mean that the illness afflicting both the rationality that founded it and its professionals afflicts the urban populations as well? Perhaps cities are deteriorating along with the procedures that organized them. But we must be careful here. The ministers of knowledge have always assumed that the whole universe was threatened by the very changes that affected their ideologies and their positions. They transmute the misfortune of their theories into theories of misfortune. When they transform their bewilderment into 'catastrophes', when they seek to enclose the people in the 'panic' of their discourses, are they once more necessarily right?

Rather than remaining within the field of a discourse that upholds its privilege by inverting its content (speaking of catastrophe and no longer of progress), one can try another path: one can analyse the microbe-like, singular and plural practices which an urbanistic system was supposed to administer or suppress, but which have outlived its decay; one can follow the swarming activity of these procedures that, far from being regulated or eliminated by panoptic administration, have reinforced themselves in a proliferating illegitimacy, developed and insinuated themselves into the networks of surveillance, and combined in accord with unreadable but stable tactics to the point of constituting everyday regulations and surreptitious creativities that are merely concealed by the frantic mechanisms and discourses of the observational organization.

This pathway could be inscribed as a consequence, but also as the reciprocal, of Foucault's analysis of the structures of power. He moved it in the direction of mechanisms and technical procedures, 'minor instrumentalities' capable, merely by their organization of 'details', of transforming a human multiplicity into a 'disciplinary' society and of managing, differentiating, classifying, and hierarchizing all deviances concerning apprenticeship, health, justice, the army, or work. 'These often minuscule ruses of discipline', these 'minor but flawless' mechanisms, draw their efficacy from a relationship between procedures and the space that they redistribute in order to make an 'operator' out of it. But what *spatial practices* correspond, in the area where discipline is manipulated, to these apparatuses that produce a disciplinary space? In the present conjuncture, which is marked by a contradiction between the collective mode of administration and an individual mode of reappropriation, this question is no less important, if one admits that spatial practices in fact secretly structure the determining conditions of social life. I would like to follow out a few of these multiform, resistant, tricky and stubborn procedures that elude discipline without being outside the field in which it is exercised, and which should lead us to a theory of everyday practices, of lived space, of the disquieting familiarity of the city.

2. THE CHORUS OF IDLE FOOTSTEPS

> The goddess can be recognized by her step
> Virgil, *Aeneid*, I, 405

Their story begins on ground level, with footsteps. They are myriad, but do not compose a series. They cannot be counted because each unit has a qualitative character: a style of tactile apprehension and kinesthetic appropriation. Their swarming mass is an innumerable collection of singularities. Their intertwined paths give their shape to spaces. They weave places together. In that respect, pedestrian movements form one of these 'real systems whose existence in fact makes up the city'. They are not localized; it is rather they that spatialize. They are no more inserted within a container than those Chinese characters speakers sketch out on their hands with their fingertips.

It is true that the operations of walking on can be traced on city maps in such a way as to transcribe their paths (here well-trodden, there very faint) and their trajectories (going this way and not that). But these thick or thin curves only refer, like words, to the absence of what has passed by. Surveys of routes miss what was: the act itself of passing by. The operation of walking, wandering, or 'window shopping', that is, the activity of passers-by, is transformed into points that draw a totalizing and reversible line on the map. They allow us to grasp only a relic set in the nowhen of a surface of projection. Itself visible, it has the effect of making invisible the operation that made it possible. These fixations constitute procedures for forgetting. The trace left behind is substituted for the practice. It exhibits the (voracious) property that the geographical system has of being able to transform action into legibility, but in doing so it causes a way of being in the world to be forgotten.

Walking rhetorics

The walking of passers-by offers a series of turns (*tours*) and detours that can be compared to 'turns of phrase' or 'stylistic figures'. There is a rhetoric of walking. The art of 'turning' phrases finds an equivalent in an art of composing a path (*tourner un parcours*). Like ordinary language, this art implies and combines styles and uses. *Style* specifies 'a linguistic structure that manifests on the symbolic level . . . an individual's fundamental way of being in the world'; it connotes a singular. Use defines the social phenomenon through which a system of communication manifests itself in actual fact; it refers to a norm. Style and use both have to do with a 'way of operating' (of speaking, walking, etc.), but style involves a peculiar processing of the symbolic, while use refers to elements of a code. They intersect to form a style of use, a way of being and a way of operating.

A friend who lives in the city of Sèvres drifts, when he is in Paris, toward the rue des Saints-*Pères* and the rue de *Sèvres*, even though he is going to see his mother in another part of town: these names articulate a sentence that his steps compose without his knowing it. Numbered streets and street numbers (112th St., or 9 rue Saint-Charles) orient the magnetic field of trajectories just as they can haunt dreams. Another friend unconsciously represses the streets which have names and, by this fact, transmit her – orders or identities in the same way as summonses and classifications; she goes instead along paths that have no name or signature. But her walking is thus still controlled negatively by proper names.

What is it then that they spell out? Disposed in constellations that hierarchize and semantically order the surface of the city, operating chronological arrangements and historical justifications, these words (*Borrégo, Botzaris, Bougainville* . . .) slowly lose, like worn coins, the value engraved on them, but their ability to signify outlives its first definition. *Saints-Pères, Corentin Celton, Red Square* . . . these names make themselves available to the diverse meanings given them by passers-by; they detach themselves from the places they were supposed to define and serve as imaginary meeting-points on itineraries which, as meta-phors, they determine for reasons that are foreign to their original value but may be recognized or not by passers-by. A strange toponymy that is detached from actual places and flies high over the city like a foggy geography of 'meanings' held in suspension, directing the physical deambulations below: *Place de l'Étoile, Concorde, Poissonnière* . . . These constellations of names provide traffic patterns: they are stars directing itineraries. 'The Place de la Concorde does not exist,' Malaparte said, 'it is an idea.' It is much more than an 'idea'. A whole series of comparisons would be necessary to account for the magical powers proper names enjoy. They seem to be carried as emblems by the travellers they direct and simultaneously decorate.

Linking acts and footsteps, opening meanings and directions, these words operate in the name of an emptying-out and wearing-away of their primary role. They become liberated spaces that can be occupied. A rich indetermination gives them, by means of a semantic rarefaction, the function of articulating a second, poetic geography on top of the geog-raphy of the literal, forbidden or permitted meaning. They insinuate other routes into the functionalist and historical order of movement. Walking follows them: 'I fill this great empty space with a beautiful name.' People are put in motion by the remaining relics of meaning, and sometimes by their waste products, the inverted remainders of great ambitions. Things that amount to nothing, or almost nothing, sym-bolize and orient walkers' steps: names that have ceased precisely to be 'proper'.

Ultimately, since proper names are already 'local authorities' or 'superstitions', they are replaced by numbers: on the telephone, one no longer dials *Opera*, but 073. The same is true of the stories and legends that haunt urban space like superfluous or additional inhabitants. They are the object of a witch-hunt, by the very logic of the techno-structure. But their extermination (like the extermination of trees, forests, and hidden places in which such legends live) makes the city a 'suspended symbolic order'. The habitable city is thereby annulled. Thus, as a woman from Rouen put it, no, here 'there isn't any place special, except for my own home, that's all. . . . There isn't anything.' Nothing 'special': nothing that is marked, opened up by a memory or a story, signed by something or someone else. Only the cave of the home remains believable, still open for a certain time to legends, still full of shadows. Except for that, according to another city-dweller, there are only 'places in which one can no longer believe in anything'.

It is through the opportunity they offer to store up rich silences and wordless stories, or rather through their capacity to create cellars and garrets everywhere, that local legends (*legenda*: what is *to be read*, but also what *can be read*) permit exits, ways of going out and coming back in, and thus habitable spaces. Certainly walking about and travelling substitute for exits, for going away and coming back, which were formerly made available by a body of legends that places nowadays lack. Physical moving about has the itinerant function of yesterday's or today's 'superstitions'. Travel (like walking) is a substitute for the legends that used to open up space to something different. What does travel ultimately produce if it is not, by a sort of reversal, 'an exploration of the deserted places of my memory', the return to nearby exoticism by way of a detour through distant places, and the 'discovery' of relics and legends: 'fleeting visions of the French countryside', 'fragments of music and poetry', in short, something like an 'uprooting in one's origins' (Heidegger)? What this walking exile produces is precisely the body of legends that is currently lacking in one's own vicinity; it is a fiction, which moreover has the double characteristic, like dreams or pedestrian rhetoric, of being the effect of displacements and condensations. As a corollary, one can measure the importance of these signifying practices (to tell oneself legends) as practices that invent spaces.

From this point of view, their contents remain revelatory, and still more so is the principle that organizes them. Stories about places are makeshift things. They are composed with the world's debris. Even if the literary form and the actantial schema of 'superstitions' correspond to stable models whose structures and combinations have often been analysed over the past thirty years, the materials (all the rhetorical details of their 'manifestation') are furnished by the leftovers from nominations, taxonomies, heroic or comic predicates, etc., that is, by fragments of scattered semantic places. These heterogeneous and even contrary elements fill the homogeneous form of the story. Things *extra* and *other* (details and excesses coming from elsewhere) insert themselves into the accepted framework, the imposed order. One thus has the very relationship between spatial practices and the constructed order. The surface of this order is everywhere punched and torn open by ellipses, drifts, and leaks of meaning: it is a sieve-order.

11 Michel Foucault

Space, power and knowledge

EDITOR'S INTRODUCTION

This interview, in which Michel Foucault talks to Paul Rabinow, makes its most general point last. Foucault argues that material changes cannot be used to explain changes in subjectivity. For instance, when, in the Middle Ages, chimneys were first walled and placed inside, rather than outside, houses, inter-personal relations were transformed. New interactions flourished around chimneys. But the building of chimneys is not enough to explain these changes – if, for instance, different discourses and values had been circulating at the time, then chimneys would have produced different kinds of changes. Generalizing from this point, Foucault argues that abstract (and in the West highly valued) words like 'liberty' and 'rationality' refer neither simply to ideas nor to practices – but to sets of complex exchanges between the two. None the less, it has been the 'practices' of liberty and reason that have been neglected by intellectual and cultural historians.

This line of thought has an important consequence. It means that architects and other social managers cannot guarantee that their designs will secure liberty or rationality. What matters is the fit between the material reorganization of space, life-practices, values and discourses: only if the fit is right will social managers be able to augment what Foucault calls 'practices of liberty'. In this light Foucault argues that intellectuals have a particular function when society is being modernized and rationalized by managers and experts: they are to remain critical of nostalgic, Utopian and overly abstract thought.

Further reading: Burgin 1990; Dreyfus and Rabinow 1983; Foucault 1980, 1988; Mitchell 1988 (a book which uses Foucault's work to describe the construction of colonial space).

S.D.

Q. Do you see any particular architectural projects, either in the past or the present, as forces of liberation or resistance?

M.F. I do not think that it is possible to say that one thing is of the order of 'liberation' and another is of the order of 'oppression'. There are a certain number of things that one can say with some certainty about a concentration camp to the effect that it is not an instrument of liberation, but one should still take into account – and this is not generally acknowledged – that, aside from torture and execution, which preclude any resistance, no matter how terrifying a given system may be, there always remain the possibilities of resistance, disobedience, and oppositional groupings.

On the other hand, I do not think that there is anything that is functionally – by its very nature – absolutely liberating. Liberty is a *practice*. So there may, in fact, always be a certain number of projects whose aim is to modify some constraints, to loosen, or even to break them, but none of these projects can simply by its nature, assure that people will have liberty automatically, that it will be established by the project itself. The liberty of men is never assured by the institutions and laws that are intended to guarantee them. This is why almost all of these laws and institutions are quite capable of being turned around. Not because they are ambiguous, but simply because 'liberty' is what must be exercised.

Q. Are there urban examples of this? Or examples where architects succeeded?

M.F. Well, up to a point there is Le Corbusier, who is described today – with a sort of cruelty that I find perfectly useless – as a sort of crypto-Stalinist. He was, I am sure, someone full of good intentions and what he did was in fact dedicated to liberating effects. Perhaps the means that he proposed were in the end less liberating than he thought, but, once again, I think that it can never be inherent in the structure of things to guarantee the exercise of freedom. The guarantee of freedom is freedom.

Q. So you do not think of Le Corbusier as an example of success. You are simply saying that his intention was liberating. Can you give us a successful example?

M.F. No. It *cannot* succeed. If one were to find a place, and perhaps there are some, where liberty is effectively exercised, one would find that this is not owing to the order of objects, but, once again, owing to the practice of liberty. Which is not to say that, after all, one may as well leave people in slums, thinking that they can simply exercise their rights there.

Q. Meaning that architecture in itself cannot resolve social problems?

M.F. I think that it can and does produce positive effects when the liberating intentions of the architect coincide with the real practice of people in the exercise of their freedom.

Q. But the same architecture can serve other ends?

M.F. Absolutely. Let me bring up another example: the *Familistère* of Jean-Baptiste Godin at Guise [1859]. The architecture of Godin was clearly intended for the freedom of people. Here was something that manifested the power of ordinary workers to participate in the exercise of their trade. It was a rather important sign and instrument of autonomy for a group of workers. Yet no one could enter or leave the place without being seen by everyone – an aspect of the architecture that could be totally oppressive. But it could only be oppressive if people were prepared to use their own presence in order to watch over others. Let's imagine a community of unlimited sexual practices that might be established there. It would once again become a place of freedom. I think it is somewhat arbitrary to try to dissociate the effective practice of freedom by people, the practice of social relations, and the spatial distributions in which they find themselves. If they are separated, they become impossible to understand. Each can only be understood through the other.

Q. Yet people have often attempted to find utopian schemes to liberate people, or to oppress them.

M.F. Men have dreamed of liberating machines. But there are no machines of freedom, by definition. This is not to say that the exercise of freedom is completely indifferent to spatial distribution, but it can only function when there is a certain convergence; in the case of divergence or distortion, it immediately becomes the opposite of that which had been intended. The panoptic qualities of Guise could perfectly well have allowed it to be used as a prison. Nothing could be simpler. It is clear that, in fact, the *Familistère* may well have served as an instrument for discipline and a rather unbearable group pressure.

Q. So, once again, the intention of the architect is not the fundamental determining factor.

M.F. Nothing is fundamental. That is what is interesting in the analysis of society. That is why nothing irritates me as much as these enquiries – which are by definition metaphysical – on the foundations of power in a society or the self-institution of a society, etc. These are not fundamental phenomena. There are only reciprocal relations, and the perpetual gaps between intentions in relation to one another.

Q. You have singled out doctors, prison wardens, priests, judges, and psychiatrists as key figures in the political configurations that involve domination. Would you put architects on this list?

M.F. You know, I was not really attempting to describe figures of domination when I referred to doctors and people like that, but rather to describe people through whom power passed or who are important in the fields of power relations. A patient in a mental institution is placed within a field of fairly complicated power relations, which Erving Goffman analysed very well. The pastor in a Christian or Catholic church (in Protestant churches it is somewhat different) is an important link in a set of power relations. The architect is not an individual of that sort.

After all, the architect has no power over me. If I want to tear down or change a house he built for me, put up new partitions, add a chimney, the architect has no control. So the architect should be placed in another category – which is not to say that he is not totally foreign to the organization, the implementation, and all the techniques of power that are exercised in a society. I would say that one must take *him* – his mentality, his attitude – into account as well as his projects, in order to understand a certain number of the techniques of power that are invested in architecture, but he is not comparable to a doctor, a priest, a psychiatrist, or a prison warden.

Q. 'Postmodernism' has received a great deal of attention recently in architectural circles. It is also being talked about in philosophy, notably by Jean-François Lyotard and Jürgen Habermas. Clearly, historical reference and language play an important role in the modern episteme. How do you see postmodernism, both as architecture and in terms of the historical and philosophical questions that are posed by it?

M.F. I think that there is a widespread and facile tendency, which one should combat, to designate that which has just occurred as the primary enemy, as if this were always the principal form of oppression from which one had to liberate oneself. Now this simple attitude entails a number of dangerous consequences: first, an inclination to seek out some cheap form of archaism or some imaginary past forms of happiness that people did not, in fact, have at all. For instance, in the areas that interest me, it is very amusing to see how contemporary sexuality is described as something absolutely terrible. To think that it is only possible now to make love after turning off the television! and in mass-produced beds! 'Not like that wonderful time when . . .' Well, what about those wonderful times when people worked eighteen hours a day and there were six people in a bed, if one was lucky enough to have a bed! There is in this hatred of the present or the immediate past a dangerous tendency to invoke a completely mythical past. Second, there is the problem raised by Habermas: if one abandons the work of Kant or Weber, for example, one runs the risk of lapsing into irrationality.

I am completely in agreement with this, but at the same time, our question is quite different: I think that the central issue of philosophy and critical thought since the eighteenth century has always been, still is, and will, I hope, remain the question: *What* is this Reason that we use? What are its historical effects? What are its limits, and what are its dangers? How can we exist as rational beings, fortunately committed to practising a rationality that is unfortunately crisscrossed by intrinsic dangers? One should remain as close to this question as possible, keeping in mind that it is both central and extremely difficult to resolve. In addition, if it is extremely dangerous to say that Reason is the enemy that should be eliminated, it is just as dangerous to say that any critical questioning of this rationality risks sending us into irrationality. One should not forget – and I'm not saying this in order to criticize rationality, but in order to show how ambiguous things are – it was on the basis of the flamboyant rationality of social Darwinism that racism was formulated, becoming one of the most enduring and powerful ingredients of Nazism. This was, of course, an irrationality, but an irrationality that was at the same time, after all, a certain form of rationality. . . .

This is the situation that we are in and that we must combat. If intellectuals in general are to have a function, if critical thought itself has a function, and, even more specifically, if philosophy has a function within critical thought, it is precisely to accept this sort of spiral, this sort of revolving door of rationality that refers us to its necessity, to its indispensability, and at the same time, to its intrinsic dangers.

Q. All that being said, it would be fair to say that you are much less afraid of historicism and the play of historical references than someone like Habermas is; also, that this issue has been posed in architecture as almost a crisis of civilization by the defenders of modernism, who contend that if we abandon modern architecture for a frivolous return to decoration and motifs, we are somehow abandoning civilization. On the other hand, some postmodernists have claimed that historical references per se are somehow meaningful and are going to protect us from the dangers of an overly rationalized world.

M.F. Although it may not answer your question, I would say this: one should totally and absolutely suspect anything that claims to be a return. One reason is a logical one; there is in fact no such thing as a return. History, and the meticulous interest applied to history, is certainly one of the best defences against this theme of the return. For me, the history of madness or the studies of the prison . . . were done in that precise manner because I knew full well – this is in fact what aggravated many people – that I was carrying out a historical analysis in such a manner that people *could* criticize the present, but it was impossible for them to say, 'Let's go back to the good old days when madmen in the eighteenth century . . .' or, 'Let's go back to the days when the prison was not one of the principal instruments. . . .' No; I think that history preserves us from that sort of ideology of the return.

Q. Hence, the simple opposition between reason and history is rather silly . . . choosing sides between the two. . . .

M.F. Yes. Well, the problem for Habermas is, after all, to make a transcendental mode of thought spring forth against any historicism. I am, indeed, far more historicist and Nietzschean. I do not think that there is a proper usage of history or a proper usage of intrahistorical analysis – which is fairly lucid, by the way – that works precisely against this ideology of the return. A good study of peasant architecture in Europe, for example, would show the utter vanity of wanting to return to the little individual house with its thatched roof. History protects us from historicism – from a historicism that calls on the past to resolve the questions of the present.

Q. It also reminds us that there is always a history; that those modernists who wanted to suppress any reference to the past were making a mistake.

M.F. Of course.

Q. Your next two books deal with sexuality among the Greeks and the early Christians. Are there any particular architectural dimensions to the issues you discuss?

M.F. I didn't find any; absolutely none. But what is interesting is that in imperial Rome there were, in fact, brothels, pleasure quarters, criminal areas, etc., and there was also one sort of quasi-public place of pleasure: the baths, the *thermes*. The baths were a very important place of pleasure and encounter, which slowly disappeared in Europe. In the Middle Ages, the baths were still a place of encounter between men and women as well as of men with men and women with women, although that is rarely talked about. What were referred to and condemned, as well as practised, were the encounters between men and women, which disappeared over the course of the sixteenth and seventeenth centuries.

Q. In the Arab world it continues.

M.F. Yes; but in France it has largely ceased. It still existed in the nineteenth century. One sees it in *Les Enfants du Paradis*, and it is historically exact. One of the characters, Lacenaire, was – no one mentions it – a swine and a pimp who used young boys to attract older men and then blackmailed them; there is a scene that refers to this. It required all the naiveté and anti-homosexuality of the Surrealists to overlook that fact. So the baths continued to exist, as a place of sexual encounters. The bath was a sort of cathedral of pleasure at the heart of the city, where people could go as often as they want, where they walked about, picked each other up, met each other, took their pleasure, ate, drank, discussed. . . .

Q. So sex was not separated from the other pleasures. It was inscribed in the centre of the cities. It was public; it served a purpose. . . .

M.F. That's right. Sexuality was obviously considered a social pleasure for the Greeks and the Romans. What is interesting about male homosexuality today – this has apparently been the case of female homosexuals for some time – is that their sexual relations are immediately translated into social relations and the social relations are understood as sexual relations. For the Greeks and the Romans, in a different fashion, sexual relations were located within social relations in the widest sense of the term. The baths were a place of sociality that included sexual relations.

One can directly compare the bath and the brothel. The brothel is in fact a place, and an architecture, of pleasure. There is, in fact, a very interesting form of sociality that was studied by Alain Corbin in *Les Filles de noces*. The men of the city met at the brothel; they were tied to one another by the fact that the same women passed through their hands, that the same diseases and infections were communicated to them. There was a sociality of the brothel, but the sociality of the baths as it existed among the ancients – a new version of which could perhaps exist again – was completely different from the sociality of the brothel.

Q. We now know a great deal about disciplinary architecture. What about confessional architecture – the kind of architecture that would be associated with a confessional technology?

M.F. You mean religious architecture? I think that it has been studied. There is the whole problem of a monastery as xenophobic. There one finds precise regulations concerning life in common; affecting sleeping, eating, prayer, the place of each individual in all of that, the cells. All of this was programmed from very early on.

Q. In a technology of power, of confession as opposed to discipline, space seems to play a central role as well.

M.F. Yes. Space is fundamental in any form of communal life; space is fundamental in any exercise of power. To make a parenthetical remark, I recall having been invited, in 1966, by a group of architects to do a study of space, of something that I called at that time 'heterotopias', those singular spaces to be found in some given social spaces whose functions are different or even the opposite of others. The architects worked on this, and at the end of the study someone spoke up – a Sartrean psychologist – who firebombed me, saying that *space* is reactionary and capitalist, but *history* and *becoming* are revolutionary. This absurd discourse was not at all unusual at the time. Today everyone would be convulsed with laughter at such a pronouncement, but not then.

Q. Architects in particular, if they do choose to analyse an institutional building such as a hospital or a school in terms of its disciplinary function, would tend to focus primarily on the walls. After all, that is what they design. Your approach is perhaps more concerned with space, rather than architecture, in that the physical walls are only one aspect of the institution. How would you characterize the difference between these two approaches, between the building itself and space?

M.F. I think there is a difference in method and approach. It is true that for me, architecture, in the very vague analyses of it that I have been able to conduct, is only taken as an element of support, to ensure a certain allocation of people in space, a *canalization* of their circulation, as well as the coding of their reciprocal relations. So it is not only considered as an element in space, but is especially thought of as a plunge into a field of social relations in which it brings about some specific effects.

For example, I know that there is a historian who is carrying out some interesting studies of the archaeology of the Middle Ages, in which he takes up the problem of architecture, of houses in the Middle Ages, in terms of the problem of the chimney. I think that he is in the process of showing that beginning at a certain moment it was possible to build a chimney inside the house – a chimney with a hearth, not simply an open room or a chimney outside the house; that at that moment all sorts of things changed and relations between individuals became possible. All of this seems very interesting to me, but the conclusion that he presented in an article was that the history of ideas and thoughts is useless.

What is, in fact, interesting is that the two are rigorously indivisible. Why did people struggle to find the way to put a chimney inside a house? Or why did they put their techniques to this use? So often in the history of techniques it takes years or even centuries to implement them. It is certain, and of capital importance, that this technique was a formative influence on new human relations, but it is impossible to think that it would have been developed and adapted had there not been in the play and strategy of human relations something which tended in that direction. What is interesting is always interconnection, not the primacy of this over that, which never has any meaning.

12 Jean-François Lyotard

Defining the postmodern

EDITOR'S INTRODUCTION

The claim that we live in the postmodern era has three separate grounds: (i) that the ideas of progress, rationality and scientific objectivity which legitimated Western modernity are no longer acceptable in large part because they take no account of cultural differences; (ii) that there is no confidence that 'high' or avant-garde art and culture has more value than 'low' or popular culture; and (iii) that it is no longer possible securely to separate the 'real' from the 'copy', or the 'natural' from the 'artificial', in a historical situation where technologies (including technologies which produce and disseminate information and images) have so much control and reach.

Jean-François Lyotard, who has been responsible for influential critiques of modernist and universalist ideas of progress and rationality, as well as illuminating defences of the avant-garde, here argues against a historical reading of the 'post' in 'postmodernism'. For him, the postmodern does not follow the modern in time: rather, modernity had always contained its 'postmodern' moments.

Further reading: Collins 1989; Connor 1989; During 1987; Harvey 1989; Hutcheon 1989; Jameson 1990; Lyotard 1986.

S.D.

I should like to make only a small number of observations, in order to point to – and not at all to resolve – some problems surrounding the term 'postmodern'. My aim is not to close the debate, but to open it, to allow it to develop by avoiding certain confusions and ambiguities, as far as this is possible.

There are many debates implied by, and implicated in, the term 'postmodern'. I will distinguish three of them.

First, the opposition between postmodernism and modernism, or the Modern Movement (1910–45), in architectural theory. According to Paolo Portoghesi (*Dell'architectura moderna*), there is a rupture or break, and this break would be the abrogation of the hegemony of Euclidean geometry, which was sublimated in the plastic poetry of the movement known as De Stijl, for example. According to Victorio Grigotti, another Italian architect, the difference between the two periods is characterized by what is possibly a more interesting fissure. There is no longer any close linkage between the architectural project and socio-historical progress in the realization of human emancipation on the larger scale. Postmodern architecture is condemned to generate a multiplicity of small transformations in the space it inherits, and to give up the project of a last rebuilding of the whole space occupied by humanity. In this sense, a perspective is opened in the larger landscape.

In this account there is no longer a horizon of universalization, of general emancipation before the eyes of postmodern man, or in particular, of the postmodern architect. The disappearance of this idea of progress within rationality and freedom would explain a certain tone, style or modus which are specific to postmodern architecture. I would say a sort of *bricolage*: the high frequency of quotations of elements from previous styles or periods (classical or modern), giving up the consideration of environment, and so on.

Just a remark about this aspect. The 'post-', in the term 'postmodernist' is in this case to be understood in the sense of a simple succession, of a diachrony of periods, each of them clearly identifiable. Something like a conversion, a new direction after the previous one. I should like to observe that this idea of chronology is totally modern. It belongs to Christianity, Cartesianism, Jacobinism. Since we are beginning something completely new, we have to re-set the hands of the clock at zero. The idea of modernity is closely bound up with this principle that it is possible and necessary to break with tradition and to begin a new way of living and thinking. Today we can presume that this 'breaking' is, rather, a manner of forgetting or repressing the past. That's to say of repeating it. Not overcoming it.

I would say that the quotation of elements of past architectures in the new one seems to me to be the same procedure as the use of remains coming from past life in the dream-work as described by Freud, in the *Interpretation of Dreams*. This use of repetition or quotation, be it ironical or not, cynical or not, can be seen in the trends dominating contemporary painting, under the name of 'transavantgardism' (Achille Bonito

Oliva) or under the name of neo-expressionism. I'll come back to this question in my third point.

The second point. A second connotation of the term 'postmodern', and I admit that I am at least partly responsible for the misunderstanding associated with this meaning.

The general idea is a trivial one. One can note a sort of decay in the confidence placed by the two last centuries in the idea of progress. This idea of progress as possible, probable or necessary was rooted in the certainty that the development of the arts, technology, knowledge and liberty would be profitable to mankind as a whole. To be sure, the question of knowing which was the subject truly victimized by the lack of development – whether it was the poor, the worker, the illiterate – remained open during the 19th and 20th centuries. There were disputes, even wars, between liberals, conservatives and leftists over the very name of the subject we are to help to become emancipated. Nevertheless, all the parties concurred in the same belief that enterprises, discoveries and institutions are legitimate only insofar as they contribute to the emancipation of mankind.

After two centuries, we are more sensitive to signs that signify the contrary. Neither economic nor political liberalism, nor the various Marxisms, emerge from the sanguinary last two centuries free from the suspicion of crimes against mankind. We can list a series of proper names (names of places, persons and dates) capable of illustrating and founding our suspicion. Following Theodor Adorno, I use the name of Auschwitz to point out the irrelevance of empirical matter, the stuff of recent past history, in terms of the modern claim to help mankind to emancipate itself. What kind of thought is able to sublate (*Aufheben*) Auschwitz in a general (either empirical or speculative) process towards a universal emancipation? So there is a sort of sorrow in the *Zeitgeist*. This can express itself by reactive or reactionary attitudes or by utopias, but never by a positive orientation offering a new perspective.

The development of techno-sciences has become a means of increasing disease, not of fighting it. We can no longer call this development by the old name of progress. This development seems to be taking place by itself, by an autonomous force or 'motricity'. It doesn't respond to a demand coming from human needs. On the contrary, human entities (individual or social) seem always to be destabilized by the results of this development. The intellectual results as much as the material ones. I would say that mankind is in the condition of running after the process of accumulating new objects of practice and thought. In my view it is a real and obscure question to determine the reason of this process of complexification. It's something like a destiny towards a more and more complex condition. Our demands for security, identity and happiness, coming from our condition as living beings and even social beings appear today irrelevant in the face of this sort of obligation to complexify, mediate, memorize and synthesize every object, and to change its scale. We are in this techno-scientific world like Gulliver: sometimes too big, sometimes too small, never at the right scale. Consequently, the claim for simplicity, in general, appears today that of a barbarian.

From this point, it would be necessary to consider the division of mankind into two parts: one part confronted with the challenge of complexity; the other with the terrible ancient task of survival. This is a major aspect of the failure of the modern project (which was, in principle, valid for mankind as a whole).

The third argument is more complex, and I shall present it as briefly as possible. The question of postmodernity is also the question of the expressions of thought: art, literature, philosophy, politics. You know that in the field of art for example, and more especially the plastic arts, the dominant idea is that the big movement of avant-gardism is over. There seems to be general agreement about laughing at the avant-gardes, considered as the expression of an obsolete modernity. I don't like the term avant-garde any more than anyone else, because of its military connotations. Nevertheless I would like to observe that the very process of avant-gardism in painting was in reality a long, obstinate and highly responsible investigation of the presuppositions implied in modernity. The right approach, in order to understand the work of painters from, say, Manet to Duchamp or Barnett Newman is to compare their work with the anamnesis which takes place in psychoanalytical therapy. Just as the patient elaborates his present trouble by freely associating the more imaginary, immaterial, irrelevant bits with past situations, so discovering hidden meanings of his life, we can consider the work of Cézanne, Picasso, Delaunay, Kandinsky, Klee, Mondrian, Malevitch and finally Duchamp as a working through – what Freud called *Durcharbeitung* – operated by modernity on itself. If we give up this responsibility, it is certain that we are condemned to repeat, without any displacement, the modern neurosis, the Western schizophrenia, paranoia, and so on. This being granted, the 'post-' of postmodernity does not mean a process of coming back or flashing back, feeding back, but of *ana*-lysing, *ana*-mnesing, of reflecting.

Part III *Nation*

13 David Forgacs

National-popular: genealogy of a concept

EDITOR'S INTRODUCTION

This essay describes some ideas first formulated by Antonio Gramsci, the Italian Marxist, when he was imprisoned by Mussolini's fascist government. Unlike the other essays in this collection, it is mainly intended to offer an interpretation of an important past theorist. But it is an appropriate essay for a cultural studies reader because Gramsci has been the thinker that the Birmingham school, in its immediate post-Hoggart/Williams phase, turned to most often. As David Forgacs notes, his ideas remain important because they help us think about the emergence of a popular new right. The reason for this is not that the new right is an equivalent to fascism, but that alternatives to the new right are as dispersed and fragmented as they were to fascism. In this situation, 'educative alliances' which call upon minority and 'subaltern' (but *not* 'unpopular') cultural values and discourses rather than monocultural and scientific/expert values and skills have real potential. It is these alliances which constitute the 'national popular'.

Gramsci, unlike Louis Althusser, thought about culture and power more than ideology and science. David Forgacs describes the conditions in Italy that enabled this – in particular the absence of a national culture and language. Again these historical conditions are especially worth recalling because they anticipate the multicultural condition in which most post-industrial nation-states now exist.

Further reading: Bhabha 1990; Gramsci 1971, 1978; Laclau 1977; Laclau and Mouffe 1985.

S.D.

1

The term 'national-popular' is a relatively new addition to the conceptual luggage of the British left and, of concepts originating in the work of
Gramsci, it has been one of the slowest to arrive here. Its presence in the
late '70s and '80s can be partly explained, I believe, by the toughening of
the political climate which has taken place in this period and by the
weakening of the grip of Althusserian Marxism upon certain sectors of
the new left. In the mid-seventies, the Gramsci being discussed was
mediated through the filter of Althusser, whose writings became widely
known in English during the same period (the early '70s) and who had
drawn on the Italian communist's work in several important respects.
Yet the figure that emerged through this 'French connection' was one
that was sanitized by Althusserian scientism. One paid this Gramsci due
homage for having brought ideology from heaven to earth by incarnat-
ing it in material institutions and social practices and for having developed a non-economistic model for analysing conjunctures as
asymmetrical relations of forces not reducible to a single all-englobing
contradiction. But his 'absolute historicism', his collapsing together of
philosophy, politics, religion and ideology, and his conception of
Marxism as involving an intellectual and moral reformation were considered too embarrassingly primitive to be given serious attention by
rigorous Marxist theoreticians. For as long as Althusserianism retained
its cultural prestige as a kind of orthodoxy, the distinguishing wedge
that Althusser and Poulantzas had driven between Gramsci's positive
work of political analysis and his historicist Marxism remained operative
and effectively served to suppress parts of his writings. The turn-about
that is now taking place, by which these suppressed parts are coming
to the fore, involves a reaction against the political impasse towards
which Althusser's later formulations on ideology, science and the subject tend. For Althusser's radical anti-historicism and anti-humanism
make problematical the moment of acquisition of mass revolutionary
consciousness by implicitly polarizing on the one hand a mass of
subjects-in-ideology and on the other the bearers of science, the intellectuals working in the van of the party. The moment of a liberatory mass
action against oppression is thus radically deferred, taken off the
agenda. Yet, at a time when the tough and flexible ideological resources
of Thatcherism have proved capable of mobilizing a large popular base,
the dangers of this kind of impasse become clear. Moreover, the last
decade in Britain has seen a renewed spate of militancy among groups

and social elements without a strict party or uniform class collocation – the women's movement, black people, lesbians and gay men, unemployed youth, students, nuclear disarmament, community pressure groups and so on – which the traditional left has been uncertain of how to relate to itself or to channel, and which have tended to jostle together in a relatively loose and unco-ordinated way beneath or alongside the ideological umbrella of the Labour Party. It is these two things arrayed against one another – the new state formation and the heterogeneous oppositional forces – which produce the need for a concept like the national-popular.

2

In Italy, where published extracts of Gramsci's prison writings began circulating immediately after the end of the Second World War, the national-popular was treated largely as a *cultural* concept and associated with progressive realist forms in literature, cinema and the other arts, which the Italian Communist Party (PCI) began to back in the '40s and '50s. 'National-popular' became a sort of slogan for forms of art that were rooted both in the national tradition and in popular life, and as such it became identified with an artistic style or styles. In this form, the term was to become the symbolic target of stringent criticism in the '60s from the Italian new left, who interpreted it as the cornerstone of a 'typically idealist operation' by which Gramsci had allegedly cast the intellectuals and their collective incarnation, the PCI, in the role of inheritors of nineteenth century radical bourgeois culture. 'Gramsci's national-popular', a critic wrote, 'ends up . . . being the cage within which all attempts at renewal turn out to be constrained by the iron laws of tradition and the Italian social "status quo".' The concept was seen as involving a double terminological slide – *national* replaced *international* and *popular* replaced *proletarian*. This in turn was symptomatic of a political elision of revolution into reformism, the parliamentary road and a form of political democracy based on broad class alliances: in short, the strategy of the PCI since the end of the war.

In Britain, the national-popular has been received and used as a *political* concept and identified with the notion of popular-democratic struggles without a specific class character which can be articulated in relation to the struggle of labour against capital. In this form, the concept has been involved in discussions of whether certain ideologies have a necessary class-belonging or whether an economistic perspective can be transcended and a broad ideological front theorized in its stead. It has also been involved in debate about how various forms of oppression are related to each other and to the class struggle, about whether the state in capitalist society is an instrument of bourgeois class rule or a site of class compromises with space for expansive democratization, and about how statist models of socialist struggle might be overcome by a broader theorization of struggle on several fronts in civil society and the state.

These two applications or interpretations of the national-popular concept make curious bedfellows. Although in each case practices of class alliance are involved, there is a substantial difference of emphasis: the first is cultural, the second political. How did this come about? And how is it that, in its cultural form, it was accused of being a conservative notion, inhibiting cultural change? I suggest that Gramsci's concept is in fact an integral one, whose cultural and political faces overlap and fuse; that not to understand this is to make only a partial reading and therefore to lay oneself open to a misreading of it (as the early, culturalist, reading was); and that the only way to reappropriate the concept in full is to make an excursus through Gramsci's writings, to see how the term emerges and the meanings it assumes within them. The present article is intended to do no more than provide the spade-work of textual reconstruction that will make this reappropriation possible.

3

It was in response to the conjuncture of ascendant fascism in Italy and the ebb-tide of revolution in the West that Gramsci began to elaborate the concept of the national-popular. The period was between 1924 and 1926. Within these two years leading up to his arrest, he returned from Moscow and Vienna, took over the leadership of the PCI from Amadeo Bordiga, and imposed a new strategic line on the party. This involved an implicit self-criticism of his own earlier 'workerism', his concentration, in the period 1919–21, on the factory councils in northern industry as organs of workers' control and as political units of socialist democracy.

Gramsci identified in Italy a highly advanced, but very small, industrial proletariat concentrated in the north-west of the peninsula; a large, but often ideologically backward peasantry, much of it located in the south and islands; a large stratum of petty-bourgeois intellectuals who exercised a degree of ideological control over the proletariat and peasantry and who, although themselves traditionally hegemonized by the bourgeoisie, tended to waver in the way they identified their class interest. By the time Gramsci launched his turn against Bordiga's leadership, fascism had installed itself in power by a class alliance between the northern industrial bourgeoisie and the large landowners with the crucial support of the petty bourgeoisie. Although it had not yet outlawed the PCI and other opposition parties, it had been conducting systematic repression of Communist activities and arresting Communist personnel. On Gramsci's reckoning, a political strategy based exclusively on the proletariat led by a vanguard party in isolation from other social forces was quite inadequate as a strategy to defeat fascism. It was necessary, rather, to construct a class alliance between three principal groups – the northern proletariat, the southern peasantry and the petty-bourgeois intelligentsia – under the hegemony of the proletariat, in order not only to provide a mass base for political action but also to prise open the interstices of the north–south industrial–landowner alliance.

For Gramsci, an immediate transition from fascism to socialism was improbable, not least because 'the existing armed forces, given their composition, cannot at once be won over' (Gramsci 1978: 406). An interlude was therefore necessary in which the liberal-democratic political structures were restored to power. It is thus in a context of a disarticulation and ideological disintegration of consent for fascism, a context in which, nevertheless, direct seizure of power is ruled out because 'the state apparatus is far more resistant than is often possible to believe' (Gramsci 1978: 409), that Gramsci puts forward the concept of the national-popular in an embryonic, tactical form:

> For all the capitalist countries a fundamental problem is posed – the problem of the transition from the united front tactic, understood in a general sense, to a specific tactic which confronts the concrete problems of national life and operates on the basis of the popular forces as they are historically determined. (Gramsci 1978: 410)

In the prison notebooks, written between 1929 and 1935, the national-popular concept is closely bound up with that of Jacobinism, which in Gramsci means a form of political domination based on the ability to overcome a narrow economic-corporate conception of a class or class-fraction and form *expansive, universalizing* alliances with other classes and class-fractions whose interests can be made to be seen as coinciding with those of the hegemonic class. Hegemony, in turn, differs from Lenin's conception of proletarian dictatorship because it involves ideological and not just political domination – in other words a coming to consciousness of a coincidence of interests. Only by breaking with an economistic correlation between ideology and class was Gramsci able to think this expansion of the concept of hegemony. Only one of the two fundamental classes – bourgeoisie and proletariat – can, however, be hegemonic. In the French Revolution, the radical bourgeoisie became hegemonic in the phase of Jacobin domination by universalizing and expanding its class interests to incorporate those of the urban artisans and the peasantry. The same process must be repeated in Italy, for Gramsci, by the proletariat in a socialist revolution. The class must secure hegemony over the peasants and the other intermediate social strata by making them conscious of a shared interest. Hegemony is thus a process of radiating out from the Communist Party and the working class a *collective will* which is national-popular:

> Any formation of a national-popular collective will is impossible, unless the great mass of peasant farmers bursts *simultaneously* into political life. That was Machiavelli's intention through the reform of the militia, and it was achieved by the Jacobins in the French Revolution. . . . All history from 1815 onwards shows the efforts of the traditional classes to prevent the formation of a collective will of this kind, and to maintain 'economic-corporate' power in an international system of passive equilibrium. (Gramsci 1971: 132)

In his notes on the Risorgimento, Gramsci observed how the democratic republican leaders around Mazzini and the Action Party failed to generalize their struggle beyond the radical bourgeoisie and win the support of the peasantry. They were thus subsumed and defeated by the Moderates under Cavour, who were able to construct a hegemonic alliance of the bourgeoisie with the southern landowners, an alliance whose continuation was secured in the state through transformism (*ad hoc* ministerial coalitions) and by the economic subjection of the South to the North in a colonial relationship offset for the big landowners by protectionist policies. This 'chapter of past history' bears on the concrete relations of force in the 1920s and '30s because of its historical parallel with the PCI at the time of the rise to power of fascism. This party too had failed to become hegemonic because of its inability to carry out the Jacobin task of linking countryside to city – peasantry to proletariat, south to north – to form a national-popular collective will. In its place, the Fascist Party had carried out a reform-revolution or passive revolution, based on the defensive, transformist alliance of the industrial bourgeoisie, big landowners and petty bourgeoisie, which involved no fundamental reorganization of the economic structure – only its technical modernization along rational 'Fordist' lines – coupled with an increase in state coercion and the securing of mass popular consent in civil society.

At a political level, then, there are four points to be noted about the national-popular concept. It was elaborated in response to fascism, a conservative social bloc made up of heterogeneous economic groups with a permanently mobilized mass base, possessing organizational reserves (military, ideological) which rule out a frontal attack (war of manoeuvre) and favour a construction of hegemony (war of position) as the correct strategy to defeat it. It was dependent on the relative numerical weakness of the Italian proletariat. It involved the formation of a collective will through the building of a mass party, where a number of social classes and class-fractions are successfully hegemonized by the party and the proletariat. It was conceived of as a transitional stage leading to the dictatorship of the proletariat, to socialist democracy (soviets) as opposed to bourgeois democracy (parliament). These concepts underwent no substantial modification at a political level, as a strategic perspective, between the period in which they were first formulated (1924–26) and the time of Gramsci's death in 1937. They were, however, qualitatively deepened by being developed in cultural and ideological terms.

4

The entry in the prison notebooks headed 'Concept of national-popular' has no overtly political content. It discusses, instead, the problem of why Italian literature did not, with a few exceptions, have a wide popular readership in Italy and why Italian newspapers, which since the late nineteenth century had adopted the practice of serializing fiction to increase circulation, were publishing predominantly French and not Italian authors. Gramsci's answer is that in Italy

> neither a popular artistic literature nor a local production of 'popular' literature exists because 'writers' and 'people' do not have the same conception of the world. In other words the feelings of the

people are not lived by the writers as their own, nor do the writers have a 'national educative' function: they have not and do not set themselves the problem of elaborating popular feelings after having relived them and made them their own. (Gramsci 1985: 206–7)

Italian readers therefore turn to French writers, who had this national function, because in France there existed a 'close and dependent relationship between people-nation and intellectuals' which Italian readers feel.

In several notes containing the phrase 'national-popular' (or 'popular-national', 'people-nation', 'nation-people') one finds this theme of the separation between intellectuals and the people in Italy (which is often, as here, contrasted with France). This separation was traditional both in that it went back a long way into Italian history and in that it had been traditionally remarked upon, notably in the Risorgimento where it had become a leitmotif among democratic intellectuals (Mazzini, De Sanctis and so forth) who had seen the Renaissance as producing a cleavage between culture and the people, between knowledge and popular life. In fact, much of what Gramsci writes about the national-popular is a materialist recasting of these abstract and idealist formulations by a re-reading of Italian cultural history.

In a long discussion of the Renaissance in notebook 5, he traces the dualism back to a separation, occurring in the fourteenth and fifteenth centuries, of a literary and philosophical élite from the commercial, manufacturing and financial bourgeoisie. The latter had acquired political domination in the period of the Communes (from the twelfth to the fourteenth century) but had been unable to consolidate it because it had failed to go beyond its economic-corporate limits and become hegemonic as a class. The return at a cultural level to classicism – humanism – was therefore a restoration which

like every restoration, . . . assimilated and developed, better than the revolutionary class it had politically suffocated, the ideological principles of the defeated class, which had not been able to go beyond its corporate limits and create the superstructures of an integral society. Except that this development was 'abstract', it remained the patrimony of an intellectual caste and had no contact with the people-nation. (Gramsci 1985: 234)

Humanism and the Renaissance in Italy were thus 'the phenomenon of an aristocracy removed from the people-nation'. Whereas in the other European countries the exported Renaissance produced a progressive scientific intelligentsia which played a crucial role in the formation of the modern national states, in Italy itself it led to the involutionary Counter-Reformation and the ideological triumph of the Catholic intellectual hierarchy. This outcome was itself linked to two factors to which Gramsci's analysis assigns great importance. The first was the fact that Italy had been the centre of the Roman Empire and then, by 'translation', of the Catholic Church, both of which exercised their power through cosmopolitan (international) intellectual castes. The second was the failure of a common national vernacular to develop in the peninsula, where instead two culturally prestigious written cosmopolitan languages (first Latin and then, after the sixteenth century, literary Tuscan) had dominated over a large number of less prestigious spoken dialects. The political disunity of Italy, of which Machiavelli complained in *The Prince*, was compounded by these factors. In the sixteenth century, the Papacy blocked the Protestant Reformation and with it the possibility of forming a modern national state. In the nineteenth century, it again constituted a major obstacle to national unification by its anti-liberalism and by jealously guarding its temporal power over central Italy. At the same time, the regional and cultural heterogeneity of the peninsula could be read off from the multiplicity of dialects, which acted as a practical obstacle to the diffusion of any national culture. The Italian nation had thus been more a rhetorical or legal entity than a felt cultural reality, existing at most for the intellectual and ruling élites but not for the masses. 'Nation' and 'people' did not coincide in Italian history:

> One should note that in many languages 'national' and 'popular' are either synonymous or nearly so (they are in Russian, in German, where *völkisch* has an even more intimate meaning of race, and in the Slavonic languages in general; in France the meaning of 'national' already includes a more politically elaborated notion of 'popular' because it is related to the concept of 'sovereignty': national sovereignty and popular sovereignty have, or had, the same value). In Italy, the term 'national' has an ideologically very restricted meaning, and does not in any case coincide with 'popular' because in Italy the intellectuals are distant from the people, i.e. from the 'nation'. They are tied instead to a caste tradition that has never been broken by a strong popular or national political movement from below. (Gramsci 1985: 208)

What is the aim of these meanderings through Italian history and culture, meanderings that make up a substantial proportion of the prison notes as a whole? The answer is that they flow into Gramsci's *political* project. They are readings of Italian cultural history undertaken in order to understand the structural reasons for the lack of any organic national-popular movement in the past and thus in order to work out the preconditions for such a movement in the present. 'Culture' in Gramsci is the sphere in which ideologies are diffused and organized, in which hegemony is constructed and can be broken and reconstructed. An essential part of the process by which the party builds the apparatuses of its social power is the molecular diffusion of a new humanism, an intellectual and moral reformation – in other words a new ideology, a new common sense based on historical materialism. A popular reformation of this kind is what has been lacking in Italian history, and Gramsci's notes on the national-popular reveal the extent to which the cosmopolitan traditions of the Italian intellectuals had impeded the molecular ideological activity by which such a reformation could be brought about:

> The lay forces have failed in their historical task as educators and elaborators of the intellect and the moral awareness of the people-nation. They have been incapable of satisfying the intellectual needs of the people precisely because they have failed to represent a lay culture, because they have not known how to elaborate a modern 'humanism' able to reach right to the simplest and most uneducated classes, as was necessary from the national point of view, and because they have been tied to an antiquated world, narrow, abstract, too individualistic or caste-like. (Gramsci 1985: 211)

When the prison notebooks were first published in Italy between 1948 and 1951, there was much talk on the left there about a 'national-popular culture' and the need for the intellectuals to contribute to the production of such a culture. As I have mentioned, this culture was identified with realism, and thus the national-popular slogan was neatly inserted into the discussions on socialist realism and progressive or critical bourgeois realism that were common currency among left literary circles around that period. Yet, though Gramsci's prison notes on literature certainly reveal that his own personal tastes ran to progressive realism, such as the nineteenth century Russian novel, and that he tended to see modernist writing as intellectualistic, coterie art, it was a fundamental misappropriation of the national-popular concept to identify it with a particular type of art in this way. When Gramsci wrote that the model of national-popular literature was constituted by the Greek tragedians, Shakespeare and the great Russian novelists, he did not mean that an Italian national-popular literature would have to resemble those kinds of text. 'National-popular' designates not a cultural content but, as we have seen, the possibility of an alliance of interests and feelings between different social agents which varies according to the structure of each national society. A future Italian national-popular literature, which will result from a socialist transformation of society in which the working class creates its own organic intellectuals, cannot therefore resemble the national-popular literature that developed in the era of bourgeois revolutions elsewhere in Europe. It has clearly been one of the hardest points for Gramsci's interpreters to grasp that he cannot specify the content of a national-popular culture that has not yet formed, but only the social preconditions of its formation. It is, as he points out, an idealist error to think that a national-popular culture will resemble any hitherto existing cultural style, because those past styles have all been the product of social formations in which culture has been stratified into high and low and dominated by specialist intellectuals without organic links with the broad popular masses. 'Popular culture' has thus been constructed as the culture of the dominated classes in antithesis to 'artistic culture', a division that is perpetuated and reproduced daily by capitalist control of the organs of both high and popular culture. The theoretical break Gramsci made with his contemporaries in Marxist cultural theory was to think of a whole cultural formation or cultural space as a unity in which to intervene. As he points out, discussing the question of how to create a new literature:

> The most common prejudice is this: that the new literature should be identified with an artistic school of intellectual origins, as was the case with Futurism. The premiss of the new literature cannot but be historical, political and popular: it must work towards the elaboration of what already exists, whether polemically or in other ways does not matter. What matters is that it sink its roots in the humus of popular culture as it is, with its tastes and tendencies and with its moral and intellectual world, even if it is backward and conventional. (Gramsci 1985: 102)

The formation of a national-popular culture in Italy would mean confronting and overcoming the same obstacles (dialects, folklore, local particularisms) as the formation of a national language. Because of this, what Gramsci says about language gives us the clearest example of how he conceptualized cultural change as a whole. In the prison notebooks, parallels are implicitly established between a series of dominant–subordinate couplings: language–dialects, philosophy–common sense (or folklore), high culture–popular culture, intellectuals–people, party–masses. The point in each case is not to impose the former on the latter but to construct an educative alliance between them ('Every relationship of "hegemony" is necessarily an educational relationship') so that one establishes an 'organic unity between theory and practice, between intellectual strata and popular masses, between rulers and ruled' which constitutes democratic centralism. The spreading of a national language is the paradigm for all these other relationships:

> Since the process of formation, spread and development of a unified national language occurs through a whole complex of molecular processes, it helps to be aware of the entire process as a whole in order to be able to intervene actively in it with the best possible results. One need not consider this intervention as 'decisive' and imagine that the ends proposed will all be reached in detail, i.e. that one will obtain a *specific* unified language. One will obtain *a unified language*, if it is a necessity, and the organized intervention will speed up the already existing processes. What this language will be, one cannot foresee or establish: in any case, if the intervention is 'rational', it will be organically tied to tradition, and this is of no small importance in the economy of culture. (Gramsci 1971: 350)

As well as being a paradigm for the other hegemonic relationships, language is also their social medium. Thus what Gramsci is talking about here is a process of constructing ideological hegemony among a wide range of social strata. Just as, at present, 'the national-popular mass is excluded from learning the educated language, since the highest level of the ruling class, which traditionally speaks standard Italian, passes it on from generation to generation', so the popular masses are excluded from high culture and '"official" conceptions of the world' and possess instead the unelaborated and unsystematic conceptions of folklore and common sense. Hence in order to be hegemonized, these strata must be addressed through a medium adapted to their different cultural positions. There will not, for instance, be a single party newspaper but a whole party press whose various organs can adapt their tone and content to different readerships.

5

With these cultural dimensions, then, the national-popular concept clearly developed beyond the immediate conjunctural considerations from which it had originated in 1924–26, where it was linked to the Comintern tactic of the united front with the socialists (1921–26), and beyond the political expedient of inter-class and inter-party alliances as a temporary anti-fascist strategy – the Popular Front line of 1935, to which it has often been reductively and polemically assimilated. It became a *historical* strategy, dependent both on the historic absence in Italy of a revolution from below, on a specifically Italian economic and social structure with special disequilibria (combining advanced and third world characteristics, for example) and also on the development of capitalist societies in the West generally, as Gramsci witnessed them being transformed by American forms of social and economic management and elaborating extensive ideological resistances.

Nor is it hard to see why, at a general level, the concept retains its validity. It recognizes the specificity of national conditions and traditions. It valorizes civil society as a key site of struggle. It emphasizes the role of ideological reorganization and struggle. It identifies struggles common to more than one social class, fraction or group which can be strategically linked together. It recognizes that different social elements can, and do, act in terms not only of economic or ideological self-interest but also in terms of shared interests. Yet it also leaves a number of problematical questions very much open. By what means does one initially win the consent of other forces and movements? How can what Gramsci called the economic-corporate interests of a class or social group then be transcended in a higher collective will? How can this will, once established, be secured and prevented from disintegrating back into competing sectoral interests? For Gramsci these problems were, after 1926, posed largely in theory, and they tended to be resolved in the notebooks within the formula of party centralism and the belief in the transitional nature of any form of interclassist alliance: in other words within a still essentially Leninist perspective of the single party and the replacement of parliament by soviets.

The crucial practical problem of the national-popular lies in this: that there is often a narrow distinction between class alliances that are effectively hegemonic for the working class, class alliances that are merely federative groupings around particular issues or at particular times (for instance elections), and class alliances that can be tipped the other way and reorganized under the hegemony of the bourgeoisie. The PCI in the 1944–48 period, after Gramsci's death (1937), not only conceded too much to its alliance partners in terms of the restoration of the old economic and political infrastructures and the maintenance of fascist personnel, notably in the police and militia. It also failed to radiate a collective will of a genuinely oppositional type into the rank and file at a time when the relations of forces were regrouping to the right, and it thus ended up excluded from the executive in 1947 and defeated at the polls in 1948.

That these practices were not simple realizations of Gramsci's theories but political choices overdetermined by all sorts of strategic choices need not be spelt out. Gramsci had not only stressed, as we saw, the essentially transitional nature of the constituent assembly under proletarian leadership but he had also emphasized that the assembly was to have been a site of struggle against 'all projects of peaceful reform, demonstrating to the Italian working class how the only possible solution in Italy resides in the proletarian revolution'. Nevertheless, the questions of when a class alliance contains or does not contain a collective will and of when it lays itself open to reorganization under bourgeois hegemony were posed starkly by the Italian Communists' practical development of Gramsci's theories. And they remain of great actuality in the West today.

Part IV Ethnicity and multiculturalism

4 Gayatri Chakravorty Spivak and Sneja Gunew

Questions of multiculturalism

EDITOR'S INTRODUCTION

Originally recorded for Australian radio, this exchange mentions a number of writers unknown outside Australia – and those not familiar with Australian literature should note that Beverley Farmer and Patrick White are WASP writers. The local references, however, support an insightful discussion of some ethical and political problems posed by the recent diasporas from poor to rich countries. It focuses on questions of authenticity and representation. Once a society is recognized as being heterogeneous – and in particular multicultural – then central institutions (art-funding bodies, universities, state policy and advisory committees, professional associations, even boards of large corporations) begin to choose representatives from minority communities to help in the work of administration. How to deal with the 'speaking as' (e.g. as an African-American, a woman, a gay, a Chicano, a Jew, a Caribbean) and the 'unauthenticities' that this process of selection entails?

Gayatri Spivak suggests that it is important to recognize that tokenism, and by implication the whole multiculturalist shift, forces us all into positions in which we are distanced both from dominant ideology and from our cultural heritages, and that this proliferation of 'unauthenticity' has a positive aspect. This shift makes it harder to ignore the history and the material forces that underpin the construction of cultural identities, especially those that underpin the decline of monoculturalism. Equally, it makes it harder to accept the traditional monoculturalist division between, on the one hand, a private sphere sheltering authenticity and, on the other, a public sphere dominated by members of the hegemonic social fraction. Finally, it makes it easier to accept that 'others' (those who do not fit the dominant embodiment of the national citizen) also have subjectivities constructed across many registers, which do not necessarily work in harmony.

Further reading: Amin 1989; Gunew 1990; Minh-ha 1989; Sangari 1987; Spivak 1988a, 1988b, 1990.

S.D.

SG We might begin with the whole notion of authenticity – a question that keeps coming up in relation to the kind of writing that I am publicizing at the moment. I now refer to it as non-Anglo-Celtic rather than Migrant writing, since within Australia, Migrant connotes an inability to speak English. Thus, it is the writing of non-Anglo-Celts but in English. The question that keeps arising in relation to this is the question of authenticity. And it takes various forms, but I suppose one way of, in a sense, caricaturing it but, also, making it accessible is: 'Aren't Patrick White's Middle Europeans or Beverley Farmer's Greeks just as authentic as the Greeks created by πO's poetry or by Antigone Kefala?' In a sense, putting the question this way covers over, or makes invisible, other forms, other questions that could be posed, such as: 'But why do these Anglo-Celts have access to publishing, to writing, to be part of Australian literature, and why are other writers like Kefala, Ania Walwicz, Rosa Cappiello, etc., not seen as part of these cultural productions, why aren't they given a full measure of cultural franchise?' In fact, in some senses, far from being invisible, the Migrant has always been constructed within Australian discursive formations, not just literature; and in literary forms the first such construction was Nino Culotta, who was an Irish journalist posing as an Italian, and wrote the most famous book for many, many decades about being an Italian immigrant trying to make it in Australia. And this book, I remember, was given to numerous immigrants as they arrived in Australia as some kind of explication of their status within the community, and is quite horrendous in all sorts of ways.

GCS For me, the question 'Who should speak?' is less crucial than 'Who will listen?' 'I will speak for myself as a Third World person' is an important position for political mobilization today. But the real demand is that, when I speak from that position, I should be listened to seriously; not with that kind of benevolent imperialism, really, which simply says that because I happen to be an Indian or whatever . . . A hundred years ago it was impossible for me to speak, for the precise reason that makes it only too possible for me to speak in certain circles now. I see in that a kind of reversal, which is again a little suspicious. On the other hand, it is very important to hold on to it as a slogan in our time. The question of 'speaking *as*' involves a distancing from oneself. The moment I have to think of the ways in which I will speak as an Indian, or as a feminist, the ways in which I will speak as a woman, what I am doing is trying to generalize myself, make myself a representative, trying to distance myself from some kind of inchoate speaking *as such*. There are many subject positions which one must inhabit; one is not just one thing. That is when a political consciousness comes in. So that in fact, for the person who does the 'speaking as' something, it is a problem of distancing from one's self, whatever that self might be. But when the cardcarrying listeners, the hegemonic people, the dominant people, talk about listening to someone 'speaking as' something or the other, I think *there* one encounters a problem. When *they* want to hear an Indian speaking as an Indian, a Third World woman speaking as a Third World woman, they cover over the fact of the ignorance that they are allowed to possess, into a kind of homogenization.

SG Yes, and they choose what parts they want to hear, and they choose what they then do with this material; and what seems to happen in very crude ways, within the context of multiculturalism, is that certain people are elevated very quickly to those who speak for *all* immigrants: in terms of funding, and in terms of the dissemination of their work, etc. As a result, you don't hear about the rest, because 'we have covered that', and those few token figures function as a very secure alibi. If you look at the proportion of, for example, multicultural, non-Anglo-Celtic artists who get funded by the Australia Council, they are a very small percentage, and often the same ones every year. Because it is, in fact, an incredible job to educate oneself to know just what is in the field, and who else is doing things. It requires a lot of labour; it is so much easier to have these recurrent token figures.

GCS Proust in *A la recherche*, when someone is criticizing Françoise's French, writes 'What is French but bad Latin?' So from that point of view, one can't distinguish, you can't say that it is a French position or a Roman position. This is what he is pointing at – the moment you say, 'This is a white position', again you are homogenizing. I think there is safety in specificity rather than in those labels.

SG This is what I was trying to refer to earlier when I was saying the question usually gets posed in the ways of asking: 'Yes, but aren't Patrick White's Middle Europeans authentic?' That is not the issue, because the whole *notion* of authenticity, of the authentic migrant experience, is one that comes to us constructed by hegemonic voices; and so, what one has to tease out is what is *not* there. One way of doing this (if one has knowledge from a particular culture), is to say: But look, this is what is left out, this is what is covered over; this kind of construction is taking place, this kind of reading is being privileged or, these series of readings are being privileged; and then to ask, What readings are not privileged, what is not there, what questions can't be asked?

GCS Subordinate people use this also; and we are not without a sense of irony: we use it. I talk a lot, right? And when I get very excited I interrupt people; and I am making a joke, but in fact it is never perceived as a joke unless I tell them. I will quite often say, 'You know, in my culture it shows interest and respect if someone interrupts': and immediately there are these very pious faces, and people allow me to interrupt. It is not as if we don't perceive the homogenization; we exploit it, why not?

SG So that what you have as one of the strategies of some of the writers that I work with, is that they play a kind of stage Migrant and poke fun at, and parody in all sorts of ways, these so-called authentic Migrant constructions. I am thinking here of the work of πO, the work of Ania Walwicz . . .

GCS In fact, tokenization goes with ghettoization. These days, I am constantly invited to things so that I will present the Third World point of view; when you are perceived as a token, you are also silenced in a certain way because, as you say, if you have been brought there it has been covered, they needn't worry about it anymore, you salve their conscience. In the United States, being an Indian also brings a certain very curious problem. Over the centuries we have had histories of, let's say, Indian indentured labour being taken to the Afro-Caribbean. After the change of regimes in certain African nations, Indians moved from Africa, then to Britain; then Indians in waves in the early '60's, professional Indians, went to the United States as part of the brain drain. These Indians who are spread out over the world, for different kinds of historical reasons, they are diasporic . . .

SG You could multiply this by the Greeks and the Italians in Australia, and numerous other ethnic groups who, for various reasons, have had to leave their original countries and move to other ones.

GCS The Indian community in the United States is the only coloured community which came in with the brain drain. This is quite different from Indians and Pakistanis in Britain, and certainly very different from Indians of the Afro-Caribbean diaspora. And therefore we are used as an alibi, since we don't share the same history of oppression with the local Blacks, the east Asians, and the Hispanics; on the other hand, our skins are not white, and since most of us are post-colonials we were trained in the British way, so there is a certain sort of Anglomania in the United States, we can be used as affirmative-action alibis.

SG Yes, this happens to some extent, too, with Jewish immigrants, often refugees, who came at various stages to Australia. They too, are used in that sort of sense of affirmative action. For all sorts of reasons they have, some of them, come to very prominent positions and so they can be wheeled in very easily to say: 'Of course, this is not an Anglo establishment, a predominantly Anglo establishment, – we've got x, y, z.' So a similar kind of alibi operates. One of the things, though, that I wanted to hear you talk about more was a notion you brought up yesterday, about this idea of earning the right to criticize. As I understand it, this can be a trap that is provided by a certain kind of privilege that comes with being this sort of token who is constantly brought in. I wonder if you could say more about that.

GCS It is a problem that is very close to my heart because I teach, after all, abroad. I will have in an undergraduate class, let's say, a young, white male student, politically-correct, who will say: 'I am only a bourgeois white male, I can't speak.' In that situation – it's peculiar, because I am in the position of power and their teacher and, on the other hand, I am not a bourgeois white male – I say to them: 'Why not develop a certain degree of rage against the history that has written such an abject script for you that you are silenced?' Then you begin to investigate what it is that silences you, rather than take this very deterministic position – since my skin colour is this, since my sex is this, I cannot speak. I call these things, as you know, somewhat derisively, chromatism: basing everything on skin colour – 'I am white, I can't speak' – and genitalism: depending on what kind of genitals you have, you can or cannot speak in certain situations. From this position, then, I say you will of course not speak in the same way about the Third World material, but if you make it your task not only to learn what is going on there through language, through specific programmes of study, but also at the same time through a *historical* critique of your position as the investigating person, then you will see that you have earned the right to criticize, and you will be heard. When you take the position of not doing your homework – 'I will not criticize because of my accident of birth, the historical accident' – that is a much more pernicious position. In one way you take a risk to criticize, of criticizing something which is *Other* –

something which you used to dominate. I say that you have to take a certain risk: to say 'I won't criticize' is salving your conscience, and allowing you not to do any homework. On the other hand, if you criticize having earned the right to do so, then you are indeed taking a risk and you will probably be made welcome, and can hope to be judged with respect.

SG Perhaps the other side of the dilemma, though, is the sort of trap that people who are wheeled in as token figures speaking for those marginalized groups can fall into, where they deny their own privileged position. You were saying earlier, for example, that in a classroom situation you are the one with the power *vis-à-vis* the white Anglo-Saxon student. Similarly, I think that one forgets when one speaks within very obviously privileged academic contexts about, say, immigrant groups within Australia, that one is also very much in danger of homogenizing, and of misrepresenting, and of not really following through those questions carefully enough; distinguishing carefully enough between those differences that one speaks 'in the name of'. That business of speaking 'in the name of' is something about which I have a real phobia, and it is very difficult to think up strategies for undermining that.

GCS And I don't think, really, that we will solve the problem today talking to each other; but, on the other hand, I think it has to be kept alive as a problem. It is not a solution, the idea of the disenfranchised speaking for themselves, or the radical critics speaking for them; this question of representation, self-representation, representing others, is a problem. On the other hand, we cannot put it under the carpet with demands for authentic voices; we have to remind ourselves that, as we do this, we might be compounding the problem even as we are trying to solve it. And there has to be a persistent critique of what one is up to, so that it doesn't get all bogged down in this homogenization; constructing the Other simply as an object of knowledge, leaving out the real Others because of the ones who are getting access into public places due to these waves of benevolence and so on. I think as long as one remains aware that it is a very problematic field, there is some hope.

SG Yes, and one of the strategies that one has learnt from the Women's Movement, for example, is to make sure that you are constantly involved in political campaigns, that you are in touch with what is happening, that you are in touch with the very specific politics of trying to bring about certain reforms. So in a similar way, I suppose, one of the ways in the area of multiculturalism is to be very alert to what is happening with the various immigrant groups in terms of cultural politics. The kinds of things that are going on, the kinds of questions that are not being asked, what people are doing that has never been heard or seen – these are the sorts of issues.

GCS Can you give some specific examples of problems of cultural politics in the Australian context?

SG Well, for example, I was walking along Glebe Road, last week, and looked in a shop window and suddenly saw, amongst the clothing (this was a tailor's shop), a poem hanging there. And I walked in, and found a wonderful friend of mine, Nihat Ziyalan, who is a Turkish poet; and this is his way – one of the few ways that he can get heard – of making his work accessible to whoever is passing by. And people do apparently come in and talk to him about his work; but he certainly is not receiving any funding at the moment. Always there is this sense of voices in the wilderness, that are never going to get heard, not through the regular channels, be it the Australia Council, be it SBS. In the case of the latter, the ethnic broadcasting television station which is supposed to be serving multiculturalist Australia, in reality they get most of their programmes from overseas, so it is Europe imported back into Australia, rather than seeing certain kinds of European or Asian or Middle Eastern groups within Australia and latching into those.

GCS This is the real problem, isn't it? We are back to some extent to where we started, the way in which one actually keeps talking about the same old things, that is to say: rather than look at the real problem of imperialism, to make it identical with the problems of immigrants; rather than look at the Third World at large, to make everything identical with the problem at home. This is, in fact, simply the old attitudes disguised in one way or another. This is the real difficulty with cultural politics. If you go, as I do, to African Literature Association conventions, what you notice is that the Black Americans – of course, when I generalize like this there are always notable exceptions – Black Americans are much more interested in the question of any Black tradition, whereas the Continental Africans are much more interested in the problems that they and their colleagues are making for themselves, in the problems of the various African nations, in the problems existing between European language productions in Africa, and what is happening to African languages as it's all getting organized into philosophy, the discipline of literature, and so on and so forth. What you really mark, is that it is the ones with United States passports who are trying to identify the problem of racism in the United States with what is happening in decolonized Africa.

SG So again, that's the question of homogenization and that refusal of specificity.

GCS Yes.

SG And I think another thing that you have been referring to, that notion of a diaspora, that the diasporic cultures are quite different from the culture that they came from originally, and that sort of distinction – an elementary distinction, and also one, of course, that history teaches us is not made, and needs to be made.

GCS You see these differences, in fact you feel them in the details of your daily life, because actually the system is not so blind – it's the benevolent ones who become blind in this way. I'll tell you a little story. I was at the Commonwealth Institute in London in March, to discuss some films made by Black Independent Film-makers in London (a wonderful group of people, I was very pleased they asked me), and one of the points I made to them was in fact (I am a bit of a broken record on this issue): 'You are diasporic Blacks in Britain, and you are connecting to the local lines of resistance in Britain, and you are therefore able to produce a certain kind of idiom of resistance; but don't forget the Third World at large, where you won't be able to dissolve everything into Black against White, as there is also Black against Black, Brown against Brown, and so on.' These young men and women thought I was asking them to connect with some kind of mystical ethnic origin because, of course, when they were brought into the places which they inhabit, their sense of the old country was from the nostalgic longing towards customs, cooking, and so on and so forth, that they saw in their families. And so they were rebelling against what is basically a generational problem, and transforming it into a total ignoring of what is going on in the Third World at large. On the other hand, the system knows I am a resident alien in the United States; at that point I was actually lecturing in Canada, at the University of Alberta. I crossed from upstate New York into Toronto (I carry an Indian passport) with no problem because, of course, an Indian resident in the United States would not, the thinking goes, want to become an illegal immigrant in Canada. Two days later, I went to London, I did my programme, and was returning back to Canada with the same passport, same resident alien's visa in the United States, and I was supposed to take a plane from Heathrow on Sunday. Air Canada says to me: 'We can't accept you.' I said: 'Why?' and she said: 'You need a visa to go to Canada.' I said: 'Look here, I am the same person, the same passport . . .' Indian cultural identity, right? but you become different. When it is from London, Indians can very well want to jump ship to Canada; I need a visa to travel from London to Canada on the same passport, but not from the United States. To cut a long story short, I was talking about a related problem to the Black men and women who had made the films, and then it happened in my own life. In the end, I had to stay another day, and telephone Canada and tell them that I could not give my seminar. I said to the woman finally before I left, in some bitterness: 'Just let me tell you one small thing: Don't say "We can't accept you", that sounds very bad from one human being to another; next time you should say: "The regulations are against it"; then we are both victims.' And the woman looked at me with such astonishment because, in Heathrow, a coloured woman wearing a sari does not speak to a white woman like this. There, I was indeed speaking as an Indian, in that particular situation. So in those kinds of things, once you begin to look at the way regulations work, you will see the differences *are* made among different kinds of Third World peoples – but not when one is being benevolent.

SG What is very much a question for me at the moment is that if you are constructed in one particular kind of language, what kinds of violence does it do to your subjectivity if one then has to move into another language, and suppress whatever selves or subjectivities were constructed by the first? And of course, some people have to pass through this process several times. And a small gesture towards beginning to understand this would be to create a demand for multi-lingual anthologies within Australia. There is an incredible and disproportionate resistance to presenting the general Australian public with immigrant writing *in English* even, but to have it in conjunction with the remainder of these repressed languages seems to be another battle which still has to be fought.

GCS One hears, for example, that some of the theoretical stuff that's produced, let's say, in France, is naturally accessible to people from Africa, from India, from these so-called natural places. If one looks at the history of post-Enlightenment theory, the major problem has been the problem of autobiography: how subjective structures can, in fact, give objective truth. During these same centuries, the Native Informant, who was found in these other places, his stuff was unquestioningly treated as the objective evidence for the founding of so-called sciences like ethnography, ethno-linguistics, comparative religion, and so on. So that, once again, the theoretical problems only relate to the person who knows. The person who *knows* has all of the problems of selfhood. The person who is *known*, somehow seems not to have a problematic self. These days, it is the same kind of agenda that is at work. Only the dominant self can be problematic; the self of the Other is authentic without a problem, naturally available to all kinds of complications. This is very frightening.

15 Cornel West

The new cultural politics of difference

EDITOR'S INTRODUCTION

Cornel West's essay can be read as a manifesto for intellectuals who work on behalf of the 'culture of difference'. It is aimed at helping us avoid the reductive ways of thinking that endanger such work – that is, it helps us to avoid those 'one-factor analyses' which 'lose touch' with the complexities of thought and action in the world, and which, in their simplifications, provide props for racism, sexism and monoculturalism. To escape such simplifications and to begin to provide an ethics for cultural workers, West turns to history. He presents a brief 'genealogy' of the decline of Eurocentrism and white suprematism – 'genealogy' being a word he borrows from Michel Foucault to refer to a history that supports current political practice. He argues that the task of 'demystification' (or ideology-critique) can only be carried out by those whose confidence and sense of the contemporary cultural-political structures is supported by a knowledge of Eurocentrism's history. Here cultural studies and history become indivisible.

Further reading: CCCS 1982; Gates 1986, 1987; Gilroy 1987; JanMohamed and Lloyd 1987; Spivak 1988a, 1988b.

S.D.

In the last few years of the twentieth century, there is emerging a significant shift in the sensibilities and outlooks of critics and artists. In fact, I would go so far as to claim that a new kind of cultural worker is in the making, associated with a new politics of difference. These new forms of intellectual consciousness advance new conceptions of the vocation of critic and artist, attempting to undermine the prevailing disciplinary divisions of labour in the academy, museum, mass media, and gallery networks while preserving modes of critique within the ubiquitous commodification of culture in the global village. Distinctive features of the new cultural politics of difference are to trash the monolithic and homogeneous in the name of diversity, multiplicity, and heterogeneity; to reject the abstract, general, and universal in light of the concrete, specific, and particular; and to historicize, contextualize, and pluralize by highlighting the contingent, provisional, variable, tentative, shifting, and changing. Needless to say, these gestures are not new in the history of criticism or art, yet what makes them novel – along with the cultural politics they produce – is how and what constitutes difference, the weight and gravity it is given in representation, and the way in which highlighting issues like exterminism, empire, class, race, gender, sexual orientation, age, nation, nature, and region at this historical moment acknowledges some discontinuity and disruption from previous forms of cultural critique. To put it bluntly, the new cultural politics of difference consists of creative responses to the precise circumstances of our present moment – especially those of marginalized First World agents who shun degraded self-representations, articulating instead their sense of the flow of history in light of the contemporary terrors, anxieties, and fears of highly commercialized North Atlantic capitalist cultures (with their escalating xenophobias against people of colour, Jews, women, gays, lesbians, and the elderly). The thawing, yet still rigid Second World ex-communist cultures (with increasing nationalist revolts against the legacy of hegemonic party henchmen), and the diverse cultures of the majority of inhabitants on the globe smothered by international communication cartels and repressive postcolonial elites (sometimes in the name of communism, as in Ethiopia), or starved by austere World Bank and IMF policies that subordinate them to the North (as in free-market capitalism in Chile), also locate vital areas of analysis in this new cultural terrain.

The new cultural politics of difference are neither simply oppositional in contesting the mainstream (or *male*stream) for inclusion, nor transgressive in the avant-gardist sense of shocking conventional bourgeois audiences. Rather, they are distinct articulations of talented (and usually privileged) contributors to culture who desire to align themselves with demoralized, demobilized, depoliticized, and disorganized people in order to empower and enable social action and, if possible, to enlist collective insurgency for the expansion of freedom, democracy, and individuality. This perspective impels these cultural critics and artists to reveal, as an integral component of their production, the very operations of power within their immediate work contexts (i.e., academy, museum, gallery, mass media). This strategy, however, also puts them in an inescapable double bind – while linking their activities to the fundamental, structural overhaul of these institutions, they often remain financially dependent on them. (So much for 'independent' creation.) For these critics of culture, theirs is a gesture that is simultaneously progressive *and* coopted. Yet, without social movement or political pressure from outside these institutions (extra-parliamentary and extra-curricular actions like the social movements of the recent past), transformation degenerates into mere accommodation or sheer stagnation, and the role of the 'coopted progressive' – no matter how fervent one's subversive rhetoric – is rendered more difficult. In this sense there can be no artistic breakthrough or social progress without some form of crisis in civilization – a crisis usually generated by organizations or collectivities that convince ordinary people to put their bodies and lives on the line. There is, of course, no guarantee that such pressure will yield the result one wants, but there is a guarantee that the status quo will remain or regress if no pressure is applied at all.

The new cultural politics of difference faces three basic challenges – intellectual, existential, and political. The intellectual challenge – usually cast as a methodological debate in these days in which academicist forms of expression have a monopoly on intellectual life – is how to think about representational practices in terms of history, culture, and society. How does one understand, analyse, and enact such practices today? An adequate answer to this question can be attempted only after one comes to terms with the insights and blindness of earlier attempts to grapple with the question in light of the evolving crisis in different histories, cultures, and societies. I shall sketch a brief genealogy – a history that highlights the contingent origins and often ignoble outcomes – of exemplary critical responses to the question.

THE INTELLECTUAL CHALLENGE

An appropriate starting point is the ambiguous legacy of the Age of Europe. Between 1492 and 1945, European breakthroughs in oceanic transportation, agricultural production, state consolidation, bureaucratization, industrialization, urbanization, and imperial dominion shaped the makings of the modern world. Precious ideals like the dignity of persons (individuality) or the popular accountability of institutions (democracy) were unleashed around the world. Powerful critiques of illegitimate authorities – of the Protestant Reformation against the Roman Catholic Church, the Enlightenment against state churches, liberal movements against absolutist states and feudal guild constraints, workers against managerial subordination, people of colour and Jews against white and gentile supremacist decrees, gays and lesbians against homophobic sanctions – were fanned and fuelled by these precious ideals refined within the crucible of the Age of Europe. Yet, the discrepancy between sterling rhetoric and lived reality, glowing principles and actual practices, loomed large.

By the last European century – the last epoch in which European domination of most of the globe was uncontested and unchallenged in a substantive way – a new world seemed to be stirring. At the height of England's reign as the major imperial European power, its exemplary cultural critic, Matthew Arnold, painfully observed in his 'Stanzas from the Grand Chartreuse' that he felt some sense of 'wandering between two worlds, one dead/the other powerless to be born'. Following his Burkean sensibilities of cautious reform and fear of anarchy, Arnold acknowledged that the old glue – religion – that had tenuously and often unsuccessfully held together the ailing European regimes could not do so in the mid-nineteenth century. Like Alexis de Tocqueville in France, Arnold saw that the democratic temper was the wave of the future. So he proposed a new conception of culture – a secular, humanistic one – that could play an integrative role in cementing and stabilizing an emerging bourgeois civil society and imperial state. His famous castigation of the immobilizing materialism of the declining aristocracy, the vulgar philistinism of the emerging middle classes, and the latent explosiveness of the working-class majority was motivated by a desire to create new forms of cultural legitimacy, authority, and order in a rapidly changing moment in nineteenth-century Europe.

The second historical coordinate of my genealogy is the emergence of the United States as *the* world power (in the words of André Malraux, the first nation to do so without trying to do so). The United States was unprepared for world power status. However, with the recovery of Stalin's Russia (after losing twenty million lives), the United States felt compelled to make its presence felt around the globe. Then, with the Marshall Plan to strengthen Europe, it seemed clear that there was no escape from world power obligations.

The first significant blow was dealt when assimilated Jewish Americans entered the higher echelons of the cultural apparatuses (academy, museums, galleries, mass media). Lionel Trilling is an emblematic figure. This Jewish entrée into the anti-Semitic and patriarchal critical discourse of the exclusivistic institutions of American culture initiated the slow but sure undoing of the male WASP cultural hegemony and homogeneity. Trilling's project was to appropriate Matthew Arnold's for his own political and cultural purposes – thereby unravelling the old male WASP consensus while erecting a new post-World War II liberal academic consensus around cold war, anticommunist renditions of the values of complexity, difficulty, variousness, and modulation. This suspicion of the academicization of knowledge is expressed in Trilling's well-known essay, 'On the Teaching of Modern Literature'.

Trilling laments the fact that university instruction often quiets and domesticates radical and subversive works of art, turning them into objects 'of merely habitual regard'. This process of 'the socialization of the anti-social, or the acculturation of the anti-cultural, or the legitimization of the subversive' leads Trilling to 'question whether in our culture the study of literature is any longer a suitable means for developing and refining the intelligence'. He asks this question not in the spirit of denigrating and devaluing the academy, but rather in the spirit of highlighting the possible failure of an Arnoldian conception of culture to contain what he perceives as the philistine and anarchic alternatives becoming more and more available to students of the '60s – namely, mass culture and radical politics.

This threat is partly associated with the third historical coordinate of my genealogy – the decolonization of the Third World. It is crucial to recognize the importance of this world-historical process if one wants to grasp the significance of the end of the Age of Europe and the emergence of the United States as a world power. With the first defeat of a western nation by a non-western nation – in Japan's victory over Russia (1905); revolutions in Persia (1905), Turkey (1908), Mexico (1911–12), China (1912); and much later the independence of India (1947), China (1948); and the triumph of Ghana (1957) – the actuality of a decolonized globe loomed large. Born of violent struggle, consciousness-raising, and the reconstruction of identities, decolonization simultaneously brings with it new perspectives on that long festering underside of the Age of Europe (of which colonial domination represents the *costs* of 'progress', 'order', and 'culture'), as well as requiring new readings of the economic boom in the United States (wherein the Black, Brown, Yellow, Red, White, female, gay, lesbian, and elderly working class live the same *costs* as cheap labour at home as well as in U.S.-dominated Latin American and Pacific rim markets).

The impetuous ferocity and moral outrage that motors the decolonization process is best captured by Frantz Fanon in *The Wretched of the Earth* (1906):

Decolonization, which sets out to change the order of the world, is obviously a program of complete disorder. . . . Decolonization is the meeting of two forces, opposed to each other by their very nature, which in fact owe their originality to that sort of substantification which results from and is nourished by the situation in the colonies. Their first encounter was marked by violence and their existence together – that is to say the exploitation of the native by the settler – was carried on by dint of a great array of bayonets and cannons.

Fanon's strong words describe the feelings and thoughts between the occupying British Army and the colonized Irish in Northern Ireland, the occupying Israeli Army and the subjugated Palestinians on the West Bank and Gaza Strip, the South African Army and the oppressed Black South Africans in the townships, the Japanese police and the Koreans living in Japan, the Russian Army and subordinated Armenians, and others in southern and eastern Russia. His words also partly invoke the sense many Black Americans have toward police departments in urban centres. In other words, Fanon is articulating century-long, heartfelt, human responses to being degraded and despised, hated and hunted, oppressed and exploited, and marginalized and dehumanized at the hands of powerful, xenophobic European, American, Russian, and Japanese imperial countries.

During the late 1950s, '60s, and early '70s in the United States, these decolonized sensibilities fanned and fuelled the Civil Rights and Black Power movements, as well as the student antiwar, feminist, grey, brown, gay, and lesbian movements. In this period we witnessed the shattering of male WASP cultural homogeneity and the collapse of the short-lived liberal consensus. The inclusion of African Americans, Latino/a Americans, Asian Americans, Native Americans, and American women in the culture of critical discourse yielded intense intellectual polemics and inescapable ideological polarization that focused principally on the exclusions, silences, and blindnesses of male WASP cultural homogeneity and its concomitant Arnoldian notions of the canon.

In addition, these critiques promoted three crucial processes that affected intellectual life in the country. First is the appropriation of the theories of postwar Europe – especially the work of the Frankfurt School (Marcuse, Adorno, Horkheimer), French/Italian Marxisms (Sartre, Althusser, Lefebvre, Gramsci), structuralisms (Lévi-Strauss, Todorov), and poststructuralisms (Deleuze, Derrida, Foucault). These diverse and disparate theories – all preoccupied with keeping alive radical projects after the end of the Age of Europe – tend to fuse versions of transgressive European modernisms with Marxist or post-Marxist left politics, and unanimously shun the term 'postmodernism'. Second, there is the recovery and revisioning of American history in light of the struggles of White male workers,

African Americans, Native Americans, Latino/a Americans, gays and lesbians. Third is the impact of forms of popular culture such as television, film, music videos, and even sports on highbrow, literate culture. The Black-based hip-hop culture of youth around the world is one grand example.

After 1973, with the crisis in the international world economy, America's slump in productivity, the challenge of OPEC nations to the North Atlantic monopoly of oil production, the increasing competition in hi-tech sectors of the economy from Japan and West Germany, and the growing fragility of the international debt structure, the United States entered a period of waning self-confidence (compounded by Watergate), and a nearly contracted economy. As the standards of living for the middle classes declined – owing to runaway inflation and escalating unemployment, underemployment, and crime – the quality of living fell for most everyone, and religious and secular neoconservatism emerged with power and potency. This fusion of fervent neonationalism, traditional cultural values, and 'free market' policies served as the groundwork for the Reagan–Bush era.

The ambiguous legacies of the European Age, American preeminence, and decolonization continue to haunt our postmodern moment as we come to terms with both the European, American, Japanese, Soviet, and Third World *crimes against* and *contributions to* humanity. The plight of Africans in the New World can be instructive in this regard.

By 1914, European maritime empires had dominion over more than half of the land and a third of the peoples in the world – almost 72 million square kilometres of territory and more than 560 million people under colonial rule. Needless to say, this European control included brutal enslavement, institutional terrorism, and cultural degradation of Black diaspora people. The death of roughly 75 million Africans during the centuries-long, transatlantic slave trade is but one reminder, among others, of the assault on Black humanity. The Black diaspora condition of New World servitude – in which they were viewed as mere commodities with production value, who had no proper legal status, social standing, or public worth – can be characterized as, following Orlando Patterson, natal alienation. This state of perpetual and inheritable domination that diaspora Africans had at birth produced the *modern Black diaspora problematic of invisibility and namelessness*. White supremacist practices – enacted under the auspices of the prestigious cultural authorities of the churches, print media, and scientific academics – promoted Black inferiority and constituted the European background against which Black diaspora struggles for identity, dignity (self-confidence, self-respect, self-esteem), and material resources took place.

The modern Black diaspora problematic of invisibility and namelessness can be understood as the condition of *relative lack of Black power to present themselves to themselves and others as complex human beings, and thereby to contest the bombardment of negative, degrading stereotypes put forward by White supremacist ideologies*. The initial Black response to being caught in this whirlwind of Europeanization was to resist the misrepresentation and caricature of the terms set by uncontested non-Black norms and models, and fight for self-recognition. Every modern Black person, especially cultural disseminators, encounters this problematic of invisibility and namelessness. The initial Black diaspora response was a mode of resistance that was *moralistic in content* and *communal in character*. That is, the fight for representation and recognition highlighted moral judgements regarding Black 'positive' images over and against White supremacist stereotypes. These images 're-presented' monolithic and homogeneous Black communities in a way that could displace past misrepresentations of these communities. Stuart Hall has discussed these responses as attempts to change the 'relations of representation'.

These courageous yet limited Black efforts to combat racist cultural practices uncritically accepted non-Black conventions and standards in two ways. First, they proceeded in an *assimilationist manner* that set out to show that Black people were really like White people – thereby eliding differences (in history and culture) between Whites and Blacks. Black specificity and particularity was thus banished in order to gain White acceptance and approval. Second, these Black responses rested upon a *homogenizing impulse* that assumed that all Black people were really alike – hence obliterating differences (class, gender, region, sexual orientation) between Black peoples. I submit that there are elements of truth in both claims, yet the conclusions are unwarranted owing to the basic fact that non-Black paradigms set the terms of the replies.

The insight in the first claim is that Blacks and Whites are in some important sense alike – i.e., in their positive capacities for human sympathy, moral sacrifice, service to others, intelligence, and beauty; or negatively, in their capacity for cruelty. Yet, the common humanity they share is jettisoned when the claim is cast in an assimilationist manner that subordinates Black particularity to a false universalism, i.e., non-Black rubrics and prototypes. Similarly, the insight in the second claim is that all Blacks are in some significant sense 'in the same boat' – that is, subject to White supremacist abuse. Yet, this common condition is stretched too far when viewed in a *homogenizing* way that overlooks how racist treatment vastly differs owing to class, gender, sexual orientation, nation, region, hue, and age.

The moralistic and communal aspects of the initial Black diaspora responses to social and psychic erasure were not simply cast into simplistic binary oppositions of positive/negative, good/bad images that privileged the first term in light of a White norm so that Black efforts remained inscribed within the very logic that dehumanized them. They were further complicated by the fact that these responses were also advanced principally by anxiety-ridden, middle-class Black intellectuals (predominantly male and heterosexual) grappling with their sense of double-consciousness – namely their own crisis of identity, agency, audience – caught between a quest for White approval and acceptance and an endeavour to overcome the internalized association of Blackness with inferiority. And I suggest that these complex anxieties of modern Black diaspora intellectuals partly motivate the two major arguments that ground the assimilationist moralism and homogeneous communalism just outlined.

Kobena Mercer has talked about these two arguments as the *reflectionist* and the *social engineering* arguments. The reflectionist argument holds that the fight for Black representation and recognition – against White racist stereotypes – must reflect or mirror the real Black community, not simply the negative and depressing representations of it. The social engineering argument claims that since any form of representation is constructed – i.e., selective in light of broader aims – Black representation (especially given the difficulty of Blacks gaining access to positions of power to produce any Black imagery) should offer positive images, thereby countering racist stereotypes. The hidden assumption of both arguments is that we have unmediated access to what the 'real Black community' is and what 'positive images' are. In short, these arguments presuppose the very phenomena to be interrogated, and thereby foreclose the very issues that should serve as the subject matter to be investigated.

Any notions of 'the real Black community' and 'positive images' are value-laden, socially loaded, and ideologically charged. To pursue this discussion is to call into question the possibility of such an uncontested consensus regarding them. Hall has rightly called this encounter 'the end of innocence or the end of the innocent notions of the essential Black subject . . . the recognition that "Black" is essentially a politically and culturally *constructed* category'. This recognition – more and more pervasive among the postmodern Black diaspora intelligentsia – is facilitated in part by the slow but sure dissolution of the European Age's maritime empires, and the unleashing of new political possibilities and cultural articulations among ex-colonized peoples across the globe.

One crucial lesson of this decolonization process remains the manner in which most Third World authoritarian bureaucratic elites deploy essentialist rhetorics about 'homogeneous national communities' and 'positive images' in order to repress and regiment their diverse and heterogeneous populations. Yet in the diaspora, especially among First World countries, this critique has emerged not so much from the Black male component of the left, but rather from the Black women's movement. The decisive push of postmodern Black intellectuals toward a new cultural politics of difference has been made by the powerful critiques and constructive explorations of Black diaspora women (e.g., Toni Morrison). The coffin used to bury the innocent notion of the essential Black subject was nailed shut with the termination of the Black male monopoly on the construction of the Black subject. In this regard, the Black diaspora womanist critique has had a greater impact than the critiques that highlight exclusively class, empire, age, sexual orientation, or nature.

This decisive push toward the end of Black innocence – though prefigured in various degrees in the best moments of James Baldwin, Amiri Baraka, Anna Cooper, W. E. B. DuBois, Frantz Fanon, C. L. R. James, Claudia Jones, the later Malcolm X, and others – forces Black diaspora cultural workers to encounter what Hall has called the 'politics of representation'. The main aim now is not simply access to representation in order to produce positive images of homogeneous communities – though broader access remains a practical and political problem. Nor is the primary goal here that of contesting stereotypes – though contestation remains a significant though limited venture. Following the model of the Black diaspora traditions of music, athletics, and rhetoric, Black cultural workers must constitute and sustain discursive and institutional networks that deconstruct earlier modern Black strategies for identity formation, demystify power relations that incorporate class, patriarchal, and homophobic biases, and construct more multivalent and multidimensional responses that articulate the complexity and diversity of Black practices in the modern and postmodern world.

Furthermore, Black cultural workers must investigate and interrogate the other of Blackness/Whiteness. One cannot deconstruct the binary oppositional logic of images of Blackness without extending it to the contrary condition of Blackness/Whiteness itself. However, a mere dismantling will not do – for the very notion of a deconstructive social theory is oxymoronic. Yet, social theory is what is needed to examine and *explain* the historically specific ways in which 'Whiteness' is a politically constructed category parasitic on 'Blackness', and thereby to conceive of the profoundly hybrid character of what we mean by 'race', 'ethnicity', and 'nationality'. Needless to say, these enquiries must traverse those of 'male/female', 'colonizer/colonized', 'heterosexual/ homosexual', *et al.*, as well.

Demystification is the most illuminating mode of theoretical enquiry for those who promote the new cultural politics of difference. Social structural analyses of empire, exterminism, class, race, gender, nature, age, sexual orientation, nation, and region are the springboards – though not landing grounds – for the most desirable forms of critical practice that take history (and herstory) seriously. Demystification tries to keep track of the complex dynamics of institutional and other related power structures in order to disclose options and alternatives for transformative praxis; it also attempts to grasp the way in which representational strategies are creative responses to novel circumstances and conditions. In this way, the central role of human agency (always enacted under circumstances not of one's choosing) – be it in the critic, artist, or constituency, and audience – is accented.

I call demystificatory criticism 'prophetic criticism' – the approach appropriate for the new cultural politics of difference – because while it begins with social structural analyses it also makes explicit its moral and political aims. It is partisan, partial, engaged, and crisis-centred, yet always keeps open a sceptical eye to avoid dogmatic traps, premature closures, formulaic formulations, or rigid conclusions. In addition to social structural analyses, moral and political judgements, and sheer critical consciousness, there indeed is evaluation. Yet the aim of this evaluation is neither to pit art-objects against one another like race-horses nor to create eternal canons that dull, discourage, or even dwarf contemporary achievements. We listen to Laurie Anderson, Kathleen Battle, Ludwig Beethoven, Charlie Parker, Luciano Pavarotti, Sarah Vaughan, or Stevie Wonder; read Anton Chekhov, Ralph Ellison, Gabriel García Márquez, Doris Lessing, Toni Morrison, Thomas Pynchon, William Shakespeare; or see the works of Ingmar Bergman, Le Corbusier, Frank Gehry, Barbara Kruger, Spike Lee, Martin Puryear, Pablo Picasso, or Howardena Pindell – not in order to undergird bureaucratic assents or enliven cocktail party conversations, but rather to be summoned by the styles they deploy for their profound insights, pleasures, and challenges. Yet, all evaluation – including a delight in Eliot's poetry despite his reactionary politics, or a love of Zora Neale

Hurston's novels despite her Republican party affiliations – is inseparable, though not identical or reducible to social structural analyses,
moral and political judgements, and the workings of a curious critical
consciousness.

The deadly traps of demystification – and any form of prophetic
criticism – are those of reductionism, be it of the sociological, psychological, or historical sort. By reductionism I mean either one-factor
analyses (i.e., crude Marxisms, feminisms, racialisms, etc.) that yield a
one-dimensional functionalism or a hyper-subtle analytical perspective
that loses touch with the specificity of an art work's form and the context
of its reception. Few cultural workers of whatever stripe can walk the
tightrope between the Scylla of reductionism and the Charybdis of
aestheticism – yet, demystificatory (or prophetic) critics must. Of course,
since so many art practices these days also purport to be criticism, this
also holds true for artists.

THE EXISTENTIAL CHALLENGE

The existential challenge to the new cultural politics of difference can be
stated simply: how does one acquire the resources to survive and the
cultural capital to thrive as a critic or artist? By cultural capital (Pierre
Bourdieu's term), I mean not only the high-quality skills required to
engage in critical practices, but more important, the self-confidence,
discipline, and perseverance necessary for success without an undue
reliance on the mainstream for approval and acceptance. This challenge
holds for all prophetic critics, yet it is especially difficult for those of
colour. The widespread modern European denial of the intelligence,
ability, beauty, and character of people of colour puts a tremendous
burden on critics and artists of colour to 'prove' themselves in light of
norms and models set by White elites whose own heritage devalued and
dehumanized them. In short, in the court of criticism and art – or any
matters regarding the life of the mind – people of colour are guilty (i.e.,
not expected to meet standards of intellectual achievement) until 'proven' innocent (i.e., acceptable to 'us').

This is more a structural dilemma than a matter of personal attitudes. The profoundly racist and sexist heritage of the European Age
has bequeathed to us a set of deeply ingrained perceptions about people
of colour including, of course, the self-perceptions that people of colour
bring. It is not surprising that most intellectuals of colour in the past

exerted much of their energies and efforts to gain acceptance and approval by 'White normative gazes'. The new cultural politics of difference advises critics and artists of colour to put aside this mode of mental bondage, thereby freeing themselves both to interrogate the ways in which they are bound by certain conventions and to learn from and build on these very norms and models. One hallmark of wisdom in the context of any struggle is to avoid knee-jerk rejection and uncritical acceptance.

There are four basic options for people of colour interested in representation – if they are to survive and thrive as serious practitioners of their craft. First, there is the Booker T. Temptation, namely the individual preoccupation with the mainstream and its legitimizing power. Most critics and artists of colour try to bite this bait. It is nearly unavoidable, yet few succeed in a substantive manner. It is no accident that the most creative and profound among them – especially those with staying power beyond mere flashes in the pan to satisfy faddish tokenism – are usually marginal to the mainstream. Even the pervasive professionalization of cultural practitioners of colour in the past few decades has not produced towering figures who reside within the established White patronage system that bestows the rewards and prestige for chosen contributions to American society.

It certainly helps to have some trustworthy allies within this system, yet most of those who enter and remain tend to lose much of their creativity, diffuse their prophetic energy, and dilute their critiques. Still, it is unrealistic for creative people of colour to think they can sidestep the White patronage system. And though there are indeed some White allies conscious of the tremendous need to rethink identity politics, it is naive to think that being comfortably nested within this very same system – even if one can be a patron to others – does not affect one's work, one's outlook, and, most important, one's soul.

The second option is the Talented Tenth Seduction, namely, a move toward arrogant group insularity. This alternative has a limited function – to preserve one's sanity and sense of self as one copes with the mainstream. Yet, it is, at best, a transitional and transient activity. If it becomes a permanent option it is self-defeating in that it usually reinforces the very inferiority complexes promoted by the subtly racist mainstream. Hence it tends to revel in a parochialism and encourage a narrow racialist and chauvinistic outlook.

The third strategy is the Go-It-Alone option. This is an extreme rejectionist perspective that shuns the mainstream and group insularity. Almost every critic and artist of colour contemplates or enacts this option at some time in his or her pilgrimage. It is healthy in that it reflects the presence of independent, critical, and sceptical sensibilities toward perceived constraints on one's creativity. Yet, it is, in the end, difficult if not impossible to sustain if one is to grow, develop, and mature intellectually, as some semblance of dialogue with a community is necessary for almost any creative practice.

The most desirable option for people of colour who promote the new cultural politics of difference is to be a Critical Organic Catalyst. By this I mean a person who stays attuned to the best of what the mainstream has to offer – its paradigms, viewpoints, and methods – yet maintains a grounding in affirming and enabling subcultures of criticism. Prophetic critics and artists of colour should be exemplars of what it means to be intellectual freedom fighters, that is, cultural workers who simultaneously position themselves within (or alongside) the mainstream while clearly aligned with groups who vow to keep alive potent traditions of critique and resistance. In this regard, one can take clues from the great musicians or preachers of colour who are open to the best of what other traditions offer, yet are rooted in nourishing subcultures that build on the grand achievements of a vital heritage. Openness to others – including the mainstream – does not entail wholesale cooptation, and group autonomy is not group insularity. Louis Armstrong, Ella Baker, W. E. B. DuBois, Martin Luther King, Jr., Jose Carlos Mariatequi, Wynton Marsalis, M. M. Thomas, and Ronald Takaki have understood this well.

The new cultural politics of difference can thrive only if there are communities, groups, organizations, institutions, subcultures, and networks of people of colour who cultivate critical sensibilities and personal accountability – without inhibiting individual expressions, curiosities, and idiosyncrasies. This is especially needed given the escalating racial hostility, violence, and polarization in the United States. Yet, this critical coming-together must not be a narrow closing of ranks. Rather, it is a strengthening and nurturing endeavour that can forge more solid alliances and coalitions. In this way, prophetic criticism – with its stress on historical specificity and artistic complexity – directly addresses the intellectual challenge. The cultural capital of people of colour – with its emphasis on self-confidence, discipline, perseverance, and subcultures of criticism – also tries to meet the existential requirement. Both are mutually reinforcing. Both are motivated by a deep commitment to individuality and democracy – the moral and political ideals that guide the creative response to the political challenge.

THE POLITICAL CHALLENGE

Adequate rejoinders to intellectual and existential challenges equip the practitioners of the new cultural politics of difference to meet the political ones. This challenge principally consists of forging solid and reliable alliances of people of colour and White progressives guided by a moral and political vision of greater democracy and individual freedom in communities, states, and transnational enterprises – i.e., corporations, and information and communications conglomerates. Jesse Jackson's Rainbow coalition is a gallant, yet flawed effort in this regard – gallant due to the tremendous energy, vision, and courage of its leader and followers; flawed because of its failure to take seriously critical and democratic sensibilities within its own operations.

The time has come for critics and artists of the new cultural politics of difference to cast their nets widely, flex their muscles broadly, and thereby refuse to limit their visions, analyses, and praxis to their particular terrains. The aim is to dare to recast, redefine, and revise the very notions of 'modernity', 'mainstream', 'margins', 'difference', 'otherness'. We have now reached a new stage in the perennial struggle for freedom and dignity. And while much of the First World intelligentsia adopts retrospective and conservative outlooks that defend the crisis-ridden present, we promote a prospective and prophetic vision with a sense of possibility and potential, especially for those who bear the social costs of the present. We look to the past for strength, not solace; we look at the present and see people perishing, not profits mounting; we look toward the future and vow to make it different and better.

NOTE

This is a version of an essay that appears in Russel Ferguson, Martha Gever, Trinh T. Minh-ha, and Cornel West, eds, *Out There: Marginalization and Contemporary Cultures*, New York, The New Museum of Contemporary Art; and Cambridge, MIT Press, 1990.

Part V *Sexuality*

16 Andrew Ross

The popularity of pornography

EDITOR'S INTRODUCTION

Andrew Ross's essay on pornography is primarily concerned with intellectuals' relation to pornography. It makes two distinctions – the first between sexuality and gender, arguing that the economy of sexual fantasy and desire has no fixed relation to gender divisions; and the second between the traditional liberal values of tolerance and pluralism on the one hand, and the recently influential 'liberatory' and the 'libertinist' imaginations on the other. The liberatory imagination wishes actively to support and produce different pleasures and practices rather than just tolerate them in the way that classic liberalism does; the libertinist imagination aims to use theory to increase the cultural areas open to complex pleasures (the prime example being Roland Barthes's notion of 'jouissance' or the bliss which – supposedly – follows reading radically polysemous texts, and which we have seen John Fiske using in the introduction).

Ross offers a sympathetic critique of these more recent projects, pointing out that they have to come to terms with structures of desire embedded in the psyche as well as with the way in which pleasures are produced industrially and disseminated as commodities in the market.

In a topic of such moment to women, and so actively researched, theorized, and engaged by women, it may seem insensitive to have chosen an essay by a man. There were two reasons for this: first Ross's essay contains an excellent, brief overview of work on pornography and second, like the essays by Eve Sedgwick, Gayatri Spivak, and Cornel West collected here, it insists on the importance of what Sedgwick calls 'allo-identification' – identification with the other. It is important, in the current situation of cultural studies, not to remain trapped within those ways of thinking for which a particular gender, sexual, or ethnic identity is required in order to speak on a particular topic. For that reason, I hope that the essay also works as an example of 'men in feminism'.

Further reading: Kappeler 1986; MacKinnon 1987; Ross 1989; Snitow *et al.* 1983; Watney 1987; Williams, L. 1990; Willis, E. 1986.

S.D.

Pornography from a woman's point of view? Yes, said the owner of my local video store, of course he could recommend some, and rattled off the titles of a few of the more popular 'couples' films currently being rented. Could he describe them? Longer, romantic sequences, with appropriate mood music, and lots of emphasis on feelings. Does this mean that there's no hard core? No, not at all, he said, and this time, his business instincts aroused, he leaned toward me, after a ritual glance over his shoulder, and proceeded to assure me, man to man, that the actors eventually did get down to the real stuff; it just took a little longer, and it was, sort of, different.

This 'sort of' difference has been exerting its pressure on the porn industry for over ten years now, ever since female consumers were acknowledged as the largest potential growth market for pornographic entertainment and sex accessories. While recent video titles like *Every Woman Has A Fantasy* and *In All the Right Places* reflect this shift in the heterosexual market, women themselves are beginning to stake out positions of power within the industry, not just as stars, commanding larger fees and various kinds of 'artistic control' over their work, but also as producers and directors.

Back in the mid-fifties, the upmarket *Playboy* had attracted an audience of aspiring pre-executive men, for whom its philosophy of 'fun' and 'swinging' promoted and celebrated the good life, ushering in a culture of consumption that represented a revolt against the stability of suburban breadwinning life. By 1980, over 200 hard-core and 165 soft-core straight male magazines (50 hard-core and a dozen soft-core gay) were established in more or less legitimate markets and submarkets that had surfaced and flourished by democratizing elements of the *Playboy* discourse for more popular or speciality audiences.

So too, the U.S. porn film industry was galvanized by the crossover success, in 1972, of *Deep Throat,* largely because of the stir it created among intellectuals – 'Not to have seen it', Nora Ephron wrote in *Esquire,* 'seemed somehow . . . derelict.' Its pseudo-Freudian subtext and its narrative focus on the *educational* and psychotherapeutic benefits of sexual liberation was addressed, nominally, at least, to an audience with higher interests than the simple pleasures of arousal.

Playboy, a suburban men's magazine, *Deep Throat*, a psychobabble film for swingers, and *Christine's Dream*, a yuppie couples' video, may not be wholly representative of the pornography made for popular consumption; they each contain an appeal to what we could call the educated body. The cultural history spanned by these three products reflects large changes in the patterns of popular consumption, in the development of visual technology, and in investment trends in an industry which in 1984 was estimated to be worth as much as $7 billion, larger than the film and the record industries put together. But their respective cultural forms are much more than just reflections of changes in the economic organization of an American mass cultural industry. They also speak and respond to a continuing debate among intellectuals and legislators about the political nature of the *popularity of sexually explicit representations*, a debate whose twists and turns have been constitutive of the ideological fabric of our recent cultural history.

In replacing the standard use of professional models from the sex industry for its pinups with images recruited from the suburban 'girl next door', *Playboy* ensured that its appeal would not be downmarket. On the contrary, it was marked, at all levels, from the celebrity *Playboy* interview to the luxury milieu of its nightclubs, by quality consumption as defined by the gentlemanly realm of acceptable sexual conduct. In this respect, *Playboy*, and, to a certain extent, *Cosmpolitan* (founded in 1965), its female challenger in the lists of consumer capitalism, predate the more radical, democratizing claims promoted by the so-called sexual revolution of the decade from the late sixties to the late seventies. For Al Goldstein, the ebullient publisher of *Screw*, who functions as one of the industry's pornographer-intellectuals, pornography's newfound political significance in the late sixties was seen as part of a zealous crusade on behalf of the popular (*Screw*, 'the world's greatest, filthiest newspaper', was actually conceived in 1968 in the offices of the *New York Free Press* as a 'sexpol' moneymaker for radical political causes):

> Not only does today's pornography serve to liberate us in our attitudes toward sex; it is also shattering the elitism that has traditionally surrounded pornography itself. Once pornography was acceptable only if it was sold in fancy, expensive editions that claimed to be 'erotic art' from India or Japan. To me pornography is what the truck driver wants, what the sanitation worker reads, what the bus driver buys.

As always, Goldstein's comments are unapologetically populist, and directed against the double standards of those who enter the debate about pornography from the perspective of the higher aesthetic realm of 'erotica', and who have had little or no contact with more popular pornographic forms which they consider to be both aesthetically and politically degrading.

But Goldstein is also the man who boasted, in 1973, that if he caught his wife cheating on him, he would 'probably break her legs and pull her clit off and shove it in her left ear'. This second comment of Goldstein's, while obviously horrific, can be read as a contextual reference, unconscious or otherwise, to the displacement of the clitoris into the throat of the heroine of *Deep Throat*, the film which had recently sought to represent the sexual revolution's two newly 'discovered' adventure zones as if they were one and the same – the centrality of the clitoris for women, and the action of fellatio for men. If this film offered the spectacle of a woman actively seeking sexual pleasure, as some argued, its exploitative underside would be fully revealed years later in *Ordeal*, the autobiography of Linda Lovelace, which describes the coercive conditions under which her career as the first legitimate porn star had proceeded.

This relation between the representations offered by the porn film and the exploitative work conditions faced by its actors and actresses has been a critical subtext of the debate about pornography among feminist intellectuals which was enjoined in the late seventies. On the one hand, this debate has been playing itself out in the law courts and in the intellectual press. On the other hand, it has resulted in the responses and political actions of sex workers themselves, who have broken into the business of production and persuasion, whether as elite film directors, like the women at Femme Productions, or as public voices on media forums such as television talk shows. So too, the industry has publicly cleaned up its act, and, in pursuit of the women's market, it has come to quite openly address the question of the representation of female pleasure and desire. Unlike other organized forms of degrading labour, however, the porn industry has had to emphasize that its conditions of paid employment are not just contractual – the only kind of labour relation which liberal capitalism ordinarily recognizes – but also that they are entirely *consensual*.

What has taken precedence in the intellectuals' debate, however, has been the more academic and philosophical question of the vexed relationship between sexual performances and real sexual conduct: often abstract questions about representation, its distance from the real, its place in and its effect upon the real, and its relation to fantasy and the construction of sexuality. Intellectuals, in other words, have felt more comfortable discussing questions that are familiar to them, and about which they are traditionally called upon to adjudicate on behalf of society as a whole.

The result, as I will argue, has been to neglect the actual conditions under which the great bulk of pornography has been produced and consumed as an object of popular taste. If, in the realm of consumption, Al Goldstein's male truck driver signifies one side of the popular, a side which is uncritically celebrated by industry intellectuals, then the female sex worker, who, for many antiporn feminists, needs to be saved from the degrading fate of her labour, signifies the pejorative side of the popular in the realm of production. For the most part, however, the respective opinions, desires, and economic roles of the truck driver and the sex worker have either been taken for granted, morally patronized, or else consigned to the flames of 'false consciousness' by intellectuals. In a rare enlightened moment, the 1976 Meese Commission on Pornography noted with regret that virtually all of the historical study of pornography has not been about 'the social practice of pornography', but rather about the 'control of that social practice by government', and recommended that 'the scope of thinking about the issue should be broadened considerably'.

There are other reasons, of course, why pornography, today, cannot be considered *simply* as an object of popular taste, rendered illicit by the dominant culture while it is exploited to provide the profits and capital which support that dominant culture. The public consciousness raised by the feminist antiporn movement has challenged this tidy model on at least two major counts. First, it has made its claims against pornography against *all men*, and on behalf of *all women*, of all classes, colours, and sexual orientations. In this respect, the feminist critique, in defining the pornographic itself as a 'dominant' culture, claims to cut across the class-specific lines traditionally drawn between the 'popular' and the 'dominant'. Second, in challenging the juridical distinction between public and private – a distinction that underpins the liberal doctrine of individual rights – the antiporn critique has also challenged the way in which the popular has been contained, in modern times, in the interests of that repository of individual rights – the 'liberal imagination', to use Lionel Trilling's term.

About the first claim, I will argue that while it proposes to redefine cultural conflict along gender rather than class lines, it reproduces the same languages of mass manipulation, systematic domination, and victimization which had been the trademark of the Cold War liberal critique of mass culture. Both share a picture of a monolithic culture of standardized production and standardized effects, and of normalized brutality, whether within the mind or against the body. While lack of mutual affection has replaced lack of aesthetic complexity as the standard grounds of disapproval in the antiporn analysis, the charge of propagandism is repeated, and the renewed use of the rhetoric of protection and reform has sustained the privilege of intellectuals to 'know what's good' for others.

Again,
see
"How to
read
Hustler"

About the second claim, I will argue that the insistence of feminism that 'the personal is the political', has successfully helped to redefine the 'private' as a realm of experience that ought, in certain instances, to be subject to public enquiry. This is a direct challenge to the doctrine of 'negative liberty' under which liberal law protects the freedom of the individual to live and act in the absence of undue external restraint. The principle of 'negative liberty' traditionally protects areas of the 'private' in which women had little in the way of privileges to defend. As a result of the feminist challenge, questions about sexuality can no longer be relegated to a quarantine area where policing has been most effectively exercised, usually against the interests of women and sexual minorities. So too, the private can no longer be seen as a realm of privilege for guaranteeing the immunity of the individual (liberal) imagination to the various 'contagions' of popular culture. But, as Beverley Brown has argued, if feminism is to consider where the 'reform' of sexual representations is appropriate, then it will have to decide 'whether or not phantasy is "private"', and what it would mean to distinguish between 'a reform of phantasy or a reform of manners'.

Trudeau

To make that distinction, however, is to raise questions about the sexual which cannot be tied exclusively to the agenda of combating gender oppression or inequality. Sex, sexuality, and sexual difference cannot be simply mapped onto categories of gender. Gayle Rubin, for example, has argued that feminism, a theory and a politics of gender oppression, does not necessarily involve the best way of thinking about sexuality, just as marxism often cannot provide the most useful analyses of inequalities which are not class-based. Rubin points out that sexual minorities, often classed as 'perverts' and thus part of pornography itself, are affected by sexual stratification as much as by gender stratification. Gender-based reforms, such as those proposed by antiporn groups, are likely to be antagonistic to the interests of sexual minorities, and have, in fact, already added to the suppression of minority rights only tentatively extended under the protection of the privacy of sexual conduct. A politics of sexuality that is relatively autonomous from categories of gender may be needed to achieve and guarantee the full sexual rights of sexual minorities.

Such a politics is the domain of what I will call the *liberatory imagination*. Unlike the liberal imagination, which exercises and defends autonomous rights and privileges already achieved and possessed, the liberatory imagination is *pragmatically* linked to the doctrine of 'positive liberty', which entails the fresh creation of legal duties to ensure that individuals will have the means that they require in order to pursue liberty and equality. But it is also this liberatory imagination which sets the agenda of radical democracy beyond liberal pragmatism in pursuit of claims, actions, rights, desires, pleasures, and thoughts that are often still considered too illegitimate to be recognized as political. Such claims, actions, and rights, etc., invariably do not arise out of liberalism's recognition of the *universal* rights of individuals. Instead, they spring from expressions of difference, from the differentiated needs and interests of individuals and groups who make up the full spectrum of democratic movements today. These differences do not necessarily converge, and they can rarely be posed in relation to rights that would concern or embrace all individuals.

Until the feminist antiporn movement changed the rules of legal engagement in the mid-eighties, the debate in the highest courts of the land about art, censorship, and pornography was one in which intellectuals, in their capacity as 'expert' witnesses, were summoned from their habitual role as 'hidden persuaders' in civil society to appear as more or less overt legitimists of juridical or state power. Partly because of this, it was also a debate which demonstrated the close, almost cognate, links between the 'metacritical' practice of juridical interpretation and the canonical judgements, according to the 'objective' laws of aesthetics, which literary critics were accustomed to make in the process of discriminating literature of permanent value from the ephemeral and the worthless. At times, participants in these debates found it impossible to avoid alluding to this elimination of professional distance.

A good example was the Supreme Court decision of *U.S. v. Samuel Roth* (1956), in which Roth was convicted of violating the federal obscenity statute by mailing 'obscence, lewd, lascivious or filthy' materials. Roth challenged the constitutionality of the statute, and while the Court of Appeals upheld the statute, one member of the Court, Judge Jerome Frank, expressed his reservations at length, among which was his disagreement with the exemption of books of 'literary distinction' from statutory censorship. Frank questioned not only the ethical but also the aesthetic grounds upon which such a distinction could be made between 'classics', and what the statute referred to as 'books which are dull and without merit':

> The contention would scarcely pass as rational that the 'classics' will be read or seen solely by an intellectual or artistic elite; for, even ignoring the snobbish, undemocratic, nature of this contention, there is no evidence that that elite has a moral fortitude (an immunity from moral corruption) superior to that of the 'masses'. And if the exception, to make it rational, were taken as meaning that a contemporary book is exempt if it equates in 'literary distinction' with the 'classics', the result would be amazing: Judges would have to serve as literary critics; jurisprudence would merge with aesthetics; authors and publishers would consult the legal digests for legal-artistic precedents; we would some day have a Legal Restatement of the Canons of Literary Taste.

In evoking this future apocalyptic state of affairs in which the professional separation of powers between 'free' intellectuals and judges has altogether eroded, Judge Frank cautions us against concluding that the role of the judge may be no more than the juridical equivalent of the function of 'free-thinking' intellectuals in civil society. But perhaps it is the corollary of this thought which harbours the idea, equally pernicious in the eyes of the Law, that intellectuals might merely function as the 'soft' agents of juridical coercion.

Judge Frank, however, was on safe ground in merely *imagining* that 'the result would be amazing'. As the obscenity statute came to be revised in successive decisions, the actual burden upon judges to consistently make such fine discriminations of 'value' has eased off. In *Memoirs v. Massachusetts* (1966), it was decided that a work had to be clearly proven to be worthless – 'utterly without redeeming social value' – before it could be considered obscene. *Miller v. California* (1973) challenged the absolutism of this ruling, and took as its constitutional standard 'whether the work, taken as a whole, lacks serious literary, artistic, political or scientific value'. For over twenty years now, written speech has been *de facto* exempt from obscenity rulings, while the heavy burden of proof placed on the prosecutor in the case of visual materials has meant that the 'value' of images in a text has been more difficult to question in the courts.

In perhaps the most infamous legal statement ever advanced about 'obscenity' or pornography, Supreme Court Justice Potter Stewart in 1964 (*Jacobellis v. Ohio*) announced that although he could not define what pornography was: 'I know it when I see it.' While the courts have not abandoned the subjective right of judges to deploy this privileged knowledge, the objective model of obscenity since *Miller v. California* has been 'the average person, applying contemporary community standards'. If judges were thus spared the professional anguish of the literary critic bent on canonizing a relatively new work of literature, it was because they, like the literary critic over the same period of time, have come to acknowledge that there are no universal, let alone national, standards for interpreting cultural representations. They have yet to fully recognize, however, that there are only specific communities and subcultures of interpreters, whose diversity of interpretation and use of cultural material are hardly suggested by universal categories like 'the average person', or 'contemporary community standards'.

For traditional intellectuals, vying to have their say on pornography, the question of value was clearer because there were so many ways of taking the high ground. Here, for example, is the appeal to aestheticism of Lord Clark: 'The moment art becomes an incentive to action, it loses its true character. This is my objection to painting with a communist programme, and it would also apply to pornography.' Steven Marcus also perceives that pornography's 'singleness of intention' is 'to move us in the direction of action' and 'away from language' and this is what relegates it to such 'simpler forms of literary utterance as propaganda and advertising'. Pornography, which, for Marcus, takes place in a pornotopian never-never land, out of social time and place, can never be true 'literature' because it cannot provide gratification and fulfilment; its effect is not finite.

For every argument about singleness of intention, there was a confessional argument about effect from the likes of George Steiner, who wrote a weary diatribe against what he saw as the boring and repetitive configurations of the pornographic – 'as predictable as a Boy Scout manual' – which extended, as he saw it, from 'the fathomless tide of straight trash' of today to the literary erotica, 'above the pulp-line', produced by most of the respected authors of the nineteenth century. For Steiner, pornography could only create new conditions of servitude, not freedom: 'The actions of the mind when we masturbate are not a dance; they are a treadmill.' Commenting on the heated response to his essay, Steiner fully drew out the classic Cold War features of his argument. Pornography, he concluded, was an erosion of our private erotic rights, a threat to the free imagination that can be mobilized alternately by the threat to individual style 'in a mass consumer civilization' *or* by 'the making naked and anonymous of the individual in the totalitarian state (the concentration camp being the logical epitome of that state)'.

Steiner's case against pornography, then, became a defence of the liberal imagination and of Western 'freedom' alike. The familiar Cold Warrior fear that popular culture already *contains* our response to it, and that it therefore has 'no respect for the reader's' imaginative rights, is presented as a brutish threat wielded by consumer capitalism and monopoly statism alike. Only Literature with its plurality of high intentions allows us to respond with the imaginative freedom that we are accustomed, in the West, to enjoy. So too, this freedom had to be of a mature nature, as opposed to pornography's activation of fantasies of infantile sexual life. Portnoy's 'complaint', as Irving Kristol put it, was simply that he was 'incapable of having an adult sexual relationship with a woman'. Pornography, whether high or low, would never grow up.

There is, of course, a specific historical context for the assumed antiliterary bias of pornography, invoked by Marcus's observation that the tendency of pornography is 'to move ideally away from language'. Such complaints appeared at a time when the written word was again becoming a minority medium associated with a saving 'literate' remnant, and thus exempt, after centuries as *the* democratizing, levelling medium, from all modes of State suppression and proscription. The private activity of reading was now seen as embattled and in need of protection from the growing hegemony exercised by visual technology over a mass population. Where, in the nineteenth century, the private act of reading (especially popular literature), on the part of the new reading public, was infernally associated with masturbation, reading was now a redemptionary exercise, a promise of deliverance from the orgiastic public rites of the spectacle and mass pornography.

Similar assumptions about elite taste are deployed in the avantgarde intellectual's case for high-class pornography as 'serious literature'. Susan Sontag, for example, praises the quality of experience offered by sophisticated erotic literature like *The Story of O*. For her, this is a literature of extremity, bravely testing and exploring the transgression of social limits by libertines. In its quest for sensual absolutes, the modernist transgression of social taboo is the best hope for a negation of everyday capitalist personality structures; it is a profoundly traumatic, subversive, and quasi-religious act of the imagination.

But Sontag makes it clear that this capacity to lead the way in transgression is not for everyone:

> Perhaps most people don't need a 'wider scale of experience'. It may be that, without subtle and extensive psychic preparation, any widening of experience and consciousness is destructive for most people. . . . Pornography is only one item among the many danger- ous commodities being circulated in this society and, unattractive as it may be, one of the less lethal, the less costly to the community in terms of human suffering. Except perhaps in a small circle of writer- intellectuals in France, pornography is an inglorious and mostly despised department of the imagination. (Sontag 1982: 233)

This charmed circle brings together the guardians of what we could call the _libertinist imagination_: theirs is a Reichian revolution of the body through the minds of intellectuals. In fact, Sontag is alluding to the avant-garde tradition in France of Georges Bataille, Jean Genet, Roland Barthes, and later, Philippe Sollers, Julia Kristeva, Hélène Cixous, Monique Wittig, and others whose common patron saint in the field of libertinage is Sade. It is a tradition in which the limited and mundane libidinal economy of _plaisir_ is contrasted with the higher, transgressive experience of _jouissance_, to use Barthes's well-known opposition, itself based on the Freudian distinction between the 'economic' pleasure principle and the destructively 'spendthrift' death drive. _Plaisir_ is thus linked to the controlled hedonism of consumer capitalism, an economy which the avant-garde pornographic imagination seeks to disrupt by pursuing pain and pleasure in excess of its conventional limits; as Sontag puts it approvingly elsewhere, 'having one's sensorium chal- lenged or stretched hurts'.

What Sontag, then, calls the 'pornographic imagination' is clearly a realm of radical chic pleasure, far removed from the semen-stained squalor of the peep show, the strip joint, the video arcade, and other sites of popular pornotopian fantasy. But it claims to be an egalitarian theatre all the same, where, as Angela Carter notes in her study of Sade, the participants are _accomplices_ in crimes of passion, not lovers or partners or servants or masters, and where pornography promises to be even more 'deeply subversive' the more it comes to be like 'real litera- ture' and 'real art' by facing up to the 'moral contradictions inherent in real sexual encounters'. Carter proposes the kind of 'moral pornographer' who would liberate the power of pornography and put it in the service of a critique of current sexual relations, terrorizing the imagination with a world of social and gender mobility. Such a pornographer would be the 'unconscious ally' of women. In fact, Carter argues that because Sade represented women as 'beings of power' with certain rights to sexual freedom, he 'put pornography in the service of women, or perhaps, allowed it to be invaded by an ideology not inimical to women'.

Antiporn feminists have hardly been willing to accept this image of the Marquis de Sade, connoisseur of mutilation and gourmet of sexual humiliation, as women's best friend in spite of himself. Nonetheless, the appeal to a *higher consciousness*, which allows both Carter and Sontag to redeem Sade, seemed to play an equally important, if somewhat different, role in the famous distinction between pornography and erotica which Gloria Steinem first advanced in 1978, and which has since become an article of faith in the ensuing feminist debate and transformed representational practices around pornography. As a women's alternative to the perceived inequalities of masculinist pornography, erotica was posed in terms of the representational codes of romantic love, with an emphasis on traditionally 'feminine' qualities like tenderness, softness, wholeness, sentiment, sensuality, and passion. 'Erotica is about sexuality, but pornography is about power and sex-as-weapon,' wrote Steinem. Erotica, which had long been used to describe a class act for well-heeled male voyeurs, would now be transformed into a purified realm of sexual freedom and equality, with higher, and more complex, holistic intentions than the singular and mundane one of arousal.

Anti-antiporn feminists who were sceptical of Steinem's distinction pointed out that this new definition of erotica rested upon a utopian orthodoxy of 'good sex', and implied, at its core, a campaign for the reform of sexuality itself. Ellen Willis described its emphasis on wholesome relationships as a 'goody-goody concept' and a 'ladylike activity', associated with the 'feminine' and not with the 'feminist' (Willis 1986: 56). Ann Snitow pointed out that soft-core, soft-focus, 'good sex' excludes the infantilism, wayward desire, and aggressivity of pre-Oedipal sexual activity that is played out, in fantasy or otherwise, in all adult life and culture (Snitow *et al.* 1983: 256). Gayle Rubin criticized the erotic chauvinism of the 'erotica' model – calling it the 'missionary position of the women's movement' – because of its exclusion of a whole range of sexual variations – running from casual promiscuity to lesbian

S/M (Rubin 1984: 267–319). While agreeing with the reformist platform, Susanne Kappeler insisted that the replacement of the content of representations – 'bad sex' by 'good sex' – changes very little; what is needed is the reform of the very structure of looking and gazing that organizes visual representation (Kappeler 1986: 49–53).

These, and many other objections to the erotica/pornography distinction, have helped to set the agenda of the contemporary debate about pornography. None of them appeals directly to the terms and categories that characterized the earlier phase of the debate about art, obscenity, and elitist/popular taste. For it is no longer the threat to the autonomy of the liberal imagination that is at stake. The *liberatory imagination* has come to the fore, bringing with it a new set of contradictions, protectionist and conservative on the one hand, and exploratory and radical on the other, posed against the backdrop of consumer capitalism in which new social and sexual identities have tentatively come into being at the cost of ever greater modes of social and cultural control. Facing up to these new contradictions has required intellectuals to rethink their allegiances and/or their allergies to popular pornography.

While the wide range of feminist critiques of pornography covers ground that cannot be easily unified, the philosophical core of the critique to be found in the work of Andrea Dworkin, Catherine MacKinnon, and WAP rests upon the principle that patriarchal oppression is *systematic* and *all-inclusive*, and that it is exercised universally and transhistorically. To look for evidence of this oppression is to demonstrate an unbroken continuum of male violence against women which stretches from the operations of pimps and pornographers to corporate executives and traffickers of 'international sexual slavery'; from incest to clitoridectomy, and from soft-core pornography to rape and sexual murder. The essentialist-biologist categories of the WAP critique posit 'male sexuality' as naturally rapacious and gynocidal – 'Men love death,' writes Dworkin, and adds, 'men especially love murder' – and 'female sexuality' as nurturing, arising from *natural* or spontaneous interests and instincts. The universal hold of male power over female autonomy is thus seen as an ongoing encroachment and invasion of a realm of natural feminine freedom. Power, manipulation, and victimage are the masculine reward, and freedom to be protected and nurtured are the feminine. A systematic threat is assumed, and an alternative world is imagined which would be invulnerable to such a threat.

These are the rhetorical terms in which antiporn feminism redefined the old defence of the liberal imagination (against the brutish threat of a pervasive mass culture) within a context provided by the countercultural alternatives that had flourished in the late sixties. The utopian result was to be a female counterculture with no ties to the 'system' and a guaranteed immunity to its rules and games of power and resistance. There would be a world, on the one hand, in which only male power could be enjoyed or suffered, and a different world in which male power no longer mattered. Such a scenario assumed that little could be done about the everyday life culture which had inevitably made women into passive, inert victims. Instead, it promoted the creation of a no-go area, or no man's land, prophylactically separate from the contaminated culture of ordinary people and popular culture. In this way, the vestigial Cold War opposition between the advanced minority of an 'adversary culture' and the monolithically victimized mass was being played out by the new feminist intellectuals.

Like many Cold War liberals, antiporn feminists also seized on a specifically *cultural* object of attention as the *causal* subject of their critique of power relations. Just as 'mass culture' has been diagnosed as containing all of the reasons for everyday life domination in the postwar 'mass society', so popular pornography came to be seen as the singular cause of sexist oppression in a patriarchal society. Robin Morgan's well-known slogan, 'pornography is the theory, rape is the practice', codified the link between the anti-violence movement and the fully visible and demonstrably concrete object of pornographic images and literature.

As has often been pointed out, the new, exclusive focus on pornography came at a time when the unity of the women's movement was in question. Interpretation of the porn industry's growth as a direct backlash against the claims of feminism helped to mobilize a newly unified voice within the women's movement. Better than any abstract critique of patriarchy, the evidentiary nature of pornography provided a spectacular point of convergence for many different interests and struggles, and therefore it came to be isolated as the *essential* issue of radical feminist attention – the primary site for the creation and normalization of violence against women. Thus, from the point of view of its (male) user, the broad range of pornographic materials was held to offer a spectrum of ideological addiction, from the soft-core *Playboy* to the 'snuff' film; from the point of view of its (female) victims, pornography offered no representation of their true desires, and every single reason for their enslavement and powerlessness. Consequently, the represented scenarios of pornographic images came to bear a clear and literally direct responsibility for their assumed effects in a world in which universally destructive and predatory male consumers were licensed to interpret these scenarios as if they were real.

Critical response, feminist and otherwise, to the antiporn critique has been extensive, and I will briefly summarize the chief arguments. Because of its fixed analysis of cause and effects in a fixed world of gendered power relations, the antiporn critique was seen as having no interest in the wide variety of uses to which pornography was put by diverse consumers and taste subcultures. Because of its acceptance of an ahistorical patriarchal logic, it had no analysis of the specific influence of consumer capitalism's volatility upon the human capacity for erotic stimulation. Because of its literalist interpretation of images, it could not account for the interplay between the complex constructions of representation and fantasy in the consumption of pornography. Because of its proponents' unfamiliarity with the full range of materials of pornographic consumption, it could not understand the shifting configurations of pleasure and desire which accounted for pornography's vast popularity. Because of its essentialist and reductionist view of sexual difference, it could not accommodate the testimony of women who enjoyed pornography, or sex workers for whom exhibitionism was an empowering experience. Because of its moralism, it had no explanatory response, other than a principled condemnation, of pornography's sexual arousal of both men and women who perhaps perceived this arousal as 'wrong' in some way, and were further aroused by this perception.

On the basis of these criticisms and others, an anti-antiporn movement of feminist intellectuals has established itself. In its challenge to a social critique that subscribes to a monolithic, undifferentiated analysis of popular culture, and that advocates collusion with censorial State power, anti-antiporn has had to make many of the same kind of arguments (including the charge of red-baiting) as anti-anticommunism did in the sixties. In particular, it has had to combat the moral panic and conspiracy mania that are shared features of the discoures of both anticommunist and antiporn intellectuals. In promoting the idea of an *expansive* popular culture for women – as opposed to a *restrictive* mass culture – the anti-antiporn movement has also had to negotiate two knotty problems for a liberatory sexual politics: first, the conservatism of the unconscious, and second, the fickleness of capital.

On the one hand, there is the integral importance of 'regressive' but unreformable fantasies of aggressivity to the construction of sexuality, and more generally, the resistance of psychic life to any *directly* imposed pressure towards social change. And on the other, there is the profit that consumer capitalism draws from ever finer marketplace discriminations between social and sexual identities even as these discriminations lend themselves to further extensions of social control. The intransigence of these two factors hardly promises to deliver a utopian culture of sexual freedom, equality, and mutuality, or at least not one that would take the form of a 'love story'. The first affirms that violence and aggressivity are likely to remain constitutive elements of our sexuality, and that we should always be prepared to take their effects into account or at least make allowance for them. The second explains how the creation of new sexual identities (women, gays and lesbians) in the liberation movements was partially achieved through the agency of a consumer capitalism which stood to profit from the exploitation of markets formed around these identities. But while neither of these factors seems to lend itself to traditional forms of 'progressive' politics, neither threatens in itself to stand in the way of a radical democratic agenda for full sexual rights. The unconscious does not distinguish between fantasies on the basis of superior quality or political correctness. And capital *per se* does not discriminate against profitable minority tastes and pleasures on the basis of morality alone, which is why a *moral* agenda à la Reagan/ Thatcher always has to be grafted onto the ideology of an enterprise culture, with all of the resulting contradictions.

It may be that sex will have to become fully capitalist before it can be anything else. But to realize the potential of that 'anything else' will involve recognizing where the *liberatory* imagination parts company with the *libertarian* view that pleasure is natural and ought to be freely pursued. The anarchic, laissez-faire sexual marketplace that was associated in particular with the pre-AIDS gay community has often been criticized on the left as a typical model of the libertarian doctrines of free will and choice. On the other hand, this marketplace has been strongly contested by conservative pressure groups on the right. Consequently, it has become a guarantee, at least until legal equality is won, that the existence of sexual minorities and their struggle for sexual rights remain in the realm of public visibility. More often than not, the first to suffer from any moral regulation of the sexual marketplace are those sexual minorities who survive, for lack of civil legitimacy, on its margins, and this has certainly been one of the first effects of the AIDS crisis.

In this respect, the liberatory imagination must exploit the short-term pragmatic benefits of libertarian principles (wherever they are still in practice) because its eyes are on the prize of full sexual rights; it has no ultimate, long-term interest in the principle of free will or free trade. This is not to sanction the commodification of sex, it is to salvage any available gains, under circumstances that are never ideal, from the contradictions of a capitalist culture. Whether or not one rejects the fundamental principles of a market economy, the limited though positive features of market legitimacy cannot be historically dismissed in the case of pornography. There is little doubt that the most unsavoury – violent and/or misogynistic – features of pornographic representation flourished in conditions when pornography was underground, and marketed illicitly. Pornography's increasingly legitimate legal status in the marketplace over the last two decades has been accompanied by the gradual disappearance of these features and a limited improvement in working conditions in the sex industry generally.

What, then, is characteristic of pornographic pleasure? If we listen to traditional intellectuals, the story we hear is one of repetition, sameness, and monotony – the qualities of standardized effects attributed to popular culture generally. But this could hardly account for the enormously differentiated range of pornography, nor for the practised power of discrimination which consumers of pornography show in their endless search for new sources of arousal which will 'repeat' familiar pleasures. While an image, shot, or sequence that is arousing in one instance may lose its power to arouse repeatedly, each fresh set of images is addressed to our carnal knowledge and memory of similar or related images. So too, while our bodies may recognize or acquire fixed, or generic tastes for certain activities or representations, they are rarely so specific as to exclude the possibility of arousal by a different genre of images or activities. The erotic body is not transhistorical, and the grammar of its response to pornography, while informed by a 'deep structure' of primal and infantile fantasies held, more or less, in common, is inflected by a personal psycho-sexual history of social experiences which ensures that its articulated sexuality is as unique as a thumbprint, while never so fixed in its contours as to be a reliable guarantee of identity.

To consider further what this grammar of responses entails for particular social subjects, I will first make one or two points about the formal organization of pornography. My comments, here and throughout, are directed more or less exclusively towards Western porn culture. Both the traditional intellectual and the antiporn feminist find grounds for disapproval in classical male pornography's lack of respect for narrative; for the former, it is a serious organic flaw, while for the latter, it demonstrates a callous scorn for the holistic experience of a properly loving and sexually fulfilling human relationship.

In fact, pornography is not at all inattentive to narrative, especially when considered within the context of its markets of consumption. Pornography's narrative form, in each of its many genres, is very closely tailored to the demands of its traditional male market, broadly based around the activity of masturbation. Whether in the 8mm stag film or video loop viewed in a booth, or in the sequence of images laid out in a magazine or 'stroke book', the suggested duration and emphasis of a narrative of encounter, arousal, and ejaculation is more or less linked to the temporality of male masturbation, which mediates the viewing process. This does not mean that the images, as if in accord with the model of behaviour conditioning, strictly determine and invoke a mechanical response in the masturbator. Even in contexts, like the video booths or peep shows in porn stores, where the consumer's contact with pornography is limited to the finite time which he pays for, his response is never simply determined by what he is offered in the way of images; it is always mediated, and thus is more likely to be determined by the fact that his arousal and pleasure is conditional upon his desire and/or his monetary capacity to pay more to extend his allotted time.

Here, then, in these conditions under which the less privileged are obliged to consume, pleasure is concretely tied to the necessity of exchanging small amounts of petty cash, a necessity spared the wealthier consumer for whom the transactional act of exchange – a 'dirty' act for the non-needy generally – can be distanced from the pleasures of consumption. For the consumer on the street, then, his pleasure is tied to what he can afford there and then, on the pornographer's premises. This does not make his pleasure qualitatively or quantitatively inferior to that of the wealthier consumer who can pay for the conditions under which he may choose to use pornography which he has either bought or rented. It does, however, explain the particular narrative form exhibited by certain kinds of pornography made to be consumed in specific contexts and under specific conditions. Different altogether, is the case of the post-1972 full-length narrative films, made for theatrical distribution. They are punctuated with sexual sequences that are set apart in time – at least ten minutes – and thus offer an economic series of masturbatory possibilities. More recently, VCR technology has allowed the consumer to isolate and to further control the masturbatory sequences offered by the home video market.

Pornography, in whatever commercial form or package, or in whatever cultural context, can never absolutely determine the nature of arousal and pleasure; it merely *aims at the market-targeted body (usually male) in ways which are likely to excite that body*, and the popularity of this or that film or magazine is evidence of its success. The same might be said of the long, seductively drawn out narrative of the romance novel, whose virtue for female readers has been claimed to reside in the qualities of waiting, breathless anticipation, and anxiety – all features of a seemingly endless discursive foreplay which is held to be more germane to the rhythms and economy of female pleasure than the sparse libidinal narrative of male pornography, but which strives after the same effect of arousal nonetheless. Here, then is a definition of what are conventionally taken to be the respective staple quotients of 'male' and 'female' pornography – a maximum of sex and minimum of foreplay in one, and the very opposite mixture in the other.

Many arguments could be posed in favour of rejecting this distinction *tout court*, and many more could be deployed to question whether such a distinction, even if it were accepted as conventional currency, could be assumed to be based upon biological or socially constructed differences. As it is, this distinction primarily applies to and derives from a comparison between visual and literary forms of production respectively, at least within the last two decades, and therefore reflects the uneven development of cultural *technology* across gender-specific markets during that time – promoting visual images for men and literature for women. Nonetheless, it is widely accepted, even by the new feminist pornmakers, that 'women-oriented' pornography is characterized by a greater emphasis on 'plot' and development of narrative. Recent advances in cable and in VCR technology have brought visual pornography directly into the domestic space. As a result, the adult video for home rental by couples is economically designed to cater to both modes or narratives of sexual response. Enjoying access to cheaper technology, the industry has been able to lavish time, money, and production values on stylized, romantic settings, more intricate narrative frames and build-ups, extended foreplay, and scenarios of mutual pleasure. On the other hand, the fast-forward feature of VCR technology ensures that the more graphic 'bits' can still be rapidly located if required for a hard-core fix.

Porn films, moreover, do not lend themselves easily to discussion among film theorists about the visual pleasure afforded by narrative in the classical realist cinema. It makes little sense to treat pornography as if it were a realist text, for this tends to discount the work of fantasy that is more directly brought into play during the viewing and use of pornography. The plot of realist films is often recounted to others in the same way as we reconstruct dreams out loud to friends, but pornography is like fantasies in this respect; no one would dream of recounting the narrative form of either. Pornography, for the most part, provides a stimulus, base, or foundation for individual fantasies to be built upon and elaborated. It merely provides the conditions – stock, generic, eroticizable components such as poses, clothing, and sounds – under which the pleasure of fantasizing, a pleasure unto itself, can be pursued. It cannot, of course, determine the precise nature or shape of the viewer's fantasies; it is aimed in the direction of his or her fantasmatic pleasure. As a result, it does not possess anything like the power of a realist Hollywood film to shape or control the effect of its representations, whether 'harmful', to use the terms of the antiporn critique, or aesthetically spurious, to the mind of the traditional intellectual.

This is not to say, of course, that pornography is anti-realist in the same way as the non-narrative avant-garde film, which deliberately sets out to disrupt the linear narratives of realism. The avant-garde film is addressed, for the most part, to intellectuals who are generally not tied, in their everyday lives, to the fixed narrative of the weekly work patterns that govern and demarcate the leisure activities of a working population. An audience of intellectuals has the time and the training to 'work' at its response to avant-garde film, while an audience of non-intellectuals is more likely to view the cultural work demanded by non-narrative film either as an unwanted imposition of overtime labour or as an obstacle in the way of the emotional gratification provided by the realist narrative.

As for the workplace itself, traditional pornography presents a special case because of its widespread use there. The exhibition of pornographic pinups in the workplace, while it is increasingly contested in the mixed workplace (by women and men, although it is also frequently *used* to reassert male privilege in that milieu) attests to the fact that their traditional male use as a fantasmatic stimulus crosses the often strictly observed divide between the world of work and the world of leisure. So too, while a television show or a film, or even the recounting of a personal sexual encounter often provides a focus for communal discussion among groups of men or women in the workplace, a pornographic image, 'cheesecake' for men or 'beefcake' for women, is offered largely as an invitation to indulge in personal fantasy. It may be passed around communally, and will be commented upon in a ribald way, but usually in a consensus of appreciation as if to affirm that even if such an image speaks to their everyday needs and desires, it represents a realm of experience that is above and beyond the possible experience of that group of men or women.

Pornography is used in this way to confirm the solidarity or cohesiveness of class taste by representing conditions of experience that are recognized as superior to those with which these social groups are likely to be familiar. Anything which threatens to demystify the superiority of the pinup invites ruthless criticism. In my own experience of all-male workplaces, this criticism, when it occurs, is usually directed not at female pinups themselves but at representations of men in especially awkward positions, or, in the case of film images depicting sexual performance, when the actor is shown to be temporarily impotent or incapacitated in such a way as to detract from his prodigious dramatization of sexual prowess. In contrast to the case of realist entertainment, where a film can draw criticism because it is 'too unrealistic' or far fetched, pornography can be criticized for a surfeit of realism which brings its fantasy world uncomfortably close to home. So too, it is likely that the porn film spectacle of hard-working bodies, repetitiously pursuing, with muscle and sweat and sperm, the performance and productivity levels required by the genre has as much to do with the libidinal economy of labour as with the popular aesthetic of athletic prowess. In this respect, the use of pornography might be said to challenge any tidy division between labour and leisure, or productivity and pleasure; its use speaks, at some level, to the potential power of fantasy to locate pleasure in work (even to eroticize work) as well as in play.

It is difficult, then, to discuss pornography as *entertainment* in the conventionally organized sense in which the culture industries demarcate leisure time from work time. So too, it holds an equally problematic relation to the categories with which intellectuals have discussed the 'progressive' features of narrative and editing in filmmaking that challenges the codes of Hollywood realism. In a discussion of the gay porn film, for example, Richard Dyer notes that its narrative and editing is seldom organized around 'the desire to be fucked', and almost always subscribes to the 'active' ejaculatory model of linear male pleasure. Can gay male sexuality be represented differently? asks Dyer. Can its pleasure be invoked in non-narrative ways? Citing the non-narrative, non-linear lesbian sequences at the end of Chantal Akerman's *Je Tu Il Elle* (1974) as a praiseworthy example of an alternative representation of sexuality, he proposes that male pornography, which, for better or worse, has cornered the market on the representation of sexuality, ought to be used for the 'education of desire', and the 'experimental education of the body', and consequently, ought to think about absorbing some of the lessons of the experimental counter-cinema.

This call for an 'education of desire' is likely to resonate most seriously within the gay community, where the need for eroticizing representations of safe sex has been most paramount, where pornography is of central political importance anyway, and where its production and consumption is ethically marked by an equality of participation among producers, performers, and consumers that is still barely evident in the straight industry and market. But the call to 'educate' desire, or anything else for that matter, is one which comes instinctively to intellectuals, all too willing to propose or act out their reformist zeal on behalf of others. Even if there can be no doubt about the urgent need, today, to think about the framework of possibilities within which pornography can be used to address the issue of safe sex, it is still a surprise to find Dyer making such a proposal, since his work on popular culture manages so carefully to avoid the moral presumptions that usually accompany campaigns for 'educational' reform.

What, then, is so different about pornography that it can be considered a respectful way to think about educating the popular body? One possible answer to that question is that the education of desire through pornography, however it is conceived and practised, would have to involve *producing* pleasure, rather than *reducing* or combating pleasure. Reform through pornography cannot proceed, at least with any hope of success, at the expense of pleasure, and, least of all, if it takes a militant path of anti-pleasure. Even the most carefully planned attempts are at pains to avoid any intrusive didacticism.

See p. 271

17 Eve Kosofsky Sedgwick

Axiomatic

EDITOR'S INTRODUCTION

In this subtle piece of methodological ground-clearing (or mine-sweeping), part of the introduction to her book *Epistemology of the Closet*, Eve Sedgwick elaborates some deceptively simple axioms from which queer studies might proceed. Of particular interest is her discussion of the Foucauldian claim that 'homosexuality' begins around 1870. What this means, of course, is that individuals who preferred sex with people of their own sex were then for the first time defined or identified as (fundamentally pathological) 'homosexuals'. But, as Sedgwick argues, even as we try to dismantle the category 'homosexual' we are playing a game in which one large model is being replaced with another large model. In this situation it is important to take the banality 'We are all different people' (Axiom 1) very seriously.

This banal proposition contains a pun: we're all different from each other, and we're not always the same ourselves. It is because the first is true that 'allo-identification' (identification with the other) should take place, however rarely it does; and it is because the second is true that the first *can* take place: we cannot simply 'auto-identify' once and for all. Thus same-sex sex, like different-sex sex, involves a mixture of both kinds of identification. At a more general level, for Sedgwick, auto-identification requires narratives which try to account for *how* we came to be what we are and, more than that, to establish *what* we are – though, of course, this can never be finally determined. Such narratives can also trigger further identifications by and with others. More particularly, Sedgwick implies, lesbian and gay studies need a particular mix of auto- and allo-identification if they are to remain different from, but not radically other to, each other.

Further reading: Butler 1990; Foucault 1980; Halperin 1989; Heath 1982; Rubin 1975, 1984; Sedgwick 1987, 1990; Weeks 1985.

S.D.

Epistemology of the Closet proposes that many of the major nodes of thought and knowledge in twentieth-century Western culture as a whole are structured – indeed, fractured – by a chronic, now endemic crisis of homo/heterosexual definition, indicatively male, dating from the end of the nineteenth century. The book will argue that an understanding of virtually any aspect of modern Western culture must be, not merely incomplete, but damaged in its central substance to the degree that it does not incorporate a critical analysis of modern homo/ heterosexual definition; and it will assume that the appropriate place for that critical analysis to begin is from the relatively decentred perspective of modern gay and antihomophobic theory.

The passage of time, the bestowal of thought and necessary political struggle since the turn of the century have only spread and deepened the long crisis of modern sexual definition, dramatizing, often violently, the internal incoherence and mutual contradiction of each of the forms of discursive and institutional 'common sense' on this subject inherited from the architects of our present culture. The contradictions I will be discussing are not in the first place those between prohomosexual and antihomosexual people or ideologies, although the book's strongest motivation is indeed the gay-affirmative one. Rather, the contradictions that seem most active are the ones internal to all the important twentieth-century understandings of homo/heterosexual definition, both heterosexist and antihomophobic. Their outlines and something of their history are sketched in Chapter 1. Briefly, they are two. The first is the contradiction between seeing homo/heterosexual definition on the one hand as an issue of active importance primarily for a small, distinct, relatively fixed homosexual minority (what I refer to as a minoritizing view), and seeing it on the other hand as an issue of continuing, determinative importance in the lives of people across the spectrum of sexualities (what I refer to as a universalizing view). The second is the contradiction between seeing same-sex object choice on the one hand as a matter of liminality or transitivity between genders, and seeing it on the other hand as reflecting an impulse of separatism – though by no means necessarily political separatism – within each gender. The purpose of this book is not to adjudicate between the two poles of either of these contradictions, for, if its argument is right, no epistemological grounding now exists from which to do so. Instead, I am trying to make the strongest possible introductory case for a hypothesis about the centrality of this nominally marginal, conceptually intractable set of definitional issues to the important knowledges and understandings of twentieth-century Western culture as a whole.

The word 'homosexual' entered Euro-American discourse during the last third of the nineteenth century – its popularization preceding, as it happens, even that of the word 'heterosexual'. It seems clear that the sexual behaviours, and even for some people the conscious identities, denoted by the new term 'homosexual' and its contemporary variants already had a long, rich history. So, indeed, did a wide range of other sexual behaviours and behavioural clusters. What *was* new from the turn of the century was the world-mapping by which every given person, just as he or she was necessarily assignable to a male or a female gender, was now considered necessarily assignable as well to a homo- or a hetero-sexuality, a binarized identity that was full of implications, however confusing, for even the ostensibly least sexual aspects of personal existence. It was this new development that left no space in the culture exempt from the potent incoherences of homo/heterosexual definition.

New, institutionalized taxonomic discourses – medical, legal, literary, psychological – centring on homo/heterosexual definition proliferated and crystallized with exceptional rapidity in the decades around the turn of the century, decades in which so many of the other critical nodes of the culture were being, if less suddenly and newly, nonetheless also definitively reshaped. Both the power relations between the genders and the relations of nationalism and imperialism, for instance, were in highly visible crisis. For this reason, and because the structuring of same-sex bonds can't, in any historical situation marked by inequality and contest *between* genders, fail to be a site of intensive regulation that intersects virtually every issue of power and gender, lines can never be drawn to circumscribe within some proper domain of sexuality (whatever that might be) the consequences of a shift in sexual discourse. Furthermore, in accord with Foucault's demonstration, whose results I will take to be axiomatic, that modern Western culture has placed what it calls sexuality in a more and more distinctively privileged relation to our most prized constructs of individual identity, truth, and knowledge, it becomes truer and truer that the language of sexuality not only intersects with but transforms the other languages and relations by which we know.

An assumption underlying the book is that the relations of the closet – the relations of the known and the unknown, the explicit and the inexplicit around homo/heterosexual definition – have the potential for being peculiarly revealing, in fact, about speech acts more generally.

But, in the vicinity of the closet, even what *counts* as a speech act is problematized on a perfectly routine basis. As Foucault says: 'there is no binary division to be made between what one says and what one does not say; we must try to determine the different ways of not saying such things. . . . There is not one but many silences, and they are an integral part of the strategies that underlie and permeate discourses' (Foucault 1978: 27). 'Closetedness' itself is a performance initiated as such by the speech act of a silence – not a particular silence, but a silence that accrues particularity by fits and starts, in relation to the discourse that surrounds and differentially constitutes it. The speech acts that coming out, in turn, can comprise are as strangely specific. And they may have nothing to do with the acquisition of new information. I think of a man and a woman I know, best friends, who for years canvassed freely the emotional complications of each other's erotic lives – the man's eroticism happening to focus exclusively on men. But it was only after one particular conversational moment, fully a decade into this relationship, that it seemed to either of these friends that permission had been given to the woman to refer to the man, in their conversation together, as *a gay man*. Discussing it much later, both agreed they had felt at the time that this one moment had constituted a clear-cut act of coming out, even in the context of years and years beforehand of exchange predicated on the man's *being* gay. What was said to make this difference? Not a version of 'I am gay', which could only have been bathetic between them. What constituted coming out for this man, in this situation, was to use about himself the phrase 'coming out' – to mention, as if casually, having come out to someone else. (Similarly, a T-shirt that ACT UP sells in New York bearing the text 'I am out, therefore I am', is meant to do for the wearer, not the constative work of reporting that s/he *is* out, but the performative work of coming out in the first place.) And the fact that silence is rendered as pointed and performative as speech, in relations around the closet, depends on and highlights more broadly the fact that ignorance is as potent and as multiple a thing there as is knowledge.

Anyone working in gay and lesbian studies, in a culture where same-sex desire is still structured by its distinctive public/private status, at once marginal and central, as *the* open secret, discovers that the line between straining at truths that prove to be imbecilically self-evident, on the one hand, and on the other hand tossing off commonplaces that turn out to retain their power to galvanize and divide, is weirdly unpredictable. In dealing with an open-secret structure, it's only by being shameless about risking the obvious that we happen into the vicinity of the transformative. I have methodically to sweep into one little heap some of the otherwise unarticulated assumptions and conclusions from a long-term project of antihomophobic analysis. These nails, these scraps of wiring: will they bore or will they shock?

Under the rule that most privileges the most obvious:

Axiom 1: People are different from each other.

It is astonishing how few respectable conceptual tools we have for dealing with this self-evident fact. A tiny number of inconceivably coarse axes of categorization have been painstakingly inscribed in current critical and political thought: gender, race, class, nationality, sexual orientation are pretty much the available distinctions. They, with the associated demonstrations of the mechanisms by which they are constructed and reproduced, are indispensable, and they may indeed override all or some other forms of difference and similarity. But the sister or brother, the best friend, the classmate, the parent, the child, the lover, the ex-: our families, loves, and enmities alike, not to mention the strange relations of our work, play, and activism, prove that even people who share all or most of our own positionings along these crude axes may still be different enough from us, and from each other, to seem like all but different species.

Everybody has learned this, I assume, and probably everybody who survives at all has reasonably rich, unsystematic resources of nonce taxonomy for mapping out the possibilities, dangers, and stimulations of their human social landscape. It is probably people with the experience of oppression or subordination who have most *need* to know it; and I take the precious, devalued arts of gossip, immemorially associated in European thought with servants, with effeminate and gay men, with all women, to have to do not even so much with the transmission of necessary news as with the refinement of necessary skills for making, testing, and using unrationalized and provisional hypotheses about what *kinds of people* there are to be found in one's world. The writing of a Proust or a James would be exemplary here: projects precisely of *nonce* taxonomy, of the making and unmaking and *re*making and redissolution of hundreds of old and new categorical imaginings concerning all the kinds it may take to make up a world.

I don't assume that all gay men or all women are very skilled at the nonce-taxonomic work represented by gossip, but it does make sense to

suppose that our distinctive needs are peculiarly disserved by its devaluation. For some people, the sustained, foregrounded pressure of
loss in the AIDS years may be making such needs clearer: as one
anticipates or tries to deal with the absence of people one loves, it seems
absurdly impoverishing to surrender to theoretical trivialization or to
'the sentimental' one's descriptive requirements that the piercing bou-
quet of a given friend's particularity be done some justice. What is more
dramatic is that – in spite of every promise to the contrary – every single
theoretically or politically interesting project of postwar thought has
finally had the effect of delegitimating our space for asking or thinking
in detail about the multiple, unstable ways in which people may be like
or different from each other. This project is not rendered otiose by any
demonstration of how fully people may differ also from themselves.
Deconstruction, founded as a very science of *différ(e/a)nce*, has both so
fetishized the idea of difference and so vaporized its possible embodiments that its most thoroughgoing practitioners are the last people to
whom one would now look for help in thinking about particular differ-
en*ces*. The same thing seems likely to prove true of theorists of postmodernism. Psychoanalytic theory, if only through the almost
astrologically lush plurality of its overlapping taxonomies of physical
zones, developmental stages, representational mechanisms, and levels
of consciousness, seemed to promise to introduce a certain becoming
amplitude into discussions of what different people are like – only to
turn, in its streamlined trajectory across so many institutional boundaries, into the sveltest of metatheoretical disciplines, sleeked down to
such elegant operational entities as *the* mother, *the* father, *the* preoedipal,
the oedipal, *the* other or Other. Within the less theorized institutional
confines of intrapsychoanalytic discourse, meanwhile, a narrowly and
severely normative, difference-eradicating ethical programme has long
sheltered under developmental narratives and a metaphorics of health
and pathology. In more familiar ways, Marxist, feminist, postcolonial,
and other engagé critical projects have deepened understandings of a
few crucial axes of difference, perhaps necessarily at the expense of
more ephemeral or less global impulses of differential grouping. In each
of these enquiries, so much has been gained by the different ways we
have learned to deconstruct the category of *the individual* that it is easy
for us now to read, say, Proust as the most expert operator of our
modern technologies for dismantling taxonomies of the person. For the
emergence and persistence of the vitalizing worldly taxonomic energies
on which Proust also depends, however, we have no theoretical support

to offer. And these defalcations in our indispensable antihumanist discourses have apparently ceded the potentially forceful ground of profound, complex variation to humanist liberal 'tolerance' or repressively trivializing celebration at best, to reactionary suppression at worst.

In the particular area of sexuality, for instance, I assume that most of us know the following things that can differentiate even people of identical gender, race, nationality, class, and 'sexual orientation' – each one of which, however, if taken seriously as pure *difference*, retains the unaccounted-for potential to disrupt many forms of the available thinking about sexuality.

- Even identical genital acts mean very different things to different people.
- To some people, the nimbus of 'the sexual' seems scarcely to extend beyond the boundaries of discrete genital acts; to others, it enfolds them loosely or floats virtually free of them.
- Sexuality makes up a large share of the self-perceived identity of some people, a small share of others'.
- Some people spend a lot of time thinking about sex, others little.
- Some people like to have a lot of sex, others little or none.
- Many people have their richest mental/emotional involvement with sexual acts that they don't do, or even don't *want* to do.
- For some people, it is important that sex be embedded in contexts resonant with meaning, narrative, and connectedness with other aspects of their life; for other people, it is important that they not be; to others it doesn't occur that they might be.
- For some people, the preference for a certain sexual object, act, role, zone, or scenario is so immemorial and durable that it can only be experienced as innate; for others, it appears to come late or to feel aleatory or discretionary.
- For some people, the possibility of bad sex is aversive enough that their lives are strongly marked by its avoidance; for others, it isn't.
- For some people, sexuality provides a needed space of heightened discovery and cognitive hyperstimulation. For others, sexuality provides a needed space of routinized habituation and cognitive hiatus.
- Some people like spontaneous sexual scenes, others like highly scripted ones, others like spontaneous-sounding ones that are nonetheless totally predictable.
- Some people's sexual orientation is intensely marked by autoerotic pleasures and histories – sometimes more so than by any aspect of

alloerotic object choice. For others the autoerotic possibility seems secondary or fragile, if it exists at all.

- Some people, homo-, hetero-, and bisexual, experience their sexuality as deeply embedded in a matrix of gender meanings and gender differentials. Others of each sexuality do not.

Axiom 2: The study of sexuality is not coextensive with the study of gender; correspondingly, antihomophobic enquiry is not coextensive with feminist enquiry. But we can't know in advance how they will be different.

Sex, gender, sexuality: three terms whose usage relations and analytical relations are almost irremediably slippery. The charting of a space between something called 'sex' and something called 'gender' has been one of the most influential and successful undertakings of feminist thought. For the purposes of that undertaking, 'sex' has had the meaning of a certain group of irreducible, biological differentiations between members of the species Homo sapiens who have XX and those who have XY chromosomes. These include (or are ordinarily thought to include) more or less marked dimorphisms of genital formation, hair growth (in populations that have body hair), fat distribution, hormonal function, and reproductive capacity. 'Sex' in this sense – what I'll demarcate as 'chromosomal sex' – is seen as the relatively minimal raw material on which is then based the social construction of *gender*. Gender, then, is the far more elaborated, more fully and rigidly dichotomized social production and reproduction of male and female identities and behaviours – of male and female *persons* – in a cultural system for which 'male/female' functions as a primary and perhaps model binarism affecting the structure and meaning of many, many other binarisms whose apparent connection to chromosomal sex will often be exiguous or non-existent. Compared to chromosomal sex, which is seen (by these definitions) as tending to be immutable, immanent in the individual, and biologically based, the meaning of gender is seen as culturally mutable and variable, highly relational (in the sense that each of the binarized genders is defined primarily by its relation to the other), and inextricable from a history of power differentials between genders. This feminist charting of what Gayle Rubin refers to as a 'sex/gender system', the system by which chromosomal sex is turned into, and processed as, cultural gender, has tended to minimize the attribution of people's various behaviours and identities to chromosomal sex and to maximize their attribution to socialized gender constructs. The purpose of that strategy has been to gain analytic and critical leverage on the female-disadvantaging social arrangements that prevail at a given time in a given society, by throwing into question their legitimative ideological grounding in biologically based narratives of the 'natural'.

'Sex' is, however, a term that extends indefinitely beyond chromosomal sex. That its history of usage often overlaps with what might, now, more properly be called 'gender' is only one problem. ('I can only love someone of my own sex.' Shouldn't 'sex' be 'gender' in such a sentence? 'M. saw that the person who approached was of the opposite sex.' Genders – insofar as there are two and they are defined in contradistinction to one another – may be said to be opposite; but in what sense is XX the opposite of XY?) Beyond chromosomes, however, the association of 'sex', precisely through the physical body, with reproduction and with genital activity and sensation keeps offering new challenges to the conceptual clarity or even possibility of sex/gender differentiation. There is a powerful argument to be made that a primary (or *the* primary) issue in gender differentiation and gender struggle is the question of who is to have control of women's (biologically) distinctive reproductive capability. Indeed, the intimacy of the association between several of the most signal forms of gender oppression and 'the facts' of women's bodies and women's reproductive activity has led some radical feminists to question, more or less explicitly, the usefulness of insisting on a sex/gender distinction. For these reasons, even usages involving the 'sex/gender system' within feminist theory are able to use 'sex/gender' only to delineate a problematical *space* rather than a crisp distinction. My own loose usage in this book will be to denominate that problematized space of the sex/gender system, the whole package of physical and cultural distinctions between women and men, more simply under the rubric 'gender'. I do this in order to reduce the likelihood of confusion between 'sex' in the sense of 'the space of differences between male and female' (what I'll be grouping under 'gender') and 'sex' in the sense of sexuality.

For meanwhile the whole realm of what modern culture refers to as 'sexuality' and *also* calls 'sex' – the array of acts, expectations, narratives, pleasures, identity-formations, and knowledges, in both women and men, that tends to cluster most densely around certain genital sensations but is not adequately defined by them – that realm is virtually impossible to situate on a map delimited by the feminist-defined sex/gender distinction. To the degree that it has a centre or starting point in certain physical sites, acts, and rhythms associated (however

Biological	Cultural
Essential	Constructed
Individually immanent	Relational

Constructivist Feminist Analysis

chromosomal sex ———————————————— gender
gender inequality

Radical Feminist Analysis

chromosomal sex
reproductive relations ———————————— reproductive relations
sexual inequality sexual inequality

Foucault-influenced Analysis

chromosomal sex ——————— reproduction ——————— sexuality

Figure 1 Some mappings of sex, gender, and sexuality

contingently) with procreation or the potential for it, 'sexuality' in this sense may seem to be of a piece with 'chromosomal sex': biologically necessary to species survival, tending toward the individually imma-nent, the socially immutable, the given. But to the extent that, as Freud argued and Foucault assumed, the distinctively sexual nature of human sexuality has to do precisely with its excess over or potential difference from the bare choreographies of procreation, 'sexuality' might be the very opposite of what we originally referred to as (chromosomal-based) sex: it could occupy, instead, even more than 'gender' the polar position of the relational, the social/symbolic, the constructed, the variable, the representational (see Figure 1). To note that, according to these different findings, *something* legitimately called sex or sexuality is all over the experiential and conceptual map is to record a problem less resolvable than a necessary choice of analytic paradigms or a determinate slippage of semantic meaning; it is rather, I would say, true to quite a range of contemporary worldviews and intuitions to find that sex/sexuality *does* tend to represent the full spectrum of positions between the most intimate and the most social, the most predetermined and the most aleatory, the most physically rooted and the most symbolically infused, the most innate and the most learned, the most autonomous and the most relational traits of being.

If all this is true of the definitional nexus between sex and sexuality, how much less simple, even, must be that between sexuality and gender. It will be an assumption of this study that there is always at least the potential for an analytic distance between gender and sexuality, even if particular manifestations or features of particular sexualities are among the things that plunge women and men most ineluctably into the discursive, institutional, and bodily enmeshments of gender definition, gender relation, and gender inequality. This book will hypothesize that the question of gender and the question of sexuality, inextricable from one another though they are in that each can be expressed only in the terms of the other, are nonetheless not the same question, that in twentieth-century Western culture gender and sexuality represent two analytic axes that may productively be imagined as being as distinct from one another as, say, gender and class, or class and race. Distinct, that is to say, no more than minimally, but nonetheless usefully.

It would be a natural corollary to Axiom 2 to hypothesize, then, that gay/lesbian and antihomophobic enquiry still has a lot to learn from asking questions that feminist enquiry has learned to ask – but only so long as we don't demand to receive the same answers in both interlocutions. In a comparison of feminist and gay theory as they currently stand, the newness and consequent relative underdevelopment of gay theory are seen most clearly in two manifestations. First, we are by now very used to asking as feminists what we aren't yet used to asking as antihomophobic readers: how a variety of forms of oppression intertwine systematically with each other; and especially how the person who is disabled through one set of oppressions may *by the same positioning* be enabled through others. For instance, the understated demeanour of educated women in our society tends to mark both their deference to educated men and their expectation of deference from women and men of lower class. Again, a woman's use of a married name makes graphic at the same time her subordination as a woman and her privilege as a presumptive heterosexual. Or, again, the distinctive vulnerability to rape of women of all races has become in this country a powerful tool for the racist enforcement by which white people, including women, are privileged at the expense of Black people of both genders. That one is *either* oppressed *or* an oppressor, or that if one happens to be both, the two are not likely to have much to do with each other, still seems to be a common assumption, however, in at any rate male gay writing and activism, as it hasn't for a long time been in careful feminist work.

Indeed, it was the long, painful realization, *not* that all oppressions are congruent, but that they are *differently* structured and so must intersect in complex embodiments that was the first great heuristic breakthrough of socialist-feminist thought and of the thought of women of colour. This realization has as its corollary that the comparison of different axes of oppression is a crucial task, not for any purpose of ranking oppressions, but to the contrary because each oppression is likely to be in a uniquely indicative relation to certain distinctive nodes of cultural organization. The *special* centrality of homophobic oppression in the twentieth century, I will be arguing, has resulted from its inextricability from the question of knowledge and the processes of knowing in modern Western culture at large.

The second and perhaps even greater heuristic leap of feminism has been the recognition that categories of gender and, hence, oppressions of gender can have a structuring force for nodes of thought, for axes of cultural discrimination, whose thematic subject isn't explicitly gendered at all. Through a series of developments structured by the deconstructive understandings and procedures sketched above, we have now learned as feminist readers that dichotomies in a given text of culture as opposed to nature, public as opposed to private, mind as opposed to body, activity as opposed to passivity, etc. etc., are, under particular pressures of culture and history, likely places to look for implicit allegories of the relations of men to women; more, that to fail to analyse such nominally ungendered constructs in gender terms can itself be a gravely tendentious move in the gender politics of reading. This has given us ways to ask the question of gender about texts even where the culturally 'marked' gender (female) is not present as either author or thematic.

Axiom 3: There can't be an a priori decision about how far it will make sense to conceptualize lesbian and gay male identities together. Or separately.

The lesbian interpretive framework most readily available at the time this project began was the separatist-feminist one that emerged from the 1970s. According to that framework, there were essentially no valid grounds of commonality between gay male and lesbian experience and identity; to the contrary, women-loving women and men-loving men must be at precisely opposite ends of the gender spectrum. The assumptions at work here were indeed radical ones: most important, the stunningly efficacious re-visioning, in female terms, of same-sex desire as being at the very definitional centre of each gender, rather than as occupying a cross-gender or liminal position between them. Thus, women who loved women were seen as *more* female, men who loved men as quite possibly more male, than those whose desire crossed boundaries of gender. The axis of sexuality, in this view, was not only exactly coextensive with the axis of gender but expressive of its most heightened essence: 'Feminism is the theory, lesbianism is the practice.' By analogy, male homosexuality could be, and often was, seen as the practice for which male supremacy was the theory. A particular reading of modern gender history was, of course, implicit in and in turn propelled by this gender-separatist framework. In accord with, for instance, Adrienne Rich's understanding of many aspects of women's bonds as constituting a 'lesbian continuum', this history, found in its purest form in the work of Lilian Faderman, deemphasized the definitional discontinuities and perturbations between more and less sexualized, more and less prohibited, and more and less gender-identity-bound forms of female same-sex bonding. Insofar as lesbian object-choice was viewed as epitomizing a specificity of female experience and resistance, insofar as a symmetrically opposite understanding of gay male object-choice also obtained, and insofar also as feminism necessarily posited male and female experiences and interests as different and opposed, the implication was that an understanding of male homo/heterosexual definition could offer little or no affordance or interest for any lesbian theoretical project. Indeed, the powerful impetus of a gender-polarized feminist ethical schema made it possible for a profoundly antihomophobic reading of lesbian desire (as a quintessence of the female) to fuel a correspondingly homophobic reading of gay male desire (as a quintessence of the male).

Since the late 1970s, however, there have emerged a variety of challenges to this understanding of how lesbian and gay male desires and identities might be mapped against each other. Each challenge has led to a refreshed sense that lesbians and gay men may share important though contested aspects of one another's histories, cultures, identities, politics, and destinies. These challenges have emerged from the 'sex wars' within feminism over pornography and s/m, which seemed to many pro-sex feminists to expose a devastating continuity between a certain, theretofore privileged feminist understanding of a resistant female identity, on the one hand, and on the other the most repressive nineteenth-century bourgeois constructions of a sphere of pure femininity. Such challenges emerged as well from the reclamation and relegitimation of a courageous history of lesbian trans-gender role-playing and identification. Along with this new historical making-visible of self-defined mannish lesbians came a new salience of the many ways in which male and female homosexual identities had in fact been constructed through and in relation to each other over the last century – by the variously homophobic discourses of professional expertise, but also and just as actively by many lesbians and gay men. The irrepressible, relatively class-non-specific popular culture in which James Dean has been as numinous an icon for lesbians as Garbo or Dietrich has for gay men seems resistant to a purely feminist theorization. It is in these contexts that calls for a theorized axis of sexuality as distinct from gender have developed. And after the anti-s/m, antipornography liberal-feminist move toward labelling and stigmatizing particular sexualities joined its energies with those of the much longer-established conservative sanctions against all forms of sexual 'deviance', it remained only for the terrible accident of the HIV epidemic and the terrifyingly genocidal overdeterminations of AIDS discourse to reconstruct a category of the pervert capacious enough to admit homosexuals of any gender. The newly virulent homophobia of the 1980s, directed alike against women and men even though its medical pretext ought, if anything, logically to give a relative exemptive privilege to lesbians, reminds urgently that it is more to friends than to enemies that gay women and gay men are perceptible as distinct groups. Equally, however, the internal perspective of the gay movements shows women and men increasingly, though far from uncontestingly and far from equally, working together on mutually antihomophobic agendas. The contributions of lesbians to current gay and AIDS activism are weighty, not despite, but because of the intervening lessons of feminism. Feminist perspectives on medicine and health-care issues, on civil disobedience, and on the politics of class and race as well as of sexuality have been centrally enabling for the recent waves of AIDS activism. What this activism returns to the lesbians involved in it may include a more richly pluralized range of imaginings of lines of gender and sexual identification.

Thus, it can no longer make sense, if it ever did, simply to assume that a male-centred analysis of homo/heterosexual definition will have no lesbian relevance or interest. At the same time, there are no algorithms for assuming a priori what its lesbian relevance could be or how far its lesbian interest might extend.

Axiom 4: The immemorial, seemingly ritualized debates on nature versus nurture take place against a very unstable background of tacit assumptions and fantasies about both nurture and nature.

If there is one compulsory setpiece for the Introduction to any gay-oriented book written in the late 1980s, it must be the meditation on and attempted adjudication of constructivist versus essentialist views of homosexuality. My demurral has two grounds. The first is that any such adjudication is impossible to the degree that a conceptual deadlock between the two opposing views has by now been built into the very structure of every theoretical tool we have for undertaking it. The second one is already implicit in a terminological choice I have been making: to refer to 'minoritizing' versus 'universalizing' rather than to essentialist versus constructivist understandings of homosexuality. I prefer the former terminology because it seems to record and respond to the question, 'In whose lives is homo/heterosexual definition an issue of continuing centrality and difficulty?' rather than either of the questions that seem to have gotten conflated in the constructivist/essentialist debate: on the one hand what one might call the question of phylogeny, 'How fully are the meaning and experience of sexual activity and identity contingent on their mutual structuring with other, historically and culturally variable aspects of a given society?'; and on the other what one might call that of ontogeny, 'What is the cause of homo- [or of hetero-] sexuality in the individual?' I am specifically offering minoritizing/universalizing as an *alternative* (though not an equivalent) to essentialist/constructivist, in the sense that I think it can do some of the same analytic work as the latter binarism, and rather more tellingly. I think it may isolate the areas where the questions of ontogeny and phylogeny most consequentially overlap. I also think, as I suggested in Axiom 1, that it is more respectful of the varied proprioception of many authoritative individuals. But I am additionally eager to promote the obsolescence of 'essentialist/constructivist' because I am very dubious about the ability of even the most scrupulously gay-affirmative thinkers to divorce these terms, especially as they relate to the question of ontogeny, from the essentially gay-genocidal nexuses of thought through which they have developed. And beyond that: even where we may think we know the conceptual landscape of their history well enough to do the delicate, always dangerous work of prying them loose from their historical backing to attach to them newly enabling meanings, I fear that the special volatility of postmodern bodily and technological relations may make such an attempt peculiarly liable to tragic misfire. Thus, it would seem to me that gay-affirmative work does well when it aims to minimize its reliance on any particular account of the origin of sexual preference and identity in individuals.

In particular, my fear is that there currently exists no framework in which to ask about the origins or development of individual gay identity that is not already structured by an implicit, trans-individual Western project or fantasy of eradicating that identity. It seems ominously symptomatic that, under the dire homophobic pressures of the last few years, and in the name of Christianity, the subtle constructivist argument that sexual aim is, at least for many people, not a hard-wired biological given but, rather, a social fact deeply embedded in the cultural and linguistic forms of many, many decades is being degraded to the blithe ukase that people are 'free at any moment to' (i.e., must immediately) 'choose' to adhere to a particular sexual identity (say, at a random hazard, the heterosexual) rather than to its other. (Here we see the disastrously unmarked crossing of phylogenetic with ontogenetic narratives.) To the degree – and it is significantly large – that the gay essentialist/constructivist debate takes its form and premises from, and insistently refers to, a whole history of other nature/nurture or nature/culture debates, it partakes of a tradition of viewing culture as malleable relative to nature: that is, culture, unlike nature, is assumed to be the thing that can be changed; the thing in which 'humanity' has, furthermore, a right or even an obligation to intervene. This has certainly been the grounding of, for instance, the feminist formulation of the sex/gender system described above, whose implication is that the more fully gender inequality can be shown to inhere in human culture rather than in biological nature, the more amenable it must be to alteration and reform. I remember the buoyant enthusiasm with which feminist scholars used to greet the finding that one or another brutal form of oppression was not biological but 'only' cultural! I have often wondered what the basis was for our optimism about the malleability of culture by any one group or programme. At any rate, never so far as I know has there been a sufficiently powerful place from which to argue that such manipulations, however triumphal the ethical imperative behind them, were not a right that belonged to anyone who might have the power to perform them.

The number of persons or institutions by whom the existence of gay people – never mind the existence of *more gay people* – is treated as a precious desideratum, a needed condition of life, is small, even compared to those who may wish for the dignified treatment of any gay people who happen already to exist. Advice on how to make sure your kids turn out gay, not to mention your students, your parishioners, your therapy clients, or your military subordinates, is less ubiquitous than you might think. By contrast, the scope of institutions whose programmatic undertaking is to prevent the development of gay people is unimaginably large. No major institutionalized discourse offers a firm resistance to that undertaking; in the United States, at any rate, most sites of the state, the military, education, law, penal institutions, the church, medicine, mass culture, and the mental health industries enforce it all but unquestioningly, and with little hesitation even at recourse to invasive violence. So for gay and gay-loving people, even though the space of cultural malleability is the only conceivable theatre for our effective politics, every step of this constructivist nature/culture argument holds danger: it is so difficult to intervene in the seemingly natural trajectory that begins by identifying a place of cultural malleability; continues by inventing an ethical or therapeutic mandate for cultural manipulation; and ends in the overarching, hygienic Western fantasy of a world without any more homosexuals in it.

That's one set of dangers, and it is against them, I think, that essentialist understandings of sexual identity accrue a certain gravity. The resistance that seems to be offered by conceptualizing an unalterably *homosexual body*, to the social engineering momentum apparently built into every one of the human sciences of the West, can reassure profoundly. Furthermore, it reaches deeply and, in a sense, protectively into a fraught space of life-or-death struggle that has been more or less abandoned by constructivist gay theory: that is, the experience and identity of gay or proto-gay children. The ability of anyone in the culture to support and honour gay kids may depend on an ability to name them as such, notwithstanding that many gay adults may never have been gay kids and some gay kids may not turn into gay adults. It seems plausible that a lot of the emotional energy behind essentialist historical work has to do not even in the first place with reclaiming the place and eros of Homeric heroes, Renaissance painters, and medieval gay monks, so much as with the far less permissible, vastly more necessary project of recognizing and validating the creativity and heroism of the effeminate boy or tommish girl of the fifties (or sixties or seventies or eighties) whose sense of constituting precisely a *gap* in the discursive fabric of the given has not been done justice, so far, by constructivist work.

At the same time, however, just as it comes to seem questionable to assume that cultural constructs are peculiarly malleable ones, it is also becoming increasingly problematical to assume that grounding an identity in biology or 'essential nature' is a stable way of insulating it from societal interference. If anything, the gestalt of assumptions that

undergird nature/nurture debates may be in the process of direct reversal. Increasingly it is the conjecture that a particular trait is genetically or
biologically based, *not* that it is 'only cultural', that seems to trigger an
oestrus of manipulative fantasy in the technological institutions of the
culture. A relative depressiveness about the efficacy of social engineering techniques, a high mania about biological control: the Cartesian
bipolar psychosis that always underlay the nature/nurture debates has
switched its polar assignments without surrendering a bit of its hold
over the collective life. And in this unstable context, the dependence on
a specified *homosexual body* to offer resistance to any gay-eradicating
momentum is tremblingly vulnerable. AIDS, though it is used to proffer
every single day to the news-consuming public the crystallized vision of
a world after the homosexual, could never by itself bring about such a
world. What whets these fantasies more dangerously, because more
blandly, is the presentation, often in ostensibly or authentically gay-
affirmative contexts, of biologically based 'explanations' for deviant
behaviour that are absolutely invariably couched in terms of 'excess',
'deficiency', or 'imbalance' – whether in the hormones, in the genetic
material, or, as is currently fashionable, in the fetal endocrine environment. If I had ever, in any medium, seen any researcher or popularizer
refer even once to any supposed gay-producing circumstance as the
proper hormone balance, or the *conducive* endocrine environment, for gay
generation, I would be less chilled by the breezes of all this technological
confidence. As things are, a medicalized dream of the prevention of gay
bodies seems to be the less visible, far more respectable underside of the
AIDS-fuelled public dream of their extirpation. In this unstable balance
of assumptions between nature and culture, at any rate, under the
overarching, relatively unchallenged aegis of a culture's desire that gay
people *not be*, there is no unthreatened, unthreatening conceptual home
for a concept of gay origins. We have all the more reason, then, to keep
our understanding of gay origin, of gay cultural and material reproduction, plural, multi-capillaried, argus-eyed, respectful, and endlessly
cherished.

*Axiom 5: The historical search for a Great Paradigm Shift may obscure the
present conditions of sexual identity.*

Since 1976, when Michel Foucault, in an act of polemical bravado,
offered 1870 as the date of birth of modern homosexuality, the most
sophisticated historically oriented work in gay studies has been offering

ever more precise datings, ever more nuanced narratives of the development of homosexuality 'as we know it today'. The great value of this scholarly movement has been to subtract from that 'as we know it today' the twin positivist assumptions (1) that there must be some *transhistorical* essence of 'homosexuality' available to modern knowledge, and (2) that the history of understandings of same-sex relations has been a history of increasingly direct, true knowledge or comprehension of that essence. To the contrary, the recent historicizing work has assumed (1) that the differences between the homosexuality 'we know today' and previous arrangements of same-sex relations may be so profound and so integrally rooted in other cultural differences that there may be no continuous, defining essence of 'homosexuality' to *be* known; and (2) that modern 'sexuality' and hence modern homosexuality are so intimately entangled with the historically distinctive contexts and structures that now count as *knowledge* that such 'knowledge' can scarcely be a transparent window onto a separate realm of sexuality but, rather, itself constitutes that sexuality.

These developments have promised to be exciting and productive in the way that the most important work of history or, for that matter, of anthropology may be: in radically defamiliarizing and denaturalizing, not only the past and the distant, but the present. One way, however, in which such an analysis is still incomplete – in which, indeed, it seems to me that it has tended inadvertently to *re*familiarize, *re*naturalize, damagingly reify an entity that it could be doing much more to subject to analysis – is in counterposing against the alterity of the past a relatively unified homosexuality that 'we' *do* 'know today'. It seems that the topos of 'homosexuality as we know it today', or even, to incorporate more fully the antipositivist finding of the Foucauldian shift, 'homosexuality as we *conceive of it* today', has provided a rhetorically necessary fulcrum point for the denaturalizing work on the past done by many historians. But an unfortunate side effect of this move has been implicitly to underwrite the notion that 'homosexuality as we conceive of it today' itself comprises a coherent definitional field rather than a space of overlapping, contradictory, and conflictual definitional forces. Unfortunately, this presents more than a problem of oversimplification. To the degree that power relations involving modern homo/heterosexual definition have been structured by the very tacitness of the double-binding force fields of conflicting definition – to that degree these historical projects, for all their immense care, value, and potential, still risk reinforcing a dangerous consensus of knowingness about the genuinely *un*known, more than vestigially contradictory structurings of contemporary experience.

As an example of this contradiction effect, let me juxtapose two programmatic statements of what seem to be intended as parallel and congruent projects. In the foundational Foucault passage to which I alluded above, the modern category of 'homosexuality' that dates from 1870 is said to be

> characterized . . . less by a type of sexual relations than by a certain quality of sexual sensibility, a certain way of inverting the masculine and the feminine in oneself. Homosexuality appeared as one of the forms of sexuality when it was transposed from the practice of sodomy onto a kind of interior androgyny, a hermaphrodism of the soul. The sodomite had been a temporary aberration; the homosexual was now a species.

In Foucault's account, the unidirectional emergence in the late nineteenth century of 'the homosexual' as 'a species', of homosexuality as a minoritizing identity, is seen as tied to an also unidirectional, and continuing, emergent understanding of homosexuality in terms of gender inversion and gender transitivity. This understanding appears, indeed, according to Foucault, to underlie and constitute the common sense of the homosexuality 'we know today'. A more recent account by David M. Halperin, on the other hand, explicitly in the spirit and under the influence of Foucault but building, as well, on some intervening research by George Chauncey and others, constructs a rather different narrative – but constructs it, in a sense, *as if it were the same one*:

> Homosexuality and heterosexuality, as we currently understand them, are modern, Western, bourgeois productions. Nothing resembling them can be found in classical antiquity. . . . In London and Paris, in the seventeenth and eighteenth centuries, there appear . . . social gathering-places for persons of the same sex with the same socially deviant attitudes to sex and gender who wish to socialize and to have sex with one another. . . . This phenomenon contributes to the formation of the great nineteenth-century experience of 'sexual inversion', or sex-role reversal, in which some forms of sexual deviance are interpreted as, or conflated with, gender deviance. The emergence of homosexuality out of inversion, the formation of a sexual orientation independent of relative degrees of masculinity and femininity, takes place during the latter part of the

nineteenth century and comes into its own only in the twentieth. Its highest expression is the 'straight-acting and -appearing gay male', a man distinct from other men in absolutely no other respect besides that of his 'sexuality'. (Halperin 1989: 8–9)

Halperin offers some discussion of why and how he has been led to differ from Foucault in discussing 'inversion' as a stage that in effect preceded 'homosexuality'. What he does not discuss is that his reading of 'homosexuality' as 'we currently understand' it – his presumption of the reader's commonsense, present-tense conceptualization of homo-sexuality, the point from which all the thought experiments of differen-tiation must proceed – is virtually the opposite of Foucault's. For Halperin, what is presumed to define modern homosexuality 'as we understand' it, in the form of the straight-acting and -appearing gay male, is gender intransitivity; for Foucault, it is, in the form of the feminized man or virilized woman, gender transitivity.

What obscures this difference between two historians, I believe, is the underlying structural congruence of the two histories: each is a unidirectional narrative of supersession. Each one makes an overarching point about the complete conceptual alterity of earlier models of same-sex relations. In each history one model of same-sex relations is super-seded by another, which may again be superseded by another. In each case the superseded model then drops out of the frame of analysis. For Halperin, the power and interest of a postinversion notion of 'sexual orientation independent of relative degrees of masculinity and feminin-ity' seem to indicate that that notion must necessarily be seen as supersed-ing the inversion model; he then seems to assume that any elements of the inversion model still to be found in contemporary understandings of homosexuality may be viewed as mere historical remnants whose pro-cess of withering away, however protracted, merits no analytic atten-tion. The end point of Halperin's narrative differs from that of Foucault, but his proceeding does not: just as Halperin, having discovered an important *intervening* model, assumes that it must be a *supervening* one as well, so Foucault had already assumed that the nineteenth-century intervention of a minoritizing discourse of sexual identity in a previously extant, universalizing discourse of 'sodomitic' sexual acts must mean, for all intents and purposes, the eclipse of the latter.

This assumption is significant only if – as I will be arguing – the most potent effects of modern homo/heterosexual definition tend to spring precisely from the inexplicitness or denial of the gaps *between* long-coexisting minoritizing and universalizing, or gender-transitive and gender-intrasitive, understandings of same-sex relations. If that argument is true, however, then the enactment performed by these historical narratives has some troubling entailments. For someone who lives, for instance, as I do, in a state where certain acts called 'sodomy' are criminal regardless of the gender, never mind the homo/heterosexual 'identity', of the persons who perform them, the threat of the juxtaposition *on* that prohibition against *acts* of an additional, unrationalized set of sanctions attaching to *identity* can only be exacerbated by the insistence of gay theory that the discourse of acts can represent nothing but an anachronistic vestige. The project of the present book will be to show how issues of modern homo/heterosexual definition are structured, not by the supersession of one model and the consequent withering away of another, but instead by the relations enabled by the unrationalized coexistence of different models during the times they do coexist. This project does not involve the construction of historical narratives alternative to those that have emerged from Foucault and his followers. Rather, it requires a reassignment of attention and emphasis within those valuable narratives – attempting, perhaps, to denarrativize them somewhat by focusing on a performative space of contradiction that they both delineate and, themselves performative, pass over in silence. I have tended, therefore, in these chapters not to stress the alterity of disappeared or now-supposed-alien understandings of same-sex relations but instead to invest attention in those unexpectedly plural, varied, and contradictory historical understandings whose residual – indeed, whose renewed – force seems most palpable today. My first aim is to denaturalize the present, rather than the past – in effect, to render less destructively presumable 'homosexuality as we know it today'.

Axiom 6: The paths of allo-identification are likely to be strange and recalcitrant. So are the paths of auto-identification.

What would make a good answer to implicit questions about someone's group-identification across politically charged boundaries, whether of gender, of class, of race, of sexuality, of nation? It could never be a version of 'But everyone *should* be able to make this identification.' Perhaps everyone should, but everyone does not, and almost no one makes more than a small number of very narrowly channelled ones. (A currently plausible academic ideology, for instance, is that everyone in a position of class privilege *should* group-identify across lines of class; but who hasn't noticed that of the very few U.S. scholars under 50 who have been capable of doing so productively, and over the long haul, most also 'happen to have been' red diaper babies?) If the ethical prescription is explanatory at all – and I have doubts about that – it is anything but a full explanation. It often seems to me, to the contrary, that what these implicit questions really ask for is narrative, and of a directly personal sort. When I have experimented with offering such narrative, in relation to this ongoing project, it has been with several aims in mind. I wanted to disarm the categorical imperative that seems to do so much to promote cant and mystification about motives in the world of politically correct academia. I wanted to try opening channels of visibility – toward the speaker, in this case – that might countervail somewhat against the terrible one-directionality of the culture's spectacularizing of gay men, to which it seems almost impossible, in any powerful gay-related project, not also to contribute. I meant, in a sense, to give hostages, though the possible thud of them on the tarmac of some future conflict is not something I can contemplate. I also wanted to offer (though on my own terms) whatever tools I could with which a reader who needed to might begin unknotting certain overdetermined impactions that inevitably structure these arguments. Finally, I have come up with such narrative because I desired and needed to, because its construction has greatly interested me, and what I learned from it has often surprised me.

A note appended to one of these accounts suggested an additional reason: 'Part of the motivation behind my work on it', I wrote there, 'has been a fantasy that readers or hearers would be variously – in anger, identification, pleasure, envy, "permission", exclusion – stimulated to write accounts "like" this one (whatever that means) of their own, and share those' (Sedgwick 1987:137). My impression, indeed, is that some readers of that essay have done so. An implication of that wishful note was that it is not only identifications *across* definitional lines that can evoke or support or even require complex and particular narrative explanation; rather, the same is equally true of any person's identification with her or his 'own' gender, class, race, sexuality, nation. I think, for instance, of a graduate class I taught a few years ago in gay and lesbian literature. Half the students in the class were men, half women. Throughout the semester all the women, including me, intensely uncomfortable with the dynamics of the class and hyperconscious of the problems of articulating lesbian with gay male perspectives, attributed our discomfort to some obliquity in the classroom relations between ourselves and the men. But by the end of the semester it seemed clear that we were in the grip of some much more intimate dissonance. It seemed that it was among the group of women, all feminists, largely homogeneous in visible respects, that some nerve of individually internal difference had been set painfully, contagiously atremble. Through a process that began, but *only* began, with the perception of some differences among our mostly inexplicit, often some- what uncrystallized sexual self-definitions, it appeared that each woman in the class possessed (or might, rather, feel we were possessed by) an ability to make one or more of the other women radically and excruciat- ingly doubt the authority of her own self-definition as a woman; as a feminist; and as the positional subject of a particular sexuality.

I think it probable that most people, especially those involved with any form of politics that touches on issues of identity – race, for instance, as well as sexuality and gender – have observed or been part of many such circuits of intimate denegation, as well as many circuits of its opposite. The political or pedagogical utility or destructiveness of those dissonant dynamics is scarcely a given, though perhaps it must always be aversive to experience them. Such dynamics – the denegating ones along with the consolidating ones – are not epiphenomenal to identity politics, but constitute it. After all, to identify *as* must always include multiple processes of identification *with*. It also involves identification *as against*; but even did it not, the relations implicit in *identifying with* are, as psychoanalysis suggests, in themselves quite sufficiently fraught with intensities of incorporation, diminishment, inflation, threat, loss, repa- ration, and disavowal. For a politics like feminism, furthermore, effec- tive moral authority has seemed to depend on its capacity for conscientious and non-perfunctory enfoldment of women alienated from one another in virtually every other relation of life. Given this, there are strong political motives for obscuring any possibility of differ- entiating between one's identification *as* (a woman) and one's identifi- cation *with* (women very differently situated – for bourgeois feminists, this means radically less privileged ones). At least for relatively privi- leged feminists of my generation, it has been an article of faith, and a deeply educative one, that to conceive of oneself as a woman at all must mean trying to conceive oneself, over and over, as if incarnated in ever more palpably vulnerable situations and embodiments. The costs of this pressure toward mystification – the constant reconflation, as one mono- lithic act, of *identification with/as* – are, I believe, high for feminism, though its rewards have also been considerable. (Its political efficacy in actually broadening the bases of feminism is still, it seems to me, very much a matter of debate.) *Identification with/as* has a distinctive resonance for women in the oppressively tidy dovetailing between old ideologies of women's traditional 'selflessness' and a new one of feminist commitment that seems to begin with a self but is legitimated only by wilfully obscuring most of its boundaries.

For better and for worse, mainstream, male-centred gay politics has tended not to be structured as strongly as feminism has by that particular ethical pressure. Yet, there is a whole different set of reasons why a problematics of *identification with/as* seems to be distinctively resonant with issues of male homo/heterosexual definition. *Between Men* tried to demonstrate that modern, homophobic constructions of male heterosexuality have a conceptual dependence on a distinction between men's *identification* (with men) and their *desire* (for women), a distinction whose factitiousness is latent where not patent. The (relatively new) emphasis on the 'homo-', on the dimension of sameness, built into modern understandings of relations of sexual desire within a given gender, has had a sustained and active power to expose that factitiousness, to show how close may be the slippage or even the melding between identification and desire. Thus, an entire social region of the vicarious becomes peculiarly charged in association with homo/heterosexual definition. I will argue that processes of homosexual attribution and identification have had a distinctive centrality, in this century, for many stigmatized but extremely potent sets of relations involving projective chains of vicarious investment: sentimentality, kitsch, camp, the knowing, the prurient, the arch, the morbid.

There may, then, be a rich and conflictual salience of the vicarious embedded within gay definition. I don't point that out to offer an excuse for the different, openly vicariating cathexis from outside that motivates this study; it either needs or, perhaps, can have none. But this in turn may suggest some ways in which the particular obliquities of my approach to the subject may bias what I find there. I can say generally that the vicarious investments most visible to me have had to do with my experiences as a woman; as a fat woman; as a non-procreative adult; as someone who is, under several different discursive regimes, a sexual pervert; and, under some, a Jew. To give an example: I've wondered about my ability to keep generating ideas about 'the closet', compared to a relative inability, so far, to have new ideas about the substantive differences made by post-Stonewall imperatives to rupture or vacate that space. (This, obviously, despite every inducement to thought provided by the immeasurable value of 'out' liberatory gay politics in the lives around me and my own.) May it not be influenced by the fact that my own relation, as a woman, to gay male discourse and gay men echoes most with the pre-Stonewall gay self-definition of (say) the 1950s? – something, that is, whose names, where they exist at all, are still so exotically coarse and demeaning as to challenge recognition, never mind acknowledgement; leaving, in the stigma-impregnated space of refused recognition, sometimes also a stimulating ether of the unnamed, the lived experiment.

Part VI Carnival and utopia

18 Richard Dyer

Entertainment and utopia

EDITOR'S INTRODUCTION

Richard Dyer's short article has been very influential in cultural studies. Originally published in the magazine *Movie* in 1977, it was one of the first attempts to move out of the combinations of semiotic/Althusserian and Gramscian thinking dominant at the time.

Dyer's article can be read as a theoretical meditation on the Hollywood musical – a genre which differs from most other Hollywood film in that it contains a relatively high proportion of non-narrative moments and belongs firmly to the larger form 'show-biz'. As a starting point, Dyer reminds us that the entertainment industry, being 'relatively autonomous', does not simply reproduce patriarchal capitalism. Developing this familiar proposition in a new direction, he goes on to argue that the industry expresses its audiences' real needs – in particular their needs for a different and better social order. How does show-biz fulfil such utopian desires? Not by literally representing a perfect society (like Sir Thomas More's *Utopia*) but (i) by 'non-representational means' – through music, colour, movement, and so on, and (ii) by picturing relations between people more simply and directly than they exist in actuality. Here the 'escapism' and 'one-dimensionality' of the culture industry are (within limits) positively affirmed.

Dyer's recuperation of entertainment shares something with Bakhtin's notion of the carnivalesque, as well as with the theories of Ernst Bloch, Adorno's German Marxist contemporary. Within current cultural studies, it has helped pave the way for the cultural populism now so important a force in the discipline.

Further reading: Bloch 1988; Chambers 1986; Dyer 1979; Fiske 1987b, 1989; Walkerdine 1986.

S.D.

This article is about musicals as entertainment. I don't necessarily want to disagree with those who would claim that musicals are also 'something else' (e.g., 'Art') or argue that entertainment itself is only a product of 'something more important' (e.g., political/economic manipulation, psychological forces), but I want to put the emphasis here on entertainment as entertainment. Musicals were predominantly conceived of, by producers and audiences alike, as 'pure entertainment' – the *idea* of entertainment was a prime determinant on them. Yet because entertainment is a commonsense, 'obvious' idea, what is really meant and implied by this never gets discussed.

Musicals are one of a whole string of forms – music hall, variety, TV spectaculars, pantomime, cabaret, etc. – that are usually summed up by the term 'show biz'. The idea of entertainment I want to examine here is most centrally embodied by these forms, although I believe that it can also be seen at work, *mutatis mutandis*, in other forms and I suggest below, informally, how this might be so. However, it is probably true to say that 'show biz' is the most thoroughly entertainment-oriented of all types of performance, and that notions of myth, art, instruction, dream and ritual may be equally important, even at the conscious level with regard to, say, Westerns, the news, soap opera, or rock music.

It is important, I think, to stress the cultural and historical specificity of entertainment. The kinds of performance produced by professional entertainment are different in audience, performers and above all intention from the kinds of performance produced in tribal, feudal or socialist societies. It is not possible here to provide the detailed historical and anthropological argument to back this up, but I hope the differences will suggest themselves when I say that entertainment is a type of performance produced for profit, performed before a generalized audience (the 'public') by a trained, paid group who do nothing else but produce performances which have the sole (conscious) aim of providing pleasure.

Because entertainment is produced by professional entertainers, it is also largely defined by them. That is to say, although entertainment is part of the coinage of everyday thought, nonetheless how it is defined, what it is assumed to be, is basically decided by those people responsible (paid) for providing it in concrete form. Professional entertainment is the dominant agency for defining what entertainment is. This does not mean, however, that it *simply* reproduces and expresses patriarchal capitalism. There is the usual struggle between capital (the backers) and labour (the performers) over the control of the product, and professional entertainment is unusual in that: (1) it is in the business of producing forms, not things, and (2) the work force (the performers themselves) is in a better position to determine the form of its product than are, say, secretaries or car workers. The fact that professional entertainment has been by and large conservative in this century should not blind us to the implicit struggle within it, and looking beyond class to divisions of sex and race, we should note the important role of structurally subordinate groups in society – women, blacks, gays – in the development and definition of entertainment. In other words, show business's relationship to the demands of patriarchal capitalism is a complex one. Just as it does not simply 'give the people what they want' (since it actually defines those wants), so, as a relatively autonomous mode of cultural production, it does not simply reproduce unproblematically patriarchal capitalist ideology. Indeed, it is precisely on seeming to achieve both these often opposed functions simultaneously that its survival largely depends.

Two of the taken-for-granted descriptions of entertainment, as 'escape' and as 'wish-fulfilment', point to its central thrust, namely, utopianism. Entertainment offers the image of 'something better' to escape into, or something we want deeply that our day-to-day lives don't provide. Alternatives, hopes, wishes – these are the stuff of utopia, the sense that things could be better, that something other than what is can be imagined and maybe realized.

Entertainment does not, however, present models of utopian worlds, as in the classic utopias of Sir Thomas More, William Morris, *et al*. Rather the utopianism is contained in the feelings it embodies. It presents, head-on as it were, what utopia would feel like rather than how it would be organized. It thus works at the level of sensibility, by which I mean an effective code that is characteristic of, and largely specific to, a given mode of cultural production.

This code uses both representational and, importantly, non-representational signs. There is a tendency to concentrate on the former, and clearly it would be wrong to overlook them – stars are nicer than we are, characters more straightforward than people we know, situations more soluble than those we encounter. All this we recognize through representational signs. But we also recognize qualities in non-representational signs – colour, texture, movement, rhythm, melody, camerawork – although we are much less used to talking about them. The nature of non-representational signs is not however so different from that of representational. Both are, in C. S. Peirce's terminology, largely iconic; but whereas the relationship between signifier and signified in a representational icon is one of resemblance between their appearance, their look, the relationship in the case of the non-representational icon is one of resemblance at the level of basic structuration.

This concept has been developed (among other places) in the work of Suzanne K. Langer, particularly in relation to music. We feel music (arguably more than any other performance medium), yet it has the least obvious reference to 'reality' – the intensity of our response to music can only be accounted for by the way music, abstract, formal though it is, still embodies feeling. Langer puts it thus in *Feeling and Form*:

> The tonal structures we call 'music' bear a close logical similarity to the forms of human feeling – forms of growth and of attenuation, flowing and slowing, conflict and resolution, speed, arrest, terrific excitement, calm or subtle activation or dreamy lapses – not joy and sorrow perhaps, but the poignancy of both – the greatness and brevity and eternal passing of everything vitally felt. Such is the pattern, or logical form, of sentience; and the pattern of music is that same form worked out in pure measures, sound and silence. Music is a tonal analogue of emotive life.
>
> Such formal analogy, or congruence of logical structures, is the prime requisite for the relation between a symbol and whatever it is to mean. The symbol and the object symbolized must have some common logical form.

Langer realizes that recognition of a common logical form between a performance sign and what it signifies is not always easy or natural: 'The congruence of two given perceptible forms is not always evident upon simple inspection. The common *logical* form they both exhibit may become apparent only when you know the principle whereby to relate them.' This implies that responding to a performance is not spontaneous – you have to learn what emotion is embodied before you can respond to it. A problem with this as Langer develops it is the implication that the emotion itself is not coded, is simply 'human feeling'. I would be inclined, however, to see almost as much coding in the emotions as in the signs for them. Thus, just as writers such as E. H. Gombrich and Umberto Eco stress that different modes of representation (in history and culture) correspond to different modes of perception, so it is important to grasp that modes of experiential art and entertainment correspond to different culturally and historically determined sensibilities.

This becomes clear when one examines how entertainment forms come to have the emotional signification they do: that is, by acquiring their signification in relation to the complex of meanings in the social-cultural situation in which they are produced. Take the extremely complex history of tap dance – in black culture, tap dance has had an improvisatory, self-expressive function similar to that in jazz; in minstrelsy, it took on an aspect of jolly mindlessness, inane good humour, in accord with minstrelsy's image of the Negro; in vaudeville, elements of mechanical skill, tap dance as a feat, were stressed as part of vaudeville's celebration of the machine and the brilliant performer. Clearly there are connections between these different significations, and there are residues of all of them in tap as used in films, television and contemporary theatre shows. This has little to do however with the intrinsic meanings of hard, short, percussive, syncopated sounds arranged in patterns and produced by the movement of feet, and everything to do with the significance such sounds acquire from their place within the network of signs in a given culture at a given point of time. Nevertheless, the signification is essentially apprehended through the coded non-representational form (although the representational elements usually present in a performance sign – a dancer is always 'a person dancing' – may help to anchor the necessarily more fluid signification of the non-representational elements; for example, a black man, a white man in blackface, a troupe, or a white woman tap-dancing may suggest different ways of reading the taps, because each relates to a slightly different movement in the evolution of the non-representational form, tap dance).

I have laboured this point at greater length than may seem warranted partly with polemic intent. Firstly, it seems to me that the reading of non-representational signs in the cinema is particularly undeveloped. On the one hand, the *mise-en-scène* approach (at least as classically developed in *Movie*) tends to treat the non-representational as a function of the representational, simply a way of bringing out, emphasizing, aspects of plot, character, situation, without signification in their own right. On the other hand, semiotics has been concerned with the codification of the representational. Secondly, I feel that film analysis remains notoriously non-historical, except in rather lumbering, simplistic ways. My adaptation of Langer seeks to emphasize not the connection between signs and historical events, personages or forces, but rather the history of signs themselves as they are produced in culture and history. Nowhere here has it been possible to reproduce the detail of any sign's history (and I admit to speculation in some instances), but most of the assertions are based on more thorough research, and even where they are not, they should be.

The categories of entertainment's utopian sensibility are sketched in the accompanying table together with examples of them. The three films used will be discussed below; the examples from Westerns and television news are just to suggest how the categories may have wider application; the sources referred to are the cultural, historical situation of the code's production.

The categories are, I hope, clear enough, but a little more needs to be said about 'intensity'. It is hard to find a word that quite gets what I mean. What I have in mind is the capacity of entertainment to present either complex or unpleasant feelings (e.g., involvement in personal or political events, jealousy, loss of love, defeat) in a way that makes them seem uncomplicated, direct and vivid, not 'qualified' or 'ambiguous' as day-to-day life makes them, and without those intimations of self-deception and pretence. (Both intensity and transparency can be related to wider themes in the culture, as 'authenticity' and 'sincerity' respectively; see Lionel Trilling's *Sincerity and Authenticity*.)

The obvious problem raised by this breakdown of the utopian sensibility is where these categories come from. One answer, at a very broad level, might be that they are a continuation of the utopian tradition in Western thought. George Kateb, in his survey of utopian thought, *Utopia and Its Enemies*, describes what he takes to be the dominant motifs in this tradition, and they do broadly overlap with those outlined above. Thus:

> . . . when a man [sic] thinks of perfection . . . he thinks of a world permanently without strife, poverty, constraint, stultifying labour, irrational authority, sensual deprivation . . . peace, abundance, leisure, equality, consonance of men and their environment.

We may agree that notions in this broad conceptual area are common throughout Western thought, giving it, and its history, its characteristic dynamic, its sense of moving beyond what is to what ought to be or what we want to be. However, the very broadness, and looseness, of this common ground does not get us very far – we need to examine the specificity of entertainment's utopia.

One way of doing so is to see the categories of the sensibility as temporary answers to the inadequacies of the society which is being escaped from through entertainment. This is proposed by Hans Magnus Enzensberger in his article, 'Constituents of a Theory of the Media' (in *Sociology of Mass Communication,* edited by Dennis McQuail). Enzensberger takes issue with the traditional left-wing use of concepts of 'manipulation' and 'false needs' in relation to the mass media:

> The electronic media do not owe their irresistible power to any sleight-of-hand but to the elemental power of deep social needs which come through even in the present depraved form of these media. . . .
>
> Consumption as spectacle contains the promise that want will disappear. The deceptive, brutal and obscene features of this festival derive from the fact that there can be no question of a real fulfilment of its promise. But so long as scarcity holds sway, use-value remains a decisive category which can only be abolished by trickery. Yet trickery on such a scale is only conceivable if it is based on mass need. This need – it is a utopian one – is there. It is the desire for a new ecology, for a breaking-down of environmental barriers, for an aesthetic which is not limited to the sphere of the 'artistic'. These desires are not – or are not primarily – internalized rules of the games as played by the capitalist system. They have physiological roots and can no longer be suppressed. Consumption as spectacle is – in parody form – the anticipation of a utopian situation.

This does, I think, express well the complexity of the situation. However Enzensberger's appeal to 'elemental' and 'physiological' demands, although we do not need to be too frightened by them, is lacking in both historical and anthropological perspectives. I would rather suggest, a little over-schematically, that the categories of the utopian sensibility are related to specific inadequacies in society as follows:

Social Tension/Inadequacy/Absence	*Utopian Solution*
Scarcity (actual poverty in the society; poverty observable in the surrounding societies, e.g., Third World); unequal distribution of wealth	Abundance (elimination of poverty for self and others; equal distribution of wealth)

Exhaustion (work as a grind, alienated labour, pressures of urban life)	Energy (work and play synonymous), city dominated (*On the Town*) or pastoral return (*The Sound of Music*)
Dreariness (monotony, predictability, instrumentality of the daily round)	Intensity (excitement, drama, affectivity of living)
Manipulation (advertising, bourgeois democracy, sex roles)	Transparency (open, spontaneous, honest communications and relationships)
Fragmentation (job mobility, rehousing and development, high-rise flats, legislation against collective action)	Community (all together in one place, communal interests, collective activity)

The advantage of this analysis is that it does offer some explanation of why entertainment *works*. It is not just left-overs from history, it is not *just* what show business, or 'they', force on the rest of us, it is not simply the expression of eternal needs – it responds to real needs *created by society*. The weakness of the analysis (and this holds true for Enzensberger too) is in the give-away absences from the left-hand column – no mention of class, race or patriarchy. That is, while entertainment is responding to needs that are real, at the same time it is also defining and delimiting what constitutes the legitimate needs of people in this society.

I am not trying to recoup here the false needs argument – we are talking about real needs created by real inadequacies, but they are not the only needs and inadequacies of the society. Yet entertainment, by so orienting itself to them, effectively denies the legitimacy of other needs and inadequacies, and especially of class, patriarchal and sexual struggles. (Though once again we have to admit the complexity and contradictions of the situation – that, for instance, entertainment is not the only agency which defines legitimate needs, and that the actual role of women, gay men and blacks in the creation of show business leaves its mark in such central oppositional icons as, respectively, the strong woman type, e.g., Ethel Merman, Judy Garland, Elsie Tanner, camp humour and sensuous taste in dress and decor, and almost all aspects of dance and music. Class, it will be noted, is still nowhere.)

Class, race and sexual caste are denied validity as problems by the dominant (bourgeois, white, male) ideology of society. We should not expect show business to be markedly different. However, there is one further turn of the screw, and that is that, with the exception perhaps of community (the most directly working class in source), the ideals of entertainment imply wants that capitalism itself promises to meet. Thus abundance becomes consumerism, energy and intensity personal free-dom and individualism, and transparency freedom of speech. In other (Marcuse's) words, it is a partially 'one-dimensional' situation. The categories of the sensibility point to gaps or inadequacies in capitalism, but only those gaps or inadequacies that capitalism proposes itself to deal with. At our worse sense of it, entertainment provides alternatives *to* capitalism which will be provided *by* capitalism.

However, this one-dimensionality is seldom so hermetic, because of the deeply contradictory nature of entertainment forms. In variety, the essential contradiction is between comedy and music turns; in musicals, it is between the narrative and the numbers. Both these contradictions can be rendered as one between the heavily representational and verisi-militudinous (pointing to the way the world is, drawing on the audience's concrete experience of the world) and the heavily non-representational and 'unreal' (pointing to how things could be better). In musicals, contradiction is also to be found at two other levels – within numbers, between the representational and the non-representational, and within the non-representational, owing to the differing sources of production inscribed in the signs.

To be effective, the utopian sensibility has to take off from the real experiences of the audience. Yet to do this, to draw attention to the gap between what is and what could be, is, ideologically speaking, playing with fire. What musicals have to do, then (not through any conspirator-ial intent, but because it is always easier to take the line of least resistance, i.e., to fit in with prevailing norms), is to work through these contradictions at all levels in such a way as to 'manage' them, to make them seem to disappear. They don't always succeed.

I have chosen three musicals which seem to me to illustrate the three broad tendencies of musicals – those that keep narrative and number clearly separated (most typically, the backstage musical); those that retain the division between narrative as problems and numbers as escape, but try to 'integrate' the numbers by a whole set of papering-over-the-cracks devices (e.g., the well-known 'cue for a song'); and musicals which try to dissolve the distinction between narrative and numbers, thus implying that the world of the narrative is also (already) utopian.

The clear separation of numbers and narrative in *Golddiggers of 1933* is broadly in line with a 'realist' aesthetic: the numbers occur in the film in the same way as they occur in life, that is, on stages and in cabarets. This 'realism' is of course reinforced by the social-realist orientation of the narrative, settings and characterization, with their emphasis on the Depression, poverty, the quest for capital, 'gold-digging' (and prostitution). However, the numbers are not wholly contained by this realist aesthetic – the way in which they are opened out, in scale and in cinematic treatment (overhead shots, etc.), represents a quite marked shift from the real to the non-real, and from the largely representational to the largely non-representational (sometimes to the point of almost complete abstraction). The thrust of the narrative is towards seeing the show as a 'solution' to the personal, Depression-induced problems of the characters; yet the non-realist presentation of the numbers makes it very hard to take this solution seriously. It is 'just' escape, 'merely' utopian.

If the numbers embody (capitalist) palliatives to the problems of the narrative – chiefly, abundance (spectacle) in place of poverty, and (non-efficacious) energy (chorines in self-enclosed patterns) in place of dispiritedness – then the actual mode of presentation undercuts this by denying it the validity of 'realism'.

However, if one then looks at the contradiction between the representational and non-representational within the numbers, this becomes less clear-cut. Here much of the representational level reprises the lessons of the narrative – above all, that women's only capital is their bodies as objects. The abundant scale of the numbers is an abundance of piles of women; the sensuous materialism is the texture of femaleness; the energy of the dancing (when it occurs) is the energy of the choreographic imagination, to which the dancers are subservient. Thus, while the non-representational certainly suggests an alternative to the narrative, the representational merely reinforces the narrative (women as sexual coinage, women – and men – as expressions of the male producer).

Finally, if one then looks at the non-representational alone, contradictions once again become apparent – e.g., spectacle as materialism and metaphysics (that is, on the one hand, the sets, costumes, etc. are tactile, sensuous, physically exhilarating, but on the other hand, are associated with fairy-land, magic, the by-definition immaterial), dance as human creative energy and sub-human mindlessness.

In *Funny Face*, the central contradiction is between art and entertainment, and this is further worked through in the antagonism between the central couple, Audrey Hepburn (art) and Fred Astaire (entertainment).

The numbers are escapes from the problems, and discomforts, of the contradiction – either by asserting the unanswerably more pleasurable qualities of entertainment (e.g., 'Clap Yo' Hands' following the dirge-like Juliette Greco-type song in the 'empathicalist', i.e., existentialist, *soirée*), or in the transparency of love in the Hepburn–Astaire numbers.

But it is not always that neat. In the empathicalist cellar club, Hepburn escapes Astaire in a number with some of the other beats in the club. This reverses the escape direction of the rest of the film (i.e., it is an escape from entertainment/Astaire into art). Yet within the number, the contradiction repeats itself. Before Hepburn joins the group, they are dancing in a style deriving from Modern Dance, angular, oppositional shapes redolent in musical convention of neurosis and pretentiousness (*cf*. Danny Kaye's number, 'Choreography', in *White Christmas*). As the number proceeds, however, more show biz elements are introduced – use of syncopated clapping, forming in a vaudeville line-up, and American Theatre Ballet shapes. Here an 'art' form is taken over and infused with the values of entertainment. This is a contradiction between the representational (the dreary night club) and the non-representational (the oomph of music and movement) but also, within the non-representational, between different dance forms. The contradiction between art and entertainment is thus repeated at each level.

In the love numbers, too, contradictions appear, partly by the continuation in them of troubling representational elements. In *Funny Face*, photographs of Hepburn as seen by Astaire, the fashion photographer, are projected on the wall as background to his wooing her and her giving in. Again, their final dance of reconciliation to "S Wonderful' takes place in the grounds of a chateau, beneath the trees, with doves fluttering around them. Earlier, this setting was used as the finish for their fashion photography sequence. In other words, in both cases, she is reconciled to him only by capitulating to his definition of her. In itself, there is nothing contradictory in this – it is what Ginger Rogers always had to do. But here the mode of reconciliation is transparency and yet we can see the strings of the number being pulled. Thus the representational elements, which bespeak manipulation of romance, contradict the non-representational, which bespeaks its transparency.

The two tendencies just discussed are far more common than the third, which has to suggest that utopia is implicit in the world of the narrative as well as in the world of the numbers.

The commonest procedure for doing this is removal of the whole film in time and space – to turn-of-the-century America (*Meet Me in St. Louis, Hello Dolly!*), Europe (*The Merry Widow, Gigi, Song of Norway*), cockney London (*My Fair Lady, Oliver!, Scrooge*), black communities (*Hallelujah!, Cabin in the Sky, Porgy and Bess*), etc. – to places, that is, where it can be believed (by white urban Americans) that song and dance are 'in the air', built into the peasant/black culture and blood, or part of a more free-and-easy stage in American development. In these films, the introduction of any real narrative concerns is usually considerably delayed and comes chiefly as a temporary threat to utopia – thus reversing the other two patterns, where the narrative predominates and numbers function as temporary escapes from it. Not much happens, plot-wise, in *Meet Me in St. Louis* until we have had 'Meet Me in St. Louis', 'The Boy Next Door', 'The Trolley Song' and 'Skip to My Lou' – only then does father come along with his proposal to dismantle this utopia by his job mobility.

Most of the contradictions developed in these films are over-ridingly bought off by the nostalgia or primitivism which provides them with the point of departure. Far from pointing forwards, they point back, to a golden age – a reversal of utopianism that is only marginally offset by the narrative motive of recovery of utopia. What makes *On the Town* interesting is that its utopia is a well-known modern city. The film starts as an escape – from the confines of Navy life into the freedom of New York, and also from the weariness of work, embodied in the docker's refrain, 'I feel like I'm not out of bed yet', into the energy of leisure, as the sailors leap into the city for their day off. This energy runs through the whole film, *including the narrative*. In most musicals, the narrative represents things as they are, to be escaped from. But most of the narrative of *On the Town* is about the transformation of New York into utopia. The sailors release the *social* frustrations of the women – a tired taxi driver just coming off shift, a hard-up dancer reduced to belly-dancing to pay for ballet lessons, a woman with a sexual appetite that is deemed improper – not so much through love and sex as through energy. This sense of the sailors as a transforming energy is heightened by the sense of pressure on the narrative movement suggested by the device of a time-check flashed on the screen intermittently.

This gives a historical dimension to a musical, that is, it shows people making utopia rather than just showing them from time to time finding themselves in it. But the people are men – it is still men making history, not men and women together. (And the Lucy Schmeeler role is unforgivably male chauvinist.) In this context, the 'Prehistoric Man' number is particularly interesting. It centres on Ann Miller, and she leads the others in the take-over of the museum. For a moment, then, a woman 'makes history'. But the whole number is riddled with contradictions, which revolve round the very problem of having an image of a woman acting historically. If we take the number and her part in it to pieces, we can see that it plays on an opposition between self-willed and mindless modes of being; and this play is between representational (R) and non-representational (NR) at all aesthetic levels.

Self-willed	Mindless
Miller as star (R)	Miller's image ('magnificent animal') (R)
Miller character – decision-maker in narrative (R)	Number set in anthropology museum – associations with primitivism (R)
Tap as self-expressive form (NR)	Tap as mindless repetitions (NR)
Improvisatory routine (R/NR)	

The idea of a historical utopianism in narrativity derives from the work of Ernest Bloch. According to Frederic Jameson in *Marxism and Form*, Bloch 'has essentially two different languages or terminological systems at his disposition to describe the formal nature of Utopian fulfilment: the movement of the world in time towards the future's ultimate moment, and the more spatial notion of that adequation of object to subject which must characterise that moment's content. . . . [these] correspond to dramatic and lyrical modes of the presentation of not-yet-being'.

Musicals (and variety) represent an extraordinary mix of these two modes – the historicity of narrative and the lyricism of numbers. They have not often taken advantage of it, but the point is that they could, and that this possibility is always latent in them. They are a form we still need to look at if films are, in Brecht's words on the theatre, to 'organise the enjoyment of changing reality'.

NOTE

An earlier version of this article was used at a SEFT weekend school and at the BFI Summer School, where it greatly benefited from comments and criticism offered.

19 Peter Stallybrass and Allon White

Bourgeois hysteria and the carnivalesque

EDITOR'S INTRODUCTION

This edited chapter from Stallybrass and White's *The Politics and Poetics of Transgression*, develops an account of carnival put forward by Mikhail Bakhtin, who wrote while Stalin was in power. Bakhtin tacitly opposed Stalinism's strictly modernizing programme and rhetoric by arguing that carnivals and other 'survivals' of the pre-modern period expressed energies suppressed in modernized everyday life and also an alternative politics. For Bakhtin, carnival contained a utopian urge: it displaced, even inverted, the normal social hierarchies. Carnival was also a time which encouraged different bodily needs and pleasures from those called upon by the ordinary rhythm of labour and leisure.

Stallybrass and White here argue that in the modern era, carnival was 'sublimated'. On the one hand (as by Freud), the opposition between order and carnival was transposed into models of the psyche; on the other, carnival becomes spectacularized, the object of a large audience's remote and sentimental gaze. Theirs is a thesis which helps make sense of a number of seemingly disparate cultural formations, though it is important not to forget that, just as the carnivalesque does not die out in modernity, rigid social hierarchies and controls pre-date modernization and industrialization, and may be found, in some form or other, wherever carnival exists. If that is not recognized, the Bakhtinian thesis developed by Stallybrass and White settles back into nostalgia.

Further reading: Bakhtin 1981, 1987; Fiske 1987b; Hartley 1983; Stallybrass and White 1986.

S.D.

While she was being massaged she told me only that the children's governess had brought her an ethnological atlas and that some of the pictures in it of American Indians dressed up as animals had given her a great shock. 'Only think, if they came to life' (she shuddered). I instructed her not to be frightened of the pictures of the Red Indians but to laugh heartily at them. And this did in fact happen after she had woken up: she looked at the book, asked whether I had seen it, opened it at the page and laughed at the grotesque figures, without a trace of fear and without any strain in her features.

'Studies on hysteria', Frau Emmy von N. (Freud 1974: 109–10)

Carnival debris spills out of the mouths of those terrified Viennese women in Freud's 'Studies on hysteria'. 'Don't you hear the horses stamping in the circus?' Frau Emmy von N. implores Freud at a moment of particularly abject horror. It is striking how the broken fragments of carnival, terrifying and disconnected, glide through the discourse of the hysteric. Occasionally, as in the extract quoted above, it appears that Freud's therapeutic project was simply the reinflexion of this grotesque material into comic form. When Frau Emmy can at last look at the 'grotesque figures' and 'laugh without a trace of fear', it is as if Freud had managed a singular restitution, salvaging torn shreds of carnival from their phobic alienation in the bourgeois unconscious by making them once more the object of cathartic laughter.

It is of course significant that the carnivalesque practice which produced the phobic symptom in Frau Emmy is that of an alien, non-European culture. Not the least significant element in the middle-class rejection of the indigenous carnival tradition in the late nineteenth century in Europe was a compensatory plundering of ethnographic material – masks, rituals, symbols – from colonized cultures. In this respect Joseph Conrad was doing no more than Frau Emmy in placing 'savage rites' at the heart of European darkness in the 1890s.

As we know, within a very few years Freud was to abandon the cathartic approach which he used with his early hysterical patients and to lose interest in the attempt to precipitate the abreactive rituals which might reinflect the grotesque and the disgusting into a *comic* form. There is some contention that this was not necessarily a positive move (Scheff 1979), but in any event it is a notable feature of the early case histories that it is *the patients themselves* who, in their pastiche appropriations of festive, carnival, religious and pantomimic gestures, suggest kinds of alleviation to their own suffering. Anna O. is credited by Ernest Jones as being the real discoverer of the cathartic method and Breuer developed and formalized her practical notions in his own method (Scheff 1979:

28). Freud's gradual move away from abreactive ritual of a cathartic kind towards associative methods of self-consciousness is entirely consonant with his desire to produce a professional, *scientific* psychology. This is because science, particularly in the late nineteenth century, was deeply hostile to ritual. It even saw itself, on occasion, as self-consciously improving upon those areas of social life which, once governed by 'irrational' rituals, could now be brought under scientific control.

Indeed science only emerged as an autonomous set of discursive values after a prolonged struggle against ritual and it marked out its own identity by the distance which it established from 'mere superstition' – science's label for, among other things, a large body of social practices of a therapeutic kind. Scheff has suggested that there is a strongly cognitive bias against ritual and catharsis in much recent work in psychology and anthropology. A re-reading of hysteria case studies (not only Freud's) in relation to the ritualistic and symbolic material of carnival suggests new ways of interpreting the hostility, the felt incompatibility, of rational knowledge to ritual behaviour.

In the 'Studies on hysteria' many of the images and symbols which were once the focus of various pleasures in European carnival have become transformed into the morbid symptoms of private terror. Again and again these patients suffer acute attacks of disgust, literally vomiting out horrors and obsessions which look surprisingly like the rotted residue of traditional carnival practices. At the same time the patients seem to be reaching out, in their highly stylized gestures and discourses, towards a repertoire of carnival material as both expression and support. They attempt to mediate their terrors by enacting private, made-up carnivals. In the absence of social forms they attempt to produce their own by pastiche and parody in an effort to embody semiotically their distress. Once noticed, it becomes apparent that there is a second narrative fragmented and marginalized, lodged within the emergent psychoanalytic discourse. It witnesses a complex interconnection between hints and scraps of parodic festive form and the body of the hysteric. In his general remarks on hysterical attacks (Freud 1963), Freud himself even makes this 'other narrative' part of his definition of hysteria, without, however, making anything of it:

> When one psychoanalyses a patient subject to hysterical attacks one soon gains the conviction that these attacks are nothing but phanta-

sies projected and translated into motor activity and *represented in pantomime*.

(Freud 1963: 153, our italics)

Freud goes on to talk about the distortion which 'the pantomimic representation of phantasy' undergoes as a result of censorship. Yet the semiotic encoding of the hysterical symptom in pantomime mimicry is given as the very form of representation of fantasy: Freud's definition of hysteria makes pantomime the *symptomatic* locus of the Imaginary, that second-order signifying system which 'translates' and 'represents' the anterior language of the unconscious. Thus when Julia Kristeva attempted to synthesize the Bakhtinian opposition between the classical and grotesque with the Lacanian terms of the symbolic and the Imaginary, there was warrant for the connection not only at the theoretical level but in this 'other narrative' of the hysteric (Kristeva 1974). Yet such is the low status of popular ritual and dramatic representation that Freud never 'sees' his own reference to pantomime as anything other than metaphorical. Towards the end of a letter to Fliess written in 1896, Freud remarks on what Charcot had dubbed the 'clownism' phase of hysterical attacks. He writes of:

the 'clownism' in boys' hysteria, the imitation of animals and circus scenes . . . a compulsion to repeat dating from their youth [in which they] seek their satisfaction to the accompaniment of the craziest capers, somersaults and grimaces.

(Freud 1954: 182)

Even though Charcot's typology of hysterical styles is unreliable and contrived, especially for the photographic representations, the 'clownism' was frequently attested to as a symptomatic aspect of hysteria. Freud, in the explanation which he offers to Fliess in the letter, refers to the 'perversion of the seducers' (the patients themselves) who, he says, 'connect up nursery games and sexual scenes'. This is something we explored in the preceding chapter in relation to the nursemaid: here, offered as an explanation of the clownism, it does not take sufficient account of the whole range of festive material scattered through various studies on hysteria and which together create a subtext irreducible to nursery games. There are indeed deep connections between childhood rituals, games and carnivalesque practices (White 1983), but here Freud's insistence upon a purely sexual aetiology obscures a fundamental socio-historical matrix of the symptom.

The carnival material of the case studies witnesses an historical repression and return. The repression includes the gradual, relentless attack on the 'grotesque body' of carnival by the emergent middle and professional classes from the Renaissance onwards. Interestingly, scholars of European popular culture have occasionally wanted to connect up, backwards as it were, Renaissance festive form to Freud's ideas. Thus C. L. Barber claims that 'A saturnalian attitude, assumed by a clear-cut gesture toward liberty, brings mirth, an accession of wanton vitality. In terms of Freud's analysis of wit, the energy normally occupied in maintaining inhibition is freed for celebration' (Barber 1959: 7). But Barber's reference to Freud seems like a reaching after validation which confuses the historically complex relation of the discourse of psychoanalysis to festive practices. The demonization and the exclusion of the carnivalesque has to be related to the victorious emergence of specifically bourgeois practices and languages which reinflected and incorporated this material within a negative, individualist framework. In one way or another Freud's patients can be seen as enacting desperate ritual fragments salvaged from a festive tradition, *the self-exclusion from which* had been one of the identifying features of their social class. The language of bourgeois neurosis both disavows and appropriates the domain of calendrical festive practices. Thus the 'highly gifted lady' of the case studies celebrated a whole series of what she called 'festivals of remembrance', annually re-enacting the various scenes of her affliction.

It might at first seem plausible to view the discourses of neurosis as the *psychic* irruption of *social* practices which had been suppressed. Certainly, in the long-term history from the seventeenth to the twentieth century, as we have seen above, there were literally thousands of acts of legislation introduced which attempted to eliminate carnival and popular festivity from European life. In different areas of Europe the pace varied, depending upon religious, class and economic factors. But everywhere, against the periodic revival of local festivity and occasional reversals, a fundamental ritual order of western culture came under attack – its feasting, violence, drinking, processions, fairs, wakes, rowdy spectacle and outrageous clamour were subject to surveillance and repressive control. We can briefly list some particular instances of this general process. In 1855 the Great Donnybrook Fair of Dublin was abolished in the very same year that Bartholomew Fair in London finally succumbed to the determined attack of the London City Missions Society. In the decade following the Fairs Act of 1871 over 700 fairs, mops and wakes were abolished in England.

By the 1880s the Paris carnival was rapidly being transformed into a trade show cum civic/military parade (Faure 1978), and although the 'cortège du boeuf gras' processed round the streets until 1914, 'little by little it was suppressed and restricted because it was said to cause a traffic problem' (Pillement 1972: 383). In 1873 the famous Nice carnival was taken over by a 'comité des Fêtes', brought under bureaucratic bourgeois control and reorganized quite self-consciously as a tourist attraction for the increasing numbers who spent time on the Riviera and who were finding neighbouring San Remo's new casino a bigger draw (Sidro 1979: 57–62). As Wolfgang Hartmann has shown (1976), in Germany in the aftermath of the Franco-Prussian war, traditional processions and festivities were rapidly militarized and incorporated into the symbolism and 'classical body' of the State. This dramatic transformation of the ritual calendar had implications not only for each stratum of the social formation, particularly for those which were disengaging *themselves* from ongoing practices, but for the basic structures of symbolic activity in Europe: carnival was now everywhere and nowhere.

Many social historians treat the attack on carnival as a victory over popular culture, first by the Absolutist state and then by the middle classes, a process which is viewed as the more or less complete destruction of popular festivity: the end of carnival. In this vision of the complete elimination of the ritual calendar there is the implicit assumption that, in so far as it was the culture of a rural population which was disappearing, the modernization of Europe led inevitably to the supersession of traditional festivity – it was simply one of the many casualties in the movement towards an urban, industrial society. On the other hand recent literary criticism, following Bakhtin, has found elements of the carnivalesque everywhere it has looked in *modern* as well as traditional literature. Critics now discover the forms, symbols, rituals and structures of carnival to be among the fundamental elements in the aesthetics of modernism (White 1982).

By and large literary critics have not connected with the work of social historians to ask how or why this carnivalesque material should persistently inform modern art because, busy with the task of textual analysis, they move too easily from social practice to textual composition. Yet the social historians who have charted the transformations of carnival as a social practice have not registered its *displacements* into bourgeois discourses like art and psychoanalysis: adopting a naively empirical view they have outlined a simple disappearance, the elimination of the carnivalesque.

But, as we have shown, carnival did not simply disappear. At least four different processes were involved in its ostensible break-up: fragmentation; marginalization; sublimation; repression.

Carnival had always been a loose amalgam of procession, feasting, competition, games and spectacle, combining diverse elements from a large repertoire and varying from place to place. Even the great carnivals of Venice, Naples, Nice, Paris and Nuremberg were fluid and changeable in their combination of practices. During the long and uneven process of suppression (we often find that a carnival is banned over and over again, only to re-emerge each time in a slightly altered fashion), there was a tendency for the basic mixture to break down, certain elements becoming separated from others. Feasting became separated from performance, spectacle from procession: the grotesque body was fragmented. At the same time it began to be marginalized both in terms of social class and geographical location. It is important to note that even as late as the nineteenth century, in some places, carnival remained a ritual involving most classes and sections of a community – the disengaging of the middle class from it was a slow and uneven matter. Part of that process was, as we have seen, the 'disowning' of carnival and its symbolic resources, a gradual reconstruction of the idea of carnival as the culture of the Other. This act of disavowal on the part of the emergent bourgeoisie, with its sentimentalism and its disgust, *made* carnival into the festival of the Other. It encoded all that which the proper bourgeois must strive *not to be* in order to preserve a stable and 'correct' sense of self.

William Addison (1953) charts many of these geographical marginalizations in the English context in the seventeenth and eighteenth centuries. Within a town the fair, mop, wake or carnival, which had once taken over the whole of the town and permitted neither outside nor outsider to its rule, was confined to certain areas and gradually driven out from the well-to-do neighbourhoods. In the last years of the Bury St Edmunds Fair it was 'banished from the aristocratic quarter of Angel Hill and confined to St Mary's and St James's squares' (Addison 1953: 163). In and around London:

> Both regular and irregular fairs were being steadily pushed from the centre outwards as London grew and the open spaces were built over. Greenwich and Stepney were the most popular at one time. Others – Croydon's for example – came to the fore later when railways extended the range of pleasure as well as the range of

boredom, until towards the end of the nineteenth century London was encircled by these country fairs, some of which were, in fact, ancient charter fairs made popular by easier transport. . . . Most of them were regarded by the magistrates as nuisances, and sooner or later most of those without charters were suppressed. Yet such was the popularity of these country fairs round London that to suppress them in one place led inevitably to an outbreak elsewhere, and often where control was more difficult. As the legal adviser to the City Corporation had said in the 1730's, 'It is at all times difficult by law to put down the ancient customs and practices of the multitude.'

(Addison 1953: 100)

In England the sites of 'carnival' moved more and more to the coastal periphery, to the seaside. The development of Scarborough, Brighton, Blackpool, Clacton, Margate and other seaside resorts reflects a process of liminality which, in different ways, was taking place across Europe as a whole. The seaside was partially legitimated as a carnivalesque site of pleasure on the grounds of health, since it combined the (largely mythical) medicinal virtues of the spa resorts with tourism and the fairground. It can be argued that this marginalization is a *result* of other, anterior processes of bourgeois displacement and even repression. But even so, this historical process of marginalization must be seen as an historical tendency distinct from the actual elimination of carnival.

Bakhtin is right to suggest that post-romantic culture is, to a considerable extent, subjectivized and interiorized and on this account frequently related to private terrors, isolation and insanity rather than to robust kinds of social celebration and critique. Bakhtin however does not give us a convincing explanation of this *sublimation* of carnival. The social historians, on the other hand, tend not to consider processes of sublimation at all: for them carnival came to an end and that was that. They tend not to believe in the return of the repressed.

But a convincing map of the transformation of carnival involves tracing migrations, concealment, metamorphoses, fragmentations, internalization and neurotic sublimations. The *disjecta membra* of the grotesque body of carnival found curious lodgement throughout the whole social order of late nineteenth- and early twentieth-century Europe. These dispersed carnivalesque elements represent more than the insignificant nomadic residues of the ritual tradition. In the long process of disowning carnival and rejecting its periodical inversions of the body and the social hierarchy, bourgeois society problematized its own relation to the power of the 'low', enclosing itself, indeed often defining itself, by its suppression of the 'base' languages of carnival.

As important as this was the fact that carnival was being marginalized *temporally* as well as spatially. The carnival calendar of oscillation between production and consumption which had once structured the whole year was displaced by the imposition of the working week under the pressure of capitalist industrial work regimes. The semiotic polarities, the symbolic clusters of classical and grotesque, were no longer *temporally* pinned into a calendrical or seasonal cycle, and this involved a degree of unpredictability in moment and surface of emergence. The 'carnivalesque' might erupt from the literary text, as in so much surrealist art, or from the advertisement hoarding, or from a pop festival or a jazz concert.

Carnival was too disgusting for bourgeois life to endure except as sentimental spectacle. Even then its specular identifications could only be momentary, fleeting and partial – voyeuristic glimpses of a promiscuous loss of status and decorum which the bourgeoisie had had to deny as abhorrent in order to emerge as a distinct and 'proper' class.

Part VII Consumption and the market

20 Meaghan Morris

Things to do with shopping centres

EDITOR'S INTRODUCTION

Meaghan Morris's wide-ranging essay is an exemplary instance of contemporary cultural studies. It carefully considers the conditions of its own production and reception – reminding us that its author is a shopper herself. Thus it is written from a position for which both the 'grammar' of shopping centres (the way their elements are put together) and their workability are part of everyday life. But it is also written from a feminist, theoretical position where such practical considerations are not all that matter. Hence, it is not written for 'ordinary women' (who, as Morris notes, exist as such only in the social imaginary) as much as for intellectuals, students, academics. This does not mean, however, that it can either condescend to shoppers who are not also theorists or assume that its readers are exceptional.

This sense that theory can never either remain within the sites of everyday life or cut itself loose from them has another aspect. For Morris recognizes that those who design, manage, and market shopping centres are theorists too. Certainly they know a great deal about the women who constitute so much of their custom. This cannot be simply dismissed or deplored, for shopping centres are not just useful; they may also be, for Morris, 'lovable'.

Because so much information about, and theory of, shopping centres circulates; because, finally, they exist as architectural outcomes of information technologies which track and manage consumption, Morris cannot write a piece which limits 'shopping in a shopping centre' to individual pleasure and consciousness in the manner of de Certeau's 'walking in the city'. Instead she turns to a history of particular shopping-centre sites she knows.

Yet, although Morris does not delocalize shopping in the way de Certeau delocalizes urban walking, certain questions remain, most obviously: how much money do you have to have to 'love' a shopping centre? Is shopping in a shopping centre the same for an unemployed as an employed person – assuming that the first have access to them to begin with? These are old, but not tired, questions, which the essay certainly does not pre-empt – and they allow us to think about the relation between this kind of work on consumption and earlier, more obviously 'left', cultural studies themes.

Further reading: Harris 1990; Kowinski 1985; Morris 1988a, 1988b; Nava 1987; Williamson 1986.

S.D.

The first thing I want to do is to cite a definition of modernity. It comes not from recent debates in feminist theory or aesthetics or cultural studies, but from a paper called 'Development in the Retail Scene' given in Perth in 1981 by John Lennen of Myer Shopping Centres. To begin his talk (to a seminar organized by the Australian Institute of Urban Studies), Lennen told this fable: 'As Adam and Eve were leaving the Garden of Eden, Adam turned to Eve and said, "Do not be distressed, my dear, we live in times of change."' After quoting Adam, Lennen went on to say, 'Cities live in times of change. We must not be discouraged by change, but rather we must learn to manage change.' He meant that the role of shopping centres was changing from what it had been in the 1970s, and that retailers left struggling with the consequences (planning restrictions, post-boom economic conditions, new forms of competition) should not be discouraged, but should change their practices accordingly.

I want to discuss some issues for feminist criticism that emerge from a study I'm doing of the management of change in certain sites of 'cultural production' involving practices regularly, if by no means exclusively, carried out by women – shopping, driving, the organization of leisure, holiday and/or unemployment activities. By 'sites', I mean shopping centres, cars, highways, 'homes' and motels. It's a large project, and this essay is a kind of preface to one or two of its problems. The essay has a framing theme, however – the 'Edenic' allegories of consumerism in general, and of shopping centres in particular, that one can find elaborated in a number of different discourses (and cultural 'sites'). It also has an argument, which will take the form of a rambling response to three questions that I've often been asked by women with whom I've discussed the project.

One of these is very general: 'what's feminist about it?' I can't answer that in any direct or immediate way, since obviously 'feminism' is not a set of approved concerns and methods, a kind of planning code, against which one can measure one's own interests and aspirations. To be frank, it's a question that I find almost unintelligible. While I do understand the polemical, and sometimes theoretical, value of arguing that something is *not* feminist, to demand a definition of positive feminist identity seems to me to require so many final decisions to be taken, and to assume so much about shared and settled values, that it makes the very concept of a 'project' – undecided and unsettled – impossible. So I shall take this question here as an invitation to make up answers as I go, and the essay will be the response. (That's a way of saying that for me, the answer to 'what's feminist about it?' should be 'I don't know yet'.)

The other two questions are more specific, and relate particularly to shopping centres.

The first question is asked almost invariably by women with whom I've discussed the topic of shopping. They say: 'Yes, you do semiotics . . . are you looking at how shopping centres are all the same everywhere? – laid out systematically, everyone can read them?' They don't ask about shopping centres and change, or about a semiotics of the management of change.

In fact, my emphasis is rather the opposite. It's true that at one level of analysis (and of our 'practice' of shopping centres), layout and design principles ensure that all centres are minimally readable to anyone literate in their use – that is, to almost if not quite everybody in the Western suburban culture I'm concerned with here. This 'readability' may be minimal indeed: many centres operate a strategy of alternating surprise and confusion with familiarity and harmony; and in different parts of any one centre, clarity and opacity will occur in different degrees of intensity for different 'users'. To a newcomer, for example, the major supermarket in an unfamiliar centre is usually more difficult to read than the spatial relations between the speciality food shops and the boutiques. Nevertheless, there are always some basic rules of contiguity and association at work to assist you to make a selection (of shops, as well as products).

However, I am more interested in a study that differentiates particular shopping centres. Differentiating shopping centres means, among other things, looking at how particular centres produce and maintain what the architectural writer Neville Quarry calls (in an appreciation of one particular effort) 'a unique sense of place' – in other terms, a myth of identity. I see this as a 'feminist' project because it requires the predication of a more complex and localized affective relation to shopping spaces (and to the links between those spaces and other sites of domestic and familial labour) than does the scenario of the cruising grammarian reading similarity from place to place. In one way, all shoppers may be cruising grammarians. I do not need to deny this, however, in order to choose to concentrate instead on the ways that particular centres strive to become 'special', for better or for worse, in the everyday lives of women in local communities. Men, of course, may have this relation to *a* shopping centre, too. So my 'feminism' at this stage is defined in non-polemical and non-exclusive (that is, non-self-identical) terms.

Obviously, shopping centres produce a sense of place for economic, 'come-*hither*' reasons, and sometimes because the architects and planners involved may be committed, these days, to an aesthetics or even a politics of the local. But we cannot derive commentary on their function, people's responses to them, or their own cultural production of 'place' in and around them, from this economic rationale. Besides, shopping-centre identities aren't fixed, consistent or permanent. Shopping centres do get facelifts, and change their image – increasingly so as the great classic structures in any region begin to age, fade and date.

But the cost of renovating them (especially the larger ones) means that the identity effect produced by any one centre's spatial play in time is not only complex, highly nuanced and variable in detail, but also simple, massive and relatively enduring overall, and over time, in space. At every possible 'level' of analysis – and there are very many indeed with such a complex, continuous social event – shopping centres are overwhelmingly and constitutively paradoxical. This is one of the things that makes it very hard to differentiate them. On the one hand, they seem so monolithically present – solid, monumental, rigidly and indisputably on the landscape, and in our lives. On the other hand, when you try to dispute with them, they dissolve at any one point into a fluidity and indeterminacy that might suit any philosopher's delirium of an abstract femininity – partly because the shopping centre 'experience' at any one point includes the experience of crowds of people (or of their relative absence), and so of all the varied responses and uses that the centre provokes and contains.

To complicate matters, this *dual* quality is very much a part of shopping-centre strategies of appeal, their 'seductiveness', and also of their management of change. The stirring tension between the massive stability of the structure, and the continually shifting, ceaseless spectacle within and around the 'centre', is one of the things that people who like shopping centres really love about shopping centres. At the same time, shopping-centre management methods (and contracts) are very much directed towards organizing and unifying – at the level of administrative control, if not of achieved aesthetic effect – as much of this spectacle as possible by regulating tenant mix, signing and advertising styles, common space decor, festivities, and so on. This does not mean, however, that they succeed in 'managing' either the total spectacle (which includes what people do with what they provide) or the responses it provokes (and may include).

So the task of analysing shopping centres partly involves on the one hand exploring common sensations, perceptions and emotional states aroused by them (which can be negative, of course, as well as delirious), and on the other hand, battling against those perceptions and states in order to make a place from which to speak other than that of the fascinated describer – either standing 'outside' the spectacle qua ethnographer, or (in a pose which seems to me to amount to much the same thing) ostentatiously absorbed in her own absorption in it, qua celebrant of 'popular culture'.

If the former mode of description may be found in much sociology of consumerism, or 'leisure', the latter mode is the more common today in cultural studies – and it has its persuasive defenders. Iain Chambers, for example, has argued strongly that to appreciate the democratic 'potential' of the way that people live through (not 'alongside') culture – appropriating and transforming everyday life – we must first pursue the 'wide-eyed presentation of actualities' that Adorno disapproved of in some of Benjamin's work on Baudelaire. It's difficult to disagree with this as a general orientation, and I don't. But if we look more closely at the terms of Adorno's objection (and leave aside here the vexed question of its pertinence to Benjamin's work), it's possible to read in them now a description of shopping-centre mystique: 'your study is located at the crossroads of magic and positivism. That spot is bewitched.' With a confidence that feminist philosophers have taught us to question, Adorno continues that 'Only theory could break the spell . . .' (although in context, he means Benjamin's own theoretical practice, not a force of theory-in-general).

In my view, neither a strategy of 'wide-eyed presentation' nor a faith in theory as the exorcist is adequate to dealing with the critical problems posed by feminism in the analysis of 'everyday life'. If we locate our own study at that 'crossroads of magic and positivism' to be found in the grand central court of any large regional mall, then social experiences more complex than wide-eyed bewitchment are certain to occur – and to elicit, for a feminist, a more critical response than 'presentation' requires. If it is today fairly easy to reject the rationalist and gynophobic prejudice implied by Adorno's scenario (theory breaking the witch's spell), and if it is also easy to refuse the old critiques of 'consumption' as false consciousness (bewitchment by the mall), then it is perhaps not so easy at the moment *also* to question the 'wide-eyed' pose of critical amazement at the performance of the everyday.

There's a great deal to be said about that, but my one point here must be that at the very least, a feminist analysis of shopping centres will insist initially upon ambivalence about its objects rather than a simple astonishment 'before' them. Ambivalence allows a thinking of relations between contradictory states: it is also a 'pose', no doubt, but one that is probably more appropriate to an everyday practice of using the same shopping centres often, for different reasons (rather than visiting several occasionally, just in order to see the sights). Above all, it does not eliminate the moment of everyday discontent – of anger, frustration, sorrow, irritation, hatred, boredom, fatigue. Feminism is minimally a movement of discontent with 'the everyday' and with wide-eyed definitions of the everyday as 'the way things are'. While feminism too may proceed by 'staring hard at the realities of the contemporary world we all inhabit', as Chambers puts it, feminism also allows the possibility of rejecting what we see and refusing to take it as 'given'. Like effective shopping, feminist criticism includes moments of sharpened focus, narrowed gaze – of sceptical, if not paranoid, assessment. (This is a more polemical sense in which I shall consider this project to be 'feminist' in the context of cultural studies.)

Recent feminist theory in a number of academic domains has provided a great many tools for any critical study of myths of identity and difference, and the rhetoric of 'place' in everyday life. But in using them in shopping centres, I strike another difficulty: a rhetorical one this time, with resonances of interdisciplinary conflict. It's the difficulty of what can seem to be a lack, or lapse, of appropriateness between my discourse as feminist intellectual and my objects of study.

To put it bluntly: isn't there something really 'off' about mobilizing the weapons (and I use that violent metaphor deliberately) of an elite, possibly still fashionable but definitively *un*popular theoretical discourse against a major element in the lived culture of 'ordinary women' to whom that discourse might be as irrelevant as a stray copy of a book by Roland Barthes chosen to decorate a simulated yuppy apartment on display at Canberra's FREEDOM furniture showroom? And wouldn't using that discourse, and its weapons, be 'off' in a way that it isn't off to use them to reread Gertrude Stein, or other women modernists, or indeed to rewrite devalued and non-modernist writings by women so that they may be used to revise existing concepts of the literary canon?

Of course, these are not questions that any academic, even feminist, is obliged to ask or to answer. One can simply define one's 'object' strategically, in the limited way most appropriate to a determined disciplinary, and institutional, context. They are also questions that it's impossible to answer without challenging their terms – by pointing out, for example, that a politics of 'relevance', and 'appropriateness' (in so far as it can be calculated at all) depends as much on the 'from where' and the 'to whom' of any discourse as it does on its relations to an 'about'. For example, the reason that I referred to 'interdisciplinary conflict' above is that during my research, I have found the pertinence or even the 'good taste' of using a theoretical vocabulary derived from semiotics to discuss 'ordinary women's lives' questioned more severely by sociologists or historians (for whom the question becomes more urgent, perhaps, as so-called 'theory' becomes more respectable) than by non-academic (I do not say 'ordinary') women – who have been variously curious, indifferent, or amused.

Nevertheless, these are questions that feminist intellectuals do ask each other; and we will no doubt continue to do so as long as we retain some sense of a wider social (as well as 'interdisciplinary') context and political import for our work. So I want to suggest the beginnings of an answer, one 'appropriate' to a cross-disciplinary gathering of feminist intellectuals, by questioning the function of the 'ordinary woman' as a figure in our polemics. As a feminist, I cannot and do not wish the image, or the reality, of other women away. As a semiotician, however, I must notice that 'images' of other women, even those which I've just constructed in mentioning 'them' as problem ('sociologists and historians' for me, rather than 'ordinary women') are, in fact, images.

My difficulty in the shopping-centre project will thus be not simply my relation as intellectual to the culture I'm speaking 'about', but to whom I will imagine that I will be speaking. So if, in a first instance, the task of differentiating shopping centres involves a struggle with fascinated description – consuming and consumerist list-making, attempts to freeze and fix a spectacular reality – my second problem will be to produce a mode of address that will 'evade' the fascinated or mirroring relationship to both the institutional discourses 'about' women that I'm

contesting, and the imaginary figure of Everywoman that those discourses – along with many feminist arguments – keep on throwing up.

However in making that argument, I also evaded the problem of
'other' (rather than 'ordinary') women. I slid from restating the now
conventional case that an image of a woman shopping is not a 'real' (or
really representative) woman shopping to talking as though that difference absolved me from thinking about other women's ideas about their
experience in shopping centres, as 'users' and as workers there. This is a
problem of method, to which I'd like to return. First, I want to make a
detour to consider the second enquiry I've had from 'other' women:
'What's the point of differentiating shopping centres? So what if they're
not all the same?'

Here I want to make two points, about method. The first is that if
this project on 'Things To Do with Shopping Centres' could have a
subtitle, it would be *'Pedestrian Notes on Modernity'*. I agree with Alice
Jardine's argument in her book *Gynesis* that feminist criticism has much
to gain from studying recent debates about 'modernity' in thought (that
is, 'modernity' in the general European sense of life after industrialization – a sense which includes but is broader than the American aesthetic
term 'postmodernity').

Studying shopping centres should be (like studying women modernists) one way to contest the idea that you can find, for example, at
moments in the work of Julia Kristeva, that the cultural production of
'actual women' has historically fallen short of a modernity understood
as, or in terms derived from, the critical construction of modern*ism*. In
this project, I prefer to study instead the everyday, the so-called banal,
the supposedly un- or non-experimental, asking not, 'why does it fall
short of modernism?' but 'how do classical theories of modernism fall
short of women's modernity?'

Secondly, the figure of the pedestrian gives me a way of imaging a
critical method for analysing shopping centres that doesn't succumb
unequivocally to the lure of using the classical images of the Imaginary,
in the psychoanalytic sense, as a mirror to the shoppingtown spectacle.
Such images are very common now in the literature about shopping
centres: especially about big, enclosed, enveloping, 'spectacular' centres
like one of those I'm studying, Indooroopilly Shoppingtown. Like department stores before them (and which they now usually contain), they
are described as palaces of dreams, halls of mirrors, galleries of illusion
. . . and the fascinated analyst becomes identified as a theatre critic,
reviewing the spectacle, herself in the spectacle, and the spectacle in

herself. This rhetoric is closely related, of course, to the vision of shoppingtown as Eden, or paradise: the shopping centre is figured as, if not exactly utopian, then a mirror to utopian desire, the desire of fallen creatures nostalgic for the primal garden, yet aware that their paradise is now an illusion.

The pedestrian, or the woman walker, doesn't escape this dreamy ambivalence. Indeed, sociological studies suggest that women who don't come in cars to shopping centres spend much more time in them than those that do. The slow, evaluative, appreciatively critical relation is not enjoyed to the same extent by women who hit the carpark, grab the goods, and head on out as fast as possible. Obviously, different women do both at different times. But if walking around for a long time in one centre creates engagement with and absorption in the spectacle, then one sure way at least to begin from a sharply defined sense of critical estrangement is to arrive at a drive-in centre on foot – and have to find a way to walk in. (Most women non-drivers, of course, don't arrive on foot – especially with children – but by public transport: which can, in Australia, produce an acutely estranging effect.)

I have to insert a qualification here about the danger of constructing exemplary allegorical figures (even that of the 'woman walker') if they're taken to refer to some model of the 'empirical social user' of shopping centres. It's a fairly futile exercise to try to make generalizations, beyond statistical averaging, about the users of shopping centres at any particular time – even in terms of class, race, age or gender. It's true that where you find a centre in a socially homogenized area (very common in some suburban regions of most Australian cities), you do find a high incidence of regular use by specific social groups (which may contribute strongly to the centre's identity effect). At a lot of centres, nevertheless, that's not the case. And even where it is, such generalizations remain abstractions, for concrete reasons: cars, public transport, visiting and tourist practices (since shopping centres can be used for sightseeing), and day-out patterns of movement, all mean that centres do not automatically 're-flect' the composition of their immediate social environment. Also, there are different practices of use in one centre on any one day: some people may be there for the one and only time in their lives; there are occasional users choosing that centre rather than this on that day for particular, or quite arbitrary reasons; people may shop at one centre and go to another to socialize or hang around. The use of centres as meeting places (and sometimes for free warmth and shelter) by young people, pensioners, the unemployed and the homeless is a familiar part of their social function – often planned for, now, by centre management (distri-bution of benches, video games, security guards). And many of a centre's habitual users may not always live in its vicinity.

Shopping centres illustrate very well, I think, the argument that you can't treat a public at a cultural event as directly expressive of social groups and classes, or their supposed sensibility. Publics aren't stable, homogeneous entities – and polemical claims assuming that they are tell us little beyond the display of political position and identification being made by the speaker. These displays may be interesting in themselves, but they don't necessarily say much about the wider social realities such polemics often invoke.

Shopping-centre designers know this very well, in fact – and some recent retailing theory talks quite explicitly about the marketing need to break down the old standardized predication of a 'vast monolithic middle-class market' for shopping-centre product, that characterized the strategy of the 1970s. The prevailing marketing philosophy for the 1980s (especially in the United States, but visible also in parts of Australia) has been rather to develop spectacles of 'diversity and market segmen-tation'. That is, to produce images of class, ethnic, age and gender *differentiation* in particular centres – not because a Vietnamized centre, for example, would better 'express' the target culture and better serve Vietnamese (though it may well do so, particularly since retail theorists seem to have pinched the idea partly from the forms of community politics), but because the display of difference will today increase a centre's 'tourist' appeal to everyone else from elsewhere.

This is a response, of course, to the disintegration of the postwar 'middle class', and the ever-growing disparity in the developed nations between rich and poor. This change is quite menacing to the suburban shopping centres, however structurally complicit the companies that profit from them may have been in bringing the change about; and what's interesting is the attempt to 'manage' the change in terms of a differential thematization of 'shoppers' – and thus of the centres to serve them. Three years ago, one theorist imagined the future thus: 'Centres will be designed specifically to meet demands of the *economic* shopper, the *recreational* shopper, or the *pragmatic* shopper, and so on.' His scenario is already being realized, although once again this does not mean that as 'shoppers' we do in fact conform to, let alone become, the proffered image of our 'demands'.

That said, I want to make one more point about pedestrian leisure-liness and critical time. One thing that it's important to do with particular centres is to write them a (differential) history. This can be surprisingly difficult and time-consuming. The shopping centre 'form' itself – a form often described as 'one of the few new building types created in our time' – certainly has had its histories written, mostly in heroic and expansive terms. But I've found empirically that while some local residents are able to tell stories of a particular development and its effects on their lives, the people who manage centres in Australia are often disconcerted at the suggestion that *their* centre could have a history. There are several obvious reasons for that – short-term employment patterns, employee and even managerial indifference to the workplace, ideologies about what counts as proper history, the consecration of shopping centres to the perpetual present of consumption ('nowness'), suspicion of 'media enquiries' (that is, of me) in centres hostile to publicity they don't control, and also the feeling that in many cases, the history is best forgotten. For example, the building of Indooroopilly Shoppingtown required the blitzing of a huge chunk of old residential Indooroopilly.

But there's a parallel avoidance of local shopping-centre histories in much of the critical writing on centres – except for those which (like Southdale Mall or Faneuil Hall Marketplace in the United States, and Roselands in Australia) figure as pioneers in the history of development. Leaving aside for the moment the material produced by commercial interests (which tends to be dominated, as one might expect, by complex economic and futuristic speculation developed, in relation to particular centres, along interventionist lines), I'd argue that an odd gap usually appears between, on the one hand, critical writing where the shopping place becomes the metaphorical site for a practice of personal reminiscence (autobiography, the production of a written self), and on the other, the purely formal description of existing structures found in architectural criticism. Walter Benjamin's *A Berlin Chronicle* (for older market forms) and Donald Horne's memoir of the site of Miranda Fair in *Money Made Us* are examples of the first practice, and the article by Neville Quarry that I've mentioned an example of the second.

The gap between these two genres (reminiscence and formal description) may in turn correspond to one produced by so-called 'Man-Environment' studies. For example, Amos Rapoport's influential book *The Meaning of the Built Environment* depends entirely on the humanist distinction between 'users' meanings' (the personal) and 'designers' meanings' (the professional). I think that a feminist study of shopping centres should *occupy* this user/designer, memory/aesthetics gap, not, of course, to 'close' or to 'bridge' it, but to dislocate the relationship

between the poles that create it, and so dissolve their imaginary autonomy. Of course, any vaguely anti-humanist critique would want to say
as much. What is of particular interest to me as a feminist is to make
relations between on the one hand those competing practices of 'place'
(which Michel de Certeau calls 'spatial stories') that by investing sites
with meaning make them sites of social conflict, and on the other,
women's discourses of memory and local history.

A shopping centre is a 'place' combining an extreme project of
general 'planning' competence (efforts at total unification, total management) with an intense degree of aberrance and diversity in local performance. It is also a 'place' consecrated to timelessness and stasis (no
clocks, perfect weather . . .) yet lived and celebrated, lived and loathed,
in intimately historic terms: for some, as ruptural event (catastrophic or
Edenic) in the social experience of a community, for others, as the
enduring scene (as the cinema once was, and the home still may be) of
all the changes, fluctuations, and repetitions of the passing of everyday
life. For both of these reasons, a shopping centre seems to me to be a
good place to begin to consider women's 'cultural production' of
modernity.

This is also why I suggested that it can be important to write a
history of particular shopping centres. It is one way in which the clash of
conflicting programmes for the management of change, and for resisting, refusing or evading 'management', can better be understood.

Such a history can be useful in other ways. It helps to denaturalize
the myths of spectacular identity-in-place that centres produce in order
to compete with each other, by analysing how these myths, those
spectacles, are constructed for particular spaces over time. The qualification 'particular' is crucial, I think, because like many critics now I
have my doubts that polemical demonstrations of the fact that such
'myth-making' takes place have much to offer a contemporary cultural
politics. Like revelations of essentialism or, indeed, 'naturalism' in
other people's arguments, simple demythologization all too often re-
trieves, at the end of the process, its own untransformed basic premises
now masked as surprising conclusions. I also think that the project
itself is anachronistic: commercial culture today proclaims and adver-
tises, rather than 'naturalizes', its powers of artifice, myth invention,
simulation. In researching the history of myth-making in a particular
place, however, one is obliged to consider how it works in concrete
social circumstances that inflect, in turn, its workings – and one is
obliged to learn from that place, make discoveries, change the drift

of one's analysis, rather than use it as a site of theoretical self-justification.

Secondly, such a history must assume that centres and their myths are actively transformed by their 'users' (although in very ambiguous ways) and that the history itself would count as one such transformation by a user. In my study this will mean, in practice, that I'm only going to analyse shopping centres that I know personally.

I'm not going to use them to tell my life story, but I am going to refuse the discursive position of externalized visitor/observer, or ethnographer/celebrant, by setting up as my objects only those centres where I have, or have had, some practice other than that of analyst – places I've lived near or used as consumer, window-shopper, tourist, or as escapee from a passing mood (since refuge, or R&R, is one of the social functions of shopping centres, though women who just hate them may find that hard to accept). As the sociologist John Carroll reports with the cheerfulness of the true conservative, 'The Promotions Manager of one of the Shopping World chains in Australia has speculated that these centres may replace Valium.' Carroll doesn't add anything about their role in creating needs for Valium, or in selling it, but only if you combine all three functions do you get a sense, I think, of Shopping World's lived ambiguity.

And here I return to the question of 'other women' and my relation to their relation to these shopping centres. I've argued quite clearly, I hope, my objections in the present context to procedures of sampling 'representative' shoppers, framing exemplary figures, targeting empirical 'user groups', and so on. That doesn't mean that I think there's anything 'wrong' with those methods, that I wouldn't use them in another context or borrow, in this context, from studies which have used them. Nor does it mean that I think there's no way to produce knowledge of shopping centres except from 'personal experience' (which would preclude me, for example, from considering what it's like to work in one for years).

However I'm interested in something a little more fugitive – or pedestrian – than either a professionally based informatics, or a narcissistically enclosed reverie, can give me. I'm interested in impromptu shopping-centre encounters: chit-chat, with women I meet in and around and because of these centres that I know personally (ranging from close family friends at some to total strangers at others). Collecting chit-chat in situ is, of course, a pedestrian professional practice ('journalism'). But I also want to analyse it in terms of the theoretical concerns

I've outlined (rather than as 'evidence' of how others really feel) as a means of doubting and revising, rather than confirming, my own 'planning' programme.

In order to pass on to a few comments about one shopping centre 'history', I'd like first to describe the set of three to which it belongs in my project. I chose this set initially for quite personal reasons: three favourite shopping centres, one of which my family used, and two of which I had often used as a tourist; two of which I loved, and one of which I hated. But I discovered subsequently that this 'set' also conforms to a system of formal distinctions conventionally used by the people who build and manage shopping centres. These are planners' terms, 'designers' meanings'. But most of us are familiar in practice with these distinctions, and some whole cities (like Canberra) are built around them.

Until recently, there has been a more or less universally accepted classification system based on three main types of centre: the 'neighbourhood' centre, the 'community' centre, and the 'regional' centre. Some writers add extra categories, like the 'super-regional', a huge and now mostly uneconomic dinosaur (rare in Australia, but common in more populous countries) with four to six full-line department stores. With the ageing of the classic suburban form and the burgeoning of rival retail formats better adapted to current economic conditions (discount chains, hypermarkets, neo-arcades, ethnic and other 'theme' environments, history-zones, speciality malls, multi-use centres and urban megastructures), the basic schema is losing some of its reality-productive power. But it remains operative (and, in Australia, dominant) for those classic and still active structures of suburban life that I'm discussing.

The basic triad – neighbourhood/community/regional – is defined not in terms of catchment-area size, or type of public attracted, or acreage occupied. It depends instead on the type of major store that a centre offers to 'anchor' its speciality shops. (As an anchor, it is usually placed at the end of the central strip.) Neighbourhood stores have only a supermarket, while community centres have a supermarket and either a discount house or a chain store (Big W, Target). Regional centres have both of these, plus at least one full department store. The anchor store is also called the magnet: it is considered to regulate the flows of attraction, circulation and expulsion of people, commodities and cars.

For example, Indooroopilly Shoppingtown in Brisbane is a canonical example of the classical postwar regional shopping centre. It's also an aristocrat – a 'Westfield'. As Australia's leading shopping-centre developer, now achieving the ultimate goal of operating in the United States and buying into the movie business, Westfield celebrates its own norm-setting status in an art corridor at Sydney's Miranda Fair, where you can visit glorious full-colour photographs of all the other major Westfields in Australia, including Indooroopilly. Indooroopilly Shoppingtown itself is a place with a postcard – a site unto itself from which people can state their whereabouts in writing. It's an instance of the model form celebrated in the general histories I mentioned above. These are expansionist histories of postwar centrifugal movements of cars and people away from old city centres – because of urban congestion in American and Australian cases, and congestion or war damage or both in European towns and cities.

Ideally these centres, according to the histories, are so-called 'greenfield' developments on the edge of or outside towns – on that ever-receding transformation zone where the country becomes the city as suburbia. Of course, they have often in fact been the product of suburb-blitzing, not suburb-creating processes – though the blitzing of one may help to create another on the city's periphery. So strong has been the force of the centrifugal imaginary, however, that in the case of the Brisbane *Courier-Mail*'s coverage of the building of Indooroopilly Shoppingtown, the houses being moved to make way for it were represented as flying off happily like pioneers out to the far frontiers of the city. The postwar regional centre, then, is traditionally represented as the 'revolutionary', explosive suburban form.

At the opposite end of the spectrum, Fortitude Valley Plaza, again in Brisbane, is an example of a neighbourhood centre. The term 'neighbourhood' may conjure up cosy, friendly images of intimacy, but this centre is actually at a major urban transit point, over a railway station, in a high density area and on one of the most polluted roads in Australia. It's also an early example neither of greenfield nor blitzing development, but of the recently very popular practice of 'infill' (or 'twilight zone') development. 'Infill' has been filling in the central shopping districts of many country towns and old suburbs over the past few years. It means that bits of shopping centre and arcade snake around to swallow the gaps between existing structures. This practice has been important in the downtown revivals that succeeded (along with the energy crisis) the heroic age of the regional shopping centre.

Again, the *Courier-Mail*'s coverage was metaphorically apt. Because there had been an old open railway line on the site, the Valley Plaza was seen to be resourcefully filling in the 'previous useless airspace' wasted by the earlier structure. It was promoted as a thrifty, perhaps even ecologically sound, solution to a problem of resources. The Valley Plaza is also an example of a centre that has undergone an identity change. When I first studied it in 1983, it was a bit dank and dated – vintage pop futurist in style, with plenty of original but pollution-blackened 1960s orange and once-zappy geometrical trimmings. Now it's light green, and Chinatownified (with Chinese characters replacing the op-art effects), to blend in with the ethnic repackaging of Fortitude Valley as a whole.

Finally, Green Hills is an example of the mediating category, a 'community' centre in East Maitland, a town near the industrial city of Newcastle in New South Wales. It's a Woolworths centre, with a supermarket and a Big W Discount House. Unlike the other two it is a mostly open mall. It's badly signed and bordered, and in fact it's mostly hidden from view in relation to the major highway (the New England) that runs right alongside. Whatever the original considerations and/or accidents behind this design, its effect now is in fact a very appropriate paranoid country town, insiders-only identity. Like much country town cultural production, you have to know where it is to find it.

Yet it was, for many years, very successful. Generically a community centre, it has none the less had a regional function – with its Big W Discount magnet pulling in people from all over the Hunter Valley who might once have gone on through to Newcastle. People didn't just come to Maitland – they went to Green Hills. So if, in this particular triad, Indooroopilly is explosive and the Valley Plaza is thrifty in the local rhetorics of space, Green Hills was represented in terms of a go-ahead conservatism – extending and renewing the old town of Maitland, while acting to help maintain the town's traditional economic and cultural independence.

I want to examine the representation of Green Hills in more detail, and one reason for looking at the triad of formal distinctions has been to provide a context for doing so. In the short history of Green Hills that I've been able to construct, it's clear that allusions to the other shopping-centre forms, and especially to the suburban-explosive model, played a very complex role firstly in Woolworths' strategic presentation of the project to build Green Hills, and secondly, once it was built, in the promotional rhetoric used to specify an ideal public to whom the centre would appeal (something like 'the loyal citizens' of Maitland).

In presenting a couple of elements of that history now, I must make two strong qualifications about what sort of history it is (in the context of this paper), and why. First, it is primarily derived from coverage in the local newspaper, the *Maitland Mercury*. Other sources generate other stories. This version is specifically concerned with the rhetorical collusion between the local media and the interests of Woolworths; and also with the ways that this relationship cut across two pre-existing but at this point contradictory collusions of interest between the media and the council on the one hand, and the media and local small business interests on the other. (Small business, of course, was understandably most alarmed about the prospect of the Green Hills development.) Close relations between these parties – council, media, small business – are very common in nearly all country newspapers now, which tend to define the town's interests very much in terms of the doings of civic fathers on the one hand, and those of local enterprise on the other. Sport and the cycle of family life are two major sites on which those doings are played out. In that sense, country newspapers are unashamedly one long advertorial. But in the building of Green Hills, civic fathers and local business were opposed in a conflict that took the form of a debate about the meaning of 'local community'. To describe this conflict briefly, I shall give it the form of an over-coherent, paranoid story.

Second, as my choice of sources suggests, this version could be criticized as lopsidedly restricted to 'designers' meanings', planners' programmes. I don't mind too much about that, for two reasons. One is that as a long-term if irregular 'user' of Green Hills, I was more interested in pursuing what I didn't already know about it, or hadn't noticed when it was happening. This 'place' had simply appeared where once there had been a border-zone that in the 1960s had signified the joys of driving out of town and the ambivalence of returning, and was, in earlier decades, the field of the illicit outside town (the forbidden picnic-ground).

The other reason is that I actually have no clear idea of what follows from the espousal of an emphasis on 'users' meanings' (or as anti-humanists might say, 'practices of consumption') – except, perhaps, for more celebrant sociology, and/or a reinvigorated local history.

Part of the problem, perhaps, is the common substitution between 'users' meanings' and 'practices of consumption'. It's an easy slide: from user to consumer to consumption, from persons to structures and processes. A whole essay could be written about what's wrong with making this and the parallel slide from notions of individual and group 'creativity' to cultural 'production' to political 'resistance' – which can lead to the kind of criticism that a friend once parodied as 'the discovery that washing your car on Sunday is a revolutionary event'.

All I want to say here is that if the production/consumption opposition is not just a 'designer/user' relation writ large (because relations of production cannot be trivialized to 'people planning things'), then it doesn't follow that representations of a shopping-centre design project circulated by local media and consumed (creatively or otherwise) by some of its readership can be slotted away as production history. Indeed, I'm not sure that media practices can usefully be 'placed' on either 'side' of such a dichotomy. I think that the dichotomy itself needs to be re-examined, especially since it now floats free of its old anchorage in theories of social totality; and the assumption that production and consumption can be read somehow as parallel or diverging realities depends on another assumption (becoming more dubious with every chip of change in technology) that we know enough now about production and can move to the other side. As though production, somehow, stays put.

The story of Green Hills is in a way an allegory about a politics of staying put, and it begins, paranoiacally, not with the first obvious appearance of a sign staking out a site, but behind the scenes – with an article in the NSW State Planning Authority journal SPAN in January 1969 and a report about it published in the *Newcastle Morning Herald* (24 January 1969). The *Herald*'s story had the provocative title 'Will Maitland Retain Its Entity Or Become A Newcastle Suburb?'

Several general problems were facing Maitland, and many other country towns in Eastern Australia, at this time: population drift, shrinking local employment prospects, declining or anachronistic community facilities, the 'nothing to do' syndrome. Maitland also had regional problems as a former rural service centre and coalfields capital en route to becoming a dormitory suburb, menaced by residential creep towards Newcastle – then about twenty miles away and getting closer. Maitland in particular suffered as well from physical fragmentation after ruinous floods in 1949 and 1955. The 1955 flood devastated the old commercial centre and the inner residential area: houses were shifted out and away in response to a 'natural' blitzing.

So the threat of suburbanization and annexation uttered by the

Herald produced an outraged response in that afternoon's *Maitland Mercury* from the Maitland mayor who, in spurning these 'dismal prophecies', mentioned the 'hope' that Woolworths would soon name the day for a development at East Maitland. From this moment on, and during all the conflicts that followed, Woolworths never figured in the council discourse as a national chain just setting up a store in a likely spot, but as a gallant and caring saviour come to make Maitland whole again – to stop the gap, to restore definition, to contain the creeping and seeping and to save Our Town's 'Entity'. In actual fact, of course, and following a well-known law of development, Green Hills was built on the town fringe nearest Newcastle, and the ensuing growth around it took the town kilometres closer to Newcastle and helped to fragment further the old city centre.

Four months after the SPAN and *Herald* incidents, the *Mercury* published a photo of an anonymous man staring at a mystery sign behind wire in the bush, saying 'This site has been selected for another all Australian development by Woolworths' (*Maitland Mercury*, 16 May 1969). The site was at that time still a ragged border wasteland, across the hill from a notorious old 'slum' called Eastville. The *Mercury* photo initiated a long-running mystery story about the conversion of the indefinite bush-border into a 'site', the site into a place, the place into a suburb, in a process of territorialization that I'll call the fabrication of a place-name.

To summarize the episodes briefly: first, the mystery sign turned out to be not just a bait to initiate interest, but a legal loophole that allowed Woolworths to claim, when challenged by local business firms, that it had fulfilled the terms of a 1965 agreement to develop the site by a certain date (*Maitland Mercury*, 25 June 1969). The sign itself could count as a developmental structure, and it had appeared just in time. Second, the first sign was replaced by another: a board at first adorned only by the letter 'G'. Maitland 'citizens' were to participate in a guessing competition to find the name of the place, and a new letter was added each week until the full place-name, and the name of a lucky winner, emerged. This happened on 22 October 1969; and on the following Remembrance Day, 11 November, the city council abolished the name of the slum across the highway, Eastville. Eastville's name was to be forgotten, said the *Mercury*, in order to 'unify the area with East Maitland' ('Eastville To Go West', *Maitland Mercury*, 12 November 1969).

The basic Green Hills complex – at this stage a neighbourhood centre with a supermarket only – was opened in February 1972. The ceremony included ritual displays of crowd hysteria, with frenzied women fainting and making off with five thousand pairs of 8-cent pantyhose in the first five minutes (*Maitland Mercury*, 10 February 1972). This rite of baptism, or of public consent to the place-name, was repeated even more fervently in November 1977 when the Big W Discount House was added to make Green Hills a community centre. This time, women came wearing signs of Green Hills identity: said the *Mercury*, 'A sea of green mums flooded in. . . . The mums dressed in sea green, celery green, grass green, olive green, green florals – every green imaginable – to take advantage of a 2NX offer of free dinner tickets for women dressed in that colour' (*Maitland Mercury*, 14 November 1977).

That wasn't the end of it. The process now known as 'metro-nucleation' had begun. In 1972, a company associated with Woolworths began a hundred-home subdivision behind the centre. The area then acquired more parking, a pub, a motel, light industry, an old peoples' home, more speciality shops at the centre itself in 1980, and then, in 1983, a community health centre. This centre, said the *Mercury* – forgetting that the forgetting of Eastville had been to unify East Maitland – would serve 'to service people living in the Berefield, Maitland, Bolwarra, East Maitland *and* Green Hills areas' (*Maitland Mercury*, 14 November 1983). Maitland's 'entity' at this stage was still a dubious mess, but Green Hills' identity was established, its status as a place-name secure. Presented rhetorically as a gesture of community unification, it had been, in effect, suburban-explosive in function.

The story continues, of course: I shan't follow it further, except to note that after this decade of expansion (a decade of acute economic distress for Maitland, and the Hunter Valley coal towns in general) Green Hills went into a certain decline. Woolworths got into trouble nationally and their Big W discount stores failed to keep pace with newer retail styles. Green Hills in particular faced stiff competition when a few blocks of the old city centre were torn down for a Coles-Myer Super-K semi-hypermarket, and when rapid infill development brought the twilight zone to town. Even residents hostile to these changes transferred their interest to them: one said, 'It's awesome how many places they think we can use just to buy our few pounds of mince.'

I want to conclude with a few general points about things to do with this story. First, there are obviously a number of standardized elements in it that would appear in any such story set anywhere. For example, oceanic and hysterical crowd behaviour, in which the crowd itself becomes a decorative feature of the shopping centre's performance, is a traditional motif (and the *Mercury* in the late 1960s ran news features on how people behaved at shopping centres in Sydney and the United States). More generally, the process of development itself was impeccably normal.

Yet in looking at local instances of these general models, the well-known things that shopping centres do, one is also studying the practical inflections, or rewritings, of those models that can account for, and found, a regional politics. In the Green Hills case, I think that the Woolworths success story was written by the media very much in terms of a specific response to pre-existing discourses about Maitland's 'very own' problems of identity and unity. In this sense, Woolworths' 'success' was precisely to efface the similarity between what was happening in Maitland and what was going on elsewhere. That's the kind of problem I'd like to consider further: the ways in which the exploitation of the sense of 'difference' in contemporary culture can be quite as complex as, and necessarily related to, the construction and deconstruction of imaginary identities.

Second, I'd like to use the Green Hills study to question some recent accounts in cultural studies of so-called 'commodity semiosis' – the processes whereby commodities become signs, and signs become commodities – and the tendency to feminize (for example, through a theme of seduction) the terms in which that semiosis is discussed.

In an interesting critique of the work of Jean Baudrillard, Andrew Wernick writes:

> The sales aim of commodity semiosis is to differentiate the product as a valid, or at least resonant, social totem, and this would be impossible without being able to appeal to taken-for-granted systems of cultural reference (Wernick 1987: 31).

While it is inappropriate (if consonant with marketspeak) simply to equate a whole shopping centre with 'the product' in Wernick's sense, I could say that in the Green Hills case, Woolworths' strategy in selling the centre to the town was to appeal to that taken-for-granted cultural reference system of 'booster' discourse deployed by ideologues of Australian country towns – towns which have long been losing their old reasons for being, and so their sense of the meaning and aim of their 'history'. Donald Horne has defined the elements of 'booster' discourse in Australia as (1) getting bigger and (2) making it last – aims which we might rephrase in combination here as 'keeping it up'.

I can say practically nothing here about the inner workings of Green Hills: but one thing that a feminist critique of commodity semiosis might notice there is that among the taken-for-granted cultural reference systems appealed to by suburban shopping centres is a garden furniture aesthetic that not only makes all centres seem the same, but, through a play of echoing spatial analogy, makes shopping centres seem like a range of other sites consecrated to the performance of family life, to women's work, to women's work in leisure: shoppingtown, beer garden, picnic spot, used-car yard (with bunting), scenic lookout, town garden, public park, suburban backyard.

The brightly coloured benches of Green Hills – along with coloured rubbish cones, rustic borders, foliage, planters, mulch and well-spaced saplings – are all direct descendants of what in 1960 Robin Boyd called, in *The Australian Ugliness*, the 'desperately picturesque accoutrements' then just bursting out brightly as 'features' at Australian beauty-spots. There's nothing desperate about their picturesqueness now, although they may mean desperation to some of their users (as well as cheer and comfort to others, especially those who remember the unforgiving discomforts of seatless, as well as featureless, Australian country town streets). Today, I think, they work to produce a sense of 'setting' that defines an imaginary coherence of public space in Australia – or more precisely, of a 'lifestyle' space declaring the dissolution of boundaries between public and private space, between public domains of work and private spheres of leisure.

Janet Wolff has argued that the emergence of the distinction between public and private spheres in the nineteenth century made impossible a female *flâneur* – a female strolling heroine 'botanizing on the asphalt' as Walter Benjamin put it in his study of Baudelaire (Woolf 1988) . I want to argue that it is precisely the proclaimed dissolution of public and private on the botanized asphalt of shoppingtown today that makes possible, not a *flâneuse*, since that term becomes anachronistic, but a practice of modernity by women for which it is most important not to begin by identifying heroines and victims (even of conflicts with male paranoia), but a profound ambivalence about shifting roles.

Yet here again, I want to differentiate. At places 'like' Green Hills, the given function of hallucinatory spatial resemblance and recall is not, as it might be in an urban road-romance, a thinning out of significance through space so that one place ends up like any other in its drab indifference. Nor is it, as it might be in a big city, a move in a competitive game where one space says of its nearby rivals, 'We Do All the Same

Things Better'. Green Hills appeals instead to a dream of plenitude and of a paradoxically absolute yet expansive self-sufficiency: a country town (if not 'male') paranoia seeking reassurance that nothing is lacking in this one spot. It's the motherland dream of staying home, staying put: and as an uncle said to me on a stray visit to Green Hills, made simply to be sociable, waving round at the mulch and the benches and the glass facade of Big W – 'Why go elsewhere when you've got it all here?' The centre itself, in his imagination, was not a fallen land of fragmented modernity, but the Garden of Eden itself. (Two years later, however, he sent me by myself to buy him cut-price T-shirts from Super-K in town – now the place where everyone wants to shop but no one cares to visit.)

Having arrived at last at the irresistible Big W magnet, I'd like to conclude with a comment on a text which seems to me to be a 'radical' culture-criticism equivalent of the Garden of Eden fable by Myer's John Lennen with which I began.

It's a passage from Terry Eagleton's book *Walter Benjamin, or Towards a Revolutionary Criticism*; and it is also, although obliquely, a parable of modernity that depends on figuring consumption as a seductively fallen state. Paraphrasing and developing Benjamin's study of the *flâneur*, Eagleton writes:

> the commodity disports itself with all comers without its halo slipping, promises permanent possession to everyone in the market without abandoning its secretive isolation. Serializing its consumers, it nevertheless makes intimate *ad hominem* address to each. (Eagleton 1981: 27)

Now if this is not, as in Lennen's paper, a figure of Adam comforting Eve with a note on the postmodern condition, it's certainly Adam comforting himself with a certain ambivalent fantasy about Eve. It's a luscious, self-seducingly *risqué* fantasy that Adam has, a commodity thought, rather like the exquisite bottle of perfume or the pure wool jumper in the import shop, nestling deep in an upmarket neo-arcade, its ambience aglow with *Miami Vice* pastels or (since that's now been a little overdone) cooled by marbloid Italianate tiling.

But its pertinence to retailing, commodity semiosis, and shopping practices today is questionable not least because the development of forms like the neo-arcade (or the fantastically revamped prewar elegance of certain city department stores) is a response to the shopping-centre forms I've been discussing: a response which works by offering signs of old-fashioned commodity fetishism precisely because suburban shopping centres don't do so. Part of my argument has been that in suburban shopping practices it isn't necessarily or always the objects consumed that count in the act of consumption, but rather that unique sense of place. Beyond that, however, I think that the Benjamin–Eagleton style of boudoir-talk about commodities can be doubly misleading.

First, one might ask, what is the sound of an intimate *ad hominem* address from a raincoat at Big W? Where is the secretive isolation of the thongs in a pile at Super-K? The commodities in a discount house boast no halo, no aura. On the contrary, they promote a lived aesthetic of the serial, the machinic, the mass-reproduced: as one pair of thongs wears out, it is replaced by an identical pair, the same sweatshirt is bought in four different colours, or two different and two the same; a macramé planter defies all middle-class whole-earth naturalness connotations in its dyes of lurid chemical mustard and killer neon pink. Second, commodity boudoir-talk gathers up into the single and class-specific image of the elite courtesan a number of different relations women and men may invent both to actual commodities, the activity of combining them and, above all, to the changing discursive frames (like shopping centres) that invest the practices of buying, trafficking with, and using commodities with their variable local meanings.

So one of the things I'd like to do with shopping centres is to make it more difficult for 'radical' culture critics to fall back quite so comfortably on the classic image of European bourgeois luxury to articulate theories of sexual and economic exchange. If I were, for the sake of argument, to make up a fable of Adam and Eve and the fall into modernity, I wouldn't have my image of Eve taking comfort from modernist explanation (as she does from Lennen's Adam), and I wouldn't have her flattering him as she does for Eagleton's 'comers'. I'd have an image of her as a pedestrian, laughing at both of them, walking on past saying, 'Boys, you sound just like the snake.'

But of course, that's not good enough. It's the Eden story that's the problem, the fable of the management of change that's wrong – with its images of the garden, the snake, the couple, the Fall, and the terms that the story imposes, no matter how or by whom it's rewritten. To deny that shopping centres, and consumption, provide allegories of modernity as a fallen state is to claim that for feminism, some stories may be beyond salvage.

A film about these matters (and about elite courtesans) shown at the Feminist Criticism and Cultural Production Conference – *Seduction – The*

Cruel Woman by Elfi Mikesch and Monika Treut – interested me in its luxuriant difference from an imaginary text I've often wanted to write about country town familial sado-masochism, called 'Maitland S&M'.

This text is about the orchestration of modes of domestic repetition, the going back again and again over the same stories, the same terrains, the same sore spots, which I think a centre like Green Hills has successfully incorporated and mobilized in its fabrication of a myth of staying put at home. In case this sounds like feminist paranoia about, once again, planners, designers and producers, I should stress that one of the things that is fascinating about Big W aesthetics is the way that the store provides little more than a set of managerial props for the performance of inventive scenarios in a drama that circulates endlessly between home and the pub and the carpark and Green Hills and back again to home. One can emerge for a good session of ritualized pain and sorrow (as well as, of course, more pedestrian experiences) dressed in nothing more ferocious or costly than a fluffy pink top and a sweet floral skirt.

My main point, however, is that in so far as I have myself used the story of Green Hills as an allegory, it has been to argue that while it's clearly crucial, and fun, for feminist criticism to keep on rewriting the given stories of culture, to keep on revising and transforming their meanings, we must also remember that with some stories in some places, we do become cruelly bound by repetition, confined by the reiteration of the terms we're contesting. Otherwise, in an act of voluntary if painful servitude, feminist criticism ties its own hands and finds itself, again and again, at Green Hills, bound back home – to the same old story.

21 Raymond Williams

Advertising: the magic system

EDITOR'S INTRODUCTION

Raymond Williams's essay was originally written as a chapter in his 1961 book *The Long Revolution*, but was only published later and as an essay. It belongs to an older form of British-orientated cultural studies than the other essays collected here, but one that it is important not to forget.

It stands apart in two main ways: first, for Williams, cultural studies moves unproblematically back into cultural history. For him, telling the story of advertising's development allows one to grasp the forces which condition it now, and also, thus, to begin to be able to conceive of a different contemporary function for advertising. Second, Williams writes as a committed socialist; for him private-sector capitalism cannot fulfil the needs of society as a whole.

Today it is, perhaps, harder to promote state-socialism than to insist that cultural studies requires historical narratives. But it is not as though these two strands of Williams's essay are quite separate. For him, the history of advertising shows a minor mode of communication becoming a major one – a vital component in the organization and reproduction of capital. In a metaphor which goes back to Marx's belief that capitalism makes commodities 'fetishes', for Williams advertising is 'magic' because it transforms commodities into glamorous signifiers (turning a car into a sign of masculinity, for instance) and these signifiers present an imaginary, in the sense of unreal, world. Most of all, capitalism makes us forget how much work and suffering went into the production of commodities. Williams's history aims to disenchant capitalism: to show us what it really is. It might be objected, of course, that advertising's magic (like many magics) actually works: that, today, the use value of many commodities is their signifying function.

But that objection (and others which may occur to readers) does not spoil the essay's power to defamiliarize the current advertising industry through erudite narrative history.

Further reading: Ewen 1976; Lears 1983: Marchand 1985; Pope 1977; Williams 1961; Williamson 1978.

S.D.

HISTORY

It is customary to begin even the shortest account of the history of advertising by recalling the three thousand year old papyrus from Thebes, offering a reward for a runaway slave, and to go on to such recollections as the crier in the streets of Athens, the paintings of gladiators, with sentences urging attendance at their combats, in ruined Pompeii, and the fly-bills on the pillars of the Forum in Rome. This pleasant little ritual can be quickly performed, and as quickly forgotten: it is, of course, altogether too modest. If by advertising we mean what was meant by Shakespeare and the translators of the Authorized Version – the processes of taking or giving notice of something – it is as old as human society, and some pleasant recollections from the Stone Age could be quite easily devised.

The real business of the historian of advertising is more difficult: to trace the development from processes of specific attention and information to an institutionalized system of commercial information and persuasion; to relate this to changes in society and in the economy: and to trace changes in method in the context of changing organizations and intentions.

The spreading of information, by the crier or by handwritten and printed broadsheets, is known from all periods of English society. The first signs of anything more organized come in the seventeenth century, with the development of newsbooks, mercuries and newspapers. Already certain places, such as St Paul's in London, were recognized as centres for the posting of specific bills, and the extension of such posting to the new printed publications was a natural development. The material of such advertisements ranged from offers and wants in personal service, notices of the publication of books, and details of runaway servants, apprentices, horses and dogs, to announcements of new commodities available at particular shops, enthusiastic announcements of remedies and specifics, and notices of the public showing of monsters, prodigies and freaks. While the majority were the simple, basically factual and specific notices we now call 'classified', there were also direct recommendations, as here, from 1658:

> That Excellent, and by all Physicians, approved China drink, called by the Chineans Tcha, by other nations *Tay* alias *Tee*, is sold at the Sultaness Head Cophee-House in Sweeting's Rents, by the Royal Exchange, London.

Mention of the physicians begins that process of extension from the conventional recommendations of books as 'excellent' or 'admirable' and the conventional adjectives which soon become part of the noun, in a given context (as in my native village, every dance is a Grand Dance). The most extravagant early extensions were in the field of medicines, and it was noted in 1652, of the writers of copy in newsbooks:

> There is never a mountebank who, either by professing of chymistry or any other art drains money from the people of the nation but these arch-cheats have a share in the booty – because the fellow cannot lye sufficiently himself he gets one of these to do't for him.

Looking up, in the 1950s, from the British Dental Association's complaints of misleading television advertising of toothpastes, we can recognize the advertisement, in 1660, of a 'most Excellent and Approved DENTIFRICE', which not only makes the teeth 'white as Ivory', but

> being constantly used, the Parties using it are never troubled with the Tooth-ache. It fastens the Teeth, sweetens the Breath, and preserves the Gums and Mouth from Cankers and Imposthumes.

Moreover

> the right are onely to be had at Thomas Rookes, Stationer, at the Holy Lamb at the east end of St Paul's Church, near the School, in sealed papers at 12d the paper.

In the year of the Plague, London was full of

> SOVEREIGN Cordials against the Corruption of the Air.

These did not exactly succeed, but a long and profitable trade, and certain means of promoting it, were now firmly established.

With the major growth of newspapers, from the 1690s, the volume of advertisements notably increased. The great majority of them were still of the specific 'classified' kind, and were grouped in regular sections of the paper or magazine. Ordinary household goods were rarely advertised; people knew where to get these. But, apart from the wants and the runaways, new things, from the latest book or play to new kinds of luxury or 'cosmatick' made their way through these columns. By and large, it was still only in the pseudo-medical and toilet advertisements that persuasion methods were evident. The announcements were conventionally printed, and there was hardly any illustration. Devices of emphasis – the hand, the asterisk, the NB – can be found, and sailing announcements had small woodcuts of a ship, runaway notices similar cuts of a man looking back over his shoulder. But, in the early eighteenth century, these conventional figures became too numerous, and most newspapers banned them. The manufacturer of a 'Spring Truss' who illustrated his device, had few early imitators.

A more general tendency was noted by Johnson in 1758:

> Advertisements are now so numerous that they are very negligently perused, and it is therefore become necessary to gain attention by magnificence of promises and by eloquence sometimes sublime and sometimes pathetick. Promise, large promise, is the soul of an advertisement. I remember a washball that had a quality truly wonderful – it gave *an exquisite edge to the razor*! The trade of advertising is now so near to perfection that it is not easy to propose any improvement.

This is one of the earliest of 'gone about as far as they can go' conclusions on advertisers, but Johnson, after all, was sane. Within the situation he knew, of newspapers directed to a small public largely centred on the coffee-houses, the natural range was from private notices (of service wanted and offered, of things lost, found, offered and needed) through shopkeepers' information (of actual goods in their establishments) to puffs for occasional and marginal products. In this last kind, and within the techniques open to them, the puffmen had indeed used, intensively, all the traditional forms of persuasion, and of cheating and lying. The mountebank and the huckster had got into print, and, while the majority of advertisements remained straightforward, the influence of this particular group was on its way to giving 'advertising' a more specialized meaning.

DEVELOPMENT

There is no doubt that the Industrial Revolution, and the associated revolution in communications, fundamentally changed the nature of advertising. But the change was not simple, and must be understood in specific relation to particular developments. It is not true, for example, that with the coming of factory production large-scale advertising became economically necessary. By the 1850s, a century after Johnson's comment, and with Britain already an industrial nation, the advertising pages of the newspapers, whether *The Times* or the *News of the World*, were still basically similar to those in eighteenth-century journals, except that there were more of them, that they were more closely printed, and that there were certain exclusions (lists of whores, for example, were no longer advertised in the *Morning Post*).

The general increase was mainly due to the general growth in trade, but was aided by the reduction and then abolition of a long-standing Advertisement Tax. First imposed in 1712, at one shilling an announcement, this had been a means, with the Stamp Duty, of hampering the growth of newspapers, which successive Governments had good reason to fear. By the time of the worst repression, after the Napoleonic Wars, Stamp Duty was at 4d a sheet, and Advertisement Tax at 3s 6d. In 1833, Stamp Duty was reduced to 1d, and Advertisement Tax to 1s 6d. A comparison of figures for 1830 and 1838 shows the effect of this reduction: the number of advertisements in papers on the British mainland in the former year was 877,972; by the later date it stood at 1,491,991. Then in 1853 the Advertisement Tax was abolished, and in 1855 the Stamp Duty. The rise in the circulation of newspapers, and in the number of advertisements, was then rapid.

Yet still in the 1850s advertising was mainly of a classified kind, in specified parts of the publication. It was still widely felt, in many kinds of trade, that (as a local newspaper summarized the argument in 1859)

> it is not *respectable*. Advertising is resorted to for the purposes of introducing inferior articles into the market.

Rejecting this argument, the newspaper (*The Eastbourne Gazette and Fashionable Intelligencer*) continued:

> Competition is the soul of business, and what fairer or more legitimate means of competition can be adopted than the availing oneself of a channel to recommend goods to public notice which is open to all? Advertising is an open, fair, legitimate and respectable means of competition; bearing upon its face the impress of free-trade, and of as much advantage to the consumer as the producer.

The interesting thing is not so much the nature of this argument, but that, in 1859, it still had to be put in quite this way. Of course the article concluded by drawing attention to the paper's own advertising rates, but even then, to get the feel of the whole situation, we have to look at the actual advertisements flanking the article. Not only are they all from local tradesmen, but their tone is still eighteenth-century, as for example:

> To all who pay cash and can appreciate
> GOOD AND FINE TEAS
> CHARLES LEA

Begs most respectfully to solicit a trial of his present stock which has been selected with the greatest care, and paid for before being cleared from the Bonded warehouses in London . . .

In all papers, this was still the usual tone, but, as in the eighteenth century, one class of product attracted different methods. Probably the first nationally advertised product was Warren's Shoe Blacking, closely followed by Rowland's Macassar Oil (which produced the counter-offensive of the antimacassar), Spencer's Chinese Liquid Hair Dye, and Morison's Universal Pill. In this familiar field, as in the eighteenth century, the new advertising was effectively shaped, while for selling cheap books the practice of including puffs in announcements was widely extended. Warren's Shoe Blacking had a drawing of a cat spitting at its own reflection, and hack verses were widely used:

> The goose that on our Ock's green shore
> Thrives to the size of Albatross
> Is twice the goose it was before
> When washed with Neighbour Goodman's sauce.

Commercial purple was another writing style, especially for pills:

> The spring and fall of the leaf has been always remarked as the periods when disease, if it be lurking in the system, is sure to show itself. (Parr's Life Pills, 1843).

The manner runs back to that of the eighteenth-century hucksters and mountebanks, but what is new is its scale. The crowned heads of Europe were being signed up for testimonials (the Tsar of all the Russias took and recommended Revalenta Arabica, while the Balm of Syriacum, a 'sovereign remedy for both bodily and mental decay', was advertised as used in Queen Victoria's household). Holloway, of course a 'Professor', spent £5,000 a year, in the 1840s, spreading his Universal Ointment, and in 1855 exceeded £30,000.

Moreover, with the newspaper public still limited, the puffmen were going on the streets. Fly-posting, on every available space, was now a large and organized trade, though made hazardous by rival gangs (paste for your own, blacking for the others). It was necessary in 1837 to pass a London act prohibiting posting without the owner's consent (it proved extremely difficult to enforce). In 1862 came the United Kingdom Bill-posters Association, with an organized system of special hoardings, which had become steadily more necessary as the flood of paste swelled. Handbills ('throwaways') were distributed in the streets of Victorian London with extraordinary intensity of coverage; in some areas a walk down one street would collect as many as two hundred different leaflets. Advertising vans and vehicles of all sorts, such as the seven-foot lath-and-plaster Hat in the Strand, on which Carlyle commented, crowded the streets until 1853, when they were forbidden. Hundreds of casual labourers were sent out with placards and sandwich boards, and again in 1853 had to be officially removed from pavement to gutter. Thus the streets of Victorian London bore increasingly upon their face 'the impress of free trade', yet still, with such methods largely reserved to the sellers of pills, adornments and sensational literature, the basic relation between advertising and production had only partly changed. Carlyle said of the hatter, whose 'whole industry is turned to *persuade* us that he has made' better hats, that 'the quack has become God'. But as yet, on the whole, it was only the quack.

The period between the 1850s and the end of the century saw a further expansion in advertising, but still mainly along the lines already established. After the 1855 abolition of Stamp Duty, the circulation of newspapers rapidly increased, and many new ones were successfully founded. But the attitude of the Press to advertising, throughout the second half of the century, remained cautious. In particular, editors were extremely resistant to any break-up in the column layout of their pages, and hence to any increase in size of display type. Advertisers tried in many ways to get round this, but with little success.

As for products mainly advertised, the way was still led by the makers of pills, soaps and similar articles. Beecham's and Pears are important by reason of their introduction of the catch-phrase on a really large scale; 'Worth a Guinea a Box' and 'Good morning! Have you used Pears' Soap?' passed into everyday language. Behind this familiar vanguard came two heavily advertised classes: the patent food, which belongs technically to this period, and which by the end of the century had made Bovril, Hovis, Nestlé, Cadbury, Fry and Kellogg into 'household names'; and new inventions of a more serious kind, such as the sewing-machine, the camera, the bicycle and the typewriter. If we add the new department-stores, towards the end of the century, we have the effective range of general advertising in the period, and need only note that in method the patent foods followed the patent medicines, while the new appliances varied between genuine information and the now familiar technique of slogan and association.

The pressure on newspapers to adapt to techniques drawn from the poster began to be successful from the 1880s. The change came first in the illustrated magazines, with a crop of purity nudes and similar figures; the Borax nude, for example, dispelling Disease and Decay; girls delighted by cigarettes or soap or shampoos. The poster industry, with its organized hoardings, was able from 1867 to use large lithographs, and Pears introduced the 'Bubbles' poster in 1887. A mail-order catalogue used the first colour advertisement, of a rug. Slowly, a familiar world was forming, and in the first years of the new century came the coloured electric sign. The newspapers, with Northcliffe's *Daily Mail* in the lead, dropped their columns rule, and allowed large type and illustrations. It was noted in 1897 that '*The Times* itself' was permitting 'advertisements in type which three years ago would have been considered fit only for the street hoardings', while the front page of the *Daily Mail* already held rows of drawings of rather bashful women in combinations. Courtesy, Service and Integrity, as part of the same process, acquired the dignity of large-type abstractions. The draper, the grocer and their suppliers had followed the quack.

TRANSFORMATION

The strange fact is, looking back, that the great bulk of products of the early stages of the factory system had been sold without extensive advertising, which had grown up mainly in relation to fringe products and novelties. Such advertising as there was, of basic articles, was mainly by shopkeepers, drawing attention to the quality and competitive pricing of the goods they stocked. In this comparatively simple phase of competition, large-scale advertising and the brand-naming of goods were necessary only at the margin, or in genuinely new things. The real signs of change began to appear in the 1880s and 1890s, though they can only be correctly interpreted when seen in the light of the fully developed 'new' advertising of the period between the wars.

The formation of modern advertising has to be traced, essentially, to certain characteristics of the new 'monopoly' (corporate) capitalism, first clearly evident in this same period of the end and turn of the nineteenth century. The Great Depression which in general dominated the period from 1875 to the middle 1890s (though broken by occasional recoveries and local strengths) marked the turning point between two modes of industrial organization and two basically different approaches to distribution. After the Depression, and its big falls in prices, there was a more general and growing fear of productive capacity, a marked tendency to reorganize industrial ownership into larger units and combines, and a growing desire, by different methods, to organize and where possible control the market. Among the means of achieving the latter purposes, advertising on a new scale, and applied to an increasing range of products, took an important place.

Modern advertising, that is to say, belongs to the system of market-control which, at its full development, includes the growth of tariffs and privileged areas, cartel-quotas, trade campaigns, price-fixing by manufacturers, and that form of economic imperialism which assured certain markets overseas by political control of their territories. There was a concerted expansion of export advertising, and at home the biggest advertising campaign yet seen accompanied the merger of several tobacco firms into the Imperial Tobacco Company, to resist American competition. In 1901, a 'fabulous sum' was offered for the entire eight pages of *The Star*, by a British tobacco advertiser, and when this was refused four pages were taken, a 'world's record', to print 'the most costly, colossal and convincing advertisement ever used in an evening newspaper the wide world o'er'. Since the American firms retaliated, with larger advertisements of their own, the campaign was both heavy and prolonged. This can be taken as the first major example of a new advertising situation.

That this period of fundamental change in the economy is the key to the emergence of full-scale modern advertising is shown also by radical changes within the organization of advertising itself. From the eighteenth century, certain shops had been recognized as collecting agencies for advertisements, on behalf of newspapers. In the nineteenth century, this system (which still holds today for some classified advertisements) was extended to the buying of space by individual agents, who then sold it to advertisers. With the growth in the volume of advertising, this kind of space-selling, and then a more developed system of space-brokerage, led to a growth of importance in the agencies, which still, however, were virtually agents of the Press, or at most intermediaries. Gradually, and with increasing emphasis from the 1880s, the agencies began to change their functions, offering advice and service to manufacturers, though still having space to sell for the newspapers. By the turn of the century, the modern system had emerged: newspapers had their own advertising managers, who advanced quite rapidly in status from junior employees to important executives, while the agencies stopped selling space, and went over to serving and advising manufacturers, and booking space after a campaign had been agreed. In 1900 the Advertisers Protection Society, later the Incorporated Society of British Advertisers, was formed: partly to defend advertising against such attacks as those of SCAPA [Society for Checking Abuses of Public Advertising – founded 1898], partly to bring pressure on newspapers to publish their sales figures, so that campaigns might be properly planned. Northcliffe, after initial hesitations about advertising (he had wanted to run *Answers* without it), came to realize its possibilities as a new basis for financing newspapers. He published his sales figures, challenged his rivals to do the same, and in effect created the modern structure of the Press as an industry, in close relation to the new advertising. In 1917 the Association of British Advertising Agents was founded, and in 1931, with the founding of the Audit Bureau of Circulations, publishing audited net sales, the basic structure was complete.

It is in this same period that we hear first, with any emphasis, of advertising as a profession, a public service, and a necessary part of the economy. A further aspect of the reorganization was a more conscious and more serious attention to the 'psychology of advertising'. As it neared the centre of the economy, it began staking its claims to be not only a profession, but an art and a science.

The half-century between 1880 and 1930, then, saw the full development of an organized system of commercial information and persuasion, as part of the modern distributive system in conditions of large-scale capitalism. Although extended to new kinds of product, advertising drew, in its methods, on its own history and experience. There is an obvious continuity between the methods used to sell pills and washballs in the eighteenth century ('promise, large promise, a quality truly wonderful') and the methods used in the twentieth century to sell anything from a drink to a political party. In this sense, it is true to say that all commerce has followed the quack. But if we look at advertising before, say, 1914, its comparative crudeness is immediately evident. The 'most costly, colossal and convincing advertisement' of 1901 shows two badly-drawn men in tails, clinking port-glasses between announcements that the cigarettes are five a penny, and the slogan ('The Englishman's Toast – Don't be gulled by Yankee bluff, support John Bull with every puff') is in minute type by comparison with 'Most Costly' and 'Advertisement'. Play on fear of illness was of course normal, as it had been throughout quack advertising, and there were simple promises of attractiveness and reputation if particular products were used. But true 'psychological' advertising is very little in evidence before the First War, and where it is its techniques, both in appeal and in draughtsmanship and layout, are crude. Appropriately enough, perhaps, it was in the war itself, when now not a market but a nation had to be controlled and organized, yet in democratic conditions and without some of the older compulsions, that new kinds of persuasion were developed and applied. Where the badly-drawn men with their port and gaspers belong to an old world, such a poster as 'Daddy, what did you do in the Great War?' belongs to the new. The drawing is careful and detailed: the curtains, the armchair, the grim numb face of the father, the little girl on his knee pointing to her open picture-book, the boy at his feet intent on his toy-soldiers. Alongside the traditional appeals to patriotism lay this kind of entry into basic personal relationships and anxieties. Another poster managed to suggest that a man who would let down his country would also let down his sweetheart or his wife.

Slowly, after the war, advertising turned from the simple proclamation and reiteration, with simple associations, of the earlier respectable trade, and prepared to develop, for all kinds of product, the old methods of the quack and the new methods of psychological warfare. The turn was not even yet complete, but the tendencies, from the twenties, were evident. Another method of organizing the market, through consumer credit, had to be popularized, and in the process changed from the 'never-never', which was not at all respectable, to the primly respectable 'hire-purchase' and the positively respectable 'consumer credit'. By 1933, a husband had lost his wife because he had failed to take this 'easy way' of providing a home for her. Meanwhile Body Odour, Iron Starvation, Night Starvation, Listlessness and similar disabilities menaced not only personal health, but jobs, marriages and social success.

These developments, of course, produced a renewed wave of criticism of advertising, and, in particular, ridicule of its confident absurdities. In part this was met by a now standard formula: 'one still hears criticism of advertising, but it is not realized how much has been done, within the profession, to improve it' (for example, a code of ethics, in 1924, pledging the industry, *inter alia* 'to tell the advertising story simply and without exaggeration and to avoid even a tendency to mislead'. If advertisers write such pledges, who then writes the advertisements?). The 'super-sensitive faddists' were rediscovered, and the 'enemies of free enterprise'. Proposals by Huxley, Russell, Leavis, Thompson and others, that children should be trained to study advertisements critically, were described, in a book called *The Ethics of Advertising*, as amounting to 'cynical manipulation of the infant mind'.

But the most significant reply to the mood of critical scepticism was in the advertisements themselves: the development of a knowing, sophisticated, humorous advertising, which acknowledged the scepticism and made claims either casual and offhand or so ludicrously exaggerated as to include the critical response (for example, the Guinness advertisements, written by Dorothy Sayers, later a critic of advertising). Thus it became possible to 'know all the arguments' against advertising, and yet accept or write pieces of charming or amusing copy.

One sustained special attack, on an obviously vulnerable point, was in the field of patent medicines. A vast amount of misleading and dangerous advertising of this kind had been repeatedly exposed, and eventually, by Acts of 1939 and 1941, and by a Code of Standards in 1950, the advertisement of cures for certain specified diseases, and a range of misleading devices, was banned. This was a considerable step forward, in a limited field, and the Advertising Association was among its sponsors. If we remember the history of advertising, and how the sellers of ordinary products learned from the quack methods that are still used in less obviously dangerous fields, the change is significant. It is like nothing so much as the newly-crowned Henry the Fifth dismissing Falstaff with contempt. Advertising had come to power, at the centre of the economy, and it had to get rid of the disreputable friends of its youth: it now both wanted and needed to be respectable.

ADVERTISING IN POWER

Of the coming to power there was now no question. Estimates of expenditure in the inter-war years vary considerably, but the lowest figure, for direct advertising in a single year, is £85,000,000 and the highest £200,000,000. Newspapers derived half their income from advertising, and almost every industry and service, outside the old professions, advertised extensively. With this kind of weight behind it, advertising was and knew itself to be a solid sector of the establishment.

Some figures from 1935 are interesting, showing advertising expenditure as a proportion of sales:

Proprietary medicines	29.4%
Toilet goods	21.3%
Soaps, polishes etc.	14.1%
Tobacco	9.3%
Petrol and oil	8.2%
Cereals, jams, biscuits	5.9%
Sweets	3.2%
Beer	1.8%
Boots and Shoes	1.0%
Flour	0.5%

The industry's connections with its origins are evident: the three leading categories are those which pioneered advertising of the modern kind. But more significant, perhaps, is that such ordinary things as boots, shoes and flour should be in the table at all. This, indeed, is the new economy, deriving not so much from the factory system and the growth of communications, as from an advanced system of capitalist production, distribution and market control.

Alongside the development of new kinds of appeal came new media. Apart from such frills as sky-writing, there was commercial radio, not yet established in Britain (though the pressure was there) but begun elsewhere in the 1920s and beamed to Britain from the 1930s. Commercial television, in the 1950s, got through fairly easily. Among new methods, in this growth, are the product jingle, begun in commercial radio and now reaching classic status, and the open alliance between advertisers and apparently independent journalists and broadcasters. To build a reputation as an honest reporter, and then use it either openly to recommend a product or to write or speak about it alongside an advertisement for it, as in the evening-paper 'special supplements', became commonplace. And what was wrong? After all, the crowned heads of Europe, and many of our own Ladies, had been selling pills and soaps for years. The extension to political advertising, either direct or by pressure-groups, also belongs, in its extensive phase, to this period of establishment; in the 1950s it has been running at a very high rate indeed.

The only check, in fact, to this rapidly expanding industry was during the last war, though this was only partial and temporary, and the years since the war, and especially the 1950s, have brought a further spectacular extension. It is ironic to look back at a book published in wartime, by one of the best writers on advertising, Denys Thompson, and read this:

> A second reason for these extensive extracts is that advertising as we know it may be dispensed with, after the war. We are getting on very well with a greatly diminished volume of commercial advertising in wartime, and it is difficult to envisage a return to the 1919–1939 conditions in which publicity proliferated.

Mr Thompson, like Dr Johnson two centuries earlier, is a sane man, but it is never safe to conclude that puffing has reached its maximum distension. The history, rightly read, points to a further major growth, and to more new methods. The highly organized field of market study, motivation research, and retained sociologists and psychologists, is extremely formidable, and no doubt has many surprises in store for us. Talent of quite new kinds is hired with increasing ease. And there is one significant development which must be noted in conclusion: the extension of organized publicity.

'Public Relations'

Advertising was developed to sell goods, in a particular kind of economy. Publicity has been developed to sell persons, in a particular kind of culture. The methods are often basically similar: the arranged incident, the 'mention', the advice on branding, packaging and a good 'selling line'. I remember being told by a man I knew at university (he had previously explained how useful, to his profession as an advertiser, had been his training in the practical criticism of advertisements) that advertisements you booked and paid for were really old stuff; the real thing was what got through as ordinary news. This seems to happen now with goods: 'product centenaries', for example. But with persons it is even more extensive. It began in entertainment, particularly with film actors, and it is still in this field that it does most of its work. It is very difficult to pin down, because the borderline between the item or photograph picked up in the ordinary course of journalism and broadcasting, and the similar item or photograph that has been arranged and paid for, either directly or through special hospitality by a publicity agent, is obviously difficult to draw. Enough stories get through, and are even boasted about, to indicate that the paid practice is extensive, though payment, except to the agent, is usually in hospitality (if that word can be used) or in kind. Certainly, readers of newspapers should be aware that the 'personality' items, presented as ordinary news stories or gossip, will often have been paid for, in one way or another, in a system that makes straightforward advertising, by comparison, look respectable. Nor is this confined to what is called 'show business'; it has certainly entered literature, and it has probably entered politics.

The extension is natural, in a society where selling, by any effective means, has become a primary ethic. The spectacular growth of advertising, and then its extension to apparently independent reporting, has behind it not a mere pressure-group, as in the days of the quacks, but the whole impetus of a society. It can then be agreed that we have come a long way from the papyrus of the runaway slave and the shouts of the town-crier: that what we have to look at is an organized and extending system, at the centre of our national life.

THE SYSTEM

In the last hundred years, then, advertising has developed from the simple announcements of shopkeepers and the persuasive arts of a few marginal dealers into a major part of capitalist business organization. This is important enough, but the place of advertising in society goes far beyond this commercial context. It is increasingly the source of finance for a whole range of general communication, to the extent that in 1960 our majority television service and almost all our newspapers and periodicals could not exist without it. Further, in the last forty years and now at an increasing rate, it has passed the frontier of the selling of goods and services and has become involved with the teaching of social and personal values; it is also rapidly entering the world of politics. Advertising is also, in a sense, the official art of modern capitalist society: it is what 'we' put up in 'our' streets and use to fill up to half of 'our' newspapers and magazines: and it commands the services of perhaps the largest organized body of writers and artists, with their attendant managers and advisers, in the whole society. Since this is the actual social status of advertising, we shall only understand it with any adequacy if we can develop a kind of total analysis in which the economic, social and cultural facts are visibly related. We may then also find, taking advertising as a major form of modern social communication, that we can understand our society itself in new ways.

It is often said that our society is too materialist, and that advertising reflects this. We are in the phase of a relatively rapid distribution of what are called 'consumer goods', and advertising, with its emphasis on 'bringing the good things of life', is taken as central for this reason. But it seems to me that in this respect our society is quite evidently not materialist enough, and that this, paradoxically, is the result of a failure in social meanings, values and ideals.

It is impossible to look at modern advertising without realizing that the material object being sold is never enough: this indeed is the crucial cultural quality of its modern forms. If we were sensibly materialist, in that part of our living in which we use things, we should find most advertising to be of an insane irrelevance. Beer would be enough for us, without the additional promise that in drinking it we show ourselves to be manly, young in heart, or neighbourly. A washing-machine would be a useful machine to wash clothes, rather than an indication that we are forward-looking or an object of envy to our neighbours. But if these associations sell beer and washing-machines, as some of the evidence suggests, it is clear that we have a cultural pattern in which the objects are not enough but must be validated, if only in fantasy, by association with social and personal meanings which in a different cultural pattern might be more directly available. The short description of the pattern we have is *magic*: a highly organized and professional system of magical inducements and satisfactions, functionally very similar to magical systems in simpler societies, but rather strangely coexistent with a highly developed scientific technology.

This contradiction is of the greatest importance in any analysis of modern capitalist society. The coming of large-scale industrial production necessarily raised critical problems of social organization, which in many fields we are still only struggling to solve. In the production of goods for personal use, the critical problem posed by the factory of advanced machines was that of the organization of the market. The modern factory requires not only smooth and steady distributive channels (without which it would suffocate under its own product) but also definite indications of demand without which the expensive processes of capitalization and equipment would be too great a risk. The historical choice posed by the development of industrial production is between different forms of organization and planning in the society to which it is central. In our own century, the choice has been and remains between some form of socialism and a new form of capitalism. In Britain, since the 1890s and with rapidly continuing emphasis, we have had the new capitalism, based on a series of devices for organizing and ensuring the market. Modern advertising, taking on its distinctive features in just this economic phase, is one of the most important of these devices, and it is perfectly true to say that modern capitalism could not function without it.

Yet the essence of capitalism is that the basic means of production are not socially but privately owned, and that decisions about production are therefore in the hands of a group occupying a minority position in the society and in no direct way responsible to it. Obviously, since the capitalist wishes to be successful, he is influenced in his decisions about production by what other members of the society need. But he is influenced also by considerations of industrial convenience and likely profit, and his decisions tend to be a balance of these varying factors. The challenge of socialism, still very powerful elsewhere but in Britain deeply confused by political immaturities and errors, is essentially that decisions about production should be in the hands of the society as a whole, in the sense that control of the means of production is made part of the general system of decision which the society as a whole creates. The conflict between capitalism and socialism is now commonly seen in terms of a competition in productive efficiency, and we need not doubt that much of our future history, on a world scale, will be determined by the results of this competition. Yet the conflict is really much deeper than this, and is also a conflict between different approaches to and forms of socialism. The fundamental choice that emerges, in the problems set to us by modern industrial production, is between man as consumer and man as user. The system of organized magic which is modern advertising is primarily important as a functional obscuring of this choice.

Part VIII *Leisure*

22 Pierre Bourdieu

How can one be a sports fan?

EDITOR'S INTRODUCTION

This essay has been chosen as much as an example of Pierre Bourdieu's thought and method as for its argument concerning sport. Indeed, the value of the latter is rather diminished because sport in France (Bourdieu, of course, is a French theorist) has had a different social function from that in the US, Britain, or Australia. Also the essay's historical claim that 'sport' emerged as a partially autonomous field when élites began to organize folk games is problematic in the British context. It underestimates the pressures for professionalization and organization from 'below' – especially with football and cricket during the nineteenth century.

Bourdieu's is an analysis heavily dependent on notions of class and class fractions, especially that between the dominant (economic and symbolic capital-rich) and dominated (cultural capital-rich) fractions of the middle class. He argues, for instance, that workers engage in sports which depend upon, and place at risk, sheer bodily strength whereas the middle classes value sports which develop the body and skills as ends in themselves. He has made similar arguments about class differentiations in aesthetic taste (Bourdieu 1986). Indeed such homologies of dispositions and values constitute what he calls a 'habitus'. For him, class fractions differ by the amount of economic capital, symbolic capital (i.e. prestige), and cultural capital (tastes) they inherit or are in a position to acquire. Through strategies to gain advantage or to reconcile themselves to their conditions of life, a particular lifestyle 'grounded in the unity of dispositions' (i.e. habitus) emerges for each group. These strategies involve 'symbolic violence' – as in struggles between fractions of the middle class over the sport's value.

Bourdieu's work is having increasing influence in Anglophone cultural studies, and exchanges between this rather sociologically inclined research and adherents of the 'culture of difference' are of vital importance for the discipline in the near future.

Further reading: Bourdieu 1986, 1990; Cunningham 1980; Garnham and Williams 1980; Robbins 1991; Thompson 1984.

S.D.

I think that, without doing too much violence to reality, it is possible to consider the whole range of sporting activities and entertainments offered to social agents – rugby, football, swimming, athletics, tennis, golf, etc. – as a *supply* intended to meet a *social demand*. If such a model is adopted, two sets of questions arise. First, is there an area of production, endowed with its own logic and its own history, in which 'sports products' are generated, i.e. the universe of the sporting activities and entertainments socially realized and acceptable at a given moment in time? Secondly, what are the social conditions of possibility of the appropriation of the various 'sports products' that are thus produced – playing golf or reading *L'Équipe*, cross-country skiing or watching the World Cup on TV? In other words, how is the demand for 'sports products' produced, how do people acquire the 'taste' for sport, and for one sport rather than another, whether as an activity or as a spectacle? The question certainly has to be confronted, unless one chooses to suppose that there exists a natural need, equally widespread at all times, in all places and in all social milieux, not only for the expenditure of muscular energy, but more precisely, for this or that form of exertion. (To take the example most favourable to the 'natural need' thesis, we know that swimming, which most educators would probably point to as the most necessary sporting activity, both on account of its 'life-saving' functions and its physical effects, has at times been ignored or refused – e.g. in medieval Europe – and still has to be imposed by means of national 'campaigns'.) More precisely, according to what principles do agents choose between the different sports activities or entertainments which, at a given moment in time, are offered to them as being possible?

THE PRODUCTION OF SUPPLY

It seems to me that it is first necessary to consider the historical and social conditions of possibility of a social phenomenon which we too easily take for granted: 'modern sport'. In other words, what social conditions made possible the constitution of the system of institutions and agents directly or indirectly linked to the existence of sporting activities and entertainments? The system includes public or private 'sports associations', whose function is to represent and defend the interests of the practitioners of a given sport and to draw up and impose the standards governing that activity, the producers and vendors of goods (equipment, instruments, special clothing, etc.) and services required in order to pursue the sport (teachers, instructors, trainers, sports doctors, sports journalists, etc.) and the producers and vendors of sporting entertainments and associated goods (tee shirts, photos of stars, etc.). How was this body of specialists, living directly or indirectly off sport, progressively constituted (a body to which sports sociologists and historians also belong – which probably does not help the question to emerge)? And, more exactly, when did this system of agents and institutions begin to function as a *field of competition*, the site of confrontations between agents with specific interests linked to their positions within the field? If it is the case, as my questions tend to suggest, that the system of the institutions and agents whose interests are bound up with sport tends to function as a field, it follows that one cannot directly understand what sporting phenomena are at a given moment in a given social environment by relating them directly to the economic and social conditions of the corresponding societies: the history of sport is a relatively autonomous history which, even when marked by the major events of economic and social history, has its own tempo, its own evolutionary laws, its own crises, in short, its specific chronology.

One of the tasks of the social history of sport might be to lay the real foundations of the legitimacy of a social science of sport as a *distinct scientific object* (which is not at all self-evident), by establishing from what moment, or rather, from what set of social conditions, it is really possible to speak of sport (as opposed to the simple playing of games – a meaning that is still present in the English word 'sport' but not in the use made of the word in countries outside the Anglo-Saxon world where it was introduced *at the same time* as the radically new social practices which it designated). How was this terrain constituted, with its specific logic, as the site of quite specific social practices, which have defined themselves in the course of a specific history and can only be understood in terms of that history (e.g. the history of sports laws or the history of *records*, an interesting word that recalls the contribution which historians, with their task of *recording* and celebrating noteworthy exploits, make to the constitution of a field and its esoteric culture)?

The genesis of a relatively autonomous field of production and circulation of sports products

It seems to be indisputable that the shift from games to sports in the strict sense took place in the educational establishments reserved for the 'élites' of bourgeois society, the English public schools, where the sons of aristocratic or upper-bourgeois families took over a number of *popular* – i.e. *vulgar* – *games*, simultaneously changing their meaning and function in exactly the same way as the field of learned music transformed the folk dances – bourrées, sarabands, gavottes, etc. – which it introduced into high-art forms such as the suite.

To characterize this transformation briefly, i.e. as regards its *principle*, we can say that the bodily exercises of the 'élite' are disconnected from the ordinary social occasions with which folk games remained associated (agrarian feasts, for example) and divested of the social (and, *a fortiori*, religious) functions still attached to a number of traditional games (such as the ritual games played in a number of precapitalist societies at certain turning-points in the farming year). The school, the site of *skhole*, leisure, is the place where practices endowed with social functions and integrated into the collective calendar are converted into *bodily exercises*, activities which are an end in themselves, a sort of physical art for art's sake, governed by specific rules, increasingly irreducible to any functional necessity, and inserted into a specific calendar. The school is the site, *par excellence*, of what are called gratuitous exercises, where one acquires a distant, neutralizing disposition towards language and the social world, the very same one which is implied in the bourgeois relation to art, language and the body: gymnastics makes a use of the body which, like the scholastic use of language, is an end in itself. (This no doubt explains why sporting activity, whose frequency rises very markedly with educational level, declines more slowly with age, as do cultural practices, when educational level is higher. It is known that among the working classes, the abandonment of sport, an activity whose play-like character seems to make it particularly appropriate to adolescence, often coincides with marriage and entry into the serious responsibilities of adulthood.) What is acquired in and through experience of school, a sort of retreat from the world and from real practice, of which the great boarding schools of the 'élite' represent the fully developed form, is the propensity towards activity for no purpose, a fundamental aspect of the ethos of bourgeois 'élites', who always pride themselves on disinterestedness and define themselves by an elective distance – manifested in art and sport – from material interests. 'Fair play' is the way of playing the game characteristic of those who do not get so carried away by the game as to forget that it *is* a game, those who maintain the 'rôle distance', as Goffman puts it, that is implied in all the rôles designated for the future leaders.

The autonomization of the field of sport is also accompanied by a process of *rationalization* intended, as Weber expresses it, to ensure predictability and calculability, beyond local differences and particularisms: the constitution of a corpus of specific rules and of specialized governing bodies recruited, initially at least, from the 'old boys' of the public schools, come hand in hand. The need for a body of fixed, universally applicable rules makes itself felt as soon as sporting 'exchanges' are established between different educational institutions, then between regions, etc. The relative autonomy of the field of sport is most clearly affirmed in the powers of self-administration and rule-making, based on a historical tradition or guaranteed by the State, which sports associations are acknowledged to exercise: these bodies are invested with the right to lay down the standards governing participation in the events which they organize, and they are entitled to exercise a disciplinary power (banning, fines, etc.) in order to ensure observance of the specific rules which they decree. In addition, they award specific titles, such as championship titles and also, as in England, the status of trainer.

The constitution of a field of sports practices is linked to the development of a philosophy of sport which is necessarily a *political* philosophy of sport. The theory of amateurism is in fact one dimension of an aristocratic philosophy of sport as a disinterested practice, a finality without an end, analogous to artistic practice, but even more suitable than art (there is always something residually feminine about art: consider the piano and watercolours of genteel young ladies in the same period) for affirming the manly virtues of future leaders: sport is conceived as a training in courage and manliness, 'forming the character' and inculcating the 'will to win' which is the mark of the true leader, but a will to win within the rules. This is 'fair play', conceived as an aristocratic disposition utterly opposed to the plebeian pursuit of victory at all costs. What is at stake, it seems to me, in this debate (which goes far beyond sport), is a definition of bourgeois education which contrasts with the petty-bourgeois and academic definition: it is 'energy', 'courage', 'willpower', the virtues of leaders (military or industrial), and perhaps above all personal initiative, (private) 'enterprise', as opposed to knowledge, erudition, 'scholastic' submissiveness, symbolized in the great lycée-barracks and its disciplines, etc. In short, it would be a mistake to forget that the modern definition of sport is an integral part of a 'moral ideal', i.e. an ethos which is that of the dominant fractions of the dominant class and is brought to fruition in the major private schools intended primarily for the sons of the heads of private industry, such as the École des Roches, the paradigmatic realization of this ideal. To value *education* over *instruction*, *character* or *willpower* over *intelligence*, *sport* over *culture*, is to affirm, within the educational universe itself, the existence of a hierarchy irreducible to the strictly scholastic hierarchy which favours the second term in those oppositions. It means, as it were, disqualifying or discrediting the values recognized by other fractions of the dominant class or by other classes (especially the intellectual fractions of the petty bourgeoisie and the 'sons of schoolteachers', who are serious challengers to the sons of the bourgeoisie on the terrain of purely scholastic competence); it means putting forward other criteria of 'achievement' and other principles for legitimating achievement as alternatives to 'academic achievement'. Glorification of sport as the training-ground of character, etc., always implies a certain anti-intellectualism. When one remembers that the dominant fractions of the dominant class always tend to conceive their relation to the dominated fraction – 'intellectuals', 'artists', 'professors' – in terms of the opposition between the male and the female, the virile and the effeminate, which is given different contents depending on the period (e.g. nowadays short hair/long hair; 'economico-political' culture/'artistico-literary' culture etc.), one understands one of the most important implications of the exaltation of sport and especially of 'manly' sports like rugby, and it can be seen that sport, like any other practice, is an object of struggles between the fractions of the dominant class and also between the social classes.

At this point I shall take the opportunity to emphasize, in passing, that the *social definition of sport* is an object of struggles, that the field of sporting practices is the site of struggles in which what is at stake, *inter alia*, is the monopolistic capacity to impose the legitimate definition of sporting practice and of the legitimate function of sporting activity – amateurism vs. professionalism, participant sport vs. spectator sport, distinctive (élite) sport vs. popular (mass) sport; that this field is itself part of the larger field of struggles over the definition of the *legitimate body* and the *legitimate use of the body*, struggles which, in addition to the agents engaged in the struggle over the definition of sporting uses of the body, also involve moralists and especially the clergy, doctors (especially health specialists), educators in the broadest sense (marriage guidance counsellors, etc.), pacemakers in matters of fashion and taste (couturiers, etc.). One would have to explore whether the struggles for the monopolistic power to impose the legitimate definition of a particular *class* of body uses, sporting uses, present any *invariant* features. I am thinking, for example, of the opposition, from the point of view of the definition of legitimate exercise, between the professionals in physical education (gymnasiarchs, gymnastics teachers, etc.) and doctors, i.e. between two forms of specific *authority* ('pedagogic' vs. 'scientific'), linked to two sorts of *specific capital*; or the recurrent opposition between two antagonistic philosophies of the use of the body, a more ascetic one (*askesis* = training) which, in the paradoxical expression *culture physique* ('physical culture') emphasizes culture, *antiphysis*, the counter-natural, straightening, rectitude, effort, and another, more hedonistic one which privileges nature, *physis*, reducing culture to the body, physical culture to a sort of 'laisser-faire', or return to 'laisser-faire' – as *expression corporelle* ('physical expression' – 'anti-gymnastics') does nowadays, teaching its devotees to unlearn the superfluous disciplines and restraints imposed, among other things, by ordinary gymnastics.

Since the relative autonomy of the field of bodily practices entails, by definition, a relative dependence, the development within the field of practices oriented towards one or the other pole, asceticism or hedonism, depends to a large extent on the state of the power relations within the field of struggles for monopolistic definition of the legitimate body and, more broadly, in the field of struggles between fractions of the dominant class and between the social classes over morality. Thus the progress made by everything that is referred to as 'physical expression' can only be understood in relation to the progress, seen for example in parent–child relations and more generally in all that pertains to pedagogy, of a new variant of bourgeois morality, preached by certain rising fractions of the bourgeoisie (and petty bourgeoisie) and favouring liberalism in child-rearing and also in hierarchical relations and sexuality, in place of ascetic severity (denounced as 'repressive').

The popularization phase

It was necessary to sketch in this first phase, which seems to me a determinant one, because in states of the field that are nonetheless quite different, sport still bears the marks of its origins. Not only does the aristocratic ideology of sport as disinterested, gratuitous activity, which lives on in the ritual themes of celebratory discourse, help to mask the true nature of an increasing proportion of sporting practices, but the practice of sports such as tennis, riding, sailing or golf doubtless owes part of its 'interest', just as much nowadays as at the beginning, to its distinguishing function and, more precisely, to the *gains in distinction* which it brings (it is no accident that the majority of the most select, i.e. selective, clubs are organized around sporting activities which serve as a focus or pretext for elective gatherings). We may even consider that the distinctive gains are increased when the distinction between noble – distinguished and distinctive – practices, such as the 'smart' sports, and the 'vulgar' practices which popularization has made of a number of sports originally reserved for the 'élite', such as football (and to a lesser extent rugby, which will perhaps retain for some time to come a dual status and a dual social recruitment), is combined with the yet sharper opposition between participation in sport and the mere consumption of sporting entertainments. We know that the probability of practising a sport beyond adolescence (and *a fortiori* beyond early manhood or in old age) declines markedly as one moves down the social hierarchy (as does the probability of belonging to a sports club), whereas the probability of watching one of the reputedly most popular sporting spectacles, such as football or rugby, on television (stadium attendance as a spectator obeys more complex laws) declines markedly as one rises in the social hierarchy.

Thus, without forgetting the importance of taking part in sport – particularly team sports like football – for working-class and lower middle-class adolescents, it cannot be ignored that the so-called popular sports, cycling, football or rugby, *also* function as spectacles (which may owe part of their interest to imaginary participation based on past experience of real practice). They are 'popular' but in the sense this adjective takes on whenever it is applied to the material or cultural products of mass production, cars, furniture or songs. In brief, sport, born of truly popular games, i.e. games produced by the people, returns to the people, like 'folk music', in the form of spectacles produced for the people. We may consider that sport as a spectacle would appear more clearly as a mass commodity, and the organization of sporting entertainments as one branch among others of show business (there is a difference of degree rather than kind between the spectacle of professional boxing, or Holiday on Ice shows, and a number of sporting events that are perceived as legitimate, such as the various European football championships or ski competitions), if the value collectively bestowed on practising sports (especially now that sports contests have become a measure of relative national strength and hence a political objective) did not help to mask the divorce between practice and consumption and consequently the functions of simple passive consumption.

It might be wondered, in passing, whether some recent developments in sporting practices are not in part an effect of the evolution which I have too rapidly sketched. One only has to think, for example, of all that is implied in the fact that a sport like rugby (in France – but the same is true of American football in the USA) has become, through television, a mass spectacle, transmitted far beyond the circle of present or past 'practitioners', i.e. to a public very imperfectly equipped with the specific competence needed to decipher it adequately. The 'connoisseur' has schemes of perception and appreciation which enable him to see what the layman cannot see, to perceive a necessity where the outsider sees only violence and confusion, and so to find in the promptness of a movement, in the unforeseeable inevitability of a successful combination or the near-miraculous orchestration of a team strategy, a pleasure no less intense and learned than the pleasure a music-lover derives from a particularly successful rendering of a favourite work. The more superficial the perception, the less it finds its pleasure in the spectacle contemplated in itself and for itself, and the more it is drawn to the search for the 'sensational', the cult of obvious feats and visible virtuosity and, above all, the more exclusively it is concerned with that other dimension of the sporting spectacle, suspense and anxiety as to the result, thereby encouraging players and especially organizers to aim for victory at all costs. In other words, everything seems to suggest that, in sport as in music, extension of the public beyond the circle of amateurs helps to reinforce the reign of the pure professionals.

In fact, before taking further the analysis of the effects, we must try to analyse more closely the determinants of the shift whereby sport as an élite practice reserved for amateurs became sport as a spectacle produced by professionals for consumption by the masses. It is not sufficient to invoke the relatively autonomous logic of the field of production of sporting goods and services or, more precisely, the development, within this field, of a sporting entertainments industry which, subject to the laws of profitability, aims to maximize its efficiency while minimizing its risks. (This leads, in particular, to the need for specialized executive personnel and scientific management techniques that can rationally organize the training and upkeep of the physical capital of the professional players: one thinks, for example, of American football, in which the squad of trainers, doctors and public-relations men is more numerous than the team of players, and which almost always serves as a publicity medium for the sports equipment and accessories industry.)

In reality, the development of sporting activity itself, even among working-class youngsters, doubtless results partly from the fact that sport was predisposed to fulfil, on a much larger scale, the very same functions which underlay its *invention* in the late nineteenth-century English public schools. Even before they saw sport as a means of 'improving character' in accordance with the Victorian belief, the public schools, 'total institutions' in Goffman's sense, which have to carry out their supervisory task twenty-four hours a day, seven days a week, saw sport as 'a means of filling in time', an economical way of occupying the adolescents who were their full-time responsibility. When the pupils are on the sports field, they are easy to supervise, they are engaged in healthy activity and they are venting their violence on each other rather than destroying the buildings or shouting down their teachers; that is why, Ian Weiberg concludes, 'organized sport will last as long as the public schools'. So it would not be possible to understand the popularization of sport and the growth of sports associations, which, originally organized on a *voluntary* basis, progressively received recognition and aid from the public authorities, if we did not realize that this *extremely economical* means of mobilizing, occupying and controlling adolescents was predisposed to become an instrument and an objective in struggles between all the institutions totally or partly organized with a view to the mobilization and symbolic conquest of the masses and therefore competing for the symbolic conquest of youth. These include political parties, unions, and churches, of course, but also paternalistic bosses, who, with the aim of ensuring *complete and continuous containment* of the working population, provided their employees not only with hospitals and schools but also with stadiums and other sports facilities (a number of sports clubs were founded with the help and under the control of private employers, as is still attested today by the number of stadiums named after employers). We are familiar with the competition which has never ceased to be fought out in the various political arenas over questions of sport from the level of the village (with the rivalry between secular or religious clubs, or more recently, the debates over the priority to be given to sports facilities, which is one of the issues at stake in political struggles on a municipal scale) to the level of the nation as a whole (with, for example, the opposition between the Fédération du Sport de France, controlled by the Catholic Church, and the Fédération Sportive et Gymnique du Travail controlled by the left-wing parties). And indeed, in an increasingly disguised way as State recognition and subsidies increase, and with them the apparent neutrality of sports organizations and their officials, sport is an object of political struggle. This competition is one of the most important factors in the development of a social, i.e. socially constituted, need for sporting practices and for all the accompanying equipment, instruments, personnel and services. Thus the imposition of sporting needs is most evident in rural areas where the appearance of facilities and teams, as with youth clubs and senior citizens' clubs nowadays, is almost always the result of the work of the village petty bourgeoisie or bourgeoisie, which finds here an opportunity to impose its political services of organization and leadership and to accumulate or maintain a political capital of renown and honourability which is always potentially reconvertible into political power.

It goes without saying that the popularization of sport, down from the élite schools (where its place is now contested by the 'intellectual' pursuits imposed by the demands of intensified social competition) to the mass sporting associations, is necessarily accompanied by a change in the functions which the sportsmen and their organizers assign to this practice, and also by a transformation of the very logic of sporting practices which corresponds to the transformation of the expectations and demands of the public in correlation with the increasing autonomy of the spectacle vis-à-vis past or present practice. The exaltation of 'manliness' and the cult of 'team spirit' that are associated with playing rugby – not to mention the aristocratic ideal of 'fair play' – have a very different meaning and function for bourgeois or aristocratic adolescents in English public schools and for the sons of peasants or shopkeepers in south-west France. This is simply because, for example, a sporting career, which is practically excluded from the field of acceptable trajectories for a child of the bourgeoisie – setting aside tennis or golf – represents one of the few paths of upward mobility open to the children of the dominated classes; the sports market is to the boys' physical capital what the system of beauty prizes and the occupations to which they lead – hostess, etc. – is to the girls' physical capital; and the working-class cult of sportsmen of working-class origin is doubtless explained in part by the fact that these 'success stories' symbolize the only recognized route to wealth and fame. Everything suggests that the 'interests' and values which practitioners from the working and lower-middle classes bring into the conduct of sports are in harmony with the corresponding requirements of *professionalization* (which can, of course, coexist with the appearances of amateurism) and of the rationalization of preparation for and performance of the sporting exercise that are imposed by the pursuit of maximum specific efficiency (measured in 'wins', 'titles', or 'records') combined with the minimization of risks (which we have seen is itself linked to the development of a private or State sports entertainments industry).

THE LOGIC OF DEMAND: SPORTING PRACTICES AND ENTERTAINMENTS IN THE UNITY OF LIFE-STYLES

We have here a case of a supply, i.e. the particular definition of sporting practice and entertainment that is put forward at a given moment in time, meeting a demand, i.e. the expectations, interests and values that agents bring into the field, with the actual practices and entertainments evolving as a result of the permanent confrontation and adjustment between the two. Of course, at every moment each new entrant must take account of a determinate state of the division of sporting activities and entertainments and their distribution among the social classes, a state which he cannot alter and which is the result of the whole previous history of the struggles and competition among the agents and institutions engaged in the 'sporting field'. For example, the appearance of a new sport or a new way of practising an already established sport (e.g. the 'invention' of the crawl by Trudgen in 1893) causes a restructuring of the space of sporting practices and a more or less complete redefinition of the meaning attached to the various practices. But while it is true that, here as elsewhere, the field of production helps to produce the need for its own products, nonetheless the logic whereby agents incline towards this or that sporting practice cannot be understood unless their dispositions towards sport, which are themselves one dimension of a *particular relation to the body*, are reinserted into the unity of the system of dispositions, the habitus, which is the basis from which life-styles are generated. One would be likely to make serious mistakes if one attempted to study sporting practices (more so, perhaps, than with any other practices, since their basis and object is the body, the synthesizing agent *par excellence*, which integrates everything that it incorporates), without re-placing them in the universe of practices that are bound up with them because their common origin is the system of tastes and preferences that is a class habitus (for example, it would be easy to demonstrate the homologies between the relation to the body and the relation to language that are characteristic of a class or class fraction). Insofar as the 'body-for-others' is the visible manifestation of the person, of the 'idea it wants to give of itself', its 'character', i.e. its values and capacities, the sports practices which have the aim of shaping the body are realizations, among others, of an aesthetic and an ethic in the practical state. A postural norm such as uprightness ('stand up straight') has, like a direct gaze or a close haircut, the function of symbolizing a whole set of moral 'virtues' – rectitude, straightforwardness, dignity (face to face confrontation as a demand for respect) – and also physical ones – vigour, strength, health.

An explanatory model capable of accounting for the distribution of sporting practices among the classes and class fractions must clearly take account of the positive or negative determining factors, the most important of which are *spare time* (a transformed form of economic capital), *economic capital* (more or less indispensable depending on the sport), and *cultural capital* (again, more or less necessary depending on the sport). But such a model would fail to grasp what is most essential if it did not take account of the variations in the meaning and function given to the various practices by the various classes and class fractions. In other words, faced with the distribution of the various sporting practices by social class, one must give as much thought to the variations in the meaning and function of the different sports among the social classes as to the variations in the intensity of the statistical relationship between the different practices and the different social classes.

It would not be difficult to show that the different social classes do not agree as to the effects expected from bodily exercise, whether on the outside of the body (bodily hexis), such as the visible strength of prominent muscles which some prefer or the elegance, ease and beauty favoured by others, or inside the body, health, mental equilibrium, etc. In other words, the class variations in these practices derive not only from the variations in the factors which make it possible or impossible to meet their *economic or cultural costs* but also from the *variations in the perception and appreciation of the immediate or deferred profits* accruing from the different sporting practices. (It can be seen, incidentally, that specialists are able to make use of the specific authority conferred by their status to put forward a perception and appreciation defined as the only legitimate ones, in opposition to the perceptions and appreciations structured by the dispositions of a class habitus. I am thinking of the national campaigns to impose a sport like swimming, which seems to be unanimously approved by the specialists in the name of its strictly 'technical' functions, on those who 'can't see the use of it'.) As regards the profits actually perceived, Jacques Defrance convincingly shows that gymnastics may be asked to produce either a strong body, bearing the outward signs of strength – this is the working-class demand, which is satisfied by body-building – or a healthy body – this is the bourgeois demand, which is satisfied by a gymnastics or other sports whose function is essentially hygienic.

But this is not all: class habitus defines the meaning conferred on sporting activity, the profits expected from it; and not the least of these profits is the social value accruing from the pursuit of certain sports by virtue of the distinctive rarity they derive from their class distribution. In short, to the 'intrinsic' profits (real or imaginary, it makes little difference – real in the sense of being really anticipated, in the mode of belief) which are expected from sport for the body itself, one must add the social profits, those accruing from any distinctive practice, which are very unequally perceived and appreciated by the different classes (for whom they are, of course, very unequally accessible). It can be seen, for example, that in addition to its strictly health-giving functions, golf, like caviar, *foie gras* or whisky, has a *distributional significance* (the meaning which practices derive from their distribution among agents distributed in social classes), or that weight-lifting, which is supposed to develop the muscles, was for many years, especially in France, the favourite working-class sport; nor is it an accident that the Olympic authorities took so long to grant official recognition to weight-lifting, which, in the eyes of the aristocratic founders of modern sport, symbolized mere strength, brutality and intellectual poverty, in short the working classes.

We can now try to account for the distribution of these practices among the classes and class fractions. The probability of practising the different sports depends, to a different degree for each sport, primarily on economic capital and secondarily on cultural capital and spare time; it also depends on the affinity between the ethical and aesthetic dispositions characteristic of each class or class fraction and the objective potentialities of ethical or aesthetic accomplishment which are or seem to be contained in each sport. The relationship between the different sports and age is more complex, since it is only defined – through the intensity of the physical effort required and the disposition towards that effort which is an aspect of class ethos – within the relationship between a sport and a class. The most important property of the 'popular sports' is the fact that they are tacitly associated with youth, which is spontaneously and implicitly credited with a sort of *provisional licence* expressed, among other ways, in the squandering of an excess of physical (and sexual) energy, and are abandoned very early (usually at the moment of entry into adult life, marked by marriage). By contrast, the 'bourgeois' sports, mainly practised for their functions of physical maintenance and for the social profit they bring, have in common the fact that their age-limit lies far beyond youth and perhaps comes correspondingly later the more prestigious and exclusive they are (e.g. golf). This means that the probability of practising those sports which, because they demand only 'physical' qualities and bodily competences for which the conditions of early apprenticeship seem to be fairly equally distributed, are doubtless equally accessible within the limits of the spare time and, secondarily, the physical energy available, would undoubtedly increase as one goes up the social hierarchy, if the concern for distinction and the absence of ethico-aesthetic affinity or 'taste' for them did not turn away members of the dominant class, in accordance with a logic also observed in other fields (photography, for example). Thus, most of the team sports – basketball, handball, rugby, football – which are most common among office workers, technicians and shopkeepers, and also no doubt the most typically working-class individual sports, such as boxing or wrestling, combine all the reasons to repel the upper classes. These include the social composition of their public which reinforces the vulgarity implied by their popularization, the values and virtues demanded (strength, endurance, the propensity to violence, the spirit of 'sacrifice', docility and submission to collective discipline, the absolute antithesis of the 'rôle distance' implied in bourgeois rôles, etc.), the exaltation of competition and the contest, etc. To understand how the most distinctive sports, such as golf, riding, skiing or tennis, or even some less recherché ones, like gymnastics or mountaineering, are distributed among the social classes and especially among the fractions of the dominant class, it is even more difficult to appeal solely to variations in economic and cultural capital or in spare time. This is firstly because it would be to forget that, no less than the economic obstacles, it is the hidden entry requirements, such as family tradition and early training, and also the obligatory clothing, bearing and techniques of sociability which keep these sports closed to the working classes and to individuals rising from the lower-middle and even upper-middle classes; and secondly because economic constraints define the field of possibilities and impossibilities without determining within it an agent's positive orientation towards this or that particular form of practice. In reality, even apart from any search for distinction, it is the relation to one's own body, a fundamental aspect of the habitus, which distinguishes the working classes from the privileged classes, just as, within the latter, it distinguishes fractions that are separated by the whole universe of a life-style. On one side, there is the *instrumental* relation to the body which the working classes express in all the practices centred on the body, whether in dieting or beauty care, relation to illness or medication, and which is also manifested in the choice of sports requiring a considerable investment of effort, sometimes of pain and suffering (e.g. boxing) and sometimes a *gambling with the body itself* (as in motor-cycling, parachute-jumping, all forms of acrobatics, and, to some extent, all sports involving fighting, among which we may include rugby). On the other side, there is the tendency of the privileged classes to treat the body as an *end in itself*, with variants according to whether the emphasis is placed on the intrinsic functioning of the body as an organism, which leads to the macrobiotic cult of health, or on the appearance of the body as a perceptible configuration, the 'physique', i.e. the body-for-others. Everything seems to suggest that the concern to cultivate the body appears, in its most elementary form, i.e. as the cult of health, often implying an ascetic exaltation of sobriety and dietetic rigour, among the lower-middle classes, i.e. among junior executives, clerical workers in the medical services and especially primary-school teachers, who indulge particularly intensively in gymnastics, the ascetic sport *par excellence* since it amounts to a sort of training (*askesis*) for training's sake.

Gymnastics or strictly health-oriented sports like walking or jogging, which, unlike ball games, do not offer any competitive satisfaction, are highly rational and rationalized activities. This is firstly because they presuppose a resolute faith in reason and in the deferred and often intangible benefits which reason promises (such as protection against ageing, an abstract and negative advantage which only exists by reference to a thoroughly theoretical referent); secondly, because they generally only have meaning by reference to a thoroughly theoretical, abstract knowledge of the effects of an exercise which is itself often reduced, as in gymnastics, to a series of abstract movements, decomposed and reorganized by reference to a specific and technically-defined end (e.g. 'the abdominals') and is opposed to the total movements of everyday situations, oriented towards practical goals, just as marching, broken down into elementary movements in the sergeant-major's handbook, is opposed to ordinary walking. Thus it is understandable that these activities can only be rooted in the ascetic dispositions of upwardly mobile individuals who are prepared to find their satisfaction in effort itself and to accept – such is the whole meaning of their existence – the deferred satisfactions which will reward their present sacrifice.

In sports like mountaineering (or, to a lesser extent, walking), which are most common among secondary or university teachers, the purely health-oriented function of maintaining the body is combined with all the symbolic gratifications associated with practising a highly distinctive activity. This gives to the highest degree the sense of mastery of one's own body as well as the free and exclusive appropriation of scenery inaccessible to the vulgar. In fact, the health-giving functions are always more or less strongly associated with what might be called aesthetic functions (especially, other things being equal, in women, who are more imperatively required to submit to the norms defining what the body ought to be, not only in its perceptible configuration but also in its motion, its gait, etc.). It is doubtless among the professions and the well-established business bourgeoisie that the health-giving and aesthetic functions are combined with social functions; there, sports take their place, along with parlour games and social exchanges (receptions, dinners, etc.), among the 'gratuitous' and 'disinterested' activities which enable the accumulation of social capital. This is seen in the fact that, in the extreme form it assumes in golf, shooting, and polo in smart clubs, sporting activity is a mere pretext for select encounters or, to put it another way, a technique of sociability, like bridge or dancing. Indeed, quite apart from its socializing functions, dancing is, of all the social uses of the body, the one which, treating the body as a sign, a sign of one's own ease, i.e. one's own mastery, represents the most accomplished realization of the bourgeois uses of the body: if this way of comporting the body is most successfully affirmed in dancing, this is perhaps because it is recognizable above all by its *tempo*, i.e. by the measured, self-assured slowness which also characterizes the bourgeois use of language, in contrast to working-class abruptness and petty-bourgeois eagerness.

NOTES

1. A slightly longer version of this article first appeared in *Social Science Information* 17, no. 6 (1978): 819–40.
2. This article is a translation of a paper given at the International Congress of the History of Sports and Physical Education Association, held in March 1978 at the Institut National des Sports et de l'Education Physique, Paris. The original title was 'Pratiques sportives et pratiques sociales'.

   The translation is by Richard Nice.

23 Dick Hebdige

From culture to hegemony

EDITOR'S INTRODUCTION

In this essay (first published in 1979 as the introductory chapter of his book *Subculture: the Meaning of Style*), Dick Hebdige traces the history of cultural studies hitherto in order to provide a theoretical justification for his study of subcultures. The essay belongs firmly to the moment at which the Birmingham school overlaid Gramscian political theory with the semiotics promulgated by Barthes and turned to the concept of polysemy.

Hebdige argues that subcultures take up the objects, spaces, and signs available to them within the larger system of late industrial culture in order to turn such objects and signs against the system. Through processes of negotiation and hybridization, subcultures articulate their counter-hegemonic styles and identities.

In his later work, Hebdige (1989) was to rework his method, admitting that he had underestimated the power of commercial culture to appropriate, and, indeed, to produce, counter-hegemonic styles. Punk, in particular, was a unique mixture of an avant-garde cultural strategy, marketing savvy and working-class transgression produced in the face of a section of British youth's restricted access to consumer markets. The line between subculture as resistance and commercial culture as an aspect of hegemony is in fact very hard to draw – especially when youth markets are in question. One way out of this difficulty is (as, for instance, Meaghan Morris in this collection shows) to think less about the opposition between hegemony and resistance via polysemy and more about the relation between material structures and life-practices of people at particular times and places.

Further reading: Brake 1980; Brantlinger 1990; Clarke *et al.* 1976; Cohen 1980; Hall and Jefferson 1976; Hebdige 1979, 1989; Johnson 1987; McRobbie and Nava 1984; Turner 1990.

S.D.

CULTURE

> Culture: cultivation, tending, in Christian authors, worship; the action or practice of cultivating the soil; tillage, husbandry; the cultivation or rearing of certain animals (e.g. fish); the artificial development of microscopic organisms, organisms so produced; the cultivating or development (of the mind, faculties, manners), improvement or refinement by education and training; the condition of being trained or refined; the intellectual side of civilization; the prosecution or special attention or study of any subject or pursuit. (*Oxford English Dictionary*)

Culture is a notoriously ambiguous concept as the above definition demonstrates. Refracted through centuries of usage, the word has acquired a number of quite different, often contradictory, meanings. Even as a scientific term, it refers both to a process (artificial development of microscopic organisms) and a product (organisms so produced). More specifically, since the end of the eighteenth century, it has been used by English intellectuals and literary figures to focus critical attention on a whole range of controversial issues. The 'quality of life', the effects in human terms of mechanization, the division of labour and the creation of a mass society have all been discussed within the larger confines of what Raymond Williams has called the 'Culture and Society' debate. It was through this tradition of dissent and criticism that the dream of the 'organic society' – of society as an integrated, meaningful whole – was largely kept alive. The dream had two basic trajectories. One led back to the past and to the feudal ideal of a hierarchically ordered community. Here, culture assumed an almost sacred function. Its 'harmonious perfection' was posited against the Wasteland of contemporary life.

The other trajectory, less heavily supported, led towards the future, to a socialist Utopia where the distinction between labour and leisure was to be annulled. Two basic definitions of culture emerged from this tradition, though these were by no means necessarily congruent with the two trajectories outlined above. The first – the one which is probably most familiar to the reader – was essentially classical and conservative. It represented culture as a standard of aesthetic excellence: 'the best that has been thought and said in the world', and it derived from an appreciation of 'classic' aesthetic form (opera, ballet, drama, literature, art). The second, traced back by Williams to Herder and the eighteenth century, was rooted in anthropology. Here the term 'culture' referred to a

> . . . particular way of life which expresses certain meanings and values not only in art and learning, but also in institutions and ordinary behaviour. The analysis of culture, from such a definition, is the clarification of the meanings and values implicit and explicit in a particular way of life, a particular culture. (Williams 1958)

This definition obviously had a much broader range. It encompassed, in T. S. Eliot's words,

> . . . all the characteristic activities and interests of a people. Derby Day, Henley Regatta, Cowes, the 12th of August, a cup final, the dog races, the pin table, the dartboard, Wensleydale cheese, boiled cabbage cut into sections, beetroot in vinegar, 19th Century Gothic churches, the music of Elgar. . . .

As Williams noted, such a definition could only be supported if a new theoretical initiative was taken. The theory of culture now involved the 'study of relationships between elements in a whole way of life' (Williams 1958). The emphasis shifted from immutable to historical criteria, from fixity to transformation:

> . . . an emphasis [which] from studying particular meanings and values seeks not so much to compare these, as a way of establishing a scale, but by studying their modes of change to discover certain general causes or 'trends' by which social and cultural developments as a whole can be better understood. (Williams 1958)

Williams was, then, proposing an altogether broader formulation of the relationships between culture and society, one which through the analysis of 'particular meanings and values' sought to uncover the conceived fundamentals of history; the 'general causes' and broad social 'trends' which lie behind the manifest appearances of an 'everyday life'.

In the early years, when it was being established in the Universities, Cultural Studies sat rather uncomfortably on the fence between these two conflicting definitions – culture as a standard of excellence, culture as a 'whole way of life' – unable to determine which represented the most fruitful line of enquiry. Richard Hoggart and Raymond Williams portrayed working-class culture sympathetically in wistful accounts of pre-scholarship boyhoods (Leeds for Hoggart (1957), a Welsh mining village for Williams (1958)) but their work displayed a strong bias towards literature and literacy and an equally strong moral tone. Hoggart deplored the way in which the traditional working-class community – a community of tried and tested values despite the dour landscape in which it had been set – was being undermined and replaced by a 'Candy Floss World' of thrills and cheap fiction which was somehow bland *and* sleazy. Williams tentatively endorsed the new mass communications but was concerned to establish aesthetic and moral criteria for distinguishing the worthwhile products from the 'trash'; the jazz – 'a real musical form' – and the football – 'a wonderful game' – from the 'rape novel, the Sunday strip paper and the latest Tin Pan drool' (Williams 1961). In 1966 Hoggart laid down the basic premises upon which Cultural Studies were based:

> First, without appreciating good literature, no one will really understand the nature of society, second, literary critical analysis can be applied to certain social phenomena other than 'academically respectable' literature (for example, the popular arts, mass communications) so as to illuminate their meanings for individuals and their societies. (Hoggart 1966)

The implicit assumption that it still required a literary sensibility to 'read' society with the requisite subtlety, and that the two ideas of culture could be ultimately reconciled was also, paradoxically, to inform the early work of the French writer, Roland Barthes, though here it found validation in a method – semiotics – a way of reading signs (Hawkes 1977).

BARTHES: MYTHS AND SIGNS

Using models derived from the work of the Swiss linguist Ferdinand de Saussure Barthes sought to expose the *arbitrary* nature of cultural phenomena, to uncover the latent meanings of an everyday life which, to all intents and purposes, was 'perfectly natural'. Unlike Hoggart, Barthes was not concerned with distinguishing the good from the bad in modern mass culture, but rather with showing how *all* the apparently spontaneous forms and rituals of contemporary bourgeois societies are subject to a systematic distortion, liable at any moment to be dehistoricized, 'naturalized', converted into myth:

> The whole of France is steeped in this anonymous ideology: our

press, our films, our theatre, our pulp literature, our rituals, our Justice, our diplomacy, our conversations, our remarks about the weather, a murder trial, a touching wedding, the cooking we dream of, the garments we wear, everything in everyday life is dependent on the representation which the bourgeoisie *has and makes us have* of the relations between men and the world. (Barthes 1972)

Like Eliot, Barthes's notion of culture extends beyond the library, the opera-house and the theatre to encompass the whole of everyday life. But this everyday life is for Barthes overlaid with a significance which is at once more insidious and more systematically organized. Starting from the premise that 'myth is a type of speech', Barthes set out in *Mythologies* to examine the normally hidden set of rules, codes and conventions through which meanings particular to specific social groups (i.e. those in power) are rendered universal and 'given' for the whole of society. He found in phenomena as disparate as a wrestling match, a writer on holiday, a tourist guide-book, the same artificial nature, the same ideological core. Each had been exposed to the same prevailing rhetoric (the rhetoric of common sense) and turned into myth, into a mere element in a 'second-order semiological system' (Barthes 1972). (Barthes uses the example of a photograph in *Paris-Match* of a Negro soldier saluting the French flag, which has a first and second order connotation: (1) a gesture of loyalty, but also (2) 'France is a great empire, and all her sons, without colour discrimination, faithfully serve under her flag'.)

Barthes's application of a method rooted in linguistics to other systems of discourse outside language (fashion, film, food, etc.) opened up completely new possibilities for contemporary cultural studies. It was hoped that the invisible seam between language, experience and reality could be located and prised open through a semiotic analysis of this kind: that the gulf between the alienated intellectual and the 'real' world could be rendered meaningful and, miraculously, at the same time, be made to disappear. Moreover, under Barthes's direction, semiotics promised nothing less than the reconciliation of the two conflicting definitions of culture upon which Cultural Studies was so ambiguously posited – a marriage of moral conviction (in this case, Barthes's Marxist beliefs) and popular themes: the study of a society's total way of life.

This is not to say that semiotics was easily assimilable within the Cultural Studies project. Though Barthes shared the literary preoccupations of Hoggart and Williams, his work introduced a new Marxist 'problematic' which was alien to the British tradition of concerned and largely untheorized 'social commentary'. As a result, the old debate seemed suddenly limited. In E. P. Thompson's words it appeared to reflect the parochial concerns of a group of 'gentlemen amateurs'. Thompson sought to replace Williams's definition of the theory of culture as 'a theory of relations between elements in a whole way of life' with his own more rigorously Marxist formulation: 'the study of relationships in a whole way of *conflict*'. A more analytical framework was required; a new vocabulary had to be learned. As part of this process of theorization, the word 'ideology' came to acquire a much wider range of meanings than had previously been the case. We have seen how Barthes found an 'anonymous ideology' penetrating every possible level of social life, inscribed in the most mundane of rituals, framing the most casual social encounters. But how can ideology be 'anonymous', and how can it assume such a broad significance? Before we attempt any reading of subcultural style, we must first define the term 'ideology' more precisely.

IDEOLOGY: A *LIVED* RELATION

In the *German Ideology*, Marx shows how the basis of the capitalist economic structure (surplus value, neatly defined by Godelier as 'Profit . . . is unpaid work' (Godelier 1970)) is hidden from the consciousness of the agents of production. The failure to see through appearances to the real relations which underlie them does not occur as the direct result of some kind of masking operation consciously carried out by individuals, social groups or institutions. On the contrary, ideology by definition thrives *beneath* consciousness. It is here, at the level of 'normal common sense', that ideological frames of reference are most firmly sedimented and most effective, because it is here that their ideological nature is most effectively concealed. As Stuart Hall puts it:

It is precisely its 'spontaneous' quality, its transparency, its 'naturalness', its refusal to be made to examine the premises on which it is founded, its resistance to change or to correction, its effect of instant recognition, and the closed circle in which it moves which makes common sense, at one and the same time, 'spontaneous', ideological and *unconscious*. You cannot learn, through common sense, *how things are*: you can only discover *where they fit* into the existing scheme of things. In this way, its very taken-for-grantedness is what establishes it as a medium in which its own premises and presuppositions are being rendered *invisible* by its apparent transparency. (Hall 1977)

Since ideology saturates everyday discourse in the form of common sense, it cannot be bracketed off from everyday life as a self-contained set of 'political opinions' or 'biased views'. Neither can it be reduced to the abstract dimensions of a 'world view' or used in the crude Marxist sense to designate 'false consciousness'. Instead, as Louis Althusser has pointed out:

> . . . ideology has very little to do with 'consciousness'. . . . It is profoundly *unconscious*. . . . Ideology is indeed a system of representation, but in the majority of cases these representations have nothing to do with 'consciousness': they are usually images and occasionally concepts, but it is above all as *structures* that they impose on the vast majority of men, not via their 'consciousness'. They are perceived–accepted–suffered cultural objects and they act functionally on men via a process that escapes them. (Althusser 1969)

Although Althusser is here referring to structures like the family, cultural and political institutions, etc., we can illustrate the point quite simply by taking as our example a physical structure. Most modern institutes of education, despite the apparent neutrality of the materials from which they are constructed (red brick, white tile, etc.) carry within themselves implicit ideological assumptions which are literally structured into the architecture itself. The categorization of knowledge into arts and sciences is reproduced in the faculty system which houses different disciplines in different buildings, and most colleges maintain the traditional divisions by devoting a separate floor to each subject. Moreover, the hierarchical relationship between teacher and taught is inscribed in the very lay-out of the lecture theatre where the seating arrangements – benches rising in tiers before a raised lectern – dictate the flow of information and serve to 'naturalize' professorial authority. Thus, a whole range of decisions about what is and what is not possible within education have been made, however unconsciously, before the content of individual courses is even decided.

These decisions help to set the limits not only on what is taught but on *how* it is taught. Here the buildings literally *reproduce* in concrete terms prevailing (ideological) notions about what education *is* and it is through this process that the educational structure, which can, of course, be altered, is placed beyond question and appears to us as a 'given' (i.e. as immutable). In this case, the frames of our thinking have been translated into actual bricks and mortar.

Social relations and processes are then appropriated by individuals only through the forms in which they are represented to those individuals. These forms are, as we have seen, by no means transparent. They are shrouded in a 'common sense' which simultaneously validates and mystifies them. It is precisely these 'perceived–accepted–suffered cultural objects' which semiotics sets out to 'interrogate' and decipher. All aspects of culture possess a semiotic value, and the most taken-for-granted phenomena can function as signs: as elements in communication systems governed by semantic rules and codes which are not themselves directly apprehended in experience. These signs are, then, as opaque as the social relations which produce them and which they represent. In other words, there is an ideological dimension to every signification.

To uncover the ideological dimension of signs we must first try to disentangle the codes through which meaning is organized. 'Connotative' codes are particularly important. As Stuart Hall has argued, they '. . . cover the face of social life and render it classifiable, intelligible, meaningful' (Hall 1977). He goes on to describe these codes as 'maps of meaning' which are of necessity the product of selection. They cut across a range of potential meanings, making certain meanings available and ruling others out of court. We tend to live inside these maps as surely as we live in the 'real' world: they 'think' us as much as we 'think' them, and this in itself is quite 'natural'. All human societies *reproduce* themselves in this way through a process of 'naturalization'. It is through this process – a kind of inevitable reflex of all social life – that *particular* sets of social relations, *particular* ways of organizing the world appear to us as if they were universal and timeless. This is what Althusser means when he says that 'ideology has no history' and that ideology in this general sense will always be an 'essential element of every social formation' (Althusser and Balibar 1968).

However, in highly complex societies like ours, which function through a finely graded system of divided (i.e. specialized) labour, the crucial question has to do with which specific ideologies, representing the interests of which specific groups and classes will prevail at any given moment, in any given situation. To deal with this question, we must first consider how power is distributed in our society. That is, we must ask which groups and classes have how much say in defining, ordering and classifying out the social world. For instance, if we pause to reflect for a moment, it should be obvious that access to the means by which ideas are disseminated in our society (i.e. principally the mass media) is *not* the same for all classes. Some groups have more say, more opportunity to make the rules, to organize meaning, while others are less favourably placed, have less power to produce and impose their definitions of the world on the world.

Thus, when we come to look beneath the level of 'ideology-in-general' at the way in which specific ideologies work, how some gain dominance and others remain marginal, we can see that in advanced Western democracies the ideological field is by no means neutral. To return to the 'connotative' codes to which Stuart Hall refers we can see that these 'maps of meaning' are charged with a potentially explosive significance because they are traced and re-traced along the lines laid down by the *dominant* discourses about reality, the *dominant* ideologies. They thus tend to represent, in however obscure and contradictory a fashion, the interests of the *dominant* groups in society.

To understand this point we should refer to Marx:

The ideas of the ruling class are in every epoch the ruling ideas, i.e. the class which is the ruling *material* force of society is at the same time its ruling *intellectual* force. The class which has the means of material production at its disposal, has control at the same time over the means of mental production, so that generally speaking, the ideas of those who lack the means of mental production are subject to it. The ruling ideas are nothing more than the ideal expression of the dominant material relationships grasped as ideas; hence of the relationships which make the one class the ruling class, therefore the ideas of its dominance. (Marx and Engels 1970)

This is the basis of Antonio Gramsci's theory of *hegemony* which provides the most adequate account of how dominance is sustained in advanced capitalist societies.

HEGEMONY: THE MOVING EQUILIBRIUM

Society cannot share a common communication system so long as it is split into warring classes. (Brecht, *A Short Organum for the Theatre*)

The term hegemony refers to a situation in which a provisional alliance of certain social groups can exert 'total social authority' over other subordinate groups, not simply by coercion or by the direct imposition of ruling ideas, but by 'winning and shaping consent so that the power of the dominant classes appears both legitimate and natural' (Hall 1977). Hegemony can only be maintained so long as the dominant classes 'succeed in framing all competing definitions within their range' (Hall 1977), so that subordinate groups are, if not controlled, then at least contained within an ideological space which does not seem at all 'ideological': which appears instead to be permanent and 'natural', to lie outside history, to be beyond particular interests.

This is how, according to Barthes, 'mythology' performs its vital function of naturalization and normalization and it is in his book *Mythologies* that Barthes demonstrates most forcefully the full extension of these normalized forms and meanings. However, Gramsci adds the important proviso that hegemonic power, precisely *because* it requires the consent of the dominated majority, can never be permanently exercised by the same alliance of 'class fractions'. As has been pointed out, 'Hegemony . . . is not universal and "given" to the continuing rule of a particular class. It has to be won, reproduced, sustained. Hegemony is, as Gramsci said, a "moving equilibrium" containing relations of forces favourable or unfavourable to this or that tendency' (Hall and Jefferson 1976).

In the same way, forms cannot be permanently normalized. They can always be deconstructed, demystified, by a 'mythologist' like Barthes. Moreover commodities can be symbolically 'repossessed' in everyday life, and endowed with implicitly oppositional meanings, by the very groups who originally produced them. The symbiosis in which ideology and social order, production and reproduction, are linked is then neither fixed nor guaranteed. It can be prised open. The consensus can be fractured, challenged, overruled, and resistance to the groups in dominance cannot always be lightly dismissed or automatically incorporated. Although, as Lefebvre has written, we live in a society where '. . . objects in practice become signs and signs objects and a second nature takes the place of the first – the initial layer of perceptible reality' (Lefebvre 1971), there are, as he goes on to affirm, always 'objections and contradictions which hinder the closing of the circuit' between sign and object, production and reproduction.

We can now return to the meaning of youth subcultures, for the emergence of such groups has signalled in a spectacular fashion the breakdown of consensus in the post-war period. It is precisely objections and contradictions of the kind which Lefebvre has described that find expression in subculture. However, the challenge to hegemony which subcultures represent is not issued directly by them. Rather it is expressed obliquely, in style. The objections are lodged, the contradictions displayed (and 'magically resolved') at the profoundly superficial level of appearances: that is, at the level of signs. For the sign-community, the community of myth-consumers, is not a uniform body. As Volosinov has written, it is cut through by class:

> Class does not coincide with the sign community, i.e. with the totality of users of the same set of signs of ideological communication. Thus various different classes will use one and the same language. As a result, differently oriented accents intersect in every ideological sign. Sign becomes the arena of the class struggle. (Volosinov 1973)

The struggle between different discourses, different definitions and meanings within ideology is therefore always, at the same time, a struggle within signification: a struggle for possession of the sign which extends to even the most mundane areas of everyday life. 'Humble objects' can be magically appropriated; 'stolen' by subordinate groups and made to carry 'secret' meanings: meanings which express, in code, a form of resistance to the order which guarantees their continued subordination.

Style in subculture is, then, pregnant with significance. Its transformations go 'against nature', interrupting the process of 'normalization'. As such, they are gestures, movements towards a speech which offends the 'silent majority', which challenges the principle of unity and cohesion, which contradicts the myth of consensus. Our task becomes, like Barthes's, to discern the hidden messages inscribed in code on the glossy surfaces of style, to trace them out as 'maps of meaning' which obscurely re-present the very contradictions they are designed to resolve or conceal.

24 Will Straw

Characterizing rock music culture: the case of heavy metal

EDITOR'S INTRODUCTION

On the face of it, Will Straw's article, originally written about heavy metal in the 1970s and updated by the author for this collection, takes a sociological rather than a cultural studies approach. He does not write as a fan; he does not suppose that listening to heavy metal possesses any counter-hegemonic force; he is not concerned with it as a life-practice. But his point is that, despite appearances to the contrary, heavy metal is not a subculture. It is a musical genre which develops at the intersection between a particular moment in the music industry (the development of an 'oligopoly') and a kind of social space (suburbanism).

In his essay, Straw is more interested in the music industry and its reception than in living in the suburbs, and his essay is particularly insightful on the effects of oligopoly on the industry. (In 1992, there are fewer major record companies globally than there were even in the 1980s: large independents like Arista, Geffen, Island, and Virgin have all been swallowed up since.) He is especially concerned to argue that the usual Adorno-esque thesis that cultural-industry centralization leads to standardization of product does not work for heavy metal, largely because rock involves 'craft-production' techniques.

He goes on to show how the ways in which it is possible to be a metal fan are organized from other areas in the cultural industry – in particular, an imagery which dissociates masculinity from being good at archival learning. This matters to metal, because it means that to be a metal fan doesn't require a sense of the history of rock and roll like the more marginal genres of punk, grunge, and thrash do. This makes it more available to those who live far from the centres of avant-garde rock action.

Further reading: Becker 1978; Born 1987; Chambers 1985; Frith 1988; Frith and Goodwin 1990.

S.D.

The decomposition of psychedelic music, in the late 1960s, followed three principal directions. The first of these, in the United States, involved a return to traditional, largely rural musical styles, with the emergence of country rock, of which the stylistic changes in the careers of the Byrds (in 1968) and the Grateful Dead (in 1970) offer examples. In Britain, a second tendency took the form of a very eclectic reinscription of traditional and symphonic musical forms within an electric or electronic rock context, with groups such as King Crimson, Jethro Tull, Genesis, Yes, and Emerson, Lake and Palmer. The third trend, which may be found in both American and British rock music of this period, was toward the heavy metal sound, frequently based in the chord structures of boogie blues, but retaining from psychedelia an emphasis on technological effect and instrumental virtuosity. In groups on the periphery of psychedelia – such as Blue Cheer, the Yardbirds, Iron Butterfly – many of the stylistic traits that would become dominant within heavy metal were already in evidence: the cult of the lead guitarist, the 'power trio' and other indices of the emphasis on virtuosity, the 'supergroup' phenomena, and the importance in performance of extended solo playing and a disregard for the temporal limits of the pop song. Their coherence into a genre was reinforced, through the 1970s, by the sedimentation of other stylistic attributes (those associated with stage shows, album-cover design, and audience dress and lifestyle) and by the relatively stable sites of institutional support (radio formats, touring circuits, record industry structures).

INSTITUTIONS AND INDUSTRIES IN THE EARLY 1970S

Heavy metal music came to prominence at a time when institutions associated with the psychedelic period were either disappearing or being assimilated within larger structures as part of widespread changes within the music-related industries. The overriding tendency in these changes was the diminishing role of local entrepreneurs in the processes by which music was developed and disseminated. The end of the sixties meant the end of free-form radio, a large number of independent record labels, the ballroom performance circuit, and the underground press, all of which had contributed, at least initially, to the high degree of regionalization within psychedelia and associated rock movements.

For many record company analysts, the number of hit-making independent record labels is an index of the degree of 'turbulence' within the industry. The modern history of the American recording industry has thus been divided into three epochs: one running from 1940 to 1958, marked by concentration and integration within and between the electronics, recording, and publishing industries; the 1959 to 1969 period, characterized by the 'turbulence' associated with the introduction on a large scale of rock music; and, finally, the period that began in 1970, and that saw the return of oligopoly to the extent that, in 1979, the six largest corporations accounted for 86 per cent of *Billboard*'s total 'chart action'. Two other statistics are worth noting: by the late 1960s, the album had displaced the single as the dominant format in record sales, and during the 1970s, in large part as a result of the overhead costs associated with oligopoly, the break-even point for album sales went from 20,000 to nearly 100,000 copies.

While the oligopolization of the American record industry in the 1970s is undeniable, this did not result in the industry becoming more conservative or its products more standardized. Writers such as Paul Hirsch have argued that the 'centralization' of decision making in the industries producing cultural 'texts' is rarely like that found in other businesses and that entertainment industries more closely resemble the house construction industry, with its organization of production along craft lines. Within the record industry, horizontal integration has frequently meant assimilating smaller, specialized labels within conglomerates (through purchases or licensing–distribution agreements), such that those involved in the selection and production of music stay in place. The record industry in the 1970s thus relied far more on outside, contracted producers or production companies than it did in the old days of the salaried artist and repertoire director.

The defining characteristic of much rock music production in the early 1970s was, further, its domination by rock elites, by people already established in creative capacities within the industry. The supergroup phenomena of this period is symptomatic of this, as is the fact that most of the leading heavy metal bands (such as Humble Pie) were formed by remnants of groups popular in the 1960s. And many of the country-rock groups and singer-songwriters who achieved high market penetration in the early 1970s had in one capacity or another long been record company employees (for instance Leon Russell, Carole King, and the members of the Eagles).

The implications of this for the American record industry during these years are not obvious. The reliance on industry elites is indicative of industry conservatism insofar as it displaced 'street-level' talent-hunting and might be seen as a resistance to innovation. However it meant neglect too of the process whereby musicians with local followings and local entrepreneurial support established themselves regionally and proved their financial viability by recording first for minor labels. The majors were now signing acts without this form of market testing (a contributing factor in the increasingly high ratio of unprofitable to profitable records), and the selection and development of talent, the initiation of new styles, was increasingly the responsibility of the established creative personnel. Recording contracts in this period of growth gave artists unprecedented control over the choice of producers and material.

'Centralization' in this context meant, therefore, a *loosening* of divisions of labour. It is clear, for example, that many of those formerly involved in support capacities (songwriters, session musicians, etc.) achieved star status because of the ease with which they could move between divisions or combine the production, composing, and performing functions (just as members of groups now took it for granted that they could record solo albums). A loosening of roles, and the continuing prosperity of performers and the industry as a whole, also encouraged international record production, with, as one of its effects, the free movement of session personnel (and their musical concerns) between Great Britain and North America (Joe Cocker's *Mad Dogs and Englishmen* album and film remains a useful document of this). While the bases for comparison are limited, the American record industry in the 1970s was not unlike the American film industry following the antitrust decisions of the 1940s, which divorced the production and distribution companies from those involved in exhibition: in both cases, one finds a high reliance on licensing agreements between major companies and smaller production outfits; in both cases, there is a fluidity of movement between roles and a tendency (for financial – often tax-related – reasons) for stars to build corporate entities around themselves and work in a variety of international locales. Much of the rock literature of the mid- to late 1970s, describing industry growth in terms of the co-optation and destruction of the energies unleashed in the 1960s, regards this as exemplifying a process inevitable within mass culture, but it can be argued that the changes are better understood as the triumph of craft-production structures. In this regard, the punk critique of early 1970s rock – which focused on its excesses and its eclecticism, on its 'empty' virtuosity and self-indulgence rather than on an assumed standardization – was a necessary counterweight to the recuperation argument.

The changes that occurred in the programming policies of FM radio stations in the United States and Canada between the late 1960s and mid-1970s are well documented elsewhere, as is the decline of the local underground press. In both cases, rising overhead costs and an increased reliance on large advertising accounts (with record companies the prominent spenders) grew out of and furthered the desire – or need – for market expansion. Either way, both radio stations and magazines paid less attention to marginal or regional musical phenomena. The rise of overhead costs and group performance fees were, similarly, the major factor in the replacement of the mid-sized performance circuit by the large arena or stadium, a process that continued throughout the 1970s, until the emergence of punk and new wave reestablished the viability of certain types of small venues.

These developments certainly did lead to standardization on FM radio and in the rock press. Radio playlist consultants, automated stations, and satellite-based networks all became significant elements in the evolution of FM radio throughout the 1970s, and the development of the rock press from local, subculturally based publications to national magazines is evident in the history of *Rolling Stone*, one of the few rock papers to survive. It would be wrong, though, to see these developments as local examples of the general 'standardizing' trend. Radio playlist consultants became important because of the eclecticism and sheer bulk of record company product – individual station directors simply didn't have the time or skill to listen to and choose from all this product. At the same time the increasing rigidity of formats was an effect of demographic research into the expansion of the rock audience beyond its traditional youth boundaries – the recession of the 1970s called for a more accurate targeting of listening groups. It was because such targeting remained a minor aspect of record company strategy (except in the most general sense) that it became crucial in shaping the formats of radio stations and magazines, media commercially dependent on the delivery of audiences to advertisers.

HEAVY METAL AUDIENCES AND THE INSTITUTIONS OF ROCK

On one level, Led Zeppelin represents the final flowering of the sixties' psychedelic ethic, which casts rock as passive sensory involvement.

Jim Miller

In discussing heavy metal music, and its relationship to rock culture in a wider sense, I am assuming a relative stability of musical style and of institutional structures from 1969–70 until 1974–76. (Near the end of this period, dance-oriented music began to achieve popularity with segments of the white audiences, with a variety of effects on the sites within which music was disseminated, while the gradual acceptance, in the United States and Canada, of British symphonic or progressive rock resulted in a generic cross-fertilization that eroded the stylistic coherence of heavy metal.)

The processes described earlier as leading to the renewed importance of the *national* rock audience also worked to constitute it as a 'mass' audience as the media disseminating music or information about it (radio and the press) now relied on national formats rather than on their ties to local communities. These developments made more important an audience segment that had been somewhat disenfranchised by movements within rock in the late 1960s – suburban youth. In the 1970s, it was they who were the principal heavy metal constituency.

In stressing the geographical situation of heavy metal audiences rather than their regional, ethnic, racial, or class basis, I am conscious that the latter have had wider currency in theoretical studies of rock, and it is obvious that race and class are, for example, highly determinant in the audience profile for soul or opera. Nevertheless, for reasons that should become evident, habitation patterns are crucial for the relationship between music, the institutions disseminating it, and life-styles in a more general sense. The hostility of heavy metal audiences to disco in the late 1970s is indicative in this respect; the demographics of disco showed it to be dominated by blacks, Hispanics, gays, and young professionals, who shared little beyond living in inner urban areas. The high degree of interaction between punk/new-wave currents and artistic subcultures in America (when compared with Great Britain) may also be traced in large part to the basis of both in inner urban areas such as New York's Soho; those living elsewhere would have little or no opportunity to experience or become involved in either of these cultures.

Suburban life is incompatible for a number of reasons with regular attendance at clubs where one may hear records or live performers; its main sources of music are radio, retail chain record stores (usually in shopping centres), and occasional large concerts (most frequently in the nearest municipal stadium). These institutions together make up the network by which major-label albums are promoted and sold – and from which music not available on such labels is for the most part excluded.

My argument is not that this institutional network gave major labels a free hand in shaping tastes but that, in conjunction with suburban lifestyles, it defined a form of involvement in rock culture, discouraging subcultural activity of the degree associated with disco or punk, for example. Heavy metal culture may be characterized in part by the absence of a strong middle stratum between the listener and the fully professional group. Only in rare cases in the early 1970s could there be found an echelon of local heavy metal bands performing their own material in local venues. What I have referred to as the dominance of music in general by elites, in conjunction with the overall decline in small-scale live performance activity in the early 1970s, worked to block the channels of career advancement characteristic of other musical currents or other periods within rock history. It might also be suggested that the economy of North American suburbs in most cases discourages the sorts of marginality that develop in large inner urban areas and foster musical subcultures. High rents and the absence of enterprises not affiliated with corporate chains mean that venues for dancing or listening to live music are uncommon. If, for the purposes of this discussion, a music-based subculture may be defined as a group whose interaction centres to a high degree on sites of musical consumption, and within which there are complex gradations of professional or semi-professional involvement in music together with relatively loose barriers between roles (such that all members will be involved, in varying degrees, in collecting, assessing, presenting, and performing music), then heavy metal audiences do not constitute a musical subculture.

The lack of intermediary strata between heavy metal audiences and groups was further determined by another characteristic of the music. Most of the groups that were predominant – Led Zeppelin, Black Sabbath, Uriah Heep, Humble Pie, Deep Purple, and so on – were British. They were instrumental in establishing a major characteristic of North American rock culture in the 1970s: regular, large-scale touring. The dependence of certain British bands on the North American market has become a structural feature of the rock industry, and is quite different in its significance from the periodic 'British invasions' of the charts.

The American rock-critical establishment had a negative response to heavy metal, or at least to the form British musicians gave it. This had two effects on the place of heavy metal within rock culture and its discourse. On the one hand, critical dismissal encouraged heavy metal musicians to employ a populist argument, whose main tenet was that critics had lost touch with the tastes of broad sections of the rock audience. On the other hand, this placed critics in the dilemma of how to respond negatively to the music without employing the terms traditionally used to condemn rock overall (sameness, loudness, musical incompetence, etc.). Those critical terms with greater acceptability in rock culture (commercialism, conservatism) were, at least initially, inappropriate. The explicitly sociological or ethnographic bent of critical writing on heavy metal, its attention to the social/political implications of the music, were symptomatic of the cleavages heavy metal had effected within rock discourse.

In the early and mid-1970s, and particularly in *Rolling Stone*, rock criticism adopted more and more of the terms of journalistic film criticism, valorizing generic economy and a performer's links with the archives of American popular music. (The consistent high regard for singers such as Bruce Springsteen, Emmylou Harris, and Tom Waits, for performers like Lou Reed who played self-consciously with rock and roll imagery, stands out in a rereading of *Rolling Stone* from this period.) The emphasis on the individual career or the genre as the context within which records were meaningful accompanied the rise of the 'serious' record review. This not only diminished the interest of heavy metal for its own sake, but also made the audience a relatively minor focus of rock criticism, as the latter moved away from the pop-journalistic or countercultural concerns of a few years earlier.

A major characteristic of heavy metal was its consistent non-invocation of rock history or mythology in any self-conscious or genealogical sense. The iconography of heavy metal performances and album covers, and the specific reworking of boogie blues underlying the music, did not suggest the sorts of modalization (that is, ironic relationships to their design principles or retrospective evocation of origins) that country rock, glitter rock, and even disco (with its frequent play upon older motifs of urban nightlife) possessed. As well, there was nothing to indicate that heavy metal listeners were interested in tracing the roots of any musical traits back to periods preceding the emergence of heavy metal. While the terms 'rock' and 'rock and roll' recur within song lyrics and album titles, this is always in reference to the present of the performance and the energies to be unleashed now, rather than to history or to myth. Any 'rebel' or non-conformist imagery in heavy metal may be seen as a function of its masculine, 'hard' stances, rather than as a conscious participation in rock's growing self-reflexivity. That the recent neo-punk movements in Anglo-American rock have found much of their constituency within heavy metal audiences is partly due, I suspect, to the redefinition of punk's minimalism as the expression of raw energy.

Equally striking is the almost total lack of hobbyist activity surrounding heavy metal music. Observation suggests that heavy metal listeners rarely become record collectors to a significant extent, that they are not characterized by what might be called 'secondary involvement' in music: the hunting down of rare tracks, the reading of music-oriented magazines, the high recognition of record labels or producers. To the extent that a heavy metal 'archive' exists, it consists of albums from the 1970s on major labels, kept in print constantly and easily available in chain record stores. There is thus little basis for the presence in heavy metal audiences of complex hierarchies based on knowledge of the music or possession of obscure records, on relationships to opinion leaders as the determinants of tastes and purchases. An infrastructure of importers, speciality stores, and fanzines was almost non-existent in heavy metal culture during the early 1970s and emerged only in the 1980s, with the recent wave of newer heavy metal groups.

In its distance from both Top 40 pop culture and the mainstream of rock-critical discourse, heavy metal in the early 1970s was the rock genre least characterized by the culture's usual practices of contextualization. It is rarely the case, for example, that heavy metal pieces are presented on the radio for their nostalgic or 'oldie' value. Rather, they are presented as existing contemporaneously with recent material, with none of the transitory aspects of Top 40 or setting down in individual careers or generic histories which the rock press and radio bring to bear upon other forms. The specificity of the heavy metal audience, then, lies in: (1) its non-participation in the two dominant components of rock culture, the Top 40 succession of hits and hobbyist tendencies associated with record and information collecting; and (2) its difference, nevertheless, from the casual, eclectic audience for transgeneric music (such as that of Carole King or, more recently, Vangelis). It is this coexistence of relatively coherent taste, consumption, and to a certain extent, life-style with low secondary involvement in rock culture that in the 1970s most strongly distinguished audiences for heavy metal from those for other sorts of rock music.

HEAVY METAL CULTURE: MASCULINITY AND ICONOGRAPHY

> On the whole, youth cultures and subcultures tend to be some form of exploration of masculinity.
>
> Mike Brake

That the audience for heavy metal music is heavily male-dominated is generally acknowledged and easily observable, though statistical confirmation of this is based largely on the audiences for album-oriented rock (AOR). Clearly heavy metal performers are almost exclusively male (recent exceptions such as Girlschool being accorded attention most often for their singularity). Is it sufficient, then, to interpret heavy metal's gender significance simply in terms of its 'cock rock' iconography?

One problem here is how to reconcile the hypothesis that heavy involvement in rock music – as critic, record collector, reader of the rock press, or performer – is primarily a male pursuit with the observation that these activities are for the most part absent from the most 'masculine' of rock audiences, that for heavy metal. The point is that involvement in rock music is simply one among many examples of criteria by which status is assigned within youth peer groups, albeit one that involves a high degree of eroticization of certain stances and attributes.

Within male youth culture (particularly in secondary school or workplaces), a strong investment in archivist or obscurantist forms of knowledge is usually devalued, marginalized as a component of what (in North America, at least) is called 'nerd' culture. I would emphasize that this marginalization is not simply directed at intellectual or knowledgeable males; rather, it involves specific relationships between knowledge and the presentation of the physical body. In recent American youth films (such as *The Last American Virgin*), the nerd is stereotyped as unstylishly dressed and successful at school: it is precisely the preoccupation with knowledge that is seen as rendering the boy oblivious to dress, grooming, posture, and social interaction (particularly as related to sexuality).

If, within a typology of male identity patterns, heavy metal listeners are usually in a relationship of polar opposition to 'nerds', it is primarily because the former do not regard certain forms of knowledge (particularly those derived from print media) as significant components of masculinity – if the 'nerd' is distinguished by his inability to translate knowledge into socially acceptable forms of competence, heavy metal peer groups value competencies demonstrable in social situations exclusively. Interestingly, within rock culture, neither of these groups is seen to partake of what the dominant discourse surrounding rock in the 1970s has regarded as 'cool'.

'Cool' may be said to involve the eroticization and stylization of knowledge through its assimilation to an imagery of competence. There developed in the 1970s a recognizable genre of rock performance (Lou Reed, Patti Smith, Iggy Pop, even, to a lesser extent, Rod Stewart) based on the integration of street wisdom, a certain ironic distance from rock mythology, and, in some cases, sexual ambiguity (whose dominant significance was as an index of experience) within relatively coherent musical styles and physical stances. The recurrence of black leather and 'rebel' postures in the iconography surrounding such music never resulted in its full assimilation in the more masculine tendencies of rock culture, since these motifs overlapped considerably with those of gay culture or involved a significant degree of intellectualization; but in North America, much of the original constituency for punk and new wave included people whose archivist involvement in rock centred on a tradition dominated by the Velvet Underground and East Coast urban rock in general. Many of those in this current (such as Lenny Kaye and Lester Bangs) became important figures within American rock criticism, and it remains the purest example of secondary involvement in rock music becoming a component of a highly stylized subculture. Since the mid-1970s, performers on its fringes have contributed an alternative constellation of male images to those found in heavy metal, one that participates in what rock culture defines as 'cool', but that lacks the androgynous aspects of the bohemian underground. Bruce Springsteen, Bob Seger, and John Cougar Mellencamp are American rock performers who have all achieved mainstream AOR success while presenting, as important components of their styles, an archivist relationship to rock music and a tendency to play self-consciously with the mythologies that surround it.

The major stylistic components of heavy metal iconography may be inventoried as follows: long hair for both performers and audiences; denim jackets and jeans among audience members; smoke bombs as an element of stage performances; marijuana smoking and the taking of depressant drugs (Quaaludes and alcohol, etc.). On album covers: eclecticism at the beginning, but the gradual cohering of an iconography combining satanic imagery and motifs from heroic fantasy illustration, which could be found increasingly too on the backs of jean jackets, automobiles and vans, T-shirts, pinball machines (and, with the later influence of punk, on buttons). The remarkable aspect of traits such as long hair and denim jackets is their persistence and longevity within heavy metal culture long after they had ceased to be fashionable across the wider spectrum of North American youth culture. This itself reflected a decade-long shift whereby the heavy metal look came to acquire connotations of low socioeconomic position. While this might seem incompatible with my characterization of heavy metal audiences as largely suburban – and therefore, presumably, middle class – it would seem that the heavy metal audience, by the early 1980s, consisted to a significant extent of suburban males who did not acquire postsecondary education and who increasingly found that their socioeconomic prospects were not as great as those of their parents.

The iconography prevalent in heavy metal culture may be seen as the development of (1) certain tendencies emergent within psychedelia, which were in part responsible for the popularization of (2) types of fantasy and science fiction literature and illustration, which, in heavy metal iconography, saw their (3) heroic or masculine features emphasized. It is well known, for example, that, within the hippie counterculture, fantasy literature such as Tolkien's *The Lord of the Rings* was widely read and provided motifs for a wide range of poster art, songs, album covers, and so on. In progressive rock of the early 1970s, related themes dominated, and the commercialization (in poster and book form) of the album covers by artists such as Roger Dean testified to the market for this style. In many cases (Jethro Tull, Genesis) fantastic motifs accompanied the musical invocation of early British history or mythology.

However, the most successfully popularized of these styles was the 'heroic fantasy' associated with Conan and spinoff fictional characters. From the late 1960s through the 1970s, this form of fiction passed from paperback novel to high-priced illustrated magazine to conventional comic book format to, ultimately, the cinema: each step was evidence of the genre's broadening appeal and entry into mainstream youth culture. By the mid-1970s, the artwork of Frank Frazetta and others associated with the genre was widely merchandised in poster and calendar form, and on the covers of heavy metal albums by such groups as Molly Hatchett. Highly masculine (dominated by an imagery of carnage) and mildly pornographic, this illustrative style has cohered around heavy metal music and its paraphernalia.

The satanic imagery associated with heavy metal iconography

almost from its inception (by Black Sabbath) grew out of stylistic traits present within psychedelia (such as those found on early Grateful Dead albums), and its convergence with elements of heroic fantasy illustration came near the middle of the decade. However, it is arguable whether the readership of fantasy literature overlaps significantly with the audience for heavy metal music (though the audience for heroic fantasy films likely does). The readership of *Heavy Metal* magazine, for example, despite its title, includes more fans of progressive rock than of heavy metal, which is to be expected in that both the magazine and these types of music are the centres of subcultural activity. Studies have demonstrated the low involvement of heavy metal audiences in print media and their high movie attendance.

What heavy metal iconography did do was contribute to the development of a 1970s kitsch, to the proliferation of fantasy and satanic imagery as vehicle and pinball arcade decor, as poster art and T-shirt illustration. For the most part, this has meant inscribing a masculine-heroic element within the fantastic or mystical motifs that surrounded psychedelic and, later, progressive rock. These motifs increasingly stood out against the geometrical-minimalist and retro design principles that became widespread within rock music following the emergence of punk and new wave.

CONCLUSION

Heavy metal is at once the most consistently successful of forms within rock music and the most marginalized within the discourse of institutionalized rock culture. That literary criticism is not regularly unsettled by the popularity of Harlequin romances while American rock culture regards heavy metal as a 'problem' is symptomatic of the tension in the 1970s between the ascension of critical discourse on rock music to respectability and the importance to it of a rock populist reading.

Heavy metal in North America provides one of the purest examples of involvement in rock music as an activity subordinate to, rather than determinant of, peer group formation. While involvement in disco or punk may determine people's choices of types and sites of love and friendship (and even the selection of places to live and work), heavy metal – perhaps because of the inaccessibility of the institutions that produce and disseminate it – does not.

For young men, at least, involvement in rock music is perhaps the most useful index of the relationship between knowledge/competence and physical/sexual presence. Despite my concentration on heavy metal, the most male-dominated of rock's forms, and the most blatant in its associations of masculinity with physical violence and power, I regard the 1970s as significant precisely for the ways in which certain types of rock (glitter, punk) accomplished important interventions in sexual politics. That these interventions and their effects were major, while heavy metal remained the most popular form of rock during this decade, is evidence of the complexity and breadth of rock culture.

POSTSCRIPT

This article was written in the early 1980s; the rock music culture which it describes is that of the 1970s. Since then, of course, the place of heavy metal within musical culture has changed radically. Beginning in the late 1970s, an infrastructure of small-scale magazines, speciality stores and the accoutrements of fandom took shape around heavy metal. By the end of the 1980s, the gap between heavy metal and post-punk rock culture had narrowed, and heavy metal had emerged as one of the coolest, most critically respectable and most diverse of musical forms. These changes are themselves of great interest, but they are beyond the scope of my article.

25 Rey Chow

Listening otherwise, music miniaturized: a different type of question about revolution

EDITOR'S INTRODUCTION

Rey Chow's essay leads us again into the exciting, if difficult, cultural politics and cultural analysis of a world in which the centrality of the West can no longer be taken for granted.

Befittingly, her arguments work on a number of registers. She begins by arguing against the Frankfurt school tradition for which a category like 'distraction' is to be interpreted negatively. For it, cultural products which did not attract their audiences' entire attention were instruments of capitalism's disposition to make consumers passive. For Chow, on the other hand, a mode of Chinese pop music which makes few claims for itself, and does not invite a fully concentrated response, in fact works effectively against the Chinese communist authorities.

The power of this rock music – whose mode she calls 'miniature' or 'partial' – can be affirmed in relation to two discourses in particular. The first is that kind of Western theorizing which does not grant 'third world' subjects full individuality, seeing them primarily just as instances of, or determined by, a culture – and, for the most part, a fundamentally non-global culture at that. The second is the kind of history-writing which thinks in monumental terms: in the Chinese context, in terms of anti-colonial nation-building and the victory of the people. In the context of that kind of grand History, banality is dangerous – not banal at all.

So, Chow argues, Chinese rock music acquires an intensity and effect out of sync with its lack of aura and cultural value. But, as Chow also reminds us, the power of the miniature is not only dependent on its discursive or cultural-political context. It belongs to technology and the body as well – here, to a particular conjunction between the two, enabled and made concrete by the

Walkman. The Walkman, an Asian invention, screens the world out, and, without veiling us, does not let the world look in at our experiences. Here we have a portable technology that produces a mode of subjectivity which is certainly not simply on the side of those who read history monumentally.

Further reading: Appadurai 1990; Chambers 1990; Clifford and Dhareshwar 1989; During 1992.

S.D.

Hong Kong 1990: a place caught in post-colonial nostalgia, the simulacra of late capitalist technological advancement, the terror of communist takeover in barely seven years, the continual influx of unwanted refugees, the continual outflow of prized citizens. Hardly a second goes by without some commercial transaction taking place. 'Merchandise for emigration' becomes the mainstay of many stores, which are chronically offering 'sales'. Who are the oppressed of this place? There are many. They are faceless, voiceless, living in refugee camps, housing estates, rented rooms, rented beds, and other unknown corners of the overcrowded colony. Inside the packed spaces of the working city, the oppressed one most commonly encounters are the keepers of ubiquitous department stores and supermarkets – bored, unpleasant, expressionless, unhelpful salesmen and women, earning minimum wages, doing hardly anything day in and day out. These 'sales specialists' neither make, finance, nor earn profit from the merchandise they sell. To that extent they have a similar relationship to the merchandise as the buyer/consumer – with one significant difference: once the transaction is over the buyer/consumer can leave, while the sales specialists are stuck in their jobs and their boredom forever. What accompanies them is the eternal Muzak in the stores, or, if they are lucky, they might be able to listen to their Walkmans secretly once in a while.

In response to the imperative to give everyone 'a voice', it is now a trend to raise the question 'Who speaks?' in the investigations of oppressed peoples. Versions of this question include 'Can X speak?', 'What does it mean to speak?', 'Who has been silenced?', 'How to speak?', and so forth. These are questions of linguistics and narratology applied to issues of power. In one respect, such questions are based on the assumptions of classical – what some might call 'vulgar' – Marxism: superstructure (speaking) on top, infrastructure (economic privilege) at the bottom. I want to clarify at the outset that I have no problem with vulgar Marxism as such. For all the attacks it receives, the vulgar Marxist refusal to let go of the strategic role of economics in shaping social *vocal* structures continues to yield some of the most powerful (!) results of cultural criticism to date.

But while it effectively raises our consciousness in regard to the privileged positions enjoyed by those who are economically successful, the question 'Who speaks?' tends to remain useless in its capacity to change existing economic power relations. This is because the posing of the question itself is already a form of privilege, mostly affordable for those who can stand apart and view the world with altruistic concern. The question that this question cannot ask, since it is the condition of its own possibility, is the more fundamental one of the inequality between theory – the most sophisticated *speaking* instance, one might say – and the oppressed.

Like anthropologists, medical doctors, zoological researchers, and their like, theorists need 'objects' to advance their careers. The current trend is for theorists in the humanities to discover objects of oppression for the construction of a guilt-tripping discourse along the lines of 'Who speaks?' and thus win for themselves a kind of moral and/or rhetorical victory. Strictly speaking, we are not only living in the age of 'travelling theories' and 'travelling theorists', but also of *portable oppressions* and *portable oppressed objects*. Our technology – including the technology that is the academic conference, the visual and aural aids with which we present our 'objects', the field trips we take for interviewing and for archaeological purposes of every kind – is what makes portability, a result of mechanization whose effects far exceed the personal mobility of speaking humans, an inherent part of 'voices', even though this portability is often ignored in our theorizing.

The problem with the question 'Who speaks?', then, is that it is still trying to understand the world in the form of a coherent narrative grammar, with an identifiable (anthropomorphic) subject for every sentence. The emphasis of the question is always on 'who'. From that it follows that 'Who speaks?' is a rhetorical question, with predetermined answers which, however, cannot change the structure of privilege against which it is aimed. Obviously, it is those who have power who speak – this is the answer this question is meant to provoke.

What if we were to attempt another type of question, one that is not centred on 1) the act of speaking and 2) the quest for a grammatical subject? How might the issue of oppression be approached? This brings us back to the scenario with which I began this essay. In Asian cities like Hong Kong, where oppression is multifarious and contradictory in nature, the question to ask, it seems to me, is rather: what are the forms of surplus? Further, how does surplus inhabit the emotions? What is the relationship between surplus, the emotions, and the portability of oppression? *What plays*? I will lodge these questions in the realm of contemporary Chinese popular music.

THE COLLECTIVE AND THE COMPOSITE

Any attempt to construct a discourse about contemporary Chinese popular music needs to come to terms with the fact that many linguistically determined senses of 'discourse' do not work. One can even say that much of this music is about the inability or the refusal to articulate and to talk. This is not simply because humans are, after all, animals that cannot be defined by their speech alone. It is also because inarticulateness is a way of combating the talking function of the state, the most *articulate* organ that speaks for everyone.

When you listen to the songs by mainland China's young singers such as Cui Jian, you'll find that they are lively, Westernized, and full of the kind of physical, rhythmic quality that we associate with rock music. Cui Jian's music poses a familiar problem about the emotions involved in our listening – the problem of physicality. Adorno has warned us against such physicality: 'The physical aspect of music . . . is not indicative of a natural state – of an essence pure and free of all ideology – but rather it accords with the retrogression of society.' The diatribe of retrogression is a formidable heirloom in the house of popular cultural theories. But treasures of the past are most valuable when they are pawned for more pressing needs of the present. If the physicality of a particular music is indeed retrogressive, we need to ask why.

Contemporary popular Chinese music raises many issues similar to those of rock-and-roll in the West. Foremost among these is that of the music's critical function in regard to the dominant culture. Any consideration of popular cultural forms confronts questions like the following: if such forms provide alternative practical consciousnesses to the dominant ideology, are the modes of subversion and resistance in them not infinitely reabsorbed by the dominant culture? Are such forms capable of maintaining their autonomy? Furthermore, how do we come to grips with such practical consciousnesses when that category indispensable to traditional Marxist social analysis – class – seems no longer adequate in mapping the cultural differentiations that persist beyond class distinctions? Take the example of American popular music. For many critics, the problem posed by this music is how to locate in it a genuinely oppositional function when class distinctions in the United States are more often elided than clearly defined. One might say that it is the impossibility of identifying any distinct class struggle – and with that, the impossibility of legitimizing the notion of class struggle itself for social criticism – that in part accounts for Adorno's reading of American popular music as a massive numbing. The blurring of class distinctions – as reflected in 'easy listening' music – is inordinately discomforting for the sober Frankfurt School critic.

It is, thus, when we focus on what still remains for many as an indispensable category in social criticism – class struggle – that contemporary Chinese popular music, despite its resonances with Western popular music, poses the greatest enigma. China is a 'Third World' nation, and yet where do we find the expression of class struggle in its popular cultural forms these days? Instead of exhibiting the classic 'symptom' of a 'Third World' nation in the form of an obsession with 'class', contemporary Chinese popular culture 'speaks' a different language of 'oppressed' emotions. In the realm of music, we find the conscious adoption of Western models of rhythm, instrumentality, recording, and modes of distribution for the production of discourses which are *non-Western in the sense of an inattentiveness to class struggle*. Many of the motifs that surface in contemporary Chinese popular music, like their counterparts in fiction, television, and film, can be described as individualist and populist – troublesome terms for Western Marxists who at one point looked to Communist China for its utopian aspirations. Such motifs are surfacing at a time when the mainland Chinese official ideology is still firmly 'communist'. Therefore, while the perception of class is undoubtedly present in the subversive emotions of contemporary Chinese popular music, it is present less as an agency for struggle than as the disciplinary cliché of the dominant culture *to be struggled against*. This is precisely because 'class struggle' has been lived through not merely in the form of critical talk but also in everyday experience, as official ideology and national culture. (In mainland China, 'struggle' is a transitive verb, an act one performs directly on another: thus, 'to struggle someone'.)

Speaking of his inability to deal with the directly political, Roland Barthes says (in an interview): 'these days a discourse that is not impassioned can't be heard, quite simply. There's a decibel threshold that must be crossed for discourse to be heard.' Barthes's statement offers us a way of defining 'dominant' culture in musical terms, not only as that which crosses a particular decibel threshold as a rule, but also as that which collectivizes and mobilizes with its particularly loud, indeed deafening, decibel level. If revolution is, among other things, a technology of sound, then its mode of implementation is that of mechanized and institutionalized recording, repetition, and simplification. As early as 1928, the Chinese writer and critic Mao Dun used the technology of sound in a discussion of 'proletarian literature' to indicate the danger of the new political orthodoxy which based its moves on prescriptive slogans: 'I . . . cannot believe that making oneself into a gramophone shouting "This is the way out, come this way!" has any value or can leave one with an easy conscience. It is precisely because I do not wish to stifle my conscience and say things I do not believe . . . that I cannot make the characters in my novelette [*Pursuit*] find a way out.'

The past forty years of Chinese communism can be described as a history in which class struggle is used as the foundation for the official culture of a nation state. The question 'Who speaks?' underlies the most brutal of political exterminations. The 'who' that is identified through arrests, purges, and murders as the landlords, capitalists, and running dogs is replaced with the 'who' that is 'the people'. Entwined with nationalism and patriotism, and strategically deployed by the state, 'the people's speech' that supposedly results from successful class struggle forms the cadences of a sonorous music. One thinks of pieces such as the 'International Song', 'Dongfanghong' (The east is red), 'Meiyou gongchandang meiyou xin zhongguo' (There would be no new China without the Communist Party), and many others that are standardized for official celebrations to invoke patriotic sentiments. Official state culture champions an irresistible grid of emotions that can be defined by Susan Stewart's notion of 'the gigantic', which 'we find . . . at the origin of public and natural history' (Stewart 1984: 71). Gigantic emotions are the emotions of reverence, dedication, discipline, and nostalgia, all of which have to do with the preservation of history as it ought to be remembered. In a Third World nation whose history is characterized by a struggle against imperialism as well as internal turmoil, the history that 'ought to be remembered' is the history of the successful collectivization of the people for the establishment of a national community.

Many examples of contemporary Chinese popular music, however, follow a very different trajectory of sound. Here, the question about popular cultural form is not a question of its ultimate autonomy from the official culture – since that official culture is omnipresent – but how, against the single audible decibel level amplified at random with guns and tanks, popular music strikes its notes of difference.

The *words* of one of Cui Jian's most popular songs, 'Rock and Roll on the Road of the New Long March', allude to one of the founding heroic events of the Chinese communist state, the Long March to Yanan. The last few lines go as follows:

> What should I say, what should I do, in order to be the real me
> How should I play, how should I sing, in order to feel great
> I walk and think of snowy mountains and grasslands
> I walk and sing of Chairman Mao
> Oh! one, two, three, four, five, six, seven.

By recalling the words, I don't mean to imply that the truth of Cui Jian's music lies in its verbal content. Rather, the disjuncturing of words from music points to the significance of the partial – of emotions as partializing rather than totalizing activities which jar with the symphonic effects of official culture.

There is, first of all, the difference between the 'decadence' of the music and the 'seriousness' of the subject matter to which the music alludes. Without knowing the 'language', we can dance to Cui Jian's song as we would to any rock-and-roll tune; once we pay attention to the words, we are in the solemn presence of history, with its insistence on emotional meaning and depth. This is why Cui Jian's music so deeply antagonized the officials in the Chinese state bureaucracy that he was dismissed from his post in the Beijing Symphony Orchestra and prohibited from performing in Beijing a couple of years ago. The official Chinese repudiation of his music is moralistic, aiming to reinforce a kind of obligatory cultural memory in which the founding deeds of communist ancestors are properly honoured instead of being 'played with' – least of all through the music imported from the capitalist West.

But as we look closely at the words themselves, we see that even the words – the medium in which solemn historical emotions can be respectably lodged – partake of the 'play' with tradition. Instead of words with sonorous historical meanings, Cui Jian's lyrics read more like grammatically incoherent utterances. Even though they conjure up 'historical' images, his words speak against literate and literary culture by their choppiness and superficiality. The Long March, one of the nation's best-selling stories since 1949, is a signifier for something vague and distant, and Chairman Mao, a mere name to complete the rhyme. In reacting against Cui Jian's music, the Chinese authorities were therefore not clinging to solemn words as opposed to flippant music but rather to what does not exist either in the words or in the music, namely, an idealized notion of official history. Therefore, while the difference between the words and the music exists in terms of their semiotic orders, the words and music are also mutual renditions of each other insofar as they both dis-member and dis-remember official history. The words, by becoming illiterate, turn into physical sound, thus joining the music in the production of a kind of emotion that is, one might say, 'beyond words'.

By associating emotion with musicality and physicality, I may be reinvoking many of the oldest myths about each of these terms. It is often argued that it is the association of music with emotionality that is responsible for its relegation to the realm of the irrational, the feminine, and the simply pleasurable. At the same time, as we examine a non-Western culture such as the Chinese in the 1990s, we notice a resurfacing of precisely such notions about music and the emotions. The discoursing of the emotions here is therefore at an interesting crossroads. How do we describe the emotions of a music that is resisting the oppressiveness of a communist state culture when that music is relying on mythic paradigms against which theories of music in the West are currently struggling? In other words, how do we theorize the significance of music-as-emotion at a time when it is precisely the reduction of music to emotionality that must also be critiqued?

The problem of emotionality, it would seem, is the problem of surplus in the sense that emotionality is what exceeds the limits by which its functions can be rationally charted. Music, it is well-known, has always been theorized as a pure form, as that which signifies nothing. In the words of Julia Kristeva, for instance, music's semiotics is such that 'while music is a system of *differences*, it is not a system of *signs*. Its constitutive elements do not have a signified.' For Kristeva, music 'takes us to the limit of the system of the sign. Here is a system of differences that is not a system that *means* something, as is the case with most of the structures of verbal language' (Kristeva 1989: 309). Because of this 'empty', trans-linguistic status, music suits the theorizing of surplus the best because it provides a means of suggesting what goes *beyond*. One might say that it is the use of music's power as surplus (as that which cannot be safely contained) for a criticism of the straitjacket of orthodox state ideology that is most evident in the making of Chinese popular music today. And it is this surplus which is commonly recognized as the emotionality of this music.

Of course, no matter how excessive the emotions are, they can always be narrativized and thus attributed a more familiar purpose. Dong Wenhua's 'Xueyan de fengcai' (Blood-stained spirit) is a good example. This compelling song was first sung for Chinese soldiers fighting in the Sino-Vietnamese War of the sixties. A newer version, resung by Wang Hong, has since then appeared and met with tremendous success among the Chinese especially around and after the Tiananmen Massacre of 1989. The song clearly demonstrates the power of music to harmonize populist emotions. To the extent that contemporary Chinese popular music serves the function of patriotic unification, it shares with its many counterparts decidedly conventional and conservative moments as well.

In an account about rock-and-roll, pleasure, and power, Lawrence Grossberg argues that 'the affective economy of rock and roll is neither identical to, nor limited to, the production of pleasure' (Grossberg 1984: 101). If there is an undeniable affinity between emotionality and musicality, we must also add, in Grossberg's words, that 'the affective investment, while asignifying, is not a pristine origin (as the concept of libido might suggest) which precedes the ideological entanglements of the articulation of . . . differences. It is a plane of effects, a circuit of empowerment' (102). What kind of empowerment? Grossberg suggests it in these terms: 'In the rock and roll apparatus, you are not what you don't listen to (which is not necessarily the same as you are what you listen to)' (103).

This statement – 'You are not what you don't listen to' – signifies a view of human labour that is not positive but negative, but the meaning of this negativity is the defiant message that human labour cannot be reduced to a narrowly defined political goal. In contemporary Chinese fiction, the forty years of communist history are increasingly understood to be the alienation of human life *par excellence* through what poses as the 'collective' good. The collective is now perceived as that mysterious, objectified Other against which one must struggle for one's life. Such is the instinctual battle fought by the protagonist in the controversial novel *Half of Man Is Woman* by Zhang Xianliang. Working in a labour camp in the countryside where official instructions are regularly announced through loudspeakers, this man reflects on physical labour in the following terms. Describing hard labour as a 'trance', he distinguishes between labour and the officially assigned 'job': 'A job is for someone else. Labour is your own.' This insistence on the difference between the work that is performed for a public sphere with clearly organized goals and the work that is one's own, is not an insistence on 'privacy' or private property, but rather a resistance against the coercive regimentation of emotions that is carried out under the massive collectivization of human lives in the Chinese communist state. Contrary to orthodox socialist beliefs, the protest made in contemporary Chinese popular culture is that such collectivization of human lives is what produces the deepest alienation ever because it turns human labour into the useful job that we are performing for that 'other' known as the collective, the country, the people, and so forth. In his book *Noise*, Jacques Attali makes a point similar to that of Zhang Xianliang's protagonist when he comments on political economy. What he suggests is that 'use' itself, instead of being the original, inalienable part of labour, is actually the most basic form of alienation, for it is already an exchange for something else – in other words, it is predicated on an other, a collective (Attali 1985: 134).

At a time when we have become rightly alert to issues in the Third World, it is precisely the problem of 'use' that has to be rethought. Something is 'useful', we tend to think, because it serves a collective purpose. While on many occasions I have no objections to this kind of thinking, it is when we deal with the Third World that we have to be particularly careful in resorting to paradigms of the collective as such. Why? Such paradigms produce stereotypical views of members of Third World cultures, who are always seen as representatives driven solely by the cause of vindicating their own cultures. To the extent that such peoples are seen as representatives deprived of their individuality and treated as members of a collective (read 'Third World') culture, I think that the morally supportive narrativizing of the Third World by way of utilitarianism, however sophisticatedly utilitarianism is argued, repeats what it tries to criticize, namely, the subjection of entire peoples to conceptual paradigms of life activities that may have little relevance to their struggles for survival.

In the case of China, I read the paradigm of collectivity as part of the legacy of imperialism imposed upon a 'backward' nation. Like most countries in the post-imperialist era, the alternative to ultimate destruction in the early twentieth century was, for the Chinese, to 'go collective' and produce a 'national culture'. Collectivity as such was therefore never an ethnic empowerment without neuroses, and it is the neuroses which are now surfacing in popular cultural forms like music. At this point in time, the narrative of collectivity does little to explain the kinds of emotions that are played (upon) in contemporary Chinese music, apart from making us notice this music's negativity and, for some, nihilism. These emotions of negativity suggest a deliberate turning away from the collective's thematic burdens through lightheartedness, sarcasm, and physicality.

While such emotions are not capturable in any one medium alone, in this essay I want to emphasize their special connection with music, in part to criticize the privilege enjoyed by visuality in most discussions of postmodern culture. Like popular culture elsewhere, popular culture in East Asia tends to gravitate toward the image. From large-scale concerts by stars to contests for young singers, from the 'self-service' performances of the Japanese-style 'Karaoke' to the equivalents of MTV programmes on Asian television, music is bound up with the fast-pace technologizing of a part of the world which relies on spectacular images for the sustenance of commodity culture. Music is always simply an accompaniment for the visual. Even when fans go to the concerts of their favourite singing stars, one feels that it is the stars' performance on stage, rather than their singing, that the fans have come to see. Music becomes a mere pretext, and singers, instead of performing with the voice, must excel more in their inventiveness with costumes, dancing, and acrobatics.

Although contemporary Chinese popular music can definitely be pursued by way of the spectacle of performance, its interest for me lies elsewhere. While the image marks the body, in music one has to invent a different language of conceptualizing the body, that is, of perceiving its existence without marking and objectifying it as such.

The body's existence is here realized through what Attali calls 'composition', in which the body, instead of always living in an alienated relation to itself through the stockpiling effects of representation, is present for itself and for 'the pleasure outside of meaning, usage and exchange' (137).

For this new presence of the body to emerge, the previous codes in which it was written must be destroyed. We hear in a song like 'Rock and Roll on the Road of the New Long March' the physicality of such a destruction, which comes to us in the form of a composite. Often, 'destructive' songs are made up of a mixture of voice, instruments, and versions of older songs, as well as previous sayings, proverbs, and idioms. Now, we may, if we are intent on reading in what I'd call the Western Marxist way, dismiss this as a form of permissive 'pluralism'. At the same time this composite structure points to a kind of musical mutation, in which no single theme or event is allowed to monopolize the decibel level, so that it is precisely at the dissonance of these musical *parts* – in the form of debris – that the physicality of these songs makes itself heard. Often, therefore, 'destructive' songs do not distinguish themselves from noise. From the actual coarseness of a singer's voice to the insertion of moments of 'clearing the throat', from the disharmonious presence of a different musical background in the same song to the adaptation of familiar folk tunes and themes for a heavily electronic music, what we hear is a mutual 'plugging' between partial noises – between differences. This plugging is at the same time an unplugging of preceding codes in which the fundamental distinction between the human voice and the musical instrument, between rehearsing and actual performing/recording, between traditional and contemporary musical forms, becomes itself a *part of playing*.

An example of such composition in East Asia is the form of entertainment, very popular of late, called 'Karaoke'. 'Karaoke' is the singing, done either in public (Karaoke bars and clubs) or in private (with individual machines for the home), which breaks down the traditional distinction between performing and listening. A person selects a song s/he likes to sing from a collection that accompanies the Karaoke machine, then sings by following the music and the images (with lyrics) on the video screen. What is most interesting is that the common requirements of 'good' performance, such as the excellence of the voice, adequate training and practice, etc., no longer matter. The entire human body, together with its noise-producing capacity, follows the machine's sounds and images. The machine allows one to feel like – to be – an original performer, but one is literally performing as a listener, with all the 'defects' that a performer is not supposed to have. One is liberated from the myth of performance, and does not need to 'know how' in order to sing any more.

In the rest of this essay I will discuss two specific aspects of composition. First, what does it mean for composition to be read, as Attali suggests, 'as an indication of a more general mutation affecting all of the economic and political networks' (135)? Second, what does it mean to say (Attali is here referring to the musical theory of John Cage) that 'music is to be produced . . . everywhere it is possible to produce it, in whatever way it is wished, by anyone who wants to enjoy it' (137)?

LISTENING OTHERWISE

The lyrics of the 'Song of the Dwarf' ('Zhuru zhi ge'), by the Taiwanese
singer Luo Dayou, go as follows:

> We must hold hands, hold hands tight
> Beware of the giants waving at you from far away
> These history-making faces, these figures of the times
> They are always carrying guns for the sake of the people
>
> The road of the Long March is rough
> Forcing their way into Tiananmen, they arrive at Beijing
> The index is alluring in the market of 'struggle'
> Revolutionary doctrines fluctuate like stock prices
> Five thousand years of despotic rule await your cleansing
> Beware:
> The characters who revolt against others are themselves revolted
>   against
> They clutch at their clothes. They need to have face.
> How many lives has Mr. Marx destroyed
> The glorious results of war are woven in our compatriots' blood
> We dedicate the great victory to the people
> Five thousand years of despotic rule await your cleansing
> But who can wash the blood on your hands
>
> We must hold hands, hold hands tight
> Beware of the smile on the face of the dwarf who is approaching
> These faces behind [him], these great figures –
> They are always carrying guns for the sake of the people.

This song, once again, demonstrates that separation between musicality and verbality I mentioned as characteristic of many other songs. In
the remarkable lines, 'the index is alluring in the market of "struggle"/
Revolutionary doctrines fluctuate like stock prices', the mockery of the
communist state is achieved by a clever combination of the languages of
revolution and the market economy, or rather, by a rewriting of revolution in terms of the market economy, effecting a demolition of the
altruistic claims made by the practitioners of the Marxist ideology, which
is included as part of the 5000-year-old Chinese despotic tradition.

The clashing of these two usually incompatible languages, revolution and the market, suggests a fundamental need to revamp the bases
for both. Their clashing reveals the grounding of emotions not in

'nature' but in technology. Because of the ineluctability of technology, what clash are also the thematics of the 'Third World' and the 'First World'. Technology is that collectivized goal to which East Asian cultures, as part of the non-Western world that survives in the backwash of imperialism, have no choice but to adopt. In the case of mainland China, the successful technologizing of an entire nation through the regimentation of life activities in collective form was accomplished through the communist revolution. In other, non-communist Chinese communities in East Asia, notably Taiwan, Hong Kong, and Singapore, the success of technology is evident in sophisticated modes of living, inseparable from the production and consumption of commodities. The co-presence of these two meanings of technology – the collectivized and the commodified – constitutes a unique type of ethnicity in ways that exceed the orthodox paradigms of demarcating First World and Third World economic and political networks.

Contrary to the paradigms of struggle and protest – the cultural stereotypes that are being laid across Third World peoples with uniformity, soliciting them into a *coded* narrative whether or not they are willing to participate in it – the emotions that emerge here imply a new writing of ethnicity. This writing cannot consider the 'ethnic' person simply in the role of the oppressed whom we in the West, armed with questions such as 'Who speaks?', attempt to 'liberate' by giving a voice, a voice that amounts to a kind of waged labour (the permit to participate in the working world with 'choice' and 'freedom'). The presence of technology means that the deeply historical perception of the unpredictable but oppressive nature of official culture is here conveyed through instruments that are accomplices as well as resisters to that culture. Precisely because historical injustice is the very ground on which the struggle for survival takes place, such injustice is often alluded to indirectly rather than confronted directly. The music of Cui Jian and Luo Dayou is as semantically loaded with the feelings of oppression as it is electronically saturated, but the feelings of oppression impinge upon us as an inerasable, *because* invisible, referent, like a language with an insistent syntax but no obvious semiotics/signs with meanings. Official Chinese culture, on the other hand, does not only suppress such *emotions* in order to uphold the glorious version of history; as usual, it would also criticize the *electronics* in the name of protecting the integrity of Chinese culture against excessive Westernization. Operating under the domination of a patriotic rhetoric that cannot be turned off, the counter-discourse we find in many popular songs is thus deliberately inarticulate, by way of a music that is lighthearted, decadent, playing to the rhythms of expensive lifestyles in forgetfulness of the wretched of the earth. The forms of nihilism are used consciously for enervation, producing moments of positivity that restructure relations to the political state.

On the streets of Hong Kong, Taipei, and other East Asian cities, as one strolls past shop windows among crowds, in restaurants, book-stores, produce markets, streetside stalls, Chinese herbal teashops – in all such public places, it is not uncommon to hear this kind of popular music being played on the side for entertainment by the people tending the stores. What the music contributes to the public sphere is a kind of 'easy', non-verbal culture that conditions passers-by, who nonetheless never focus on it seriously. Unlike the overwhelming presence of com-modified images, popular music leads a life on the side, as a kind of distraction made possible by technology, a distraction that, moreover, is not visible.

Such listening on the streets is not merely the substitution of one kind of attention for another, the aural for the visual. Instead, because it is always played on the side, as we are doing other things, it is what I would call a 'listening otherwise'. Listening otherwise changes the meaning of music from its traditional association with a plenitude that escapes concrete articulation on account of its infinity, to that of a part object whose field is always elsewhere. At the same time, this part object is surplus; it is not reducible or graspable in the form of an externalized image. Its *excessive partiality* requires a different kind of theorizing.

'HEAR THERE AND EVERYWHERE': MUSIC MINIATURIZED

What we need, in other words, is a history of listening – a history of how listening and how the emotions that are involved in listening change with the apparatuses that make listening possible. Traditionally, listen-ing is, as a rule, public. For a piece of music to be heard – even under the most private circumstances – a certain public accessibility can always be assumed. Such public accessibility continues even when music becomes portable with the transistor radio and the portable cassette tape player. With the invention of headphones, on the other hand, listening enters an era of interiorization whose effect of 'privacy' is made possible by the thoroughly mechanized nature of its operation. But listening through headphones is still attached to relatively large pieces of machinery, which tend to remain stationary. (We use them when we don't want to disturb others occupying the same space.)

The form of listening that is a decisive break from the past is that made possible by the Walkman. One critic describes the Walkman this way: 'that neat little object . . . a pregnant zero, . . . the unobtrusive link in an urban strategy, a semiotic shifter, the crucial digit in a particular organization of sense' (Chambers 1990: 1). Even though the popular songs I am discussing may not be consciously intended for playing on the Walkman alone, what I would argue is that the conception of the Walkman is already written into these songs. The Walkman is implied in their composite mode of making, which corresponds to a composite mode of listening that involves multiple entries and exits, multiple turnings-on and turnings-off. If music is a kind of storage place for the emotions generated by cultural conflicts and struggles, then we can, with the new listening technology, talk about the production of such conflicts and struggles *on the human body* at the press of a button. In the age of the Walkman (or its more sophisticated affiliate, the Discman), the emotions have become portable.

In contrast to the gramophone or loudspeaker, without which the 'gigantic' history of the public would not have been possible, the Walkman ushers in the history of a miniaturized music. But the notion of miniature is useful here only indirectly, as a way to point to the need for us to invent another language that would more appropriately describe the partiality of music. Susan Stewart's study of the narratives of the miniature provides us with the necessary assistance. Among the most important characteristics of the miniature, according to Stewart, is that it establishes a correspondence with the things of which it is a miniature. The miniature is thus unimaginable without visuality: 'the miniature is a cultural product, the product of an eye performing certain operations, manipulating, and attending in certain ways to, the physical world' (Stewart 1984: 55). The miniature is the labour of multiplying and intensifying significance microscopically: 'That the world of things can open itself to reveal a secret life – indeed, to reveal a set of actions and hence a narrativity and history outside the given field of perception – is a constant daydream that the miniature presents. This is the daydream of the microscope: the daydream of life inside life, of significance multiplied infinitely *within* significance' (54; emphasis in original).

Insofar as Walkman music is shrunken music, music reduced to the size of the little portable machine that produces it, it is a kind of miniature. But the most important feature of music's miniaturization does not lie in the smallness of the equipment which generates it. Rather, it lies in the *revolution in listening* engendered by the equipment: while the music is hidden from others because it is compacted, this hiddenness is precisely what allows me to hear it full blast. The 'miniaturizing' that does not produce a visible body – however small – that corresponds with 'reality' leads to a certain freedom. This is the freedom to be deaf to the loudspeakers of history. We do not return to individualized or privatized emotions when we use the Walkman: rather the Walkman's artificiality makes us aware of the impending presence of the collective, which summons us with the infallibility of a sleepwalker. What the Walkman provides is the possibility of a barrier, a blockage between 'me' and the world, so that, as in moments of undisturbed sleep, I can disappear as a listener playing music. The Walkman allows me, in other words, to be missing – to be a missing part of history, to which I say: 'I am not there, not where you collect me.' In the Walkman, the hiding place for the music-operator, we find the music that, to borrow Attali's phrase, 'is to be produced everywhere it is possible to produce it . . . by anyone who wants to enjoy it'. Here, Barthes's statement that 'Politics is not necessarily just talking, it can also be listening' takes on a new meaning. For listening is not, as Adorno describes popular music in America, 'a training course in . . . passivity'; rather it is a 'silent' sabotage of the technology of collectivization with its own instruments.

As the machine of what we might call 'automatic playing', the Walkman offers a means of self-production in an age when any emphasis on individualist positions amounts to a scandal. What is scandalous is that self-production is now openly autistic. The autism of the Walkman listener irritates onlookers precisely because the onlookers find themselves reduced to the activity of looking alone. For once, voyeurism yields no secrets: one can look all one wants and still nothing is to be seen. The sight of the Walkman listener, much like the sight of some of our most brilliant scientists, artists, and theorists, is one that we cannot enter even with the most piercing of glances. (The Walkman allows us for the first time to realize that our 'geniuses' have always lived with earphones on.) Critics of the Walkman, like critics of mass culture in general, are condemned to a position of exteriority, from which all kinds of ineffectual moralistic attacks are fired. This position of exteriority amounts to the charge: 'Look at yourself! Look how stupid you look!' But the autistic sight is the one which is free of the responsibility to look, observe, and judge. Its existence does not depend on looking, especially not on looking at oneself.

The music operator's activity frankly reveals that the 'collective' is not necessarily an 'other' to be idealized from afar, but a mundane, mechanical, portable *part* of ourselves which can be tucked away in our pocket and called up at will. This 'self' production through the collective requires not so much slogans as it does AA batteries, and it takes place in the midst of other, perhaps equally insignificant, activities. It substitutes listening for the writing of music and demolishes the myth of creativity through a composite discoursing of the emotions. The noises and voices of production become ingredients of self-making. Deprived of their images and their bodily presence in on-stage performances, even singers – 'stars' and 'icons' – become part of the technologically exteriorized 'inner speech' of the listener. As such, the emotions of music are dehydrated, condensed, and encapsulated, so that they can be carried from place to place and played instantly – at 'self-service'.

NOTE

A revised version of this article appears in Rey Chow, *Writing Diaspora: Tactics of Intervention in Contemporary Cultural Studies* (Bloomington, Ind.: Indiana University Press, forthcoming).

Part IX *Media*

26 Ien Ang

Dallas *and the ideology of mass culture*

EDITOR'S INTRODUCTION

This is an edited version of a chapter of Ien Ang's book, *Watching Dallas*, based on work carried out in Holland. For her research, Ien Ang used an unusual ethnographic technique. She placed advertisements in the daily papers and analysed letters written to her in reply. 'I like watching *Dallas* but often get odd reactions,' the ad began. In this section of her book, she examines the function of the 'ideology of mass culture' for those who responded to her. By 'ideology of mass culture' she means the negative image commonly given to so-called mass culture – especially in Europe.

What she found was rather unexpected. First, the negative view of mass culture was generally accepted by all three groups she singles out: *Dallas*-haters, *Dallas*-lovers, and 'ironists'. Second, it was the *Dallas*-lovers who had the most complex and carefully negotiated relation both to this ideology and to the programme. Amongst them she found a more subtle ambivalence than among those who watched *Dallas* ironically.

Ang's study takes ideology-critique out of the hands of the theorists to examine its strategical use for viewers 'out there'. It can be read alongside a different kind of ethnographic research – as carried out by Buckingham, Hobson, and Tulloch for instance – in which television viewing is not enquired into at the level of viewer's discourse but as situated in domestic space and organized within the dynamics of domestic relations and, therefore, as an element of individual lifestyles.

Further reading: Ang 1985; Buckingham 1987; Hobson 1982; Katz and Liebes 1985; Morley 1980; Newcombe 1986; Tulloch 1990; Webster 1988.

S.D.

HATING *DALLAS*

The letters of those who dislike *Dallas* are characterized not only by a positive and self-assured tone, but also by a large measure of fury, annoyance and indignation. These people seem not just to dislike *Dallas*: they get terribly worked up by it. Many of them also make considerable use of strong language in judging the programme, as though to emphasize yet again the logic of their hatred: 'worthless rubbish', 'a stupid serial', 'the biggest nonsense', 'eyewash', 'dreadful', 'annoying', 'ghastly', 'daft', 'ridiculous', 'disgusting', etc.

But these letter-writers don't just resort to emotional expressions of anger and frustration. They often go to some length to supply a rational explanation for their dislike. For example, some justify their aversion by denouncing the *Dallas* story as 'stereotypical', especially where the representation of women is concerned.

> My personal opinion of *Dallas* is that I find it a horribly cheap serial. I do admire it, the way they can work it all out every time, how they can set up the most crazy dramas in a series like that. Every instalment the family members all go bawling on non-stop (only the women, of course, men aren't allowed to cry, apparently). (Letter 36)

Such condemnations levelled at the content of *Dallas* can also be combined with disapproval of the presumed insincere intentions of the producers. *Dallas* is a kind of fraud, these letter-writers find, because it is a commercial product:

> It really makes me more and more angry. The aim is simply to rake in money, loads of money. And people try to do that by means of all these things – sex, beautiful people, wealth. And you always have people who fall for it. To get high viewing figures. (Letter 35)

But the most comprehensive and total condemnation of *Dallas* is expressed in this letter extract:

> My opinion of *Dallas*? Well, I'd be glad to give it to you: WORTHLESS RUBBISH. I find it a typical American programme, simple and commercial, role-affirming, deceitful. The thing so many American programmes revolve around is money and sensation. Money never seems to be a problem. Everyone is living in luxury, has fantastic cars and loads of drink. The stories themselves are mostly not very

important. You never have to think for a moment: they think for you. (Letter 31)

All these condemnations have the same function. Categories like 'stereotypical' and 'commercial' are not only used in the descriptive sense, but invested with a moral status and emotional charge: they serve as explanations for the writers' dislike of *Dallas*. These explanations sound extremely convincing. But, we might ask, are they really as adequate and balanced as they appear at first sight?

It is not my aim here to cast doubt on the sincerity of the feminist and anticapitalist concerns of these letter-writers. But what can be questioned is whether it is really so logical to connect the experience of displeasure, which must in the first instance be an emotional reaction to watching *Dallas*, so directly with a rationalistic evaluation of it as a cultural product. Even if someone does like watching it, he or she can be aware of the 'commercial' or 'stereotypical' character of the programme. Thus, enjoying *Dallas* does not preclude a political or moral condemnation of its production context or its ideological content. The fact that those who hate the serial do make such a connection indicates that categories like 'commercial' and 'stereotypical' exercise a certain attraction, because using them gives the letter-writers a feeling of security. These categories enable them to legitimize their dislike, make it credible and totally comprehensible. They seem to give these letter-writers the conviction that they are right and allow them an uninhibited display of anger.

And so these categories form a central component of an ideological discourse in which the social significance of forms of popular culture is determined in a particular way. This is the ideology of mass culture. In order to understand the self-confidence of those who hate *Dallas* we need now to investigate this ideology more closely.

THE IDEOLOGY OF MASS CULTURE

Dallas is not only widely watched, but also widely discussed: a lot is said and written about the programme. These public discourses about *Dallas* provide a framework within which answers can be given to questions such as: what must I think about such a television serial? What arguments can I use to make my opinion plausible? How must I react to people who hold a different opinion? Not all existing discourses, however, are equally capable of formulating satisfactory answers to such questions. Some discourses are more prestigious than others, they sound more logical or convincing, and are more successful in determining the social image of TV programmes like *Dallas*.

In many European countries nowadays there is an official aversion to American television series: they are regarded as a threat to one's own, national culture and as an undermining of high-principled cultural values in general. Against this ideological background, professional intellectuals (television critics, social scientists, politicians) put a lot of energy into creating a consistent and elaborated 'theory' on American television series – a theory which provides a 'scientific' cloak for the aversion. A representative and revealing formulation of this theory comes from the sociology of mass communications:

> The most important characteristic of a TV series is that the film content is dependent on its economic marketability. Aiming at a very broad market means that the content must be reduced to universally consumable motifs. This applies in particular to American series which in the United States serve as 'commercial' packaging. [. . .] The commercial character of the TV series hinders the introduction of concrete social and political attitudes, because they might provoke controversies in various groups. [. . .] The film is given a 'universal appeal' character; it deals with familiar, broadly institutionalized ingredients. The necessary ingredients of a successful series include romantic love [. . .] simple patterns of good and evil and the building-up of suspense, climax and relief. [. . .] This reduction to the normal human aspects of existence means that the content is recognizable for a wider audience, but it offers a stereotypical and schematized image of reality.

As a description of the working method of the commercial, American television industry this account certainly offers some adequate insights, although one might wonder whether such a direct connection exists between the economic conditions under which TV series are produced and their aesthetic and narrative structures. Such crude economic determinism is often criticized in media studies circles. Nevertheless, the core of this theory tends to be accepted as correct. What interests us here, however, is not the correctness or adequacy of the theory itself, but the way in which some of its elements carry over into the way in which American TV series are evaluated. A theory fulfils an ideological function if it fulfils an *emotional* function in people's heads, to which the assertions contained in the theory are subordinated.[1]

Emotionally, then, the above-described theory on American TV series leads to their total rejection and condemnation. They become 'bad objects'. These then are the contours of what I would like to call the 'ideology of mass culture'. In this ideology some cultural forms – mostly very popular cultural products and practices cast in an American mould – are *tout court* labelled 'bad mass culture'. 'Mass culture' is a denigrating term, which arouses definitely negative associations. In opposition to 'bad mass culture' implicitly or explicitly something like 'good culture' is set up.

The emotional attraction of the ideology of mass culture, however, is not confined to the select circle of professional intellectuals. As we have seen, the letter-writers who dislike *Dallas* also all too easily reach for its categories. Apparently the ideology of mass culture has such a monopoly on the judging of a phenomenon like *Dallas* that it supplies ready-made conceptions, as it were, which sound self-evident and can be used without any strain or hesitation. The dominance of the ideology of mass culture apparently even extends to the common-sense of every-day thinking: for ordinary people too it appears to offer a credible framework of interpretation for judging cultural forms like *Dallas*.

The ideology of mass culture therefore not only offers a (negative) label for the programme itself, but also serves as a mould for the way in which a large number of haters of *Dallas* account for their displeasure. To put it briefly, their reasoning boils down to this: '*Dallas* is obviously bad because it's mass culture, and that's why I dislike it.' And so the ideology of mass culture fulfils a comforting and reassuring role: it makes a search for more detailed and personal explanations super-fluous, because it provides a finished explanatory model that convinces, sounds logical and radiates legitimacy.

Hating *Dallas* need not, however, necessarily coincide with sub-scribing to the ideology of mass culture. Other factors may be respon-sible for the fact that one is not attracted to the television serial itself. The letters from those who dislike it, however, are so structured by the schemas of this ideology that they offer us little insight into the way in which they watch the programme, which meanings they attach to it, etc. Hence, despite the confidence of their expressed opinions, it remains even more puzzling why some letter-writers don't like *Dallas* than why its fans do.

THE IRONICAL VIEWING ATTITUDE

But not all letter-writers who have adopted the ideology of mass culture seem to dislike *Dallas*. On the contrary, some of them state explicitly that they are fond of it, while at the same time employing the norms and judgements the ideology prescribes. How is this possible? It seems somewhat contradictory to regard *Dallas* as a 'bad object' on the one hand, but on the other to experience pleasure in watching it. But if we read the relevant letters carefully, it emerges that this apparent contradiction is resolved in an ingenious manner. How? Let me give an example.

> *Dallas*. . . . God, don't talk to me about it. I'm just hooked on it! But you wouldn't believe the number of people who say to me, 'Oh, I thought you were against capitalism?' I am, but *Dallas* is just so tremendously exaggerated, it has nothing to do with capitalists any more, it's just sheer artistry to make up such nonsense. (Letter 25)

It is clear how this letter-writer 'solves' the contradiction between the moral of the ideology of mass culture and experiencing pleasure in *Dallas*: with mockery and irony. One group of letter-writers seems to make *Dallas* the object of derision. They assume an ironic stance when watching it, an attitude they refer to in their letters at length and with obvious pleasure. An important element of this ironical viewing attitude is the supplying of commentary. According to Michel Foucault commentary is a type of discourse that has the aim of dominating the object: by supplying commentary to something one affirms a superior relation to that object. Thus *Dallas* too is 'dominated' by the mocking commentary of these viewers, 'put in the corner'.

The ironic viewing attitude makes a reconciliation possible between the rules of the ideology of mass culture ('I must find *Dallas* bad') and the experiencing of pleasure ('I find *Dallas* amusing *because* it's so bad'). As these letter-writers put it:

> My feelings are mostly very superior, such as: what a lot of idiots. And I can laugh at it. Often too I find it oversentimental. One thing in its favour: It's never dull. (Letter 29)

> As you may notice I watch it a lot, and (you may find this sounds a bit big-headed) I find it amusing precisely because it's so ghastly (if you know what I mean). (Letter 36)

By ironizing commentary a distance is created from the reality represented in *Dallas*. In this way those who subscribe to the norms of the ideology of mass culture can like *Dallas*. Irony then comes to lead its own life and this viewing attitude becomes a necessary condition for experiencing pleasure in the first place. Thus the conflict disappears between the norms of the ideology of mass culture and liking *Dallas*: ironizing, i.e. creating a distance between oneself and *Dallas* as 'bad object', *is* the way in which one likes *Dallas*. This is, for example, the case for the 'ardent *Dallas* watchers' I quoted above. But the viewing attitude of the following letter-writer is also determined to a large degree by the exorcizing power of the ironic commentary:

> Why does a person watch *Dallas* and in my case, why does a serious, intelligent feminist like watching *Dallas*? [. . .] My leisure reading consists 90 per cent of feminist books, but when I'm watching *Dallas* with my girl friend and Pamela comes down the stairs wearing a low-necked dress, then we shout wildly: just look at that slut, the way she prances around, she ought to be called Prancela. Bobby is a decent chap, like my eldest brother, and Jock is like my father, so I can hate them intensely too. I can stand Sue Ellen, neurotic as she is, and J.R. laughs just like Wiegel [Dutch right-wing politician] and that has me jumping with rage. Lucy is too beautiful to be true and I don't find Miss Ellie all that marvellous since her breast operation. [. . .] I like to let it all hang out, a sort of group therapy, mostly together with friends. (Letter 24)

The ironic viewing attitude places this viewer in a position to get the better, in a sense, of *Dallas*, to be above it. And in this way, as a 'serious, intelligent feminist', she can allow herself to experience pleasure in *Dallas*. She says in fact: 'Of course *Dallas* is mass culture and therefore bad, but precisely because I am so well aware of that I can really enjoy watching it and poke fun at it.'

Just as for the letter-writers who dislike *Dallas*, for these ironizing fans the ideology of mass culture has become common sense: for them too it is self-evident that *Dallas* is 'bad mass culture'. But the very weapon of irony makes it unnecessary for them to suppress the pleasure that watching *Dallas* can nevertheless arouse; irony enables them to enjoy it without suffering pangs of conscience. The dismissive norms of the ideology of mass culture are smoothly integrated in the ironic viewing attitude.

We have seen earlier that those who hate *Dallas* have little difficulty in giving reasons for their dislike: they can always draw on the instant judgements of the ideology of mass culture. However, the ironic fans are in a certain sense on even stronger ground. While liking *Dallas* ironically leads to euphoria and merriment, as we have seen, disliking *Dallas* is accompanied by anger and annoyance. And these are not nice feelings. Hence those who dislike *Dallas* run the risk of a conflict of feelings if, *in spite of this*, they cannot escape its seduction, i.e. if they continue to watch. This can lead to almost tragi-comic ups and downs, as this letter-writer relates:

> When the serial started I disliked it intensely. [. . .] I myself started watching the serial because I spent a lot of time in the home of people, the husband of whom was from America and the serial made him think a lot about home. So I watched a few episodes because I was forced to in a way and that's now for me the only reason I watch it. I just want to see how it turns out. The fact is that every time the disasters overlap, so I'm sitting in front of the box and now I never miss a single episode. Fortunately it's on late in the evening so before that I can do some sport or something. I must also add that in every episode there are some things that really annoy me. (Letter 38)

So disliking *Dallas* is certainly not an experience without its ambivalences!

LOVING *DALLAS*

But what about those who 'really' like *Dallas*? How do they relate to the ideology of mass culture?

Ideologies organize not only the ideas and images people make of reality, they also enable people to form an image of themselves and thus to occupy a position in the world. Through ideologies people acquire an identity, they become subjects with their own convictions, their own will, their own preferences. So, an individual living in the ideology of mass culture may qualify him or herself as, for example, 'a person of taste', 'a cultural expert' or 'someone who is not seduced by the cheap tricks of the commercial culture industry'. In addition to an image of oneself, however, an ideology also offers an image of others. Not only does one's own identity take on form in this way, but the ideology serves also to outline the identity of other people. Thus a dividing line is drawn by the ideology of mass culture between the 'person of taste', the 'cultural expert', etc. and those who, according to this ideology, are not such. Or to be more specific, between those who do recognize *Dallas* as 'bad mass culture' and those who do not.

One *Dallas*-hater thus tries to distance herself from those who like *Dallas*:

> I don't understand either why so many people watch it, as there are lots of people who find it a serious matter if they have to miss a week. At school you really notice it when you turn up on Wednesday morning then it's, 'Did you see *Dallas*, wasn't it fabulous?' Now and then I get really annoyed, because I find it just a waste of time watching it. [. . .] Then you hear them saying that they had tears in their eyes when something happened to someone in the film, and I just can't understand it. At home they usually turn it on too, but then I always go off to bed. (Letter 33)

She outlines the identity of the others, those who like *Dallas*, in a negative way, and with a particular degree of confidence: lovers of *Dallas* are almost declared idiots by this letter-writer! The ideology of mass culture therefore definitely does not offer a flattering picture of those who like *Dallas*. They are presented as the opposite of 'persons of taste', 'cultural experts' or 'people who are not seduced by the cheap tricks of the commercial culture industry'. How do lovers of *Dallas* react to this? Do they know that this negative image of them exists and does it worry them at all?

In the small advertisement which the letter-writers replied to, I included the following clause: 'I like watching the TV serial *Dallas* but often get odd reactions to it.' It seems to me that the phrase 'odd reactions' is vague at the very least: from the context of the advertisement there is no way of knowing what I meant. Yet various lovers of *Dallas* go explicitly into this clause in their letters: the words 'odd reactions' seem sufficient to effect an 'Aha!' experience in some fans.

> I have the same 'problem' as you! When I let drop in front of my fellow students (political science) that I do my utmost to be able to watch *Dallas* on Tuesday evenings, they look incredulous. (Letter 19)

> It always hits me too that people react 'oddly' when you say you like watching *Dallas*. I think everyone I know watches it but some of my friends get very worked up over this serial and even go on about the

dangerous effects on the average TV viewer. I really don't know
what I should think of this. (Letter 22)

These extracts lead one to suspect that the rules and judgements of the
ideology of mass culture are not unknown to *Dallas* fans. What is more,
they too seem to respond to this ideology. But they tend to do so in a
completely different way from those who hate *Dallas* or who love it
ironically. 'Really' loving *Dallas* (without irony) would seem to involve a
strained attitude toward the norms of the ideology of mass culture. And
it is this strained relationship which the fans have to try to resolve.

In contrast to the haters and ironic lovers, who, as we have seen,
express their attitude to the ideology of mass culture in a rather uniform
and unconflicting way, the 'real' fans use very divergent strategies to
come to terms with its norms. One strategy is to take over and internalize the judgements of the ideology of mass culture itself:

> I just wanted to react to your advertisement concerning *Dallas*. I
> myself enjoy *Dallas* and the tears roll down when something tragic
> happens in it (in nearly every episode, that is). In my circle too
> people react dismissively to it, they find it a typical commercial
> programme far beneath their standards. I find you can relax best
> with a programme like this, although you just have to keep your eye
> on the kind of influence such a programme can have, it is role-
> confirming, 'class-confirming', etc., etc. And it's useful too if you
> think what kind of cheap sentiment really does get to you. (Letter
> 14)

There is a remarkable about-face in this letter. Instead of stating why she
likes *Dallas* so much (which was the question I had put in my advertisement), the letter-writer confines herself to reiterating a reasoning which
derives from the ideology of mass culture in answer to the 'dismissive
reactions' of her milieu. She doesn't adopt an independent attitude
towards this ideology but merely takes over its morals. But whom is she
addressing with these morals? Herself? Me (she knows from my advertisement that I like watching *Dallas*)? All *Dallas* fans? It is as though she
wants to defend the fact that she enjoys *Dallas* by showing that she is in
fact aware of its 'dangers' and 'tricks': aware, in other words, that *Dallas*
is 'bad mass culture'.

But a protective strategy can also be employed by actually challenging the ideology of mass culture.

> I am replying to your advertisement as I would like to speak my

> mind about *Dallas*. I've noticed too that you get funny reactions
> when you like watching *Dallas* (and I like watching it). Many people
> find it worthless or without substance. But I think it does have
> substance. Just think of the saying: 'Money can't buy happiness',
> you can certainly trace that in *Dallas*. (Letter 13)

But what has been said here against the ideology of mass culture
remains caught within the categories of that ideology. Against the
opinion 'no substance' (= 'bad') is placed the alternative opinion 'does
have substance' (= 'good'); the category 'substance' (and thus the
difference 'good/bad') is therefore upheld. This letter-writer 'negotiates'
as it were within the discursive space created by the ideology of mass
culture, she does not situate herself outside it and does not speak from
an opposing ideological position.

But why do these *Dallas* lovers feel the need to defend themselves
against the ideology of mass culture? They obviously feel under attack.
Obviously they can't get round its norms and judgements, but must
stand out against them in order to be able to like *Dallas* and not to have
to disavow that pleasure. But it is never pleasant to be manoeuvred into
a defensive position: it shows weakness. To have to defend oneself is
nearly always coupled with a feeling of unease.

> You are right in saying that you often get these strange reactions.
> Such as 'So you like watching cheap mass entertainment, eh?' Yes, I
> watch it and I'm not ashamed of it. But I do try to defend my
> motivation tooth and nail. (Letter 7)

'Tooth and nail'; the pent-up intensity of this expression reveals the
strong desire of this letter-writer to defend herself and to justify herself,
in spite of her contention that she 'is not ashamed of it'.

Finally, yet another defence mechanism against the ideology of
mass culture is possible. That is, strangely enough, irony again. But in
this case irony is not integrated so unproblematically in the experience
of watching *Dallas* as in the case of the ironic fans we encountered
earlier. On the contrary, here irony is an expression of a conflicting
viewing experience. One letter-writer has put this psychological conflict
clearly into words. In her account there is an uncomfortable mixture of
'really' liking *Dallas* and an ironic viewing attitude:

> Just like you I often get odd reactions when I say that at the moment
> *Dallas* is my favourite TV programme. [. . .] I get carried along
> intensely with what is happening on TV. I find most figures in the

serial horrible, except Miss Ellie. The worst thing I find is how they treat one another. I also find them particularly ugly. Jock because he doesn't have an aesthetically justifiable head, Pamela because she has to seem so smart, I find that 'common'. I can't stand it that everyone (in the serial) finds her sexy when she looks like Dolly Parton with those breasts. They are a sad lot, so honest, stinking rich, they want to seem perfect but (fortunately for us!) none of them is perfect (even Miss Ellie has breast cancer, and that cowboy Ray, whom I've really fallen for, is always running into trouble). (Letter 23)

The distance from the *Dallas* characters is great for this letter-writer – witness the annihilating judgement that she passes so ironically on them. Nevertheless her account is imbued with a kind of intimacy which betrays a great involvement in the serial ('I get carried along intensely' . . ., 'I can't stand it' . . ., 'whom I've really fallen for'). The detached irony on the one hand and the intimate involvement on the other appear difficult to reconcile. So it emerges from further on in her letter that irony gains the upper hand when watching *Dallas* is a social occasion:

I notice that I use *Dallas* as a peg for thinking about what I find good and bad in my relations with others. I notice this in particular *when I'm watching with a group of people* because then we usually can't keep our mouths shut; we shout disgraceful! and bastard! and bitch! (sorry, but emotions really run high!). We also sometimes try to get an idea of how the Ewings are all doing. Sue Ellen has postnatal depression and that's why she is so against her baby. Pamela is actually very nice and suffers because of Sue Ellen's jealousy. J.R. is just a big scaredy-cat, you can see that from that uncertain little laugh of his. (Letter 23, my italics)

The ironic commentaries are presented here as a *social* practice. This is confirmed by the sudden transition from the use of 'I' to 'we' in this extract. Is it perhaps true to say that the need to emphasize an ironic attitude to viewing, thereby creating a distance from *Dallas*, is aroused in this letter-writer by the social control emanating from an ideological climate in which 'really' liking the programme is almost taboo? In any case intimacy returns further on in the letter as soon as she is talking again in terms of 'I'. And the irony then disappears into the background.

Actually they are all a bit stupid. And oversensational. Affected and genuinely American (money-appearance-relationship-maniacs –

family and nation! etc.). I know all this very well. And yet. . . . The
Ewings go through a lot more than I do. They seem to have a richer
emotional life. Everyone knows them in Dallas. Sometimes they run
into trouble, but they have a beautiful house and anything else they
might want. I find it pleasant to watch. I do realize their ideals of
beauty. I look at how their hair is done. I'm very impressed by their
brilliant dialogues. Why can't I ever think what to say in a crisis?
(Letter 23)

Real love and irony – both determine the way in which this letter-writer
relates to *Dallas*. It is clear that they are difficult to reconcile: real love
involves identification, whereas irony creates distance. This ambivalent
attitude to *Dallas* seems to stem from the fact that on the one hand she
accepts the correctness of the ideology of mass culture (at least in a
social context), but on the other hand 'really' likes *Dallas* – which is
against the rules of this ideology. The irony lies here then in the 'social
surface'; it functions, in contrast to the ironizing lovers, for whom irony
is interwoven with the way in which they experience pleasure in *Dallas*,
as a sort of screen for 'real' love. In other words, irony is here a defence
mechanism with which this letter-writer tries to fulfil the social norms
set by the ideology of mass culture, while secretly she 'really' likes
Dallas.

We can draw two conclusions from these examples. First, the fans
quoted seem spontaneously, of their own free will, to take the ideology
of mass culture into account: they come into contact with it and cannot
apparently avoid it. Its norms and prescriptions exert pressure on them,
so that they feel the necessity to defend themselves against it. Second, it
emerges from their letters that they use a very wide variety of defence
strategies: one tries simply to internalize the ideology of mass culture,
another tries to negotiate within its discursive framework, and yet
another uses surface irony. And so it would appear that there is not one
obvious defence strategy *Dallas* fans can use, that there is no clear-cut
ideological alternative which can be employed against the ideology of
mass culture – at least no alternative that offsets the latter in power of
conviction and coherence. And so the letter-writers take refuge in various discursive strategies, none of which, however, is as well worked out
and systematic as the discourses of the ideology of mass culture.
Fragmentary as they are, these strategies are therefore much more liable
to contradictions. In short, these fans do not seem to be able to take up
an effective ideological position – an identity – from which they can say

in a positive way and independently of the ideology of mass culture: 'I like *Dallas* because . . .'.

But this weak position the fans are in, this lack of a positive ideological basis for legitimizing their love of *Dallas*, has tiresome consequences. Whereas those who hate the programme can present their 'opponents' as, for example, 'cultural barbarians', 'people with no taste' or 'people who let themselves be led astray by the tricks of the commercial culture industry' (thus implying that they themselves are *not*), the fans do not have such a favourable representation to hand. They are not in a position to hit back by forming in their turn an equally negative image of those who dislike *Dallas*; they can only offer resistance to the negative identities that *others* ascribe to them.

As one of the letter-writers says: 'I personally find it terrible when I hear people saying they don't like *Dallas*' (Letter 2). As finding it 'terrible' is her only word of defence – apparently nothing else occurred to her – isn't that a form of capitulation?

THE IDEOLOGY OF POPULISM

It is wrong, however, to pretend that the ideology of mass culture exercises dictatorial powers. The discourses of this ideology are very important, culturally legitimized organizers of the way in which the social meaning of *Dallas* is constructed, but alternative discourses do exist which offer alternative points of identification for lovers of *Dallas*.

Not all letter-writers who like *Dallas* seem to be troubled by the compelling judgements produced by the ideology of mass culture. Some of them just seem to ignore the 'odd reactions' mentioned in the advertisement text, probably because they do not even know what is meant by it, as this letter-writer indicates: 'I have never yet heard odd reactions – as you wrote in *Viva*. People who didn't watch it had no opinion, and people who did watch it found it nice' (Letter 20).

Apparently this letter-writer lives in a cultural milieu in which the ideology of mass culture has little effect on the way in which people judge patterns of cultural consumption. Hating *Dallas* and loving *Dallas* are in this context positions which are relatively free of the associations evoked by the ideology of mass culture. For this letter-writer, who apparently has no idea of the constraint that the ideology of mass culture exercises on so many other lovers of *Dallas* – 'I am curious about your "odd reactions"', she writes – loving *Dallas* is a pretty carefree affair because she does not seem to be surrounded by the taboo which is created by the ideology of mass culture.

A few other letter-writers do seem to be subject to this atmosphere of taboo, but take up an attitude towards it based on deflating the standards of the ideology of mass culture itself. That can be achieved by simply refusing to let it bother them: 'When I say I like watching *Dallas*, I often get odd reactions too, but I also like eating at McDonalds and like poetry a lot, things that get just as strange a reaction' (Letter 24). This letter-writer even flirts a bit with her love for 'mass culture' (McDonalds!), so that a defence against 'odd reactions' is not necessary.

Other letter-writers again try to undermine the ideology of mass culture by not only resisting the negative identity forced on them, but by retaliating to put the position of those who hate *Dallas* in a negative light. Sometimes they do this in a rudimentary way, for example by turning the tables on those who pretend to loathe the programme: 'I have noticed that among people in my milieu they won't honestly admit that they like watching it, but I do, I really like watching it. [. . .] People often find it sugary but they would like to have a taste of that sugariness just as well, wouldn't they?' (Letter 6).

Another lover of *Dallas* goes even further. In her letter she tries to indicate the social origin of the ideology of mass culture, in order then to make her resistance to it known:

> When I ask for an opinion at school I get the same reactions as you. Does it perhaps have something to do with the fact that I am at grammar school and have my final exams this year? I think so. For you 'have to' follow current affairs programmes and 'good' films, but who decides for me what *I* find good? I myself of course. (Letter 5)

Her use of language ('I myself of course') reveals a certain degree of pugnacity in her resistance to the norms and opinions of the ideology of mass culture. Here she invokes something like an 'individual right of determination' and betrays a certain allergy to aesthetic standards determined from on high. So she speaks from an ideological position which can be aptly summed up in the well-known saying: 'There's no accounting for taste.'

This is the core of what we can call the ideology of populism, an ideology which is completely opposite to the ideology of mass culture: it arrives at its norms and judgements in a radically opposite way. But it is not impossible for the two ideologies to be united in one person. Thus one ironizing lover characterizes *Dallas* on the one hand as a 'hideously cheap serial' (a statement which fits within the discursive repertoire of the ideology of mass culture), while on the other hand she judges those who dislike *Dallas* from a populist perspective: 'I find the people who react oddly rather ludicrous – they can't do anything about someone's taste. And anyway they might find things pleasant that you just can't stand seeing or listening to' (Letter 36).

This statement clearly illustrates how the populist ideology functions. It is, first and foremost, an anti-ideology: it supplies a subject position from which any attempt to pass judgement on people's aesthetic preferences is *a priori* and by definition rejected, because it is regarded as an unjustified attack on freedom. The populist ideology therefore postulates an identity which is characterized by an appeal to total autonomy: 'But there's just one thing I'd like to make quite clear: please don't let yourself be sat on by other people with their own (odd) ideas (like me)' (Letter 36).

Viewed in this way, the populist position must be particularly attractive for lovers of *Dallas*, because it provides an identity which can be forcefully employed against the codes of the ideology of mass culture. Why is it then that we can trace so little of this position in the letters written by fans?

One explanation lies in the difference in the way both ideologies function. The populist ideology derives its attraction from its direct mode of address, from its ability to produce and ensure immediate certainty. Its discourses are anti-intellectual and consist mainly of no more than short slogans, as the saying 'There's no accounting for taste' makes clear. The populist ideology functions therefore mainly at a *practical* level: it consists of common-sense ideas which are assumed almost 'spontaneously' and unconsciously in people's daily lives. The ideology of mass culture on the other hand is mainly of a *theoretical* nature: its discourses possess great consistency and rationality, they take on the form of more or less elaborate theories. The ideology of mass culture is therefore an intellectual ideology: it tries to win people over by *convincing* them that 'mass culture is bad'.

This difference can explain why in the letters the ideology of mass culture is present in a much more pronounced way than populist ideology. At a theoretical level the latter is the subservient one. It has literally fewer words and less clear-cut 'rational' prescriptions available to defend and legitimize its general attitude that 'there's no accounting for taste'. For the opposite attitude, namely that 'mass culture is bad', very many arguments lie to hand. So it is not surprising that, if people have to account for taste, for example when they have to give reasons why they like or dislike *Dallas*, they cannot, or only with difficulty, evade the discursive power of the ideology of mass culture. This is why the ideology of mass culture succeeds in ensuring that each category of letter-writers – haters, ironizing lovers, 'real' lovers of *Dallas* – is alive to its norms and judgements and why it seems to brush aside the populist position.

POPULAR CULTURE, POPULISM AND THE IDEOLOGY OF MASS CULTURE

But the power of the ideology of mass culture is certainly not absolute. Indeed, it is precisely the markedly 'theoretical', discursive nature of this ideology that reveals the limits of its power. Its influence will be mainly restricted to people's opinions and rational consciousness, to the discourses people use when *talking* about culture. These opinions and rationalizations need not, however, necessarily prescribe people's cultural *practices*. It could even be that the dominance of the normative discourses of the ideology of mass culture – as it is expressed in all sorts of social institutions such as education and cultural criticism – has in fact a counter-productive effect on people's practical cultural preferences so that, not through ignorance or lack of knowledge, but out of self-respect they refuse to subject themselves to the prescriptions of the ideology of mass culture or to let their preferences be determined by it. The populist position offers a direct justification for such a refusal, because it rejects altogether any paternalistic distinction between 'good' and 'bad' and dismisses any feeling of guilt or shame over a particular taste. There exists then a cynical dialectic between the intellectual dominance of the ideology of mass culture and the 'spontaneous', practical attraction of the populist ideology. The stricter the standards of the ideology of mass culture are, the more they will be felt as oppressive and the more attractive the populist position will become. This position offers the possibility, contrary to the morals of the ideology of mass culture, of following one's own preferences and enjoying one's own taste.

The commercial culture industry has understood this well. It employs the populist ideology for its own ends by reinforcing the cultural eclecticism underlying it and propagating the idea that indeed there's no accounting for taste, that in other words no objective aesthetic judgements are possible. It sells its products by propagating the idea that everyone has the right to his or her own taste and has the freedom to enjoy pleasure in his or her own way.

But the populist ideology is applicable not only for the aims and interests of the commerical culture industry. It also links up with what Bourdieu has called the popular 'aesthetic': an aesthetic which is the exact opposite of the bourgeois aesthetic disposition in which an art object is judged according to extremely formal, universalized criteria which are totally devoid of subjective passions and pleasures. In the popular 'aesthetic' on the other hand, no 'judgements of Solomon' are passed on the quality of cultural artefacts. This aesthetic is of an essentially pluralist and conditional nature because it is based on the premise that the significance of a cultural object can differ from person to person and from situation to situation. It is based on an affirmation of the continuity of cultural forms and daily life, and on a deep-rooted desire for participation, and on emotional involvement. In other words, what matters for the popular aesthetic is the recognition of pleasure, and that pleasure is a personal thing. According to Bourdieu the popular aesthetic is deeply anchored in common sense, in the way in which cultural forms in everyday life are approached by ordinary people.

Pleasure, however, is *the* category that is ignored in the ideology of mass culture. In its discourses pleasure seems to be non-existent. Instead it makes things like responsibility, critical distance or aesthetic purity central – moral categories that make pleasure an irrelevant and illegitimate criterion. In this way the ideology of mass culture places itself totally outside the framework of the popular aesthetic, of the way in which popular cultural practices take shape in the routines of daily life. Thus it remains both literally and figuratively caught in the ivory towers of 'theory'.

NOTE

1. As Terry Eagleton puts it, 'what *is* important to recognize is that the cognitive structure of an ideological discourse is subordinated to its emotive structure – that such cognitions or miscognitions as it contains are on the whole articulated according to the demands [. . .] of the emotive "intentionality" it embodies'.

27 Armand Mattelart, Xavier Delcourt and Michèle Mattelart

International image markets

EDITOR'S INTRODUCTION

This essay is quite open about its political engagement: it analyses threats to the processes of 'cultural democratization' in the (so-called) new world order. In doing so it makes three crucial points: first, that the Western media are increasingly being exposed to market forces in the sense that they must target their audience more and more carefully; second, that information processing now represents about half of all value-adding economic activity in post-industrial nations; and, third, that it is no longer accurate to think in terms of a division between a controlling and centralizing first world and a deprived and marginalized third world. In the context of global communications, we must think instead about alliances across this division. However, as this division breaks down, local hierarchies between those who have access to information and media and those who do not often increase.

Unlike Ien Ang's piece, this essay does not ask, what are the pleasures and uses of cultural products?; unlike the essays by Cornel West and Michele Wallace it does not turn to theory to invite a vibrant politics of difference. Rather, it concentrates on changes in communications industry structure, in the hope that disseminating such knowledge might work towards a more flexible media regime in which a wider range of needs can be expressed and fulfilled.

Further reading: Boyd-Barrett 1977, 1982; Curran and Gurevitch 1991; Garnham 1990; Leal 1990; Mattelart 1991; Schneider and Wallis 1988; Smith 1980; Sussman and Lent 1991; Tomlinson 1991; Urry and Lash 1987.

S.D.

The increasing commercialization of the cultural sector and the parallel development of the new technologies of communication have projected culture into the heart of industrial and political structures. For the majority of European countries, this situation is radically new. The relationship between culture and industry is gradually being added to a debate formerly centred on that between culture and the state, an extension which has produced a rupture with existing definitions of 'culture'.

In countries where the networks of mass-cultural production and distribution were immediately integrated into a market philosophy, an acceleration of the commercialization process is less likely to be experienced as a radical rupture. In this respect, the influence of national conditions in the formation of a theoretical framework appears to be a main element, though generally underestimated (not to mention totally neglected). These national conditions have been marked in Europe by the historical importance of the state in the political and economic management of society, but also by political movements and social organizations for which cultural demands were primarily formulated in terms of access to the privileges of 'high culture'. The way in which, up until the 1970s, the audiovisual media were treated in France is particularly illustrative: the relationship between culture and the state monopolized everyone's attention, leading to a blockage in the industrial or commercial dimension of mass-cultural production. Theories of the state, developed at the time by radical critics, particularly in France, only confirmed this fragmented vision of a cultural apparatus confined to the ideological and political sphere.

In Europe, until the second half of the 1970s, radio–television systems were almost entirely under the thumb of the public authorities. To allow broadcasting to face the laws of the market could only, it was thought, constitute a diversion from the spirit of public service. Even when doors opened for the private sector – as in Great Britain with the independent channel ITV, or in France and Italy with the introduction of advertising as a determining element in the financing of public enterprises – these openings remained subject to a strict framework of regulation and control.

From the end of the 1970s, however, the public service has been showing evident signs of crisis, destabilized and weakened by political, financial, and technological factors. First, the spiral of inflation, combined with cuts in public spending, is eroding the financial base on which public television has traditionally rested. Second, faced with an almost saturated market for television sets, the combination of licence fee income and authorized advertising resources is no longer sufficient to absorb the increase in production costs and investment demand.

Third, the expansion of the audiovisual market through both the new communications technologies and the additional TV channels has meant the arrival in strength of the private sector. This expansion has also exposed the way in which the public service finds it difficult to satisfy the demand of users whose fragmented interests conflict with a public monopoly's mass audience profile. At the same time, the crisis within the public radio–television monopoly is itself encouraging governments to relax direct state control in favour of private initiatives.

On top of these national factors, the state of the world economy has had important repercussions in the communications field. The accent on productivity and accelerated realization of surplus value is transforming both work organization and production processes. The most significant areas are those of publishing and the press – confronted with the introduction of computers and telematics – and the audiovisual media – forced to implement an increasingly industrialized production. The growing penetration of international products into national communications markets testifies to the progress of internationalization in publishing, advertising, marketing, and audiovisual production.

In this development of new markets, both cable and satellites are crucial factors. The enormous initial investment involved, and the sheer length of time needed for them to reach profitability, has stimulated new alliances between the state, the financial sector, and private industry. The state, taking charge of providing the technological infrastructure, has thereby given the go-ahead to the development of markets and the manufacture of hardware like terminals. The financial crisis affecting public resources has therefore led to new ways of getting consumers to participate in the financing of this infrastructure. Ultimately, profitability is tending to supplant the media's traditional function of preserving the *res publica*, and in the process is transforming profoundly the rules of democracy.

Information, communications, and culture are increasingly to be found at the centre of international debates, and have formed the basis of multiple confrontations. Since 1973, through organizations like UNESCO or the Non-Aligned Movement, Third World countries have repeatedly denounced the unequal international flow of news – produced and distributed as it is by a limited number of press agencies belonging to the developed nations. The demand for a 'new world information and communications order' subsequently gave rise to a series of meetings and conferences. These meetings led up to the

General Conference of UNESCO in Belgrade in 1980, where the MacBride Report on the problems of communications was approved. Since that time, meetings of the non-aligned countries have continued to draw up a balance sheet of progress, noting for instance that new forms of alliance between the countries of the South have emerged, principally through the creation of national news agencies and regional networks of these agencies.

Initially centred on combating the imbalance of news flows, this debate on communications has progressively widened its scope under the pressure of non-aligned countries. The declaration on computers and development adopted during the meeting in New Delhi (1983) testifies to this. International organizations of an essentially technical nature have also begun to feel the political effects of an increasingly global questioning of the geopolitical distribution of power in the field of information. One example is the debate within the International Union of Telecommunications on the allocation of frequencies, an allocation which the ten biggest broadcasting countries (controlling 90 per cent of the available wavebands) thought had been resolved once and for all.

Recognition of this new phase in the political and cultural emancipation of the Third World should not, however, allow us to pass over the tensions within this movement. For are we really talking about a new information order or simply a new sharing out of the established order? The 'Third World' consensus explodes as soon as we come to the central problems of a genuinely alternative form of communication. Who will produce this information? What subject matter will emerge from this transformation? What are the means of communication best adapted to these producers and to this content? Roberto Savio, founder of Inter-American Press Service, an agency created in the wake of the international discussions on communications, drew the lessons from ten years' experience: 'The real problem', he wrote in June 1982, 'should not be posed in terms of quantitative transfers of informational capacities from North to South. Rather it should be in terms of creating new flows of information with contents, personnel, priorities, and needs which are absent from current flows. Following this logic, it is not specifically in the North/South context that the various groups making up the social fabric – unions, academic institutions, cooperatives, associations, and communities – must be situated in order to produce information that existing channels do not supply. The problem is therefore qualitative and not quantitative.'

This emphasis on quantity, which allowed certain Third World governments to pass over embarrassing questions of power within society, has so far limited the construction of a 'new order' to the provision of financial aid, technical assistance, and professional training. And it is precisely this flaw which has enabled authorities in the West to reduce the idealism and generosity of the debate's initiators to a simple manipulation of institutions, remote-controlled by the Soviet Union. Disconcerted by the growth of Third World demands, which have expanded from the distribution of news to the control of communications technologies, they finally rallied in 1981 by decreeing an embargo on further negotiations.

The Declaration of Talloires, published May 18, 1981, at the close of a meeting organized by the World Press Freedom Committee, remains the most striking document of this counterattack by 'newspapers, magazines, free radio and television stations of the West and elsewhere', uniting for the first time against the 'campaign by the Soviet Union and some Third World countries seeking to give UNESCO the power to model the future development of the media'. Analysing the meaning of this realignment of forces, the Peruvian researcher Rafael Roncagliolo wrote in June 1982:

> The time when communications bosses acted in relatively dispersed fashion through organizations like the Inter-American Press Association and the International Press Institute has now disappeared. Today, we are seeing the formation of a big transnational bloc with a strategy whose principal objective – paraphrasing the terms of the Talloires Declaration – is to 'no longer authorize discussions and activities which relate to propositions unacceptable to the West'. Their complementary objective is to take over certain suggestions for a new world information and communications order whilst abandoning democratization in favor of 'cooperation with the Third World, aiming to help it renew its production and training resources'. The qualitative problem of the role of communications in the construction of democracy is thus transformed into a quantitative problem which boils down to an increased dependence through technology and professional and ideological training.

One cannot resist on behalf of somebody else. The very idea of resistance implies an aggression felt in the very heart. Yet persuaded of the durability – even the superiority – of their culture, many in the industrialized countries have criticized the Third World for excessively politicizing the debate on the new world information and communications order, for having been caught up in the game of sorcerer's apprentice ideologues. But to challenge the choice of battlefield and the use of words, without relating them to the conditions of their selection, is surely to prevent oneself from identifying the historical origin of resistance, to understand the language it speaks and therefore to communicate.

Each form of resistance has its own language. In an age of crisis in politics, the France of the 1970s placed its confidence in the language of the economy. And it was precisely through the economy that it received the first signal of alarm. 'In post-industrial economies', wrote the President of the Inter-Ministerial Commission on Transborder Data Flows in 1980, 'where the processing of information today represents between 40 and 50 per cent of its added value, it is natural that international information exchange plays a central role . . . The current development of transborder flows establishes and amplifies the *dominance that multinational systems are achieving over individual countries*. Certainly the nation state remains vigorous. But it runs the risk of being steadily drained of its strength.'

To make the shift from this alarm call to the development of a national debate, however, required a change in the political majority in France. 'Power over communications is being concentrated in every country,' declared President Mitterand during the Versailles summit of June 1982. 'A handful of firms are expropriating all the networks necessary for electronic transmission. By controlling them, they influence in turn the traditional media: the cinema, the press, and television. Most of the new activities in which the majority of firms are engaged (production, storage, information processing) presuppose extremely heavy investment, which again leads to high concentration . . . More generally, the distribution of information developed and controlled by a few dominant countries could mean for others the loss of their history or even their sovereignty, thus calling into question their freedom to think and decide.'

At the same time, the world conference in Mexico City on cultural policies (*Mondiacult '82*) confirmed that the countries of the North, more sensitive to the imbalance of world trade because of their own recently-acquired vulnerability, had finally discovered the links between the economy and culture that the South had perceived as early as 1973.

This 'discovery' established the failure of the so-called cultural democratization policies and marked the limits of a conception of development based on the introduction of planning tools in the cultural sector:

> The past fifteen years have seen the emergence of three parallel phenomena: (a) a two, five, or ten-fold increase, according to the country, of public spending on culture; (b) despite increased spending, stagnation in the use made by the public of cultural institutions; and (c) a twenty, hundred, or thousand-fold increase in public contact with artistic works as a result of industrial cultural products . . . The conclusion that inevitably springs from this observation is that far more is being done to democratize and decentralize culture with the industrial products available on the market than with the 'products' subsidized by public authorities.

Culture and economy: the same struggle. It is useless to avert one's gaze and pretend nothing has changed: the facts are there and cannot be denied.

> Cultural and artistic creation – several delegates have argued so from the beginning – is today victim of a system of multinational financial domination against which we must organize ourselves . . .
> Is it our destiny to become the vassals of an immense empire of profit? We hope that this conference will be an occasion for peoples, through their governments, to call for genuine cultural resistance, a real crusade against this domination, against – let us call a spade a spade – this financial and intellectual imperialism.

For those familiar with international issues, such a declaration by French Minister of Culture Jack Lang speaking in Mexico City was a non-event. However, hearing these words from an official representative of a large industrial country *was* an event, amply shown by the international and national divisions created by his intervention. Apart from the 'total exasperation' registered by the United States, the speech from Lang, 'well received by the Eastern bloc and Third World countries', caused a split within the Western camp.

Ignoring Lang's conjunction between economics and culture, comment in the French media focused instead on 'American cultural imperialism' (although the United States had not been named once in the speech) and turned it into a battle of value judgements and assumptions. Lang was accused of having launched 'a war of berets, bourrées, and Breton bagpipes' against Dashiell Hammett, Chester Himes, William Irish, Orson Welles, Meredith Monk, Richard Foreman, Jackson

Pollock, Andy Warhol, Merce Cunningham, etc. 'The worst Broadway revue will always outclass the pathetic spectacle of folkloric dances in clogs,' wrote one of the most violent critics.

This outburst of 'national masochism' seemed to mark the emergence in France of an intelligentsia which, in order to denigrate its culture of origin, used the same contemptuous tone and derisory examples as many ruling-class elites in the Third World had done as they waited for previously despised popular cultural forms like reggae and salsa to return home on the wings of transnational corporations before celebrating their 'birth'. And yet this emergence is itself very much a French phenomenon. In its ability to consider culture either in its material or historical context, it anchors itself in the French tradition of antagonism between the 'cultural' and the 'technical'. As *Technology, Culture, and Communication* noted:

> Why is there such fierce resistance to the linking of culture and technology? Why is there a tendency to dissociate the two, that is to perceive the former through the exclusive outlets of literature and aesthetics – therefore as essentially prestigious – and the latter as a product of utilitarianism? Why is there this difficulty in reconciling culture with its own materiality and historical conditions of production? Why have intellectuals so long been reticent not only in analyzing the apparatuses of cultural massification but above all in critically posing, other than in terms of sheer indifference or elitism, the problem of their own relations with the media?

Of course, one does not have only the culture of one's personal taste and aesthetic leanings but also that of one's social class and professional interests. And admitting this enables us to see that there exists a dynamic link between knowledge and ignorance, between what one chooses to learn and what one cannot ignore. Paradoxically, the loudest demands for 'cosmopolitanism' are accompanied in France by a localism that borders on illiteracy.

The debate over 'American cultural imperialism' came at just the right time to remind us that within the 'Latin' countries, everyone doesn't speak the same language: 'While waiting for further episodes of *Dallas*, Moroccan television is showing another series, *The Conquest of the West*. In French! This is a double insult to the Arab World via Paris.' As the Moroccan writer Tahar Ben Jelloun recalled, the paths of cultural subjugation follow the twists and turns of the colonial heritage. But this is not all, as the vice-president of the American delegation at *Mondiacult*

'82 underlined: 'When Mr. Lang affirms "culture and economy: the same struggle", he ought to remember that multinationals flourish in France as well as in the United States, that France exports its culture like the United States and like many other countries.'

A minefield? Much more so than these declarations would lead us to believe. For the denunciation of an evil 'other' is never exempt from a certain holier-than-thou attitude to be found at the heart of the notion of cultural identity. In the area of the audiovisual media, there are at least four ways in which cultural identity serves as a screen to reality, a way of not thinking in terms of an alternative.

Example One: Exclusive recourse to simple protectionist measures like the quota system on imported films. Although somewhat justified by the 'defence of national territory', this policy has many adverse effects, not least that it establishes a geographical division between the here and the elsewhere. While it limits foreign influence, it proposes no other alternative than the limit itself. For the quota solution to be effective, it must at least be accompanied by the necessary complement of a production policy. A government that adopts the quota solutions seems to be doing a lot when it has done essentially nothing.

Example Two: The defence of cultural identity as a mask for greater profits to sectional interests – public servants, technicians, executives, artistic personnel, etc., all solidly installed in their ivory towers. When the defence of cultural identity becomes confused with the defence of a fixed past, it runs the risk of filling a strictly conservative role. It finds itself reduced to a role of complacency, reduced, in fact, to an asphyxiating localism.

Example Three: Cultural identity reduced to a national label stuck on what is essentially a transnational copy. A large number of television series, for example, have fallen into this trap. Admittedly the stories may be based on the national past, or real historical situations, but the general narrative style is still that of the big television empires. In the process, cultural identity becomes picturesque folklore.

Example Four: Cultural identity as the standard-bearer for an alternative cultural imperialism. This happens, for example, when a country presents itself as a champion of linguistic community and simply treats the latter as a market unified by common language, rather than taking account of its underlying diversity. The history of 'Latinity' is a prime example of this tendency. As Guy Martinière explains:

The concept of *Latin* America, created in France under Napoleon III, was born on the eve of the military – and scientific – expedition to Mexico. The Latin definition of the political, cultural, and economic influence of the France of Napoleon III in relation to the America formerly colonized by Spain and Portugal responded admirably to the *grand dessein* of the Emperor . . . France, heir to the European Catholic dynasty, carried in America and in the world the torch of the *Latin* races – that is the French, the Italians, the Spanish, and the Portuguese – in order to check the 'rise of the Protestant nations and the Anglo-Saxon race' while avoiding a European decline. Already at the time, in the face of this French 'cultural' initiative, reaction was not slow in coming: the notion of 'Hispanity' quickly appeared in Spain in response to this Latinity.

By approaching the issue of communications in the Third World from the point of view of dependency on the North, one often overlooks the specific nature of each country's system. Because of this, the evidence of a growing presence of Brazilian production in Italy, or even Mexican production in the United States, comes to most people as a confusing surprise. This confusion can only be dispersed by looking at the relationship in each country between culture, the state, and industry. Such an analysis would enable us to understand why, at a time when many Third World countries have yet to select their system of television, others are already in the forefront of the transnational technological system; this explains the presence in Brazil and Mexico of international multimedia groups at levels of ownership concentration scarcely paralleled in Western Europe.

Rede Globo, the largest Brazilian television network (opened in 1965), is owned by the Globo organization. This includes the newspaper *O Globo* (founded in 1925 and one of the biggest in the country); the Globo radio system (inaugurated in 1944 and composed of seventeen stations on the AM and FM bands); a publishing firm, La Rio Grafica Editora; the Globo audiovisual recording company (SIGLA); the electronics industry Telcom; a show-business promotion firm (VASGLO); the Global art gallery; and last but not least, the Globo television network, which owns five broadcasting stations, thirty-six affiliated stations, and hundreds of retransmission stations.

TV Globo's production level is such that imports make up no more than two mass-audience programmes out of ten. In 1978, Rede Globo created the Roberto Marinho Cultural Foundation to work, according to its own description, 'alongside Brazilian communities in the search for solutions to problems of common welfare'. Today, Rede Globo accounts for 70 per cent of advertising expenditure in the Brazilian media: in 1979, $760 million was spent on advertising on Brazilian television. This compares to $950 million in Great Britain, where the GNP was almost twice as big and the consumer market three times as large.

In Mexico, Televisa, a group set up in 1973, owns four television channels with sixty-one transmission stations covering almost the entire country. Out of a total of 55 million viewers, this network attained 41 million in 1979 or 7 million households. The forty-seven companies that make up Televisa cover all aspects of the cultural industries. Televisa also extends its ownership to five radio stations, including the biggest in the country; five publishing houses (books and magazines), with the largest print runs on the Mexican market; nine show-business firms, ranging from theatres to a football club, as well as pop singers and cinema chains; three film production firms, including one exclusively given over to cartoons; four record companies; a tourist agency, etc. Following the trend of Rede Globo, Televisa also owns a cultural foundation which bears its name. Televisa is also a patron of the arts through the Rufino Tamayo Museum, the newest in the Mexican capital; and finally, thanks to the above-mentioned film library, it also runs an institute of research and historical documentation.

The many arms of the Televisa empire probably make Mexico a unique case in the history of radio–television, with a degree of monopoly control by a single private conglomerate practically without equal in any capitalist country. Everything has happened as if the single political party structure which characterizes the Mexican regime has been transposed to the commercial television system.

Far from being simple appendices to a commercial empire, the cultural foundations of Televisa and Rede Globo are powerful means of penetration into the field of formal education, allowing these companies to enlarge considerably their social function. One can readily envisage their importance for the introduction of new technologies and as laboratories for new forms of cultural action. For these so-called philanthropic enterprises, an excellent means of tax avoidance for the companies, are also important examples of the state delegating some of its responsibilities to private enterprise. By means of the *Telecurso, 2e Grau* (TV Course, 2nd degree) of the Roberto Marinho foundation or the university courses of the Televisa cultural foundation (six hours a day, over 7,500 programmes broadcast since 1980), an original model of collaboration between the public and private sectors has been established.

Whether viewed in terms of the formation of multimedia groups or in terms of communications hardware production, 'Third World' appears today as an increasingly meaningless term. A whole series of interchangeable terms (the South, developing countries, peripheral countries, etc.) no longer grasp the realities they supposedly refer to. Diplomatic language now makes a distinction between firstly, the oil-exporting countries (mostly members of OPEC); secondly, those oil-importing countries with a significant industrial base (described as the 'newly industrializing countries'); and finally, those countries lacking in both energy and a sufficient industrial base, grouped under the term 'less developed countries'. This differentiation, however, does not affect in the slightest the reinforcing of the economic and financial power of the leading industrial countries. The five largest industrial economies – the United States, Japan, Federal Republic of Germany, France, and the United Kingdom – alone account for almost 40 per cent of international trade.

This strengthening of the group of industrialized countries has been accompanied by important internal shifts: the relative decline of American international investment (from 60 per cent of the world total in 1969 to 40 per cent in 1980); the increased opening up of the United States to investment from other industrialized countries (the total amount of foreign capital in the U.S. increased from 10,000 to 66,000 million dollars between 1967 and 1980); the increase in the international investment position of West Germany and Japan (each now with 10 per cent of the world total of direct investment); the decline of Great Britain (which fell from 20 per cent to 14 per cent of this total between 1960 and 1980); and the static position of France (5 per cent of the world total in 1980). But the share of the industrialized countries among the whole of direct investment increased from 69 per cent to 74 per cent between 1967 and 1975.

This redistribution within the industrialized 'club', coupled with the relative weakening of American domination, has gone hand in hand with the emergence of two new technological front-runners: Japan and to a lesser extent, the Federal Republic of Germany. If we measure technological potential by the number of scientists and engineers working in research and development per one million inhabitants, there has been an increase of almost 50 per cent over the last ten years in both these countries. By the end of the 1970s, there were 3,608 scientists and engineers for every million people in Japan, compared to 2,854 in the United States, 1,802 in West Germany, 1,419 in Great Britain, 1,327 in

France, and 674 in Italy. These figures also enable us to measure the gap still separating the 'industrialized countries' and the 'newly industrializing countries': in South Korea, this proportion falls to 418 (despite having tripled in ten years); in Brazil, 208; in Mexico, 101. In the less developed countries, it falls still further: to 74 in the Ivory Coast and 20 in Niger.

This imbalance of human potential is even more accentuated when we consider the share of each world region in electronics productions: in 1980, the United States accounted for 45 per cent of turnover in this sector, Japan 11 per cent, the whole of West Europe 28 per cent, 'the rest of the world' (excluding the Comecon countries and China) 16 per cent.

Does admittance to the relatively small club of 'newly industrializing countries' (Brazil, Mexico, Singapore, Taiwan, South Korea, Hong Kong) necessarily mean the abandonment of organic, economic, political, and cultural links with their former partners in the statistical lists? Nothing could be more foolhardy than to approach international relations in terms of this narrow economism. In fact, the progressive mastering by Brazil of high technology sectors such as aeronautics and computers, and programme industries like cinema and television, has been accompanied by a gradual redistribution among its export markets. In 1960 Brazilian exports to developing countries represented 9 per cent of its total. In 1973, this had moved to 18.1 per cent, and in 1977, to 24.1 per cent. On the other hand, its exports to the 'developed countries' fell from 84.8 per cent in 1960 to 68.1 per cent in 1977. This new type of South–South cooperation has been marked by the appearance of what have been somewhat quickly dubbed 'the multinationals of the Third World'. A recent study by the International Labour Organization (ILO) tried to identify the characteristics distinguishing them from transnationals created in the developed countries. According to this study, which analysed companies in Argentina, Brazil, Hong Kong, India, Indonesia, Mauritius, Mexico, Pakistan, Peru, the Philippines, Sri Lanka, and Thailand, these multinationals are primarily distinguished by their supply of an alternative technology to that of the industrialized giants. Their 'alternative' nature is found in their better adaptation of technologies to internal markets and greater labour intensity. By making greater use of a country's internal resources and local production methods, these companies respond better to national employment objectives.

Are 'Third World multinationals' real alternatives to transnationals from the developed countries? To answer this, we must trace the limits of this new development. On the one hand, the technologies offered, essentially in the manufacturing sector, are generally only adaptations of technologies developed in the large industrialized countries. But they do not necessarily challenge the model of social growth that favours the formation of elites whose needs alone are taken into account – at the expense of an increasingly poorer majority.

In countries where the requirements of democracy really do influence technological policy, an 'alternative communications strategy' doesn't look to factories – even those of the Third World – for a solution. Instead it looks to social experiments in the use of technologies. Thus, anxious not to import the dependent relationship attached to the audio-visual material it needed, Mozambique turned towards international alliances with groups which had a critical analysis in line with its own concerns. Nevertheless, although Mozambique is a rare example of a Third World country which has questioned the centralizing tendency of a national television system, its project has come up against the technical and scientific inequalities which plague 'less developed countries': thus the political will to set up a horizontal, non-elitist communications system must confront, in these countries, a preliminary handicap – that of the historical lack of technical experience.

The appearance on the international scene of secondary peaks of economic and political domination blurs the previous map of the international power balance. However, the elevation of a few Third World countries to the rank of 'newly industrialized country' has not led to a redistribution of financial power. For this industrialization has been carried out at the cost of a gigantic debt which reinforces financial concentration in the hands of a small number of the private banking sector. The majority of the debts of developing countries are to private banks: in 1981 commercial banks financed almost 60 per cent of the total external debt of non-oil-exporting developing countries. The average interest rate on this debt has practically doubled between 1975 and the beginning of the 1980s, increasing from 5.5 per cent to 10 per cent; whereas its total size quadrupled between 1978 and 1983 through the rise in the value of the dollar (most debts being in dollars). In 1982, interest payments alone represented about two-thirds of the current debt of these countries. For countries with huge debts like Argentina, Mexico, and Brazil, the servicing of that debt (interest plus repayments) represents respectively 153 per cent, 126 per cent, and 117 per cent of their export earnings.

This phenomenon establishes the growing and perhaps irreversible integration of the economies of developing countries into the world economy. In 1983, these countries had to import massively to maintain the level of exports necessary for the partial payment of their debt and an industrialization process (imports of equipment, pesticides, and oil). Shifts in the exchange rate have worsened this situation, reducing the quantity of imports that a given quantity of exports can finance. At the same time, the surplus of the oil-exporting countries fell from \$102 billion in 1980 to \$12 billion in 1982.

In the industrialized countries, the repercussions of the 'globalizing' of the economy on communications systems are still essentially analysed in terms of cultural and industrial dependence. For Third World countries caught in the spiral of deteriorating trade balances, the immediate requirements of sheer survival have emphasized dramatically the extent of the control of communications over consumption, particularly in the agro-food sector. By focusing solely on news sources, the debates within international organizations on the new information order have left this fundamental dimension in the shadows. And yet marketing and advertising are the backbone for any model of consumption; and their role is particularly striking in Latin America, where the extent of advertising mostly exceeds the accepted levels of tolerance in industrialized countries.

A comparison of advertising spending by media category throughout the world reveals that the press is still the largest, with 43 per cent of advertising receipts in 96 countries (1976). Television came second with 21 per cent and radio third with 7 per cent. In Western Europe and North America, television received 14 per cent and 20 per cent of takings respectively. In Latin America, this figure climbs to 41 per cent, although even this percentage is considerably exceeded by Mexico, where television accounts for 62 per cent of advertising expenditure. If we exclude government advertising, it is transnational agro-food firms which, in Mexico, spend the most on advertising. It is also in Mexico that the penetration of agro-food transnationals is the most advanced: 130 foreign enterprises own over 300 industrial establishments, 80 per cent of these being of North American origin. But, paradoxically, Mexico has to import over half of the basic foodstuffs needed by the population (e.g., wheat, beans, sorghum, corn).

Numerous studies confirm that the consumption model created by the transnational system demands, for anyone really to benefit from it, an income accessible to only 20 or 30 per cent of the population. Thus the system of commercialization, the system of production, and the system of communications all play a complementary role within the transnational framework by promoting a model of social inequality. The main patterns to emerge from the installation of new technologies in countries like Brazil show that, far from democratizing access to cultural goods, they reinforce segregations and consolidate hierarchies.

The pilot experiment for videotex in Brazil, for example, carried out under the auspices of the French firm Matra, enables us to see how an 'interactive' technology, which supposedly enables horizontal communication within a society, in fact accentuates the verticality of that society by simply updating its system of social and economic discrimination. Those chosen to benefit from the prospective videotex services were essentially recruited from the top of an already strongly concentrated financial and industrial system – a multimedia conglomerate, the banking sector, the public administration. The technological criteria for selection were thus automatically converted into criteria for social selection: to participate in this experiment, you had to have, at the very least, a telephone and a colour television, and this in a country with seven telephones per 100 inhabitants and where less than 12 per cent of households had colour television.

An export strategy which thus reduces industrial cooperation to a simple system of market penetration can only be indifferent to the political, social, and cultural dimensions of the consumption model it promotes, whether in technology or food. In so doing, it pushes international relations into a neoliberal mould which, in celebrating the era of electronic democracy, proclaims in fact the end of legitimate politics, equating individual liberty with the liberalization of the market.

In a speech to the Public Affairs Council in New York, a director of the European agro-food transnational Nestlé outlined the following argument:

The struggle in which we are engaged is of a political nature and on a political level, but it is not yet certain that the future will be one of economic, social, personal, and political liberty . . . Success in politics is not magical. Our enemies are not more intelligent than us and not supermen. And having begun a political reflection, we should give ourselves some political objectives . . . I feel it is essential that multinational firms under attack create a united group of talented and experienced professionals and, when needed, occasional consultants who, isolated from the everyday public relations of the firm, can concentrate their efforts on the political issues encountered by multinationals. In the search for a receptive public and the elimination of a critical attitude, multinational firms have an invaluable weapon at their disposal: marketing and management personnel in the field.

Thinking politically, as this 'communications strategy' shows clearly, is not only to equip oneself with tools but to think in terms of social alliances:

> We must either reactivate our traditional professional associations, or look beyond them for new allies among associations of peasants, workers, and owners of small businesses, many of whom have been suspicious of multinational capitalism in the past for good reasons. We must affirm the common interests of all institutions which create wealth – large or small, private or governmental, national or multinational; in short, we must affirm the pluralism and the diversity of the human condition, an example of which is given by democracy as well as the free market of commerce and ideas. Multinational capitalism must never appear as the dominating rival to local interests or to national or tribal sentiments.

It should not be too quickly forgotten that whereas the goal of democracy is the extension of freedoms and the multiplication of points of popular decision-making, that of the market is based on the division of labour, power, knowledge, and wealth. Previously, firms saw themselves as the standard-bearers of an apoliticism which delegated all social functions to the invisible hand of the market. Today, the privatization process is pushing firms into a totally different relation with society, transforming them into pressure groups with new social responsibilities and political concerns.

The terrain of another international space is here marked out: it is not the supposedly 'neutral' space of technological innovations but that of political will. The issue therefore extends well beyond international trading relations to encompass the very existence of democracy.

28 Janice Radway

The institutional matrix of romance

EDITOR'S INTRODUCTION

In this essay (a section of the first chapter of her book *Reading the Romance*), Janice Radway offers an analysis of the institutions in which the romance is produced. Asking the question 'what makes romances so popular?' she argues that it cannot simply be answered in terms of the pleasure the romance genre offers readers or the desires it satisfies. A business intervenes between texts and their readers.

By sketching a history of the mass-market publishing industry she shows how this industry has become increasingly sophisticated and specialized as it attempts to reduce the risks that are so great a part of all commercial cultural enterprises. Modern popular romance develops as a genre through a series of strategical decisions by publishers. Yet it is important to emphasize that Radway does not conceive of romance readers as cultural dupes (any more than Will Straw does heavy-metal listeners or Ien Ang *Dallas* viewers). For her, romance reading occurs in a tripartite structure in which readers' pleasure/choice, the publishing industry, and the writer each play a part in determining textual production.

Further reading: Cohn 1988; Modleski 1984, 1987; Radway 1984, 1988.

S.D.

Like all other commercial commodities in our industrial culture, literary texts are the result of a complicated and lengthy process of production that is itself controlled by a host of material and social factors. Indeed, the modern mass-market paperback was made possible by such technological innovations as the rotary magazine press and synthetic glue as well as by organizational changes in the publishing and bookselling industries. One of the major weaknesses of the earlier romance critique has been its failure to recognize and take account of these indisputable facts in its effort to explain the genre's growing popularity. Because literary critics tend to move immediately from textual interpretation to sociological explanation, they conclude easily that changes in textual features or generic popularity must be the simple and direct result of ideological shifts in the surrounding culture. Thus because she detects a more overtly misogynist message at the heart of the genre, Ann Douglas can argue in her widely quoted article, 'Soft-Porn Culture', that the coincidence of the romance's increasing popularity with the rise of the women's movement must point to a new and developing backlash against feminism. Because that new message is there in the text, she reasons, those who repetitively buy romances must experience a more insistent need to receive it again and again.

Although this kind of argument sounds logical enough, it rests on a series of tenuous assumptions about the equivalence of critics and readers and ignores the basic facts about the changing nature of book production and distribution in contemporary America. Douglas's explanatory strategy assumes that purchasing decisions are a function *only* of the content of a given text and of the needs of readers. In fact, they are deeply affected by a book's appearance and availability as well as by potential readers' awareness and expectations. Book buying, then, cannot be reduced to a simple interaction between a book and a reader. It is an event that is affected and at least partially controlled by the material nature of book publishing as a socially organized technology of production and distribution.

The apparent increase in the romance's popularity may well be attributable to women's changing beliefs and needs. However, it is conceivable that it is equally a function of other factors as well, precisely because the romance's recent success *also* coincides with important changes in book production, distribution, advertising, and marketing techniques. In fact, it may be true that Harlequin Enterprises can sell 168 million romances not because women suddenly have a greater need for the romantic fantasy but because the corporation has learned to address and overcome certain recurring problems in the production and distribution of books for a mass audience. If it can be shown that romance sales have been increased by particular practices newly adopted within the publishing industry, then we must entertain the alternate possibility that the apparent need of the female audience for this type of fiction may have been generated or at least augmented artificially. If so, the astonishing success of the romance may constitute evidence for the effectiveness of commodity packaging and advertising and not for actual changes in readers' beliefs or in the surrounding culture. The decision about what the romance's popularity constitutes evidence for cannot be made until we know something more about recent changes in paperback marketing strategies, which differ substantially from those that have been used by the industry for almost 150 years.

Standard book-marketing practices can be traced, in fact, to particular conceptions of the book and of the act of publication itself, both of which developed initially as a consequence of the early organization of the industry. The output of the first American press, established at Cambridge, Massachusetts, in 1639, was largely the ecclesiastical work of learned gentlemen of independent means who could afford to pay the printer to issue their books. Limitation of authorship to those with sufficient capital occurred generally throughout the colonies because most of the early presses were owned by combined printer-publishers who charged authors a flat fee for typesetting and distribution and a royalty for each book sold. Because it was the author who financed publication and thus shouldered the risk of unsold copies, the printer-publisher had relatively little interest in seeing that the book appealed to previously known audience taste. As a result, authors exerted almost total control over their works, which were then conceived as the unique products of their own individual intellects. Publication was concomitantly envisioned as the act of publicly issuing an author's ideas, an act that could be accomplished by the formal presentation of even one copy of those ideas for public review. In the early years of the printing industry, therefore, the *idea* of publication was not tied to the issue of sales or readership. As long as the work was presented in the public domain, it was considered published, regardless of whether it was read or not.

Of course, authors did concern themselves with readers, not least because they stood to lose a good deal if their books failed to sell. However, the problem was not a major one because the literate reading community was small and because publication itself was carried out on a local scale. The author very often knew who his readers were likely to be and could tailor his offering to their interests and tastes. Indeed, it was not uncommon for an early American writer to finance publication by soliciting contributions from specific, known subscribers whom he made every effort to please. It was thus relatively easy to match individual books with the readers most likely to appreciate the sentiments expressed within them.

Thus the concept of the book as a unique configuration of ideas conceived with a unique hypothetical audience in mind developed as the governing conception of the industry. Publishers prided themselves on the diversity of their offerings and conceived the strength of an individual house to be its ability to supply the American reading public with a constant stream of unique and different books. In addition, they reasoned further that because publishing houses issued so many different kinds of works, each of which was intended for an entirely different public, it was futile to advertise the house name itself or to publicize a single book for a heterogeneous national audience. In place of national advertising, then, publishers relied on editors' intuitive abilities to identify the theoretical audiences for which books had been conceived and on their skills at locating real readers who corresponded to those hypothetical groups. Throughout the nineteenth century and indeed well into the twentieth, authors, editors, and publishers alike continued to think of the process of publication as a personal, discrete, and limited act because they believed that the very particularity and individuality of books destined them for equally particular and individual publics.

Despite the continuing domination of this attitude, the traditional view of book publishing was challenged, even if only tentatively, in the early years of the nineteenth century by an alternate view which held that certain series of books could be sold successfully and continuously to a huge, heterogeneous, preconstituted public. Made possible by revolutionary developments in technology and distribution and by the changing character of the reading audience itself, this new idea of the book as a saleable commodity gradually began to alter the organization of the editorial process and eventually the conception of publishing itself. Although this new view of the book and of the proper way to distribute it was at first associated only with a certain kind of printer-publisher, it was gradually acknowledged and later grudgingly used by more traditional houses when it became clear that readers could be induced to buy quite similar books again and again.

The specific technological developments that prepared the way for the early rationalization of the book industry included the improvement of machine-made paper, the introduction of mechanical typesetting and more sophisticated flatbed presses, and the invention of the Napier and Hoe cylinder press. The inventions of the steamboat and the railroad and the extension of literacy – especially to women – combined to establish publishing as a commercial industry with the technical capacity to produce for a mass audience by 1830. What this meant was that commercially minded individuals began to enter the business with the sole purpose of turning a profit.

The first production scheme designed specifically to mass produce cheap paperbound books and to utilize the magazine distribution system was not mounted until 1937 when Mercury Publications created American Mercury Books. In fact, according to Frank Schick, American Mercury was the first paperbound book series to employ magazine distribution successfully. Packaged to look like magazines, these books were sold at newsstands and, like periodicals, remained available only for a month. American Mercury's practices, which stressed the ephemerality of this literature, clearly differentiated this publishing venture from more traditional book production, which continued to focus on the establishment of a line of diverse books of lasting worth to be kept constantly in print on a backlist and in stock at the better retail establishments. Although the company at first published a variety of titles, by 1940 the editors had decided to concentrate on mysteries in the interest of establishing better control over their market. The new series, called Mercury Mysteries, differentiated its remarkably similar covers and titles by numbering each book for the reader's convenience.

The publishers of American Mercury Books hoped to sell their paperbacks in large quantities to readers who already knew their mystery magazines. Those magazines enabled the editors to take note of reader opinion and to gauge preferences that they then sought to match in their manuscript selection. In effect, American Mercury tried to control both its audience *and* the books produced especially for that group. Despite this successful formalization of category publishing, the relatively small size of the American Mercury venture has prevented it from being credited with the mass-market paperback revolution. Although that honour is usually awarded to Robert de Graff for his founding of Pocket Books in 1939, his scheme introduced no new conceptual innovations to the industry. Like the editors at American Mercury, de Graff thought of the book as a commodity to be sold, relied on the magazine system of distribution, and gradually turned to category publication. Still, it was de Graff's ability to institute this system on a large scale that set the stage for the romance's rise to dominance within the mass-market industry. To understand exactly how and why the romance has become so important in commodity publishing, it is necessary to understand first how the economics of paperback publishing and distribution created the industry's interest in the predictability of sales.

In the years immediately preceding de Graff's entry into the field, major improvements had been made in both printing and binding techniques. The invention of magazine rotary presses made high-speed production runs possible and profitable. Although the new machinery was very expensive, the cost was born largely by the printers themselves who were, by tradition, independent from publishing firms. Because the printers had to keep the costly presses operating twenty-four hours a day to guarantee a return on their initial investment, they pressured de Graff and his competitors at Avon, Popular Library, and Dell to schedule production tightly and regularly. This practice led to a magazine-like monthly production schedule similar to American Mercury's, a practice that fitted nicely with de Graff's intention to distribute his books through the magazine network. The regularization of production further enabled the printers to buy large quantities of paper at lower rates without also having to pay to store it indefinitely. The publishers benefited in turn because they could sell their books at much lower prices.

Surprisingly enough, the invention of synthetic glue also helped to add speed to the publication of the mass-market paperback. Traditional book binding is accomplished by hand or machine sewing of folded signatures of paper to create the finished book. Even when carried out mechanically, the process is both expensive and time-consuming. 'Perfect' binding is an alternate procedure in which single leaves of paper are gathered together, cut uniformly, and then glued to the spine of the cover. The first adhesives used in the process of perfect binding were animal glues that were not only slow to dry, but once dried, were so inflexible that bindings often cracked, releasing individual pages. The glues made it necessary for a printer to obtain sufficient storage space for drying the perfect-bound books. The invention of quick-drying synthetic glues eliminated most of these problems. Fast-setting adhesives necessitated assembly-line procedures that simultaneously accelerated the whole production process and obviated the need for costly storage. The new binding machines were expensive but, once again, the printers shouldered the enormous costs and passed much of the benefit on to the publishers.

Together with the rotary presses, then, perfect binding and synthetic glues made possible the production of huge quantities of books at a very low cost per unit and contributed to the acceleration and regularization of the acquisition and editorial processes. The consequent emphasis on speed caused the paperback publishers to look with favour on category books that could be written to a fairly rigid formula. By directing their potential writers to create in this way, mass-market houses saved the time and expense of editing unique books that had as yet not demonstrated their ability to attract large numbers of readers.

The particular step taken by de Graff that made this production of vast numbers of books financially feasible was his decision to utilize the extensive magazine distribution network that had developed during the past thirty years. De Graff reasoned that if he was actually to sell the large quantities of books he could now produce so effortlessly, he would have to place books in the daily paths of many more Americans. Because he was aware of the relative lack of bookstores in the United States and of the general population's feeling that those establishments were intimidating and inhospitable, he concluded that books would have to be marketed somewhere else if they were to be sold on a grand scale. He turned to the American News Company, which had a virtual monopoly on the national distribution of magazines and newspapers, because it counted among its clients many thousands of newsstands, drugstores, candy stores, and even food outlets. De Graff felt sure that if confronted with attractively packaged and very inexpensive books at these establishments, the American magazine reader could be persuaded to become a paperback book purchaser. The phenomenal sales of his first ten titles proved him right.

Despite the advantages it offered, however, magazine distribution also posed substantial problems. De Graff and his early competitors soon discovered that few of their new book retailers knew anything about books. Uneasy about purchasing materials they might not be able to sell, these individuals at first resisted efforts to get them to stock paperback books. To overcome their hesitation, de Graff and his counterparts at other houses proposed that the entire risk of unsold books be shouldered by the publishing firms themselves. As a result, they permitted all retail outlets to return any unsold books or to certify that the books themselves had been destroyed.

The returns policy had the desired effect in that it convinced retailers that they could not be harmed by stocking paperbacks, but it proved extremely troublesome to the publishers themselves. Because they had no way to track simultaneously progressing returns and new print orders or to shift the returns from one outlet to another, many publishers found themselves sending a book through a second printing to accommodate demand, only to discover later, after all returns were completed, that eventual total sales were less than the first print order.

The resulting overproduction was very costly and caused the mass-market publishers to search for ways to make book sales more predictable. It was thus that category literature suggested itself as a means of gauging how a new version of an already-proved type of book might perform in the market.

Category or formulaic literature has been defined most often by its standard reliance on a recipe that dictates the essential ingredients to be included in each new version of the form. It therefore permits an editor to direct and control book creation in highly specific ways. It is worth emphasizing, however, that category literature is *also* characterized by its consistent appeal to a regular audience.

Not only does this kind of production obviate the need to set print orders solely on the basis of blind intuition, but it also reduces the difficulties of designing a proper advertising campaign. By relying on the subscription lists of related periodicals and on sales figures of earlier offerings in the genre, category publishers can project potential sales with some certainty. At the same time, they can use the periodicals for a specific advertising strategy and thus avoid the difficulty and expense of mounting a national effort in the hope of ferreting out the proper audience by chance.

To understand the importance of the fact that category publishing makes book advertising manageable, it is necessary to know that publishers have argued for years that books cannot be marketed or advertised as are other commodities. Because every book is individual and unique, the industry has maintained, all publishers must 'start from scratch' in the effort to build an audience for them. Assuming, therefore, that the discreteness of books necessitated that each be advertised individually, publishers concluded that the enormous expense of advertising an entire month's offering ruled out the process entirely. Furthermore, because they believed that the variety of books offered by each firm made the creation of a single image of the house impossible, they also concluded that potentially less expensive national advertising of the house imprint would do nothing for the sales of individual books. Thus the publishing industry's advertising budget has been remarkably small for many years. The situation did not change until the 1970s when corporate takeovers of independent houses by large communications conglomerates resulted in the infusion of huge amounts of capital, some of which was directed to advertising budgets. However, before explaining how and why this has occurred and its relevance for our investigation of the romance, it is necessary to return to the early years of the third paperback revolution to trace the growing importance of the romance genre within the mass-market industry.

Although the early paperback publishers relied initially on proven hardcover bestsellers to guarantee large sales, they soon found that an insufficient number of these were available to supply the demand for cheap, paper-covered books. Wary of producing huge quantities of a title that had not yet demonstrated its saleability, these mass-market houses slowly began to rely on books that were examples of categories already proven to be popular with the reading public. The trend really began with the mystery or detective story that developed as the first dominant category in modern mass-market publishing. The genre was particularly well suited for semiprogrammed issue because the writer–publisher–audience relationship had been formalized in the 1920s with the establishment of the pulps like *Black Mask*, *Dime Detective*, *Detective Story*, and *Detective Fiction Weekly*. They helped to establish a generic orthodoxy which would then guide continuous novel production in hardcover format. Paperback mystery publishing developed simply as an extension of an already established literary practice.

Unfortunately, mystery popularity declined throughout the 1950s. Although the genre occasionally gained back the readers it lost, several publishers nonetheless began to look elsewhere for new material that they could sell on an even more regular and predictable basis. Troubled by this variability in mystery sales, Gerald Gross at Ace Books recalled the consistent reprint success of Daphne du Maurier's *Rebecca*. Wondering whether its long-standing popularity (it had been published first in 1938) indicated that it struck a universal chord in female readers, he attempted to locate previously published titles resembling du Maurier's novel, which he hoped to issue in a 'gothic' series. He settled upon Phyllis Whitney's *Thunder Heights*, which he then published in 1960 as the first title in his 'gothic' line.

Since Gross and other gothic publishers were not simply inserting mass-produced reading matter into a previously formalized channel of communication as had been done with paperback mysteries, it is necessary to ask why they were almost immediately successful in establishing the gothic romance as a particular category and in creating a growing demand for new titles. Their success cannot be attributed to the mere act of offering a new product to an audience already identified and therefore 'controlled' by the fact of its common subscription to the same magazines. Although confession and romance periodicals had been supplying love stories for faithful readers since their first appearance in the 1920s, these pulps were designed for a working-class audience. Because book reading has always been correlated with high education and income levels, it seems probable that the gothic's extraordinary paperback success was the result of the publishers' ability to convert and then repetitively reach middle-class women. Although one might suspect that these publishers relied on the middle-class trade magazines – such as *Good Housekeeping* or the *Ladies' Home Journal* – to identify and retain its new audience, in fact, this does not appear to have been the case. Publishers used very little advertising to promote the sales of the early gothics.

What, then, accounts for the immediate success of the category? The achievement has much to do with the special characteristics of its audience, that is, with the unique situation of women in American society. The principal problem facing the publisher in a heterogeneous, modern society is finding an audience for each new book and developing a method for getting that book to its potential readers. By utilizing the magazine distribution network, paperback publishers substantially increased their chances of finding buyers. But the use of this network proved especially significant for those paperback houses that were newly interested in female readers because it made available for book distribution two outlets almost always visited on a regular basis by women, the local drugstore and the food supermarket. Even the growing number of women who went to work in the 1960s continued to be held responsible for child care and basic family maintenance, as were their counterparts who remained wholly within the home. Consequently, the publishers could be sure of regularly reaching a large segment of the adult female population simply by placing the gothics in drug and food stores. At the same time, they could limit advertising expenditures because the potential or theoretical audience they hoped to attract already had been gathered for them. The early success of the gothic genre is a function of the de facto but nonetheless effective concentration of women brought about by social constraints on their placement within society. This concentration had the overall effect of limiting their diffusion throughout social space. In turn, this limitation guaranteed that as a potential book-buying public, American women were remarkably easy to reach.

The popularity of gothic romances increased throughout the decade of the 1960s. While American college students were beginning to protest American involvement in Vietnam and a gradually increasing number of feminists vociferously challenged female oppression, more and more women purchased novels whose plots centred about developing love relationships between wealthy, handsome men and 'spunky' but vulnerable women. The audience for gothics grew to such proportions that by the early 1970s works of top gothic authors outsold the works of equivalent writers in all other categories of paperback fiction, including mysteries, science fiction, and Westerns. A typical Whitney or Holt paperback issued by Fawcett began with a first printing of 800,000 copies. Although most of the category's authors sold nowhere near that number, when taken together the gothic novels released by no less than eight paperback houses constituted an enormous total output.

This extraordinary sales success of gothics established them as a true cultural phenomenon and qualified them for endless analysis and satire in the news media. Many articles on 'How to Write a Gothic' can be found in the Sunday supplements and popular magazines of the period, attesting to widespread awareness of the phenomenon, if less than universal approbation of it.

The increased publicity notwithstanding, sales of gothic romances dropped off gradually between 1972 and 1974. Returns increased to such an extent that many houses cut back their gothic output. When asked to explain the decline in popularity, former publishers of gothics equivocate. Some feel that the market had simply been saturated, while others suspect that the growing visibility of the feminist movement and increasing openness about female sexuality led to a greater tolerance if not desire for stories with explicit sexual encounters. All seem to agree, however, that the nature of romance publishing changed dramatically in April 1972, when Avon Books issued *The Flame and the Flower* by Kathleen Woodiwiss.

Because Woodiwiss had sent her unsolicited manuscript to Avon without the usual agent introduction, it landed on the 'slush pile', usually considered an absolute dead end in contemporary publishing. Inexplicably, it was picked up by executive editor Nancy Coffey, who was looking for something to get her through a long weekend. As she tells the story, she could not put the manuscript down. She returned to Avon enthusiastically determined to get the book into print. Coffey eventually convinced others and the book was released in April as an Avon Spectacular. Although Woodiwiss's novel, like the gothics, followed the fortunes of a pert but feminine heroine, it was nearly three times as long as the typical gothic, included more explicit descriptions of sexual encounters and near rapes, and described much travel from place to place. Despite the differences, it ended, as did all gothics, with the heroine safely returned to the hero's arms.

A paperback original, *The Flame and the Flower* was given all the publicity, advertising, and promotion usually reserved for proven best-sellers. Such originals had been issued continuously in small quantities throughout the early years of mass-market history, but concentration on them was not widespread for the simple reason that it cost more to pay out an advance to an author and to advertise an unknown book than to buy reprint rights to an already moderately successful hardback. Avon, however, under the direction of Peter Meyer, had begun to experiment with originals and different advertising campaigns in the mid-1960s. When Coffey agreed to publish *The Flame and the Flower* without previous hardcover exposure, she was simply following a practice that had become fairly common within her firm. The house's extraordinary success with Woodiwiss's novel soon caused industry-wide reconsideration of the possibilities of paperback originals as potential bestsellers. When Avon followed this success with two more bestseller romances in 1974, the industry was convinced not only of the viability of the original but also of the fact that a new category had been created. Within the trade, the genre was dubbed the 'sweet savage romance' after the second entrant in the field, Rosemary Roger's *Sweet Savage Love*.

Once Avon had demonstrated that original romances could be parlayed into ready money, nearly every other mass-market house developed plans to issue its own 'sweet savage romances', 'erotic historicals', 'bodice-rippers', or 'slave sagas', as they were variously known throughout the industry. Virtually all recognized, as Yvonne McManus of Major Books did, that 'Avon ha[d] smartly created a demand through heavy advertising and promotion'. As she commented further, 'it . . . invented its own new trend, which is clever paperback publishing'.

Although a few houses have developed bestsellers in the 'sweet savage' category, Avon has been most successful at identifying the house imprint with this kind of romance and has established close ties with its audience by compiling a mailing list from its fan letters. Several publishers have attempted to develop other sorts of romances with the idea of creating a series or 'line' that they hope to associate in readers' minds with the house name. The creation of 'line' fiction is one more example of the familiar attempt to identify a permanent base audience in order to make better predictions about sales and to increase profit. The growing proliferation and success of such schemes, often modelled after Avon's informal techniques or the more elaborate operations of

Harlequin Enterprises, makes them an extremely important development in romance publishing specifically and in mass-market paperback
publishing generally. Before assessing several of the most important of
these, it will be helpful to mention two further developments, one in
general publishing, the other in bookselling, that help to explain why so
many paperback houses not only have found the romance market
attractive but also have been able to appeal to it successfully.

The most significant development in American publishing in the
twentieth century has been the assumption of control of once privately
owned houses by vast communications conglomerates. Begun in 1960
with the Random House 'absorption' of Knopf and continued in 1967
when the Radio Corporation of America (RCA) purchased Random
House, the merger trend has left only a few houses intact. In 1967, for
instance, the Columbia Broadcasting System (CBS) acquired Holt,
Rinehart and Winston and then later purchased Praeger Publishers,
Popular Library, and Fawcett Publications. Xerox has assumed control
of Ginn and Company, R. R. Bowker, and the trade periodical, *Publishers
Weekly*. Dell is owned by Doubleday and Company, as is the Literary
Guild. Gulf and Western has acquired both Simon and Schuster and
Pocket Books. Although by no means exhaustive, this litany at least
makes clear that the first impact of the merger trend has been the union
of hardcover and mass-market paperback companies within a single
corporate structure. Despite the fact that most individual houses have
retained editorial control over what they produce, it is also apparently
true that greater attention is paid to their profit-and-loss statements by
corporate headquarters than the houses used to devote to them
themselves.

It is not hard to understand why 'attention to the bottom line' has
begun to dominate the publishing process when one considers that
despite increased profit consciousness within the mass-market segment
of the industry, publishing remained a small, informally organized
business well into the 1970s. Once referred to as 'seat-of-the-pants'
publishing by its critics and supporters alike, the American industry
continued to make decisions about manuscript selection, print orders,
and advertising campaigns on the basis of editors' intuitions, ignoring
the availability of the computer and the development of sophisticated
market-research techniques. Much of the reluctance to adopt these
highly mechanical procedures can be traced to the lingering vision of
publishing as the province of literary gentlemen seriously devoted to the
'cause' of humane letters. Editors worried that if profit became the

principal goal, publishers would be reluctant to sponsor the first novel of a promising young writer because its financial failure would be virtually guaranteed.

In recently assessing the impact of corporate takeovers on publishing, Thomas Whiteside has observed that the 'business was indeed riddled with inefficiency'. 'Sluggish management, agonizingly slow editorial and printing processes, creaky and ill-coordinated systems of book distribution and sales, skimpy advertising budgets, and . . . inadequate systems of financing', he claims, 'prevented many publishers from undertaking major long-range editorial projects that they knew were necessary to their companies' future well-being.' Traditionally a low-profit industry, trade-book publishing was also characterized by widely varying profits because each house's fortunes fluctuated rapidly in concert with its failure or success at selling its monthly list. When the corporate managers of the new conglomerates began to scrutinize the houses' financial practices and performances, they were appalled. Most responded by forcing the publishers to adopt the procedures long familiar to the corporate world: 'efficient accounting systems, long-range planning, elimination of waste, and unnecessary duplication of services'.

Although it seems obvious that conglomerate control has had the effect of forcing trade publishers to do away almost completely with 'mid-level' books – those that perform only moderately well in both the market and in critical opinion – it has had the additional effect of providing the paperback houses with large sums of money. This has enabled them to pay huge fees for the reprint rights to bestselling novels; it has also permitted them to devote a great deal of financial attention to planning category sales by commissioning market-research studies and to the advertising of the new 'lines' created as their consequence. The logic behind this kind of financial manoeuvre is grounded on the assumption that if paperback sales can be made more predictable and steady, the newly acquired mass-market section of a conglomerate can be used to balance out the necessarily unpredictable operation of the trade process.

Corporate takeovers have had the effect, then, of adding to the pressure on paperback houses to devote increasing amounts of time and money to category sales. At the same time, because reprint rights have grown enormously expensive, it has been necessary for them to place even more emphasis on the acquisition of original manuscripts. To avoid the difficulties of training inexperienced writers and the expense of introducing their works on an individual basis to new audiences, paper-back publishers have consequently tended to seek out originals that fit closely within category patterns. They believe it is easier to introduce a new author by fitting his or her work into a previously formalized chain of communication than to establish its uniqueness by locating a special audience for it. The trend has proven so powerful, in fact, that as of 1980, 40 to 50 per cent of nearly every house's monthly releases were paperback originals. The conglomerates' quest for financial accounta-bility has had another effect besides that of increasing the emphasis on category publishing with its steady, nearly guaranteed sales. Their overwhelming interest in predictability has also helped to forge an important link between the now more profit-minded paperback houses and the increasingly successful bookstore chains, B. Dalton, Bookseller, and Waldenbooks. Together, these two developments have led to even greater industry interest in romantic novels and the women who pur-chase them.

Indeed, while the recent history of paperback publishing has been dominated by the rise to prominence of the blockbuster bestseller, it has also been characterized by this slow but inexorable transformation of the business from a relatively small, informally run enterprise still focused on the figure of the author and the event of book *reading* into a consumer-oriented industry making use of the most sophisticated mar-keting and advertising techniques to facilitate simple commodity exchange. The extraordinary popularity of the romance is in part a function of this transformation, since those very techniques have been applied most energetically to this kind of category literature. Although publishers cannot explain adequately why marketing research was ap-plied to romances rather than to spy thrillers or Westerns, it seems likely that the decision was influenced by two factors.

First, female readers constitute more than half of the book-reading public. More money is to be made, it seems, by capturing a sizable portion of that large audience than by trying to reach nearly all of a smaller one. At the same time, women are remarkably available as a book-buying public in the sense that their social duties and habits make them accessible to publishers on a regular basis. The possibility of easy and extensive distribution to an audience inadvertently gathered for them by other forces thus tends to justify the mass production of romances. Currently, one-quarter to one-third of the approximately 400 paperback titles issued each month are original romances of one kind or another. Almost all of the ten largest paperback houses include a fair proportion of romance fiction as part of their monthly releases. In addition, Harlequin now claims that its million-dollar advertising campaigns reach one out of every ten women in America and that 40 per cent of those reached can usually be converted into Harlequin readers. The huge sales figures associated with romance fiction seem to be the result of this all-important ability to get at a potential audience.

Second, romance novels obviously provide a reading experience enjoyable enough for large numbers of women so that they wish to repeat that experience whenever they can. To conclude, however, that the increasing domination of the paperback market by the romance testifies automatically to some *greater* need for reassurance among American women is to make an unjustified leap in logic. It is also to ignore the other evidence demonstrating that the domination is the consequence of a calculated strategy to make the largest profit possible by appealing to the single most important segment of the book-buying public. The romance's popularity must be tied closely to these important historical changes in the book publishing industry as a whole.

Nonetheless, that popularity is also clearly attributable to the peculiar fact that much of book reading and book buying in America *is* carried on by women. Many observers of women and book publishing alike have concluded that middle-class women are book readers because they have both the necessary money and the time. They have the time, certainly, because, until recently, social custom kept them out of the full-time paid labour force and in the home where their primary duties involved the care and nurture of the family and, in particular, children. Because children are absent from the home for part of the day after the first several years, the reasoning proceeds, their mothers have blocks of time that can be devoted to the activity of reading.

Although not all women readers are represented by these conditions, it seems highly likely that they do provide the background for the majority of women who are romance readers. Actual demographic statistics are closely guarded within the competitive publishing industry by executives who often insist that romances are read by a broad cross section of the American female population. Still, both Harlequin and Silhouette have indicated repeatedly that the majority of their readers fall within the twenty-five to forty-five age group. If this is true, the meaning of the romance-reading experience may be closely tied to the way the act of reading fits within the middle-class mother's day and the way the story itself addresses anxieties, fears, and psychological needs resulting from her social and familial position. It is to these

questions that we must turn, keeping in mind all the while that burgeoning sales do not necessarily imply increasing demand or need.
Publishers and the profit motive must be given their due in any effort to
explain the popularity of the romance or to understand its significance
as a historical and cultural phenomenon. It should also be kept in mind
that despite its relative success at gauging general audience interest,
semiprogrammed issue cannot yet guarantee perfect fit between all
readers' expectations and the publisher's product.

Bibliography

Addison, W. 1953 *English Fairs and Markets*. London: Batsford.

Adorno, T. W. 1991 *The Culture Industry: Selected Essays on Mass Culture*, ed. with intro. J. M. Bernstein. London: Routledge.

Alcoff, L. 1988 'Cultural Feminism versus Post-Structuralism: The Identity Crisis in Feminist Theory', *Signs* 13(3): 405–37.

Althusser, L. 1969 *For Marx*. London: Allen Lane.

Althusser, L. and Balibar, E. 1968 *Reading Capital*. London: New Left Books.

Ames, M. 1986 *Museums, the Public and Anthropology: A Study of the Anthropology of Anthropology*. Vancouver: University of British Columbia Press.

Amin, S. 1989 *Eurocentrism*, trans. R. Moore. New York: Monthly Review Press.

Ang, I. 1985 *Watching Dallas: Soap Opera and the Melodramatic Imagination*. London: Methuen.

—— 1991 *Watching Television*. London: Routledge.

Anzaldúa, G. and Moraga, C. (eds) 1982 *This Bridge is Called My Back: Writings of Radical Women of Color*. New York: Kitchen Table, Women of Color Press.

Appadurai, A. (ed.) 1986 *The Social Life of Things: Commodities in Cultural Perspective*. Cambridge: Cambridge University Press.

—— 1990 'Disjuncture and difference in the global cultural economy', *Public Culture* 2(2): 1–24.

Attali, J. 1985 *Noise: the Political Economics of Music*, trans. Brian Massumi. Minneapolis, Minn.: University of Minnesota Press.

Bachelard, G. 1969 *The Poetics of Space*, trans. M. Jolas. Boston: Beacon.

Bakhtin, M. 1981 *The Dialogic Imagination*. Austin, Tex.: University of Texas Press.

—— 1987 *Rabelais and His World*. Bloomington, Ind.: Indiana University Press.

Barber, C. L. 1959 *Shakespeare's Festive Comedies: a Study of Dramatic Form and its Relation to Social Custom*. Princeton, NJ: Princeton University Press.

Barthes, R. 1972 *Mythologies*. London: Jonathan Cape.

—— 1977 'Change the object itself: mythology today', in *Image Music Text*. London: Fontana: 165–9.

Baudrillard, J. 1968 *Le Système des objets*. Paris: Gallimard.

Becker, H. 1978 'Arts and crafts', *American Journal of Sociology* 83: 864–70.

—— 1982 *Art Worlds*. Berkeley, Calif.: University of California Press.

Belsey, C. 1980 *Critical Practice*. London and New York: Methuen.

—— 1982 'Re-reading the great tradition', in *Rereading English*, ed. P. Widdowson. London: Methuen: 121–35.

Benjamin, W. 1969 *Illuminations*. New York: Schocken Books.

Bennett, T. 1986 'The politics of "the popular" and popular culture', in *Popular Culture and Social Relations*, ed. T. Bennett, C. Mercer and J. Woollacott. Milton Keynes: Open University Press: 6–21.

—— 1992 'Putting policy into cultural studies', in *Cultural Studies*, ed. L. Grossberg, C. Nelson and P. Treichler. New York: Routledge: 23–34.

Bennett, T. and Woollacott, J. 1988 *Bond and Beyond: the Political Career of a Popular Hero*. London: Macmillan.

Berman, M. 1982 *All that is Solid Melts into Air: the Experience of Modernity*. New York: Simon and Schuster.

Berman, R. A. 1989 *Modern Culture and Critical Theory: Art, Politics and the Legacy of the Frankfurt School*. Madison, Wis.: University of Wisconsin Press.

Bhabha, H. K. 1986 'The other question: difference, discrimination and the discourse of colonialism', in *Literature, Politics and Theory: Papers from the Essex Conference 1976–1984*, ed. F. Barker, P. Hulme and M. Iverson. London: Methuen: 148–72.

—— (ed.) 1990 *Nation and Narration*. London: Routledge.

Blanchot, M. 1987 'Everyday speech', *Yale French Studies* 73: 12–20.

Bloch, E. 1988 *The Utopian Function of Art and Literature: Selected Essays*, trans. Jack Zipes and Frank Mecklenberg. Cambridge, Mass.: MIT Press.

Boddy, W. 1985 '"The shining centre of the home": ontologies of television in the "golden age"', in *Television in Transition*, ed. P. Drummond and R. Paterson. London: BFI.

—— 1990 'The seven dwarfs and the money grubbers: the public relations crisis of US television in the late 1950s', in *Logics of Television: Essays in Cultural Criticism*, ed. P. Mellencamp. Bloomington, Ind.: Indiana University Press: 98–116.

Born, G. 1987 'Modern music culture: on shock, pop and synthesis', *New Formations* 1(2): 51–78.

Bourdieu, P. 1977 *Outline of a Theory of Practice*. Cambridge: Cambridge University Press.

—— 1986 *Distinction: a Social Critique of the Judgement of Taste*, trans. R. Nice. Cambridge, Mass.: Harvard University Press.

—— 1990 *In Other Words: Essays Towards a Reflexive Sociology*, trans. Matthew Adamson. Stanford, Calif.: Stanford University Press.

Boyd-Barrett, O. 1977 'Mass communication in cross-cultural contexts: the case of the third world', in *Mass Communication and Society*, ed. J. Curran, M. Gurevitch and J. Woollacott. London: Edward Arnold: 79–94.

—— 1982 'Cultural dependency and the mass media', in *Culture, Society and the Media*, ed. M. Gurevitch, T. Bennett, J. Curran and J. Woollacott. London: Methuen: 175–93.

Brake, M. 1980 *The Sociology of Youth Culture and Youth Subcultures*. London: Routledge and Kegan Paul.

Brantlinger, P. 1990 *Crusoe's Footsteps: Cultural Studies in Britain and America*. New York: Routledge.

Browne, N. 1984 'The political economy of the television (super) text', *Quarterly Review of Film Studies* 9: 174–82.

Brunsdon, C. 1990 'Television: aesthetics and audience', in *Logics of Television: Essays in Cultural Criticism*, ed. P. Mellencamp. Bloomington, Ind.: Indiana University Press: 59–72.

Brunsdon, C. and Morley, D. 1978 *Everyday Television: 'Nationwide'*. London: BFI.

Buckingham, D. 1987 *Public Secrets: EastEnders and its Audience*. London: BFI.

Burgin, V. 1990 'Paranoiac space', *New Formations* 1(2): 61–75.

Butler, J. 1990 *Gender Trouble: Feminism and the Subversion of Identity*. London: Routledge.

Carby, H. 1986a 'Sometimes it jus' bes' dat way', *Radical America* 20: 9–22.

—— 1986b '"On the threshold of woman's era": lynching, empire, and sexuality in black feminist theory', in *'Race', Writing and Difference*, ed. H. L. Gates. Chicago, Ill.: University of Chicago Press: 301–16.

Carpenter, E. 1975 'Collecting northwest coast art', in *Indian Art of the Northwest Coast*, ed. B. Holm and B. Reid. Seattle, Wash.: University of Washington Press: 9–49.

Caughie, J. 1984 'Television criticism: "a discourse in search of an object"', *Screen* 25(4): 109–20.

CCCS (Centre for Contemporary Cultural Studies) 1981 *Unpopular Education: Schooling and Social Democracy in England since 1944*. London: Hutchinson.

—— 1982 *The Empire Strikes Back: Race and Racism in 70s Britain*. London: Hutchinson.

Chabram, A. 1990 'Chican/o studies as oppositional ethnography', *Cultural Studies* 4(3): 228–47.

Chambers, I. 1985 *Urban Rhythms: Pop Music and Popular Culture*. London: Macmillan.

—— 1986 *Popular Culture: the Metropolitan Experience*. London: Methuen.

—— 1990 'A miniature history of the Walkman', *New Formations* 1(1): 1–24.

Christian, B. 1987 'The race for theory', *Cultural Critique* 6: 51–63.

Clarke, J., Hall, S., Jefferson, T. and Roberts, B. 1976 'Subcultures, cultures and class', in *Resistance through Rituals: Youth Subcultures in Post-War Britain*, ed. S. Hall and T. Jefferson. London: Hutchinson: 9–79.

Clifford, J. 1986 'On ethnographic allegory', in *Writing Culture: The Poetics and Politics of Ethnography*, ed. J. Clifford and G. E. Marcus. Berkeley, Calif: University of California Press: 98–121.

—— 1988a 'Of other peoples: beyond the salvage principle', in *Discussions in Contemporary Culture*, ed. H. Foster. Seattle, Wash.: Bay Press: 121–50.

—— 1988b *The Predicament of Culture*. Cambridge, Mass.: Harvard University Press.

—— 1991 'Four northwest coast museums: travel reflections', in *Exhibiting Cultures: the Poetics and Politics of Museum Display*, ed. I. Karp and S. Lavine. Washington, DC, and London: Smithsonian Institution Press: 212–54.

Clifford, J. and Dhareshwar, V. 1989 *Traveling Theories: Traveling Theorists*. Santa Cruz: Centre for Cultural Studies.

Clifford, J. and Marcus, G. E. (eds) 1986 *Writing Culture: the Poetics and Politics of Ethnography*. Berkeley, Calif.: University of California Press.

Cohen, P. 1980 'Subcultural conflict and working-class community', in *Culture, Media, Language*, ed. S. Hall, D. Hobson, A. Lowe and P. Willis. London: Hutchinson: 78–87.

Cohn, J. 1988 *Romance and the Erotics of Property: Mass Market Fiction for Women*. Durham, NC: Duke University Press.

Collins, J. 1989 *Uncommon Cultures: Popular Culture and Post-Modernism*. New York: Routledge.

Collins, R., Garnham, N. and Locksley, G. 1988 *The Economics of Television: the UK Case*. London: Sage.

Connerton, P. 1980 *The Tragedy of Enlightenment: an Essay on the Frankfurt School*. Cambridge: Cambridge University Press.

Connor, S. 1989 *Postmodern Culture: an Introduction to Theories of the Contemporary*. Oxford: Blackwell.

Coward, R. 1984 *Female Desire: Women's Sexuality Today*. London: Paladin.

Cunningham, H. 1980 *Leisure in the Industrial Revolution*. London: Croom Helm.

Curran, J. 1977 'Capitalism and control of the press, 1800–1975', in *Mass Communication and Society*, ed. J. Curran, M. Gurevitch and J. Woollacott. London: Edward Arnold: 195–230.

Curran, J. and Gurevitch, M. (eds) 1991 *Mass Media and Society*. London: Edward Arnold.

de Certeau, M. 1984 *The Practice of Everyday Life*. Berkeley, Calif.: University of California Press.

de Lauretis, T. 1987 *Technologies of Gender: Essays on Theory, Film and Fiction*. Bloomington, Ind.: Indiana University Press.

Doyle, B. 1989 *English and Englishness*. London: Routledge.

Dreyfus, Hubert L. and Rabinow, Paul 1983 *Michel Foucault: Beyond Structuralism and Hermeneutics Second Edition. With an Afterword by and an Interview with Michel Foucault*. Chicago, Ill.: University of Chicago Press.

During, S. 1987 'Postmodernism and postcolonialism today', *Textual Practice* 1(1): 58–86.

—— 1989 'What was the west', *Meanjin* 48(4): 759–76.

—— 1992 'Postcolonialism and globalisation', *Meanjin* 51(2): 339–53.

Dwyer, K. 1979 'The dialogic of ethnology', *Dialectical Anthropology* 4: 205–24.

Dyer, R. 1979 *Stars*. London: BFI.

Eagleton, T. 1981 *Walter Benjamin, or Towards a Revolutionary Criticism*. London: Verso.

Ellis, J. 1982 *Visible Fictions: Cinema, Television, Video*. London: Routledge.

Ewen, S. 1976 *Captains of Consciousness: Advertising and the Social Roots of Consumer Culture*. New York: McGraw-Hill.

Fabian, J. 1983 *Time and the Other: How Anthropology Makes its Object*. New York: Columbia University Press.

Faure, A. 1978 *Paris Carême-frenant*, Paris: Hachette.

Fiske, J. 1987a 'British cultural studies and television', in *Channels of Discourse: TV and Contemporary Criticism*, ed. R. C. Allen. Chapel Hill, NC, and London: University of North Carolina Press: 254–90.

—— 1987b *Television Culture*. London: Methuen.

—— 1989 *Understanding Popular Culture*. Boston, Mass.: Unwin Hyman.

Fiske, J. and Hartley, J. 1978 *Reading Television*. London: Methuen.

Foucault, M. 1978 *The History of Sexuality. Volume one: an introduction*, trans. R. Hurley. New York: Pantheon.

—— 1980 *Power/Knowledge: Selected Interviews and Other Writings 1972–1977*. New York: Pantheon.

—— 1986 'Of other spaces', *Diacritics* 16: 22–7.

—— 1988 *Politics, Philosophy, Culture: Interviews and Other Writings 1977–1984*, ed. with intro. Lawrence D. Kritzman. London: Routledge.

Freud, S. 1954 *Sigmund Freud's Letters to Wilhelm Fliess, Drafts and Notes*, ed. M. Bonaparte, A. Freud and E. Kris, trans. E. Masbacher and J. Strachey. New York: Basic Books.

—— 1963 'General remarks on hysterical attacks', in *Dora: An Analysis of a Case of Hysteria*, trans. D. Bryan. New York: Macmillan: 153–7.

—— 1974 'Studies on hysteria', in *Pelican Freud Library* 3, ed. A. Richards, trans. J. Strachey and A. Strachey. Harmondsworth: Penguin.

Frith, S. 1988 *Music for Pleasure*. Cambridge: Polity.

Frith, S. and Goodwin, A. (eds) 1990 *On Record: Rock, Pop and the Written Word*. London and New York: Routledge.

Frith, S. and McRobbie, A. 1978 'Rock and sexuality', *Screen Education* 28: 1–14.

Frow, J. 1990 'Accounting for tastes: some problems in Bourdieu's sociology of culture', *Cultural Studies* 1(1): 59–73.

—— 1991 'Michel de Certeau and the practice of representation', *Cultural Studies* 3(1): 52–60.

Gallop, J. 1982 *The Daughter's Seduction: Feminism and Psychoanalysis*. Ithaca, NY: Cornell University Press.

Garnham, N. 1990 *Capitalism and Communication: Global Culture and the Politics of Information*. London: Sage.

Garnham, N. and Williams, R. 1980 'Pierre Bourdieu and the sociology of culture: an introduction', *Media, Culture and Society* 2: 209–23.

Garratt, S. 1990 'Teenage Dreams' in *On Record: Rock, Pop and the Written Word*, S. Frith and A. Goodwin (eds). London and New York: Routledge: 399–409.

Gates H. L., Jr (ed.) 1986 *'Race', Writing and Difference*. Chicago, Ill.: University of Chicago Press.

—— 1987 'Authority (white) power and the (black) critic; it's all Greek to me', *Cultural Critique* 7: 32–43.

Giddens, T. 1979 *Central Problems in Social Theory: Action, Structure and Contradiction in Social Analysis*. Berkeley, Calif.: University of California Press.

Gilroy, P. 1987 *There Ain't No Black in the Union Jack: the Cultural Politics of Race and Nation*. London: Hutchinson.

Gitlin, T. 1983 *Inside Prime Time*. New York: Pantheon.

Godelier, M. 1970 'Structure and contradiction in "Capital"', in *Structuralism: a Reader*, ed. M. Lane. London: Jonathan Cape: 112–23.

Golding, P. and Murdock, G. 1990 'Screening out the poor', in *The Neglected Audience*, ed. J. Willis and T. Wollen. London: BFI: 32–42.

Gramsci, A. 1971 *Selections from the Prison Notebooks*, ed. and trans. Quintin Hoare and Geoffrey Nowell-Smith. London: Lawrence and Wishart.

—— 1975 *Quaderni del carceri*. Turin: Finaudi.

—— 1978 *Selections from the Political Writings*, ed. and trans. Quintin Hoare. London: Lawrence and Wishart.

—— 1985 *Selections from Cultural Writings*, ed. D. Forgacs and G. Nowell-Smith. London: Lawrence and Wishart.

Gray, A. 1987 'Behind closed doors: video recorders in the home', in *Boxed In: Women and Television*, ed. H. Baehr and G. Dyer. London: Pandora.

Greimas, A. J. and Rastier, F. 1968 'The interaction of semiotic constraints', *Yale French Studies* 4: 86–105.

Grossberg, L. 1984 '"I'd rather feel bad than not feel anything at all": rock and roll, pleasure and power', *enclitic* 8(1–2): 96–112.

—— 1987 'The in-difference of television', *Screen* 28(2): 28–45.

—— 1988 'Wandering audiences, nomadic critics', *Cultural Studies* 2(3): 377–91.

Gunew, S. 1990 'Denaturalizing cultural nationalism: multicultural readings of "Australia"', in *Nation and Narration*, ed. H. Bhabha. London: Routledge: 99–120.

Hall, S. 1977 'Culture, the media and the "ideological effect" ', in *Mass Communication and Society*, ed. J. Curran, M. Gurevitch and J. Woollacott. London: Edward Arnold: 315–48.

—— 1980 'Cultural studies and the centre: some problematics and problems', in *Culture, Media, Language: Working Papers in Cultural Studies, 1972–79*, ed. S. Hall, D. Hobson, A. Love and P. Willis. London: Hutchinson: 15–48.

—— 1981 'Notes on deconstructing the popular', in *People's History and Socialist Theory*, ed. R. Samuel. London: Routledge and Kegan Paul: 227–40.

—— 1988 *The Hard Road to Renewal: Thatcherism and the Crisis of the Left*. London: Verso.

—— 1990 'The emergence of cultural studies and the crisis of the humanities', *October* 53: 11–23.

Hall, S. and Jefferson, T. (eds) 1976 *Resistance through Rituals: Youth Subcultures in Post-War Britain*. London: Hutchinson.

Hall, S. and Whannel, P. 1964 *The Popular Arts*. London: Hutchinson.

Hall, S., Critcher, C., Jefferson, T., Clarke J. and Roberts, B. 1979 *Policing the Crisis: Mugging, the State, and Law and Order*. London, Macmillan.

Halperin, D. 1989 *One Hundred Years of Homosexuality*. London and New York: Routledge.

Handler, R. 1985 'On having a culture: nationalism and the preservation of Quebec's patrimoine', in *History of Anthropology Vol. 3: Objects and Others*, ed. G. Stocking. Madison, Wis.: University of Wisconsin Press: 189–217.

Haraway, D. 1984 'Teddy bear patriarchy: taxidermy in the garden of Eden, 1908–1936', *Social Text* 11: 24–59.

—— 1988 'Situated knowledge', *Feminist Studies* 14(3): 575–99.

Harris, N. 1990 *Cultural Excursions, Marketing Appetites and Cultural Tastes in Modern America*. Chicago, Ill.: University of Chicago Press.

Hartley, J. 1983 'Encouraging signs: television and the power of dirt, speech and scandalous categories', *Australian Journal of Cultural Studies* 1(2): 62–82.

Hartmann, W. 1976 *Der Historische Festzug: Seine Enstehung und Entwicklung im 19 und 20 Jahrhunderts*, Studien zur kunst des 19 Jahrhunderts, 35: Munich: Prestel.

Harvey, D. 1985 *Consciousness and the Urban Experience*. Oxford: Blackwell.

—— 1989 *The Condition of Postmodernity*. Oxford: Blackwell.

Hawkes, T. 1977 *Semiotics and Structuralism*. London: Methuen.

Hayward, P. 1990 'How ABC capitalised on cultural logic: the moonlighting story', in *The Media Reader*, ed. M. Alvarado and J. O. Thompson. London: BFI: 265–75.

Heath, S. 1982 *The Sexual Fix*. London: Macmillan.

Heath, S. and Skirrow, G. 1977 'Television: a world in action', *Screen* 18(2): 7–59.

Hebdige, D. 1979 *Subculture: the Meaning of Style*. London: Methuen.

—— 1989 'Hiding in the light: youth surveillance and display', in *Hiding in the Light: Images and Things*. London: Routledge: 17–37.

Hirsch, M. and Fox Keller, E. (eds) 1990 *Conflicts in Feminism*. New York: Routledge.

Hobson, D. 1982 *Crossroads: the Drama of a Soap Opera*. London: Methuen.

Hoggart, R. 1957 *The Uses of Literacy*. Harmondsworth: Penguin.

—— 1966 'Literature and society', *The American Scholar* 35: 277–89.

Hunter, I. 1988 *Culture and Government: the Emergence of Literary Education*. London: Macmillan.

Hutcheon, L. 1989 *The Politics of Postmodernism*. London: Routledge.

Iyer, P. 1988 *Video Night in Kathmandu: and Other Reports from the Not-So-Far East*. New York: Vintage.

Jameson, F. 1981 *The Political Unconscious: Narrative as a Socially Symbolic Act*. Ithaca, NY: Cornell University Press.

—— 1990 *Postmodernism or the Cultural Logic of Late Capitalism*. Durham, NC: Duke University Press.

JanMohamed, A. and Lloyd, D. 1987 'Introduction: towards a theory of minority discourse', *Cultural Critique* Spring: 65–82.

Jardine, A. 1985 *Gynesis: Configurations of Woman and Modernity*. Ithaca, NY: Cornell University Press.

Jay, M. 1984a *Adorno*. Cambridge, Mass.: Harvard University Press.

—— 1984b *Marxism and Totality: the Adventures of a Concept from Lukacs to Habermas*. Berkeley, Calif.: University of California Press.

Jhally, Sut 1987 *The Codes of Advertising: Fetishism and the Political Economy of Meaning in the Consumer Society*. London: Frances Pinter.

Johnson, R. 1987 'What is cultural studies anyway?', *Social Text* 6(1): 38–90.

Jordan, J. 1981 'Black History as Myth', in *Civil Wars*. Boston: Beacon Press.

Kappeler, S. 1986 *The Pornography of Representation*. Minneapolis, Minn.: University of Minnesota Press.

Karp, I and Lavine, S. D. 1991 *Exhibiting Cultures: the Poetics and Politics of Museum Display*. Washington, DC: Smithsonian Institution Press.

Katz, E. and Liebes, T. 1985 'Mutual aid in the decoding of *Dallas*: preliminary notes from a cross-cultural study', in *Television in Transition: Papers from the First International Television Studies Conference*, ed. P. Drummond and R. Paterson. London: BFI: 183–98.

Kern, S. 1983 *The Culture of Time and Space 1880–1918*. Cambridge, Mass.: Harvard University Press.

Kowinski, W. S. 1985 *The Malling of America: an Inside Look at the Great Consumer Paradise*. New York: Pantheon.

Kristeva, J. 1974 *La Révolution du Langage Poètique*. Paris: Seuil.

—— 1989 *Language – the Unknown: an Initiation into Linguistics*, trans. Anne M. Menke. New York: Columbia University Press.

Kroeber, A. L. and Kluckhorn, C. 1952 *Culture: a Critical Review of Concepts and Definitions*. New York: Vintage.

Laclau, E. 1977 *Politics and Ideology in Marxist Theory*. London: New Left Books.

Laclau, E. and Mouffe, C. 1985 *Hegemony and Social Strategy: Towards a Radical Democratic Politics*. London: Verso.

Laing, S. 1986 *Representations of Working-class Life, 1959–64*. London: Macmillan.

Leal, O. F. 1990 'Popular taste and erudite repetoire: the place and space of television in Brazil', *Cultural Studies* 4(1): 19–29.

Lears, T. J. 1983 'From salvation to self-realisation: advertising and the therapeutic roots of consumer culture, 1880–1930', in *The Culture of Consumption: Critical Essays in American History, 1880–1980*, ed. R. J. Fox and T. J. Lears. New York: Pantheon: 3–38.

Lefebvre, H. 1971 *Everyday Life in the Modern World*. Allen Lane: London.

—— 1991 *Critique of Everyday Life*, vol. 1. London: Verso.

Levine, L. 1988 *Highbrow/Lowbrow: the Emergence of Cultural Hierarchy in America*. Cambridge, Mass.: Harvard University Press.

Lévi-Strauss, C. 1960 *Structural Anthropology*, vol. 2. New York: Basic Books.

—— 1985 *The View from Afar*. New York: Basic Books.

Lyotard, J.-F. 1986 *The Postmodern Condition: a Report on Knowledge*. Manchester: Manchester University Press.

MacCabe, C. 1981 'Memory, phantasy, identity: *Days of Hope* and the politics of the past', in *Popular Television and Film*, ed. T. Bennett, C. Mercer and J. Woollacott. London: BFI.

MacKinnon, C. 1987 *Feminism Unmodified: Discourses of Life and Law*. Cambridge, Mass.: Harvard University Press.

Macpherson, C. B. 1962 *The Political Theory of Possessive Individualism*. Oxford: Oxford University Press.

McRobbie, A. 1980 'Settling accounts with subcultures', *Screen Education* 34: 37–49.

—— 1984 'Dance and social fantasy', in *Gender and Generation*, ed. A. McRobbie and M. Nava. London: Macmillan.

McRobbie, A. and Nava, M. (eds) 1984 *Gender and Generation*. London: Macmillan.

Marchand, R. 1985 *Advertising the American Dream: Making Way for Modernity 1920–1940*. Berkeley, Calif.: University of California Press.

Marcus, G. and Fischer, M. 1986 *Anthropology as Cultural Critique*. Chicago, Ill.: University of Chicago Press.

Marx, K. and Engels, F. 1970 *The German Ideology*. London: Lawrence and Wishart.

Mattelart, A. 1991 *Advertising International: the Privatisation of Public Space*, trans. M. Chanan. London and New York: Comedia/Routledge.

Mead, M. 1971 *The Mountain Arapesh*, vol. 3. Garden City, NY: Natural History Press.

Meehan, E. R. 1988 'Technical capability vs. corporate imperatives: towards a political economy of cable television and information diversity', in *The Political Economy of Information*, ed. V. Mosco and J. Wasko. Madison, Wis.: University of Wisconsin Press.

—— 1990 'Why we don't count: the commodity audience', in *Logics of Television: Essays in Cultural Criticism*, ed. P. Mellencamp. Bloomington, Ind., and London: Indiana University Press: 117–37.

Mercer, K. 1987 'Black hair/style politics', *New Formations* 3: 33–54.

Mills, C. W. 1959 *The Sociological Imagination*, New York: Oxford University Press.

Minh-ha, T. T. 1989 *Woman, Native, Other: Writing Postcoloniality and Feminism*. Bloomington, Ind.: Indiana University Press.

Mitchell, Timothy 1988 *Colonizing Egypt*. Cambridge: Cambridge University Press.

Modleski, T. 1983 'The rhythms of reception: daytime television and women's work', in *Regarding Television. Critical Approaches – an Anthology*, ed. E. A. Kaplan. Frederick, Md.: University Publications of America.

—— 1984 *Loving with a Vengeance*. London: Methuen.

—— (ed.) 1987 *Studies in Entertainment: Critical Approaches to Mass Culture*. Bloomington, Ind.: University of Indiana Press.

Mohanty, C. T. 1984 '"Under western eyes": feminist scholarship and colonial discourses', *boundary 2* 12(3)–13(1): 333–58.

Morley, D. 1980 *The 'Nationwide' Audience: Structure and Decoding*. BFI Television Monographs, 11. London: BFI.

—— 1986 *Family Television: Cultural Power and Domestic Leisure*. London: Comedia/Roultedge.

—— 1989 'Changing paradigms in audience studies', in *Remote Control: Television, Audiences, and Cultural Power*, ed. E. Seiter, H. Borchers, G. Kreutzner and E. Warth. London: Routledge: 1–16.

—— 1990 'Behind the ratings: the politics of audience research', in *The Neglected Audience*, ed. J. Willis and T. Wollen. The Broadcasting Debate, 5. London: BFI: 5–15.

Morris, M. 1988a 'At Henry Parkes Motel', *Cultural Studies* 1(2): 1–47.

—— 1988b *The Pirate's Fiancée: Feminism, Reading, Postmodernism*. London: Verso.

—— 1990 'Banality in cultural studies', in *Logics of Television: Essays in Cultural Criticism*, ed. P. Mellencamp. Bloomington, Ind., and Indianapolis, Ind.: Indiana University Press: 14–43.

Mulvey, L. 1989 *Visual and Other Pleasures*. Bloomington, Ind.: Indiana University Press.

Nava, M. 1987 'Consumerism and its contradictions', *Cultural Studies* 1(2): 204–10.

Newcombe, H. 1986 'American television criticism 1970–1985', *Critical Studies in Communication* 3: 217–28.

Ortner, S. 1984 'Theory in anthropology since the sixties', *Comparative Studies in Society and History* 26: 126–66.

Petro, P. 1986 'Mass culture and the feminine: the "place" of television in film studies', *Cinema Journal* 25(3): 5–21.

Pillement, G. 1972 *Paris en Fête*. Paris: Grasset.

Poole, M. 1984 'The cult of the generalist: British television criticism 1936–83', *Screen* 25(2): 41–61.

Pope, D. 1977 *The Making of Modern Advertising*. New York: Basic Books.

Radway, J. 1984 *Reading the Romance: Women, Patriarchy and Popular Literature*. Chapel Hill, NC: University of North Carolina Press.

—— 1988 'Reception study: ethnography and the problems of dispersed audiences and monadic subjects', *Cultural Studies*, 2(3): 359–76.

Ray, W. 1984 *Literary Meaning: from Phenomenology to Deconstruction*. Oxford: Blackwell.

Rigby, B. 1991 *Popular Culture in Modern France: a Study of Cultural Discourse*. London: Routledge.

Robbins, D. 1991 *The Work of Pierre Bourdieu*. Milton Keynes: Open University.

Robbins, K. 1983 *The Eclipse of a Great Power: Modern Britain 1870–1975*. London: Longman.

Roberts, K. and Kidd, A. J. 1977 *The Fragmentary Class Structure*. London: Heinemann.

Rosaldo, R. 1989 *Culture and Truth: the Remaking of Social Analysis*. Boston, Mass.: Beacon Press.

Ross, A. 1988 'The work of nature in the age of electronic emission', *Social Text* 18: 116–28.

—— 1989 *No Respect: Intellectuals and Popular Culture*. London: Routledge.

Rubin, G. 1975 'The traffic in women: notes on the political economy of sex', in *Toward an Anthropology of Women*, ed. R. R. Reiter. New York: Monthly Review Press: 267–319.

—— 1984 'Thinking sex: notes for a radical theory of the politics of sexuality', in *Pleasure and Danger: Exploring Female Sexuality*, ed. Carole Vance. Boston, Mass.: Routledge and Kegan Paul: 267–319.

Saakana, A. S. 1988 'Mythology and History: An Afrocentric Perspective of the World', *Third Text* 3/4: 143–50.

Sahlins, M. 1985 *Islands in History*. Chicago, Ill.: University of Chicago Press.

Sangari, K. 1987 'The politics of the possible', *Cultural Critique* 7: 157–86.

Scheff, T. J. 1979 *Catharsis in Healing. Ritual and Drama*. Berkeley: University of California Press.

Schneider, C. and Wallis, B. 1988 *Global Television*. Cambridge, Mass.: MIT Press.

Sedgwick, E. K. 1985 *Between Men: English Literature and Male Homosocial Desire*. New York: Columbia University Press.

—— 1987 'A poem is being written', *Representations* 17: 110–43.

—— 1990 *Epistemology of the Closet*. Berkeley, Calif.: University of California Press.

Seiter, E., Borchers, H., Kreutzner, G. and Warth, E. (eds) 1989 *Remote Control: Television, Audiences, and Cultural Power*. London: Routledge.

Sidro, A. 1979 *Le Carnaval de Nice et ses Fous*. Nice: Éditions Serre.

Smith, A. 1980 *The Geopolitics of Information: How Western Culture Dominates the World*. London: Faber.

Snitow, A., Stansell, C. and Thompson, S. (eds) 1983 *The Powers of Desire: the Politics of Sexuality*. New York: Monthly Review Press.

Sontag, Susan 1982 *A Susan Sontag Reader*. New York: Farrar, Straus and Giroux.

Spigel, L. 1988 'Installing the television set: popular discourses on television and domestic space, 1948–1955', *Camera Obscura* 16: 11–47.

—— 1990 'Television in the family circle: the popular reception of a new medium', in *Logics of Television: Essays in Cultural Criticism*, ed. P. Mellencamp. Bloomington, Ind.: Indiana University Press: 73–97.

Spivak, G. C. 1988a *In Other Worlds*. London: Routledge.

—— 1988b 'Can the subaltern speak?' in *Marxism and the Interpretation of Culture*, ed. C. Nelson and L. Grossberg. Urbana, Ill.: University of Illinois Press: 217–313.

—— 1990 *The Postcolonial Critic: Interviews, Strategies, Dialogues*, ed. S. Harasym. London: Routledge.

Stallybrass, P. and White, A. 1986 *The Politics and Poetics of Transgression*. London: Methuen.

Stewart, S. 1984 *On Longing: Narratives of the Miniature, the Gigantic, the Souvenir, the Collection*. Baltimore, Md.: Johns Hopkins University Press.

Stocking, G. 1968 'Arnold, Tylor and the uses of invention', in *Race, Culture and Evolution*. New York: Free Press: 69–90.

Sussman, G. and Lent, J. A. (eds) 1991 *Transnational Communications: Wiring the Third World*. Newbury Park: Sage.

Taylor, E. 1990 *Prime-time Families: Television Culture in Postwar America*. Berkeley, Calif.: University of California Press.

Thompson, E. P. 1968 *The Making of the English Working Class*. Harmondsworth, Penguin.

Thompson, J. B. 1984 'Symbolic violence: language and power in the writings of Pierre Bourdieu', in *The Theory of Ideology*. Cambridge: Polity Press: 42–72.

Tomlinson, J. 1991 *Cultural Imperialism*. London: Pinter Publishers.

Tulloch, J. 1990 *Television Drama*. London: Routledge.

Tulloch, J. and Moran, A. 1986 *Quality Soap: a Country Practice*. Sydney: Currency.

Turner, G. 1990 *British Cultural Studies: an Introduction*. Boston, Mass.: Unwin Hyman.

Urry, J. and Lash, S. 1987 *The End of Organised Capitalism*. Cambridge: Polity Press.

Vitart-Fardoulis, A. 1986 'L'objet interrogé: ou comment faire parler une collection d'ethnographie', *Gradhiva* 1 (Autumn): 9–12.

Volosinov, V. N. 1973 *Marxism and the Philosophy of Language*. London: Seminar Press.

Walkerdine, V. 1986 'Video replay: families, films and fantasy', in *Formations of Fantasy*, ed. V. Burgin, J. Donald and C. Kaplan. London: Methuen.

Wallace, M. 1990 *Invisibility Blues: From Pop to Theory*. London: Verso.

Watney, S. 1987 *Policing Desire: Pornography, AIDS, and the Media*. Minneapolis, Minn.: University of Minnesota Press.

Webster, D. 1988 *Looka Yonder: the Imaginary America of Popular Culture*. London: Comedia/Routledge.

Weedon, C. 1987 *Feminist Practice and Poststructuralist Theory*. Oxford: Blackwell.

Weeks, J. 1985 *Sexuality and its Discontents*. London: Routledge and Kegan Paul.

Wernick, A. 1987 'Sign and Commodity: Aspects of the Cultural Dynamic of Advanced Capital', *Canadian Journal of Political and Social Theory* 8: 28–42.

White, A. 1982 'Pigs and pierrots: politics of transgression in modern fiction', *Raritan*, 2(2): 51–70.

—— 1983 'The dismal sacred word: academic language and the social reproduction of seriousness', *Literature/Teaching/Politics* 2(4): 4–15

Williams, L. 1990 *Hard Core: Power, Pleasure and the 'Frenzy of the Visible'*. New York: Pandora.

Williams, R. 1958 *Culture and Society: 1780–1950*. Harmondsworth: Penguin.

—— 1961 *The Long Revolution*, Harmondsworth: Penguin.

—— 1974 *Television: Technology and Cultural Form*. London: Fontana.

—— 1983 *Keywords*. London: Fontana.

Williamson, J. 1978 *Decoding Advertisements: Ideology and Meaning in Advertising*. London: Marion Boyers.

—— 1986 *Consuming Passions: the Dynamics of Popular Culture*. London: Marion Boyers.

Willis, E. 1986 'Feminism, moralism and pornography', in *Caught Looking: Feminism, Pornography and Censorship*, ed. Kate Ellis *et al*. New York: Caught Looking: 48–63.

Willis, P. 1977 *Learning to Labour: How Working Class Kids Get Working Class Jobs*. New York: Columbia University Press.

Willis, S. 1991 *A Primer for Daily Life*. London: Routledge.

Woolf, J. 1985 'The Invisible Flâneuse: Women and the Literature of Modernity', *Theory, Culture and Society* 2/3: 37–46.

Wright, G. and Rabinow P. 1982 'Spatialization of power: a discussion of the work of Michel Foucault' and 'Interview: space, knowledge and power', *Skyline*, 1: 14–20.

Wright, J. 1979 *Britain in the Age of Economic Management*. Oxford: Oxford University Press.

Index

Addison, William 290
advertising 320–6; global 435
Akerman, Chantal 241
Adorno, Theodor 4, 44, 172, 271, 299, 300, 368, 385, 398
African-American cultural politics 118, 209–10
African-American diaspora 209–10
African-American literary tradition 127–8
African Literature Association 199
Afro-centrism 120, 127
AIDS 236, 248, 256, 260
Alcoff, Linda 78, 82–5
Althusser, Louis 5, 177, 208, 363–4
American Museum of Natural History 59
American News Company 444
Ames, Michael 72
Anderson, Laurie 213
Ang, Ien 21, 22
anthropology 59–60, 111–17
Anzaldúa, Gloria 81
Arapesh people 61–3
architecture 163–4, 168–9; modern movement in 171
Arista Records 368
Armstrong, Louis 216
Arnold, Matthew 64, 206
art: album covers and 378–9; criticism and, 213–4; definition of 63–4; entertainment and 280–1; pornography and 229–30

Astaire, Fred 280–1
Attali, Jacques 391, 393
audience research *see* ethnography
Auschwitz 172
Austen, Jane 2
Australia: multiculturalism and 194–202; public space in 316–17
authenticity: cultural products and 55–6, 59, 61–2; migrant cultures and 194; political representation and 198
avant-garde 24; and postmodernism 173
Avon Books 443, 448–9

Bachelard, Gaston 142
Baker, Ella 216
Bakhtin, Mikhail 16, 66, 271, 284, 287, 291
Baldwin, James 212
Balibar, Etienne 364
Balzac, Honoré de 35
Bangs, Lester 378
Baraka, Amiri 212
Barber, C. L. 288
Barthes, Roland 18, 120, 221, 231, 300, 360–2, 386–7, 398; *S/Z* 121
Bataille, Georges 231
Battle, Kathleen 213
Baudelaire, Charles 39, 299, 316
Baudrillard, Jean 54–5, 130, 315
Becker, Howard 57
Beethoven, Ludwig van 35, 213